TRIBULATION

OR

TRIUMPH ?

God's Plan, Your Choice!

By

Bishop Clarence B. Harris

Apostle to the End Time Church and the Jewish Nation

Alpha Omega Productions, Inc.
P. O. Box 6641
Athens, Georgia 30604-6641

First published in 2003
By Alpha Omega Productions, Inc.

www.alphaomegapro.org

Printed in the U.S.A
Library of Congress cataloged

ISBN 0-9702658-4-0

Printed by Book Masters, Inc.
Mansfield, Ohio

Copyright © 2003 by Bishop Clarence B. Harris
Alpha Omega Productions, Inc.

Acknowledgements

I am deeply indebted to the following individuals who have helped me tremendously by proof reading, critiquing, and praying for the completion of this publication. Their services have been invaluable, and a sacrifice, on behalf of those who desire to learn and discern the difference between truth and error.

Althea Harris

Sherry Henderson, Rudolph Henderson,

Julian Harris, Naomi Palmer, Jesus Ruiz, Patricia Ruiz,

Gernie Joseph, Frederick Martin, Jackie Hooker,

Albert Woodard, William Pettiford, III, Jenell Harris

Jason Harris

I thank God for allowing me to press through the snares of intellectual dishonesty that I might know and examine truth in many areas. Perhaps I was born for such a time as this, with a tenacious desire to research, study, and investigate controversial issues; to help make the confusing paths simple and plain.

I am eternally grateful for having received many unbiased biblical truths from a First Century Jewish Christian perspective. Therefore, I attribute all my knowledge and understanding to the one the Bible identifies as He that is, He that was, and He who is to come...

The Story of Truth and Error

One Day, Truth decided to take a shower. As He stepped into the shower area, he took off his cloak, and hung it on a garment rack. He then proceeded to enjoy the refreshing aspects of a good shower. Shortly thereafter, Error, not knowing that Truth was showering came into the shower area, and placed His cloak on the same garment rack. After about twenty minutes Error got out of the shower and put on the cloak of Truth. Error paraded himself before the multitude as the Truth, and many believed him to be the Truth. However, those who knew the truth and could discern beyond the deception said, "there goes Error dressed in Truth's clothes."

When Truth came out of the shower he noticed that his cloak was missing. He then looked and saw that Error had taken his cloak. Truth being a man of integrity refused to put on the cloak of Error. So he left the shower area without any clothing on. As truth was walking down the street those who saw him shouted in a loud voice . . . "there goes the naked Truth."

Truth is light, and those who prefer to walk in light rather than darkness, should not be deceived by wolves in sheep's clothing. A true friend will speak the truth in times of adversity. Unfortunately for some, truth can be like to an unwelcomed friend, speaking what others do not want to hear. However, unless one is willing to confront truth, his sense of reality can be distorted, and he can easily be deceived. Ironicaly for some, "*truth is stranger than fiction*" therefore, they would prefer to believe fables. This book transforms Christian fiction into biblical fact, exposes error, and clearly presents the mindset of First Century Jewish Christian church doctrines.

A very good friend shared the story of truth and "Lie" with me. My modified version of the story speaks volumes about the hearts of men. Truth, Error, and the deceit of lies, propaganda, and disinformation which permeates the earth in many forms. Only the pure in heart can receive the naked Truth and discern the difference between Truth and Error. God is also light, and He is exposing darkness and bring many to the light.

The Prelude

If the world was to be expressed in musical terms and its current plight revealed by biblical lyrics it could be sung through the verses of Matthew 24:4-8 with the tune of the battle Hymn of the Republic. These verses signify the introductory prelude before the prophetic song of the biblical seven-year tribulation period begins. The prelude is about to conclude and the future events, expressed throughout the book of Revelation, are about to begin.

The setting for this global prelude was given as a panoramic view, revealed by Jesus Christ, as He prophesied to His disciples while overlooking the Old City Jerusalem from the Mount of Olives. *"And as he sat upon the Mount of Olives, the disciples came unto him privately, saying, Tell us, when shall these things be? and what shall be the sign of thy coming, and of the end of the world?"* **(Mt 24:3)**

"And Jesus answered and said unto them, Take heed that no man deceive you For many shall come in my name, saying, I am Christ; and shall deceive many.

And ye shall hear of <u>wars</u> and <u>rumours of wars</u>: see that ye be not troubled: for all these things must come to pass, but the end is not yet.

For <u>nation shall rise against nation</u>, and <u>kingdom against kingdom</u>: and there shall be <u>famines</u>, and <u>pestilences</u>, and <u>earthquakes, in divers places</u>.

All these are the beginning of sorrows."

WARS
(US- Iraq, UN-Iraq, NATO-Bosnia)

RUMORS OF WARS
(The Cold War, Pakistan-India, N. Korea-US, China-Taiwan)

DECEPTION
(Religion, politics, fraternal orders, propaganda, media, globalism)

NATION AGAINST NATION
(Russia-Chechyna, US-Iraq, Serbia-Bosnia-Croatia)

KINGDOM AGAINST KINGDOM
(Illuminati-Christian, Satan-Christ)

FAMINES
(Africa, North Korea, India, Russia)

PESTILENCES
(SARS, AIDS, Ebola, STD's, BSE, vCJD, Bird Flu)

EARTHQUAKES IN DIVERS PLACES
(Atlanta, Birmingham, Richmond, China, Iran, Iraq)

Table of Contents

Introduction 1

In The Beginning it Was Not So! 8
The Manifestation of the Sons of God 26

Tribulation? A Biblical Perspective 29
Tribulation or Triumph? 32
Why Tribulation? 46
Old Testament Roots for New Testament Tribulation 52

Understanding How the doctrine "Once Saved, Always Saved,"
Closes the Door to Divine End Time Revelation 57
The Love of God and Salvation 67
(Chart) Unconditional Salvation Vs Conditional Salvation **75**
Are Christians Born Again Sinners? 77
Biblical Non-qualifying Statements for Salvation 82
Qualifying or Conditional Statements for Salvation 83
What is Biblical Sanctification? 85
What is Biblical Justification? 87
The Unpardonable Sin 92
A New Testament Expose' on the Doctrine of Grace 93
Criteria to Receive and Maintain the Grace of God 99

Have Christians Been Appointed to the Wrath of God? 105
What About the Thief on the Cross? 124
Can a Christian be Oppressed or Possessed by a Devil? 129

The Timing of the Rapture and the Great Tribulation 138
The Wedding Sequence of the Lamb 142
   1. The Rapture shall take place at the Last Trumps 145
   2. The Tares are gathered before the Wheat 147
   3. The Lord will gather (rapture) His elect immediately
      after the tribulation of those days. 149
   4. The prophet Joel and the Apostle Peter identify the events
      that begin and conclude the Church Age. 150
   5. There is only one rapture appointed for the righteous... not multiple
      raptures or multiple resurrections. 151
   6. The Jewish feast days also give an exact sequence and
      time frame for the rapture of the church. 152

7. The Gospel of the Kingdom must be preached until the end of the
   Church Age and then the end will come. 153

8. The Manchild remnant and the Philadelphian church will judge
   the world and the angels. 156

9. The Mystery of Iniquity must be revealed and the Transgressors
   temples are made desolate. 159

The Mystery of the Natural and Spiritual Temples and the Priesthood

The Mystery of the Natural and Spiritual Temples
and the Priesthood 163
The Global Temple of Peace in Jerusalem 185

The Book of Daniel

The Last Days Witnesses and Judges of Christ 187
The Historic Gaps in Biblical Prophecy 188

1. The dual nature of Messianic prophecy always produces
   a gap in prophetic history 188

2. The 2,000-year gap of Joel confirmed by Peter 189

3. The early and latter rain of the Holy Ghost 190

4. The gap between the Feasts of Pentecost and Trumpets 191

5. The Gospel of the Kingdom begins and ends the Church Age 191

6. The priests and the Ark preceded the people (with a gap)
   into the Promise Land 192

A Chapter Breakdown of the Book of Daniel 193
   Daniel Chapter 1 193
   Daniel Chapter 9 197
The Prophetic 70th Week of Daniel 197
   (Chart) Daniel's 70th Week 206
   Daniel Chapter 10 207
   Daniel Chapter 12 209

Where are Christians (the Church) in the Book of Revelation?

Where are Christians (the Church) in the
Book of Revelation? 210
The Five Eurocentric Doctrinal Divorces that Produce Error

1. Divorce of the Name of Jesus Christ from Water Baptism 224

2. Divorce of the Baptism of the Holy Ghost from the Gospel of Salvation 225

3. Divorce of the Necessity of the Spirit, the Water, and the Blood,
   from the New Testament Covenant 227

4. Divorce of the Father, the Son, and the Holy Ghost for Belief in a Trinitarian,
   Tri-theistic, Three-person Godhead 229

5. Divorce of the Rapture of the Church from the Second Coming of Christ 231
   Are the Terms Love and Judgment Compatible? 234

**The Four Categories of Saints Found in the
Book of Revelation** 244

Behold the Revelation of Jesus Christ 247

Christians and the Church in the Book of Revelation

Revelation Chapter 1 248

Revelation Chapter 2 255

Revelation Chapter 3 259

Revelation Chapter 4 264

Revelation Chapter 5 265

Revelation Chapter 6 266

Revelation Chapter 7 268

Revelation Chapter 8 274

Revelation Chapter 9 274

Revelation Chapter 10 275

Revelation Chapter 11 277

Revelation Chapter 12 282

Revelation Chapter 13 290

Revelation Chapter 14 293

Revelation Chapter 15 296

Revelation Chapter 16 297

Revelation Chapter 17 302

Revelation Chapter 18 304

Revelation Chapter 19 306

Revelation Chapter 20 308

Revelation Chapter 21 310

Revelation Chapter 22 316

Introduction

Recently, I was fortunate to travel in the Middle East, Africa, Europe, South East Asia, and the Americas, where I conducted end time seminars with religious groups of all persuasions. I was stunned to discover that what I had been investigating for almost thirty years was more pervasive than I had ever imagined. I discovered that most of the world has become engulfed by Western culture and has been introduced to a Jesus that is foreign to the Bible. Numerous religious counterfeits have been conjured up by denominational leaders, each putting forth their own Jesus, and have **caused irreparable damage to the plight of humanity and confused their quest for eternity**.

For quite some time, people all over the world have believed that America is a Christian country. However, for those who have lived within her borders, many have found that not to be the case. Even though it was founded on Judeo-Christian ethics it application was never according to biblical standards. Shortly after America's legal and constitutional bout with segregation and integration, I went on a quest to prove that the Christian religion was false. My quest was in part an attempt to acquire an understanding and a resolution to some of the social, political, and religious events of conflict, which occurred in the nineteen fifties and nineteen sixties in America.

I saw how cities like Birmingham, Alabama, became nicknamed "Bombingham," because of individuals who tried to demonstrate Christian love, and advocate human civil rights, became unsolicited martyrs instead. Ironically, those who claimed to adhere to the Christian faith and Christianized the Negroes, were the same who often killed them. I heard the reports of how a 12 year old boy from Chicago, Emmett Till, was savagely murdered in the rural south, and an entire nation denied due-process to its victims and could not abide by its own Judeo-Christian laws to convict the guilty. All across America, Sunday morning church services were often followed by jubilant festivities and picnics around "hanging trees," which displayed the bodies of those that were lynched by "Christian" mobs who deemed Negroes not to be equal to those European descent.

When my family moved from rural Tuskegee, Alabama to upstate New York after a brief stay in Florida, injustice still flourished in migrant camps in the South and in the created ghettos of America's major northern cities. I was not raised in the Christian church, but was taught the message of Jesus Christ by my mother. However, her childhood Sunday school knowledge could not answer my complicated social, political, and religious dilemmas of the Christian religion. Years later my mother conveyed to me the tragic account of how one of her uncles was used as a human guinea pig in the US's eugenic experiments during WW I and a cousin who was castrated by a white mob. He later disappeared without a trace. In Alabama there were also the victims of the horrific US government's syphilis experiments on Black males at Tuskegee Institute. In Rochester, New York during the early sixties, I encountered an anti-Christian, anti-Caucasian organization that preached the concept of Jesus Christ as the father of white, blue-eyed devils and the enemy of people of African descent. Consequently, the Christian religion and its application among the nations of the earth became subject to microscopic scrutiny by the global press and its minority victims during the Civil Rights Movement.

During the post World War II Era, many American "Christian Nazi" and neo-Nazi groups emerged, espousing the idea that the US was the biblical New Jerusalem, the Jews came from Satan, and the Third Reich was God's kingdom on earth. Calling themselves the Aryan Nation in recent years, some were chartered as a racist church under the name "The Church of Jesus Christ – Christian." Unfortunately for the true Christian religion, many who claim to be followers of Christ not only reject biblical authority, they also reject secular history, and facts such as Christ being a Jew. Such is the anti-Semitic stance of the Aryan Nation. Apparently, this level of intellectual dishonesty and lack of spiritual integrity allows such religious groups to undermine their own religious foundation, and pervert the truth. Hence, whether blatant or subtle, the European based Christian religions have for centuries had a serious credibility problem, and made it hard for many to receive the faith.

Despite this tragic legacy, I had hope that there would be some redeeming grace to salvage the Christian religion, through examining its historic claims to see if, it could stand upon its own merit. Even though I was not raised in a Christian church, I sought diligently to discover whether the Christian religion was relatively true, or if the allegations made by minorities and the disenfranchised all over the world were legitimate? Many years of research led me to the discovery that there were many contradictions in the practice of the Christian religion; however, not within the Bible itself. For almost four centuries, most American Christian groups were obviously plagued with hypocrisy and stood in violation of their own holy book of conduct. **Forsaking their divine constitution, the Bible, they made themselves transgressors of their own religion and criminals in their household of faith.** Consequently, this behavior has given immense ammunition to those wanting to make accusations and discredit this religion. In essence, Christianity has a lingering credibility problem that did not just start yesterday.

Christianity and all of its denominational variations bear little resemblance to the original Jewish Christian church. The events and doctrines that have had the preeminence in the Western church world since the first century are quite foreign to the actual practices and teachings of the Bible. In essence, what has become known as the Christian faith over the centuries can be characterized as: "**in the beginning it was not so!**" European Christian doctrines and practices were modified when they reached American soil and used religion and economics as cloaks to exploit all who could by forced to help the conquering groups accomplish their privileged dreams.

The term Christian was initially applicable only to those who abided in the Apostles' doctrines (Acts 11:26, 2:38-42). Since Christianity does not support or abide in the apostles' doctrines it should not be a strange thing that its leaders can not decipher the prophetic word. Despite the fact that they are forever studying, they are

2

seemingly never able to come to the knowledge of the truth. The biblical Jesus claimed to be "The Way, The Truth, and The Life." He even promised those who had a heart for truth, that the truth would make them free. It is a very difficult task for many to stand in front of the mirror of one's own heart and honestly receive what they see. If the statements of Jesus Christ are true then those who can truthfully confront their history and honestly access it can unlock the mysteries concealed by the Spirit of Truth.

Historians investigate and uncover the events and circumstances of past events. Using the psychoanalytical approach to history, psychologist and sociologists not only examine what happens historically, but also contemplate the individual motives as to why certain events happen. **With the use of the academic tools of the biological sciences, history, sociology, and psychology, I discovered a model of Christ that was reflective of the biblical Jesus.** An accurate portrayal is *absolutely essential* if one is to accurately understand Bible prophecy and discover concealed end time biblical truths.

The *jugular vein* of the Christian faith, upon which its validity rests, is the concept of the resurrection. If Jesus Christ did not, or could not raise Himself from the dead, then how could He raise any that would believe on him? Hence, **if there is no resurrection of the dead, then the Christian faith is a hopeless and vain religion**. However, if the resurrection is true, then it would verify Christ's claims to be the ransom for the sins of men, confirm the future resurrection for all true Christians at the appointed time, and nullify the illegitimate claims of other religions as being truthful.

The historical evidence that I uncovered was very compelling, and could be considered by some, to be conclusive. However, the greatest evidence for the resurrection is the claims by millions of individuals who have testified over the centuries, of having received the supernatural Pentecostal experience called the baptism of the Holy Ghost. This historical event first occurred in 31 AD, in the Upper Room at Jerusalem in the presence of Mary, Jesus' mother, and His disciples. After personally receiving this supernatural impartation by the resurrected Spirit of Christ, almost 25 years ago in Washington, DC (just three blocks from the White House), I became fully persuaded of the Bible's authenticity and that the supernatural component of the New Testament is still valid today. The reality of my discovery of the biblical Jesus that was foreign to the European church world, and its anti-Semitic history, validated my faith with tangible *substance,* rather than with vain blind religious traditions. The Bible presented a supernatural Jesus (and supernatural followers of Christ), whom Europeans could not control, who were not a part of the European Christian experience, or doctrines (for almost seventeen centuries). However, Rome transformed the miraculous and supernatural Christian church into a cerebral, liturgical, and ceremonial church plagued with endless traditions contrary to the scriptures.

Consequently, the God of heaven is stirring up something in the spiritual world to compel the inhabitants of earth to fulfill His prophetic script, whether they are cognizant of it or not! A new day is on the horizon and the issues of the past are being rectified in the hearts of men to counteract the confusion and religious hypocrisy of the past. During

3

my last two trips to Israel, I spoke with Muslims and Jews whose historical encounters with the Christian world made them victims of a European Jesus that seemed to cause His followers to exterminate and exploit those deemed inferior. Neither the Muslims, nor the Jews, that I spoke with had heard an accurate account of the historical biblical Jesus. Their exposure to the Christian faith for over one thousand years were primarily through the Roman Universal (Catholic) Church, and her Eastern twin sister, the Greek Orthodox Church. During the past five hundred years, the Western European Protestant church world continued the anti-Semitic tendencies of their mother church at Rome.

I explained to both groups that people of African descent in America also had a turbulent struggle with the Christian religion, and that **they had just cause to reject the European Jesus**. One of my primary objectives was to show how Jesus (the author of the divine prophetic script) has established from the foundation of the world, the roles that nations, kindred, and tongues would portray in fulfilling Bible prophecy. Therefore, events past, present and future have contributed to a definitive destiny. An accurate portrayal of Christ helped to dispel their misconceptions, and explained how the abuses committed by Western and Eastern European Christians (**Eurocentric Christianity**) were actually a part of the biblical prophetic script. My message was well received and convinced many to examine the scriptures further to see if the information I had conveyed was true. Subsequently some have become Christians.

While in Israel, I also spoke with several German and Russian Christians who also discovered "the real Jesus." Many have come to the Holy Land to give their lives for the Jewish people, if necessary, even if the Jewish nation does not understand the prophetic script, and to be honorable witnesses of Christ. They, like myself, presented to the Jewish people the true Jesus, whom their European fathers misrepresented and did not know. God is seemingly doing a new thing in the earth and upcoming future events will be noticeably unprecedented in human history. For those who are not aware of this divine spiritual shift in human affairs, they may not realize that the final preparatory event that will set the stage for Jewish end time prophetic fulfillment, and the plight of the Eurocentric church, draws near.

In Bulgaria, France and the Philippines I presented to Christian church leaders the Hebraic roots of the biblical Jesus and conclusively showed that Christ was not the guardian of European culture. I explained that He was in fact a Jew, and reminded them that so were all the prophets and apostles. They began to understand how anti-Semitism blinds the hearts and subconsciously perverts the minds of men, causing them to error in doctrine, and misrepresent Jesus Christ. In the Philippine city of Bacolod, a former vice mayor who was disenchanted with Christianity, and was on the verge of converting to Islam, totally changed his plans after hearing the message of the biblical Jesus. My life has been thoroughly enriched after witnessing men of all religious persuasions and denominational backgrounds humble themselves, and come out of their self imposed cultural security blankets, to receive an accurate portrayal of Jesus Christ.

Christ is uniting people of all races, kindreds, and tongues on a scale that is unprecedented in human history to become biblical Christians and shed off the yokes of

4

denominational Christianity. Eastern and Western Europeans, Africans, Northern and Southern Americans, Asians, Russians, and Australian Christians are unifying through obedience to the scriptures and a newly found love for the Jewish people. **The grand-children of former Nazis, the descents of slave owners and the descendents of slaves are lifting their hands together in worship and praise to the God of Israel. Despite their past and many cultural differences, many have discovered the true and living biblical Jesus Christ.** Many have forsaken their Catholic and Protestant traditions and have united through Pentecost by receiving of the baptism of Holy Ghost.

My two recent trips to Israel were immensely exciting and hopeful because I saw a new church in the process of emerging out of the cultural and religious bondage of the past. I spoke with a company of Jews and Arabs, who had cultural scales of bondage removed from their eyes, and discovered the biblical Jesus. In the midst of a world held hostage to terrorism and religious conflicts, a quiet revolution was happening in the hearts of men, sending them on the road to truth, and the winning side of the end time prophetic scenario.

As I travel worldwide, I am overwhelmed to see Christians of many nationalities supernaturally drawn to assist the Jewish nation, pray for them, and unite with them in their feast day celebrations. **These acts do not erase the horrific legacy of Western Christianity, but it does establish an olive branch of peace and love, to show the nation of Israel another face of Jesus that is historically accurate and contrary to past misrepresentations.** The biblical Jesus is historical, alive, and changing the hearts of men. The Jewish nation has not seen a true representation of Jesus since the first century Jewish Christians. Most contemporary Jews are familiar only with the European representation of Christ that persecuted their people. **True Christians are realizing that their eternal fate and end time prophetic destiny is directly tied to the plight of natural Israel.** They have come to understand that when all scriptures have been fulfilled, both natural Israel (the Jews) and spiritual Israel (the church), will be delivered from their calamities and united as one in Christ. **Many Muslims, Jews, and Christians, though in conflict now, will understand the Messianic prophesies and walk hand in hand with Christ in the last days.**

It is nothing less than a miracle, and a major fulfillment of the divine script, how the Jews and their descendents from all over the world are being drawn to gather together in the Holy Land. The God of Adam, Noah and Abraham beckoned the animals to come into the Ark as they were gathered to fulfil His divine purpose. In the same manner the current migration to Israel by Jews, from all quadrants of the earth, is one of the most important prophecies last century to set the stage for the end time biblical scenario. This Jewish migration back to Israel is called **The Aliya**, meaning "going up," or ingathering. Jews from North America, Eastern and Western Europe, Asia, Africa and the Middle East are being led home to their Promised Land for many reasons, but some do not even know why they feel compelled to go. In 1984 and 1991, the Israeli government launched two secret operations, **Operation Moses**, and **Operation**

Solomon to smuggle over 23,000 Ethiopian Jews from Ethiopia, and resettle them in Israel. After almost two thousand years of captivity, persecution, and genocide the Jewish people no longer live in the Diaspora, had no country of homeland; but in the fullness of time, according to God's divine timing, these things are now coming to pass.

> *"Therefore thus saith the Lord GOD; Now will **I bring again the captivity of Jacob, and have mercy upon the whole house of Israel**, and will be jealous for my holy name;*
> *After that they have borne their shame, and all their trespasses whereby they have trespassed against me, when they dwelt safely in their land, and none made them afraid.*
> ***When I have brought them again from the people, and gathered them out of their enemies' lands, and am sanctified in them in the sight of many nations;***
> *Then shall they know that **I am the LORD their God, which cause them to be led into captivity among the heathen: but I have gathered them unto their own land, and have left none of them any more there.***
> *Neither will I hide my face any more from them: for I have poured out my spirit upon the house of Israel, saith the Lord GOD."* (Ezek 39:25-29)

On May 1, 1948 the Jews were reestablished as a nation again to fulfill their prophetic destiny. The key players, the US, the UN, and the USSR could not be excluded from this end time drama, even though they had no idea of their role in helping to fulfill the divine script. I must also mention that out of all the nations and civilizations that have ever existed on the face of the earth, **only the nation of Israel can boast of its miraculous rebirth after nineteen hundred years of being scattered throughout the nations of the Roman Empire. She was preserved as a nation without a homeland after the destruction of Jerusalem in 70 AD**. Even more astounding is the fact that the Jewish Prophet Zechariah stated twenty-seven hundred years ago that the nation of Israel would be a burdensome stone to the whole world before the end of the ages.

> *"**Behold, I will make Jerusalem a cup of trembling unto all the people round about**, when they shall be in the siege both against Judah and against Jerusalem.*
> ***And in that day will I make Jerusalem a burdensome stone for all people**: all that burden themselves with it shall be cut in pieces, though all the people of the earth be gathered together against it."* (Zech 12:2,3)

Zechariah wrote these prophetic statements not knowing that the nation of Israel would be a silent voice in history from 70 AD to 1948. As slaves throughout the Roman Empire, the Jewish race became the vessels of scapegoating and victims of heinous racist atrocities for centuries. Nevertheless, God has raised this nation up from the grave to fulfil His end time Bible prophecies and send true Christians to turn the nation of Israel back to Christ, their rejected Messiah. Many may choose not to believe in Bible prophecy, but the laws of probability are totally in its favor. Hundreds of prophecies concerning Christ as the Messiah were fulfilled at His first coming, and an overwhelming number of prophetic declarations will unfold in the near future. Every believing Christian and all skeptics will have an opportunity to experience firsthand, the validity of the Bible, as the divine script is implemented through contemporary world events. This modern age will conclude at the last great battle, between Christ and the Antichrist forces called the Battle of Armageddon in northern Israel as He returns with the saints of God and the hosts of heaven. He shall also touch the Mount of Olives, which faces the old city of Jerusalem, causing a mighty earthquake type split of the mountain.

"Behold, the day of the LORD cometh, and thy spoil shall be divided in the midst of thee . . .
Then shall the LORD go forth, and fight against those nations, as when he fought in the day of battle.
And his feet shall stand in that day upon the mount of Olives, which is before Jerusalem on the east, and the mount of Olives shall cleave in the midst thereof toward the east and toward the west, *and there shall be a very great valley; and half of the mountain shall remove toward the north, and half of it toward the south.*
And ye shall flee to the valley of the mountains; for the valley of the mountains shall reach unto Azal: yea, ye shall flee, like as ye fled from before the earthquake in the days of Uzziah king of Judah: and **the LORD my God shall come, and all the saints with thee.**
And it shall come to pass in that day, that the light shall not be clear, nor dark: But it shall be one day which shall be known to the LORD, not day, nor night: but it shall come to pass, that at evening time it shall be light.
And it shall be in that day, that living waters shall go out from Jerusalem; half of them toward the former sea, and half of them toward the hinder sea: in summer and in winter shall it be.
And the LORD shall be king over all the earth: in that day shall there be one LORD, and his name one . . .
And men shall dwell in it, and there shall be no more utter destruction; but Jerusalem shall be safely inhabited.
And this shall be the plague wherewith the LORD will smite all the people that have fought against Jerusalem; Their flesh shall consume away while they stand upon their feet, and their eyes shall consume away in their holes, and their tongue shall consume away in their mouth." (Zech 14:1-12)

In the Beginning It was Not So!

As we explore the subject of the true identity of Jesus Christ, several legitimate questions must be examined: How did the legacy of the European Jesus that causes people to hate and commit human carnage around the globe develop such an anti-Semitic and anti-Christ mentality? What did the Jewish prophets and apostles state would be the methods employed by Christ to rectify anti-Semitic Christianity and judge His church? What do the book of Revelation and the epistles of the Jewish Apostles have to say about the role the church will play in the last days and during the Great Tribulation? Which, if any, of the many Eurocentric theories concerning the timing of the rapture of the church and the Second Coming of Christ are accurate?

If Jesus Christ were to return today to make a declaration to the church, He would most likely utter the following words to the thousands of Christian denominational sects that currently exist. "**In the beginning it was not so!**" Can you believe that there are more Christian denominational sects than there are pages in the Bible (including the pages of large print editions for the visually impaired)? It appears that human nature causes many to despise reproof and that *people in general do not like to be told that they have been deceived or their beliefs are incorrect.* However, with so many contrary beliefs in Christianity, everyone cannot be correct and all doctrines cannot be true.

I am always astonished when I ask Christians if they have ever read the entire Bible. They, more times than not, respond by stating that they have not even read most of the Bible. Neither has most studied its contents for clarity, sound doctrine, or social issues. In essence, the confusion found in Christianity is due in part to the fact that few have ever read the guidelines of the New Covenant, but have subsequently infused their own preferred beliefs within it. Despite these apparent contradictions and self-imposed ignorance, they still claim to be Christians. With so many contrary opinions and confusion surrounding Christianity, there seems to be no uniform standard or definition for the faith. Over the centuries, there has developed a mutual degree of tolerance for each other's doctrines, even though some still call rival Christian sects, "cults."

I found that many church leaders, who are suppose to be ambassadors of Christ, actually represented themselves, and only established their own kingdoms in the name of Christ. Unfortunately, many represent their religious organization, and pledge their allegiance to their cultural religious traditions, at the expense of the biblical truth. Christian bishops, pastors, and elders are suppose to be the guardians of Christ's bride, and trustees of the mysteries of God; but instead, **they impregnate the members of the bride of Christ (the church) with their own doctrinal seeds, and pervert the mysteries of God**. Maybe this behavioral pattern is a defect found deep within the human psyche, and the religious who walk contrary to the Bible cannot escape its grasp. We find similar manifestations in the political arena when politicians betray their public trust. Noble public servants, which aspire to occupy an elected office for the betterment of society, forsake their call to be servants of the people, and represent their own self- interests. Unfortunately, pride, power, perks and special interests groups transformed them instead. Internal corruption within the hearts of men seems to cause religious leaders, as well as politicians, to swerve from their humble servitude for the people and seek their own self-preservation. Truth, honesty, and integrity are compromised, and the masses support such activities as long as the leaders tell them what they want to hear. Such is also the case concerning the religious who lay in wait to be deceived.

When truth confronts error, there must be a radical shift and departure from falsehood, or there will be an unforgiving rejection of truth in order to preserve one's comfort zone. The sincere student, who searches for truth, would not take offence at correction, but would delight in it, because it will keep him on the correct path. He realizes that truth will eventually help him accomplish his noble quest. However, few embark upon this journey. Truth is also very evasive, because one must have a sincere heart that is not tainted with preconceived biases and open to honest assessment in order to receive it. Apparently, few have scrutinized their own faith (as well as those of others) to objectively test their beliefs to see if they are full proof. Because of a lack of understanding of their own beliefs, some pronounce that polar religious views are not only compatible, they are also the same. For example, the belief by some that biblical creation and Darwinian evolution is compatible. Even something as simple as the Christian practice of water baptism illustrates the rebellion and confusion found in Christianity. Some baptize by sprinkling, some by pouring, and others by immersion; some baptize forward, some backwards, and some not at all. This also is confusion! They may even naively say that all Christian churches teach about Jesus; therefore, they must all be the same. The great dilemma found in Christianity is will the real Jesus Christ please stand up? Their lack of knowledge of the faith and rebellion to New Testament commands hampers truth and muddies the water of understanding amongst those who are not Christians.

Christianity and its many founding denominational fathers do not adhere to biblical Jewish apostolic commandments. To the contrary, they serve to the laymen, a religious buffet of doctrines based on personal preference, political correctness, and denominational traditions. All of these acts produce religious confusion and error, and ensures that few can understand the Bible, its author, and its original purpose and intent. There are seminaries all over the world with men forever studying, but seemingly *"never able to come to the knowledge of the truth."*

Again, **in the beginning it was not so!** The church world as we know it today does not resemble in doctrine or practice the tenets of the First Century Church established by the Jewish Disciples of Christ. This is primarily due to the fact that the concept of "**Christianity**" is a bi-product of European doctrines, denominationalism, and culture that is **foreign to the New Testament scriptures**. The First Century Church was able to maintain its cohesiveness even though it was comprised of both Jews and Gentiles, while operating under an apostolic *theocratic government* of apostles,

9

prophets, evangelists, pastors, and teachers. Amazingly, the Jewish apostles preached the gospel of the kingdom under the anointing of the Spirit of Christ even though they did not have a canonized New Testament. In fact, none of the original apostles ever saw the book of Revelation, except John who wrote it. The apostles of Jesus Christ came from different occupations and a variety of educational levels, yet they were able to preach the exact same gospel, reveal the same doctrine for salvation, and establish only one body of believers on three different continents. Their message was **one Lord, one faith, one baptism, and one covenant with only one eternal head of the church**. Christianity's culturally biased oath of the fourth century, the **Nicean Creed**, does not adhere to Jewish apostolic authority or the Bible. It places the central powers of the church in the hands of the *"Holy Catholic and Apostolic Church, "* and it's Roman Emperor, the Pope.

In the beginning it was not so! The church, since the second century, became infused with pagan theology, and a European-style anti-Semitic sanitizing of Jewish cultural roots, and New Testament commandments, from their Christian experience. Hence, European church founders would rival and usurp their authority over the biblical apostles of Christ, substituting their doctrines in place of scriptures. Some would even use supplemental texts, like *the Apocrypha*, the *Book of Mormons*, the *Lost Books of Eden*, the *Book of Enoch*, the *Book of Barnabas*, and the *Sixth and Seventh Books of Moses* to justify their deviant doctrines. Others would reject accurate translations of the bible and substitute them with "dummied-down" modern translations such as *The Living*, *Good News for Modern Man*, and the *New International Version*, or translations that deny the claims of Christ, the *New World Translation*. Some have even alleged though New Age philosophies found in the concept of *The da Vinci Code* that Jesus married and fathered children through Mary Magdalene or that Jesus is one of many ascended masters in the *Aquarian Gospel of Jesus Christ*.

Another twist in my investigation led to the discovery that for centuries layman could not, and were not allowed, to read the Bible. They were commanded to obey the Pope only and confess their sins to the priests at the confessionals. When layman began reading, starting in the sixteenth century, they were told that only the clergy could interpret the Bible for them, hear the voice of God, and be the mediators between God for them. **Like blind sheep, the "Christian" masses followed the clergy with a religious passion, yet having no biblical knowledge.** They simply repeated what they were taught (like a parrot) but never examined the biblical evidence themselves. Hence, every manner of evil was done in the name of Christ throughout the earth, even though men did not know Christ. **A bloody Christless religion soon emerged, and the legacy of a European Jesus that killed permeated the earth**. This was especially prominent among the persecuted Jews and those who kept the original teaching of the Jewish apostolic fathers. To the victims of religious genocide in the Americas, Africa, Asia, and India, these deeds were often done in the name of the Roman Catholic Church. They also became common among her rebellious denominational children, the Protestant churches. The inquisition, the Catholic crusades, the Russian Programs,

10

the German Holocaust, African slavery, and the doctrine Manifest Destiny for Native Americans were examples of the legacy of blood that swept the earth and gave the biblical Jesus a bad rap.

Throughout the history of the European church, there have been periods of genocide, where members of Christianity would wage doctrinal wars against each other, and massacre each other in the name of Christ. **There were Christians killing Christians over communion**, which represents the blood and body of Christ. This was madness! Hence, gang warfare developed in the churches of men, all in the name of Christ. It is no wonder that anyone who is not a Christian may find it hard to see any desirable attributes in the European Jesus. **The misrepresentation of Christ throughout the church age has been so perverted, that if Christ had to return again as a man seeking employment, He would not be able to get a job impersonating Himself.** In order for the Christian kingdoms of men to understand what God will do in the very near future **they must honestly assess their brutal history, be transformed in their hearts, and become compliant with the biblical church fathers, rather than their glorified European church fathers.**

In the past three decades the Christian media and numerous religious publications have had a tremendous global impact upon Christian thought. However, their collective effects have been both a blessing and a curse. The blessing has been the fact that through modern technology, many more people have heard of Christ and the physical needs of millions have been enhanced by expressions of love, charity, and humanitarian aid solicited through such means. The question still remains, which Jesus has been introduced through the media and the missionaries of the thousands of Christian denominational sects? Most Christian radio and television managers, newspaper editors, and book publishers still uphold the traditions of the European Jesus, and suppress material that is not considered culturally or religiously correct. However, an increasing number of individuals are escaping out of such cultural censorship, and are now reading the entire Bible. They are beginning to think outside of the "*cultural box*" in search of truth and the biblical Jesus.

Where religion failed to further the goals of European global conquest, the absence of religion appears to have completed the task. The religious monarchs of Eastern Europe and Asia were replaced by atheistic communistic states. With or without God, the Greco-Roman's desire to conquer infested the earth with a Marxist ideological twist during the fifty-year Cold War. It polarized the world into two revolutionary rival factions: NATO and the WARSAW PACT nations. Currently, **European imperialism successfully exports Western culture worldwide through religion, atheistic communism, and pseudo-scientific theories**. Both the secular and religious worlds are walking in unison, in preparation, and in anticipation of a Western utopian world order. This fourth and final upcoming European Reich of socialistic global control will establish **a one-world government, a one world religious system, and a one world economic system to fulfill the Jewish biblical prophetic script**. The God of history knew the barbaric acts that would be committed upon the nations of the earth, starting with the Greeks, and followed by the Romans, until the New World Order and the Second Coming of Christ. The Bible reveals a prophetic Jesus whom Westerners have betrayed, and even though they claim to have the Spirit of Christ, they are confused as to what role they will play in the divine plot.

Unbeknown to the sons of men, their great religious plans and secular utopian schemes are also according to the divine script. Like a wheel within a wheel, few can see the big picture of God's divine hand leading mankind to a definitive destiny. The righteous are led by the Spirit of Christ, but the wicked are manipulated by Satan to commit the sins of the flesh (pride, jealously, greed, diverse lust, fear, murder, depression, impatience, anger, strife, gossip, division, sedition, heresy, fornication, and adultery, to name a few). Therefore, both the righteous and the wicked partake in the divine script, whether they realize it or not. Those who are deists and the agnostics refuse to believe that the Creator is intimately involved in the affairs of men. However, the ignorance and unbelief of men does not negate or make void the prophetic word of God!

The following individuals, John the Baptist, Simon Peter, Judas, and the Jewish Sanhedrin, all did the will of God. Some did it for their profit, others to their demise. Regardless of the knowledge and wisdom of men, even at their technological peaks, there is no comparison to the knowledge and scope of an "all wise" God, who knows everything, and has known the conclusion of world's affairs before the world began.

Humanity and the church world have reached their pinnacle, through the prophetic word of God, which began to accelerate in frequency and intensity towards its fulfillment, through many natural signs, and the establishment of a global government. **European Christianity is on the verge of reaching its apex and destiny, as the revived Roman Empire unfolds in the form of a New World Order**. The prophetic script was written thousands of years ago by the Jewish prophets, dictating historical events and the conclusion of human history, as we know it. The church world *should* know God's divine plan and be with one accord concerning it; however, Christianity is just as confusing (and in some cases unbelieving) as the unbelievers.

For the sake of God's elect, the church is slowly and methodically being restored back to the way it was at the beginning of the first century. The Azusa Street Revivals of Los Angeles, California in 1906 was a key starting point to trace this voyage back to America's *truth and restoration* of the original doctrines of the Jewish apostolic church. Even though men have misrepresented Christ, He will soon raise up a people from all nations and tongues, who will reveal Him *in spirit and in truth*, and dispel all imposters.

Christ has already begun the systematic destruction of all denominations and will soon unfold a new line of demarcation for the final global conflict between the forces of light and the powers of darkness. For example, sexual scandals, sexual perversion, incest, and divorce within the nuclear heterosexual family structure has rocked the Western church world. The infestation of the contemporary church by male homosexuals and lesbian church leaders, and the exposure of decades of pedophile Catholic priests have sent many in Christianity scrambling for the first time, to rediscover the foundations of the Christian faith. Why? Because **in the beginning it was not so!**

Without exception, when these subjects are addressed in the New Testament, those who partake in such activities are guaranteed to receive eternal judgement. Sexual vice has been a European problem ever since the early Greek and Roman Empires; therefore, one should not be surprised that the European religious and secular worlds are beginning to walk in unison to fulfill their prophetic destiny and justify their iniquity. **Modern Rome, in the guise of Christianity, is being rocked and shakened at its religious core to expose its anti-biblical doctrines and non-biblical roots.** This too is the hand of God separating the righteous from the apostate in His kingdom.

Many people the world-over perceives America to be a Christian nation, rich in freedom, and bathed in immense wealth. However, to their dismay, some have become confused because of the media, about the exportation of graphic violence, anti-Christian morals, and sexual deviance. Some within the Islamic faith even accused America of being the "Great Satan," because of its cultural perversions, religious hypocrisies, and immoral cultural norms. Consequently, the Eurocentric Christian faith has only increased its credibility problem. Of course, not understanding the liberties and diversity of contemporary America, many non-Western religious groups have questioned the validity of the Christian faith and America's existentialistic (one can do what ever they believe is right) Christianity. Even America's rejection of polygamy is being challenged because of its soaring divorce rate and repetitive blended families. The reciprocal practice among women of having more than one husband is called polyandry. In America one may now have many spouses and yet legally claim that no polygamy or polyandry has been practiced because they did not have their spouses concurrently. Instead they have numerous wives and husbands from one marriage relationship to another. Tragically, the rate of divorce in the Christian church is the same as with the unbelievers. **In the beginning it was not so!**

While there is a systematic dismantling of Western Christianity due to sin, vice, corruption, and persecution by secular humanistic governments in many Western nations, few realize that there are also spiritual conflicts that are raging in the heavenlies for the souls of men. To hasten matters, America is rewriting history and forsaking its Judeo-Christian heritage in her schools and public places. America's current liberal activist driven courts, in conjunction with the socialistic organization, the American Civil Liberties Union (ACLU), is helping to accomplish this task. The ACLU has served literally as the devil's advocate and catalyst to challenge the American commitment to the truth of the gospel and fulfill her divine script. This current situation is in the same manner, that the disciple Judas was used by the prince of darkness, to fulfill his role in God's divine plan with Christ. The ACLU has helped to propagate the Eurocentric theory of evolution and the removal of the images of the Christian Messiah from public display. Unfortunately, one day American Christians will awaken from their materialistic slumber to discover that they have allowed themselves to accept, with little opposition, a democratic socialistic system of humanistic **World Governance**. A revived Roman Empire will be fully established and its coming global Caesar will be the Antichrist.

What many Christians fail to realize is that Christ is allowing the dismantling of Christianity through use of secular agencies and institutions.

On every front, whether religious or secular, it appears that despite the philosophies or ideologies of the European worldview, all human affairs are proceeding in accordance with the divine script. Some have tried to break the Bible code of secrecy through a kabalistic-type numerical and computer analysis of the Hebrew letters. However, if the secrets of God are concealed in numerical codes, then only skilled mathematicians could know the mysteries of God. Others have dismissed the Bible as being Jewish folklore, having no bearing on the future whatsoever. There are also religious groups, like the former Heaven's Gate religious sect, that perverted the end time message and met their demise through coordinated mass suicides. They anticipated aliens on the backside of an asteroid to catch them away from the earth. There have been various groups who prophesied the *dates* of Christ's return and have been proven wrong. Others have seen apparitions that claim to be Jesus or His mother Mary. Consequently, they produce doctrines that were totally contrary to established biblical truths.

Despite the many counterfeits, the key to knowing the truth concerning the end times is quite simple and can be clearly seen in scripture. However, it is a misconception that most will receive the truth, because they are shackled by unrepentant vices, private beliefs, and preconceived biases. Even though the biblical text is quite clear concerning the end times, scholars and theologians are in a whirlwind of confusion concerning Bible prophecy. Few can study the Bible and let it speak for itself, because it wars against their desired beliefs.

The truth can only be revealed to those who are open to receive it and willing to allow the light of **the divine constitution** to pierce through their darkness.

In the jungle of confusion, many religious leaders retreat from taking a stand on the various issues, claiming that it does not concern them, which view of the rapture is correct, believing with confidence, that they will be ready regardless. However, their concept of readiness is a paradox because, **it is impossible for one to prepare for something if he does not know how or what to prepare for**, especially, if they are admonished by Christ to endure until the end! *"He that hath an ear let him hear . . .* **Just as in the days of Noah, so shall also be the coming of the Son of Man."** There is no way, that the inhabitants of the earth prior to the flood could have prepared themselves for the cataclysmic events that would follow, except they received specific instructions from the Lord of Judgment.

Much debate and speculation persist in Christianity over the role the church and the nation of Israel will play in the last days. Needless to say, **because of extreme anti-Semitic bias, most Western end time biblical theories have displaced the Jews with their own denomination or religious sect, calling themselves the newly chosen people of God. They may even go further and claim that the tribulation period is designated only for the Jews to avenge their crucifixion of Christ.** These two major errors prohibit them from even beginning to unravel the mysteries concerning the end times. Even more important, is the fact that the Christian religion was initially a Jewish religion, fulfilling the promises God made with the Patriarch Abraham. **Western Christianity has failed to realize is that the tribulation period has been custom designed for all sectors of Christianity.** Both natural Israel and spiritual Israel will have an opportunity to come clean before a holy God. During this period there will be a major reduction of Christian denominations and religious sects. Currently there are over 25,000 denominational groups. When Jesus Christ finishes His correction and chastisement of those whom He loves, there will be only one. This period will be among the greatest days for Christ, but a nightmare for all Christians who refuse to abide in the divine constitution, the Bible. European imperialism and cultural pride will not alter God's divine script; in fact their attitudes and doctrines will help set the stage for the final conflict between the God of heaven and the forces of darkness. Cultural prejudices towards Jews have ensnared many that see only the Jews when they interpret the book of Revelation. What they fail to realize is that no one in the predominately Gentile church will be raptured until the church fulfills its primary purpose, which is to provoke the Jews to jealousy and convert them to their Messiah.

There are several theories that Western Christian theologians have developed to explain their views on the rapture of the church, the plight of the nation of Israel, and the Second Coming of Christ. Their primary areas of dispute center around: 1) when the rapture actually takes place, 2) the number of resurrections or raptures, 3) who actually represents current day Israel, 4) the literal or figurative concept of the tribulation, and 5) the millennium kingdom reign of Christ. These divergent and contradictory theories have been the source of much debate and confusion for the masses, keeping them in a *"ball of confusion."* The terms and genuine biblical doctrines that have been slanted with an anti-Semitic bias and given preferential treatment to the Gentile Eurocentric church are as follows:

The Rapture - This is not a biblical term but it is a common term used to describe a biblical concept. Biblically identified as "the *quickening*," this supernatural event is the hope of all faithful Christians. It refers to a designated time in human history that true Christian disciples of Christ will be transformed, from mortality to immortality, by the power of the resurrected Christ, and "caught up" to meet Him in the air.

The Resurrection – The process of being raised from the dead after one has experienced natural death.

The Tribulation – A seven year period of perfect judgments and wrath upon the inhabitants of the earth. It includes three and a-half years of judgment upon Satan and his kingdom, which will be cast down to earth to be judged with the rebellious and unbelieving masses of the earth.

The Millennium – This is a one thousand year reign of the Jewish Messiah on earth from the city of Jerusalem, after the Tribulation period. This is the Messiah that the Jews of the first century were looking for, as the prophesied Lion of the Tribe of Judah, whose kingdom would have no end. Jewish Christians of the first century would call this event the Second Coming of Christ and the fulfillment of the Jewish Feast of Tabernacle.

Dispensationalism – This word comes from the root word dispensation, which implies a specified time period, or several periods of time. Unfortunately this concept, once applied to the biblical interpretation of the end times, has become not only very anti-Semitic, but also purely Eurocentric. Case and point: the seven Churches of Asia found in Revelation chapters two and three, are used by European church scholars in reference to seven time periods in their Western church history. Using only the history of the Roman Catholic Church, the Protestant Reformation, and their historical development for support, the church is portrayed as a European entity. This method of rewriting church history excludes all churches with Jewish Pentecostal roots since the first century and tries to legitimize the illegitimate traditions and doctrines of the Western world. The first major error in this assessment is that the second and third chapters of the book of Revelation make no reference to any sort of time period or dispensation whatsoever. This well accepted, but biblically unfounded concept of dispensationalism is a distortion of the truth. It is also a fabrication to debase the church from its Jewish roots, and promote the myth that the God of Abraham, Isaac, and Jacob has forsaken the Jews, and put the Europeans in their stead.

The major Eurocentric theories are as follows: Dispensational Premillennialism (Pre Tribulationists), Amillennialism, Postmillennialism, Historic Premillenialism (Historic Post-tribulationism), Midtribulationism, Preterism, Posttribulationism.

Dispensational Premillennialism / Pre-Tribulationist Beliefs

■ This theory proposes that there are at least two raptures and two returns of Christ yet remaining; one before the Great Tribulation, and one seven years afterwards. Some even add a third rapture midway through the Tribulation for the "left behind" Christians. They believe that converted Jews will then be raptured at the end of the Tribulation. Hence, there could be at least three raptures for those who are in Christ.

■ Believing that the Second Coming occurs in two phases. The majority in the Western church world prescribes to the religiously correct pre-tribulation rapture of the church, and the post tribulation rapture of the *"left behind"* tribulation saints, and Jews.

■ This belief clearly draws a clear distinction between the church and Israel. It also relegates the tribulation for the Jews to contend with the Antichrist, while the predominately Gentile church, is removed from the earth to escape the havoc of God's wrath and judgment on earth.

■ This doctrine also teaches that there will be a literal one thousand-year reign of Christ at the end of the Tribulation period.

16

Amillennialist Beliefs

■ The Amillennialist believes that the rapture of the church and the Second Coming of Christ are the same event; therefore, there is no gap or elapse of time between the two events.

■ They believe that Christians are already experiencing tribulation in this present age, and there will be no Great Tribulation period of seven years to come.

■ This belief prescribes to the idea that the church is the new Israel and God has chosen the church, spiritual Israel, as His only Israel. Therefore, the natural Jews are no longer God's chosen people, because the Gentile church has been substituted in their place.

■ They also reject the idea of a literal thousand year millennial reign of Christ at the conclusion of the church age.

Postmillennialist Beliefs

■ This interpretation of scripture asserts that there is no distinction between the Second Coming of Christ and the rapture of the church; however, they believe these events occur at the end of the one thousand year millennium period.

■ They believe that the resurrection of Christians and unbelievers occur together at the end of the millennium period. They proclaim this because they hold to the idea that the church age and the millennium period has no clear line of demarcation, and is a continuance for the furtherance of the gospel.

■ Like the amillenniumist, they believe that tribulation is an on going experience for the Christian and that there will be no special period or time span for such an event.

■ Also like the amillenniumist, they adhere to notion that the church is the new Israel and the Jews are no longer the elect of God.

Historic Premillenialism / Historic Post-Tribulationists Beliefs

■ The rapture and the Second Coming of Christ occur as simultaneous events at the end of the tribulation.

■ The church will go through the seven-year tribulation period and the Antichrist reign to fulfill their prophetic destiny.

■ The church is classified as spiritual Israel and the Jews as natural Israel. God has a redemption plan for both groups that are unique and separate.

■ This view teaches that the millennium is present and future tense, because Christ currently reigns in heaven and always will; therefore, it would not be necessary for Him to reign on earth.

Midtribulationism / Mid Tribulationalists Beliefs

■ Their theory alleges that there will be a rapture of the church midway through the seven-year tribulation period and another rapture for the Jews and those left behind at its end. It is a slight modification of the dispensational pre-millennium theory.

■ Like most Eurocentric theorists, mid-tribulationalists believe that the Second Coming of Christ and the Rapture are two distinct events occurring years apart.

■ They believe that the church is raptured first, then and at the end of the tribulation, the Jews will be raptured at Christ's Second Coming. There is a clear distinction between Jews and Christians; God has a plan to deal with both, but not at the same time.

■ The millennial kingdom of Christ will be established after the Great Tribulation period, at which time Christ will reign on earth.

Preterism / Preterist Beliefs

■ The Preterist believe that there will be no rapture or future resurrection. They assert that Matthew 24 and the book of Revelation has already been fulfilled. They further claim that the prophetic events declared by other Christian groups took place during the First Century; therefore, Bible prophecy is no longer future tense.

■ Preterist also believe there will not be a literal Second Coming of Christ. They interpret these portions of scriptures to be spiritual concepts, because Christ allegedly appears daily to assist them in their activities.

■ They believe that the Tribulation took place in the First Century through the Roman siege of the city of Jerusalem and the destruction of the Jewish temple.

■ Some may even believe that the resurrection is of the body in the future is invalid because they assert that the bodily resurrection was only for Christ and first century believers to convert them to the faith.

Posttribulationism / Post Tribulationalists Beliefs

■ The Second Coming of Christ and the rapture of the Church occur simultaneously as Christ meets the church in the clouds of heaven.

■ The Tribulation period lasts for seven years, the church goes through the entire process, and is raptured at its conclusion, and defeats the spirit of death. The church is used to conquer the Antichrist and his kingdom, and the spirit of death is defeated.

■ God has not forsaken the Jews and will deliver both natural and spiritual Israel from their sins through the Great Tribulation The church will provoke the Jews to jealousy and multitudes will be converted and believe that Jesus is their Messiah, thus fulfilling the covenant of Abraham.

■ Christ will reign on earth for a thousand years after the conclusion of the Tribulation period and resurrection of the saints of God (rapture). The wicked shall be raised in the second resurrection at the end of the millennium period, and cast into the Lake of Fire and Brimstone.

With so many contradictory beliefs, it is no wonder that the Christian faith can be considered in practice, a confusing religion. In the next couple of chapters we will take the Eurocentric theories to the crucible and test them to see if they will be able to stand under intense scrutiny. The most popular of the stated end time theories is the Pre-Tributationists view; however, we will find the Post-tribulationalists view to be the most accurate. The Preterist and the Amillennialist views are the most extreme and the most inaccurate; therefore, very little will be spoken of these views. At the conclusion of this book, I will provide conclusive evidence that Gentile Christians can be found through-out the book of Revelation, and have an awesome task to perform in the earth during the end times. The true church will have a spiritual coalition with the Jewish nation, confront the Antichrist, and bring great deliverance to all who desire to flee the chains of darkness imposed on the minds and hearts of men.

When Jesus Christ came the first time as the suffering Messiah, there were several hundred scriptures He fulfilled, which were prophetically spoken hundreds of years beforehand, by the Jewish prophets. The greater number of unfulfilled prophecies found in the Old and New Testaments pertain to the end times. Despite the best attempts by men to understand the prophetic text, only the spirit of Christ (who is also called the Spirit of Truth) can reveal the concealed prophetic mysteries of God. The following scriptural list is but a snapshot of events that Christ, and historical characters of His day partook of, to fulfill the divine script declared from the foundation of the world.

New Testament Accounts, Through the Gospel's, of Scriptures Being Fulfilled

Mt 1:22,23 "Now all this was done, that it might be fulfilled which was spoken of the Lord by the prophet, saying,

Behold, a virgin shall be with child, and shall bring forth a son, and they shall call his name Emmanuel, which being interpreted is, God with us." [Isa 7:14]

Mt 2:14,15 "When he arose, he took the young child and his mother by night, and departed into Egypt:

And was there until the death of Herod: that it might be fulfilled which was spoken of the Lord by the prophet, saying, Out of Egypt have I called my son." [Hos 11:1]

Mt 2:16-18 "Then Herod, when he saw that he was mocked of the wise men, was exceeding wroth, and sent forth, and slew all the children that were in

Bethlehem, and in all the coasts thereof, from two years old and under, according to the time which he had diligently enquired of the wise men.

Then was fulfilled that which was spoken by Jeremy the prophet, saying, In Rama was there a voice heard, lamentation, and weeping, and great mourning, Rachel weeping for her children, and would not be comforted, because they are not." [Jer 31:15]

Mt 2:19-23 "But when Herod was dead, behold, an angel of the Lord appeareth in a dream to Joseph in Egypt, Saying, Arise, and take the young child and his mother, and go into the land of Israel: for they are dead which sought the young child's life.

And he arose, and took the young child and his mother, and came into the land of Israel. But when he heard that Archelaus did reign in Judaea in the room of his father Herod, he was afraid to go thither: notwithstanding, being warned of God in a dream, he turned aside into the parts of Galilee:

And he came and dwelt in a city called Nazareth: that it might be fulfilled which was spoken by the prophets, He shall be called a Nazarene." [Isa 11:1]

Mt 4:12-17 "Now when Jesus had heard that John was cast into prison, he departed into Galilee; And leaving Nazareth, he came and dwelt in Capernaum, which is upon the sea coast, in the borders of Zabulon and Nephthalim:

That it might be fulfilled which was spoken by Esaias the prophet, saying, The land of Zabulon, and the land of Nephthalim, by the way of the sea, beyond Jordan, Galilee of the Gentiles;

The people which sat in darkness saw great light; and to them which sat in the region and shadow of death light is sprung up. From that time Jesus began to preach, and to say, Repent: for the kingdom of heaven is at hand." [Isa 9:1-2]

Mt 5:17,18 "Think not that I am come to destroy the law, or the prophets: I am not come to destroy, but to fulfil.

For verily I say unto you, Till heaven and earth pass, one jot or one tittle shall in no wise pass from the law, till all be fulfilled."

Mt 8:14-17 "And when Jesus was come into Peter's house, he saw his wife's mother laid, and sick of a fever. And he touched her hand, and the fever left her: and she arose, and ministered unto them.

When the even was come, they brought unto him many that were possessed with devils: and he cast out the spirits with his word, and healed all that were sick:

That it might be fulfilled which was spoken by Esaias the prophet, saying, Himself took our infirmities, and bare our sicknesses." [Isa 53:4]

Mt 12:14-23 "Then the Pharisees went out, and held a council against him, how they might destroy him.

But when Jesus knew it, he withdrew himself from thence: and great multitudes followed him, and he healed them all; And charged them that they should not make him known:

That it might be fulfilled which was spoken by Esaias the prophet, saying, Behold my servant, whom I have chosen; my beloved, in whom my soul is well pleased: I will put my spirit upon him, and he shall shew judgment to the Gentiles.

He shall not strive, nor cry; neither shall any man hear his voice in the streets. A bruised reed shall he not break, and smoking flax shall he not quench, till he send forth judgment unto victory. And in his name shall the Gentiles trust.

Then was brought unto him one possessed with a devil, blind, and dumb: and he healed him, insomuch that the blind and dumb both spake and saw. And all the people were amazed, and said, Is not this the son of David?" [Isa 42:1-4]

Mt 13:10-17 "Why speakest thou unto them in parables? He answered and said unto them, Because it is given unto you to know the mysteries of the kingdom of heaven, but to them it is not given.

For whosoever hath, to him shall be given, and he shall have more abundance: but whosoever hath not, from him shall be taken away even that he hath. Therefore speak I to them in parables: because they seeing see not; and hearing they hear not, neither do they understand.

And in them is fulfilled the prophecy of Esaias, which saith, By hearing ye shall hear, and shall not understand; and seeing ye shall see, and shall not perceive:

For this people's heart is waxed gross, and their ears are dull of hearing, and their eyes they have closed; lest at any time they should see with their eyes, and hear with their ears, and should understand with their heart, and should be converted, and I should heal them. But blessed are your eyes, for they see: and your ears, for they hear.

For verily I say unto you, That many prophets and righteous men have desired to see those things which ye see, and have not seen them; and to hear those things which ye hear, and have not heard them." [Isa 6:9.10]

Mt 13:34,35 "All these things spake Jesus unto the multitude in parables; and without a parable spake he not unto them:

That it might be fulfilled which was spoken by the prophet, saying, I will open my mouth in parables; I will utter things which have been kept secret from the foundation of the world." [Psa 78:2]

Mt 21:1-5 "And when they drew nigh unto Jerusalem, and were come to Bethphage, unto the mount of Olives, then sent Jesus two disciples,

Saying unto them, Go into the village over against you, and straightway ye shall find an ass tied, and a colt with her: loose them, and bring them unto me.

And if any man say ought unto you, ye shall say, The Lord hath need of them;

and straightway he will send them.

All this was done, that it might be fulfilled which was spoken by the prophet, saying.

Tell ye the daughter of Sion, Behold, thy King cometh unto thee, meek, and sitting upon an ass, and a colt the foal of an ass." [Isa 62:11, Zech 9:9]

Mt 26:51-56 "And, behold, one of them which were with Jesus stretched out his hand, and drew his sword, and struck a servant of the high priest's, and smote off his ear.

Then said Jesus unto him, Put up again thy sword into his place: for all they that take the sword shall perish with the sword. Thinkest thou that I cannot now pray to my Father, and he shall presently give me more than twelve legions of angels?

But how then shall the scriptures be fulfilled, that thus it must be? In that same hour said Jesus to the multitudes, Are ye come out as against a thief with swords and staves for to take me? I sat daily with you teaching in the temple, and ye laid no hold on me.

But all this was done, that the scriptures of the prophets might be fulfilled. Then all the disciples forsook him, and fled." [Isa 53:1-12]

Mt 27:3-10 "Then Judas, which had betrayed him, when he saw that he was condemned, repented himself, and brought again the thirty pieces of silver to the chief priests and elders,

Saying, I have sinned in that I have betrayed the innocent blood. And they said, What is that to us? see thou to that. And he cast down the pieces of silver in the temple, and departed, and went and hanged himself. And the chief priests took the silver pieces, and said, It is not lawful for to put them into the treasury, because it is the price of blood.

And they took counsel, and bought with them the potter's field, to bury strangers in.

Wherefore that field was called, The field of blood, unto this day.

Then was fulfilled that which was spoken by Jeremy the prophet, saying, And they took the thirty pieces of silver, the price of him that was valued, whom they of the children of Israel did value; And gave them for the potter's field, as the Lord appointed me." [Zech 11:12,13]

Mt 27:33-35 "And when they were come unto a place called Golgotha, that is to say, a place of a skull, They gave him vinegar to drink mingled with gall: and when he had tasted thereof, he would not drink.

And they crucified him, and parted his garments, casting lots: that it might be fulfilled which was spoken by the prophet, They parted my garments among them, and upon my vesture did they cast lots." [Psa 22:18]

Mk 13:3-8 "And as he sat upon the mount of Olives over against the temple, Peter and James and John and Andrew asked him privately,

Tell us, when shall these things be? and what shall be the sign when all these things shall be fulfilled?

And Jesus answering them began to say, Take heed lest any man deceive you: For many shall come in my name, saying, I am Christ; and shall deceive many. And when ye shall hear of wars and rumours of wars, be ye not troubled: for such things must needs be; but the end shall not be yet.

For nation shall rise against nation, and kingdom against kingdom: and there shall be earthquakes in divers places, and there shall be famines and troubles: these are the beginnings of sorrows."

Mk 15:26-28 "And the superscription of his accusation was written over, THE KING OF THE JEWS. And with him they crucify two thieves; the one on his right hand, and the other on his left.

And the scripture was fulfilled, which saith, And he was numbered with the transgressors." [Isa 53:12]

Lk 4:16-22 "And he came to Nazareth, where he had been brought up: and, as his custom was, he went into the synagogue on the sabbath day, and stood up for to read.

And there was delivered unto him the book of the prophet Esaias. And when he had opened the book, he found the place where it was written,

The Spirit of the Lord is upon me, because he hath anointed me to preach the gospel to the poor; he hath sent me to heal the brokenhearted, to preach deliverance to the captives, and recovering of sight to the blind, to set at liberty them that are bruised,

To preach the acceptable year of the Lord.

And he closed the book, and he gave it again to the minister, and sat down. And the eyes of all them that were in the synagogue were fastened on him. And he began to say unto them,

This day is this scripture fulfilled in your ears. And all bare him witness, and wondered at the gracious words which proceeded out of his mouth. And they said, Is not this Joseph's son?" [Isa 61:1,2]

Lk 24:44-48 "And he said unto them, These are the words which I spake unto you, while I was yet with you, that all things must be fulfilled, which were written in the law of Moses, and in the prophets, and in the psalms, concerning me.

Then opened he their understanding, that they might understand the scriptures, And said unto them, Thus it is written, and thus it behoved Christ to suffer, and to rise from the dead the third day:

And that repentance and remission of sins should be preached in his name among all nations, beginning at Jerusalem. And ye are witnesses of these things." [Hos 6:2]

Jn 13:18-21 "I speak not of you all: I know whom I have chosen: but that the scripture may be fulfilled, He that eateth bread with me hath lifted up his heel against me.

Now I tell you before it come, that, when it is come to pass, ye may believe that I am he.

Verily, verily, I say unto you, He that receiveth whomsoever I send receiveth me; and he that receiveth me receiveth him that sent me.

When Jesus had thus said, he was troubled in spirit, and testified, and said, Verily, verily, I say unto you, that one of you shall betray me." [Psa 41:9]

Jn 15:22-25 "If I had not come and spoken unto them, they had not had sin: but now they have no cloke for their sin. He that hateth me hateth my Father also.

If I had not done among them the works which none other man did, they had not had sin: but now have they both seen and hated both me and my Father.

But this cometh to pass, that the word might be fulfilled that is written in their law, They hated me without a cause." [Psa 35:19; 69:4]

Jn 17:9-12 "I pray for them: I pray not for the world, but for them which thou hast given me; for they are thine.

And all mine are thine, and thine are mine; and I am glorified in them.

And now I am no more in the world, but these are in the world, and I come to thee. Holy Father, keep through thine own name those whom thou hast given me, that they may be one, as we are.

While I was with them in the world, I kept them in thy name: those that thou gavest me I have kept, and none of them is lost, but the son of perdition; that the scripture might be fulfilled." [Psa 41:9, Jn 6:70]

Jn 18:29-32 "Pilate then went out unto them, and said, What accusation bring ye against this man? They answered and said unto him, If he were not a malefactor, we would not have delivered him up unto thee.

Then said Pilate unto them, Take ye him, and judge him according to your law. The Jews therefore said unto him, It is not lawful for us to put any man to death:

That the saying of Jesus might be fulfilled, which he spake, signifying what death he should die. Then Pilate entered into the judgment hall again, and called Jesus, and said unto him, Art thou the King of the Jews?"

Jn 19:28-30 "After this, Jesus knowing that all things were now accomplished, that the scripture might be fulfilled, saith, I thirst.

Now there was set a vessel full of vinegar: and they filled a spunge with vinegar, and put it upon hyssop, and put it to his mouth. When Jesus therefore had received the vinegar, he said, It is finished: and he bowed his head, and gave up the ghost." [Psa 69:21]

Jn 19:32-37 "Then came the soldiers, and brake the legs of the first, and of the other which was crucified with him. But when they came to Jesus, and saw that he was dead already, they brake not his legs:

But one of the soldiers with a spear pierced his side, and forthwith came there out blood and water. And he that saw it bare record, and his record is true: and he knoweth that he saith true, that ye might believe.

For these things were done, that the scripture should be fulfilled, A bone of him shall not be broken. And again another scripture saith, They shall look on him whom they pierced." [Psa 34:20, Ex 12:46, Num 9:8-12]

The Manifestation of the Sons of God

Few Christians realize that the restoration of this temporal earth back to it's eternal, immortal realm of existence is predicated on the ministry of the manifested sons of God in the last days. **The completion of the three-and-a-half years of ministry** of the manifested sons of God parallels with the works of the Son of perdition, the Antichrist. The climax of these two opposing forces on earth **will trigger the quickening** or rapture of the church. At this juncture in human history, the bride of Christ, the church, will also be supernaturally transformed into the wife of Christ at His appearing (II Thes 2:1). The manifested Sons of God, or Manchild, will be the catalysts to prepare natural and spiritual Israel for the Second Coming of Jesus Christ.

At the beginning of creation, the world that now appears did not exist. We are told in the book of Romans chapter eight that the whole creation (the animals, plants, birds, fish, soil, water, and the atmosphere) is waiting for their redemption. Their restoration is totally connected to the state of man's existence. When Adam sinned and was transformed from immortality to mortality, all of creation changed to a corrupt state with him. Rebellion in the universe brought death, sickness, disease, bacteria, germs, viruses, parasites, blood sucking insects and vampire bats, destructive tornadoes, hurricanes, volcanoes, earthquakes and even, other destructive atmospheric forces into existence. Nature was thrown into a spiral of disarray. The life of all flesh is in the blood, and the sting of sin, which is death, takes it away. Therefore, all of creation is now subjected to corruption and death, but patiently awaits the hope of restoration.

"But if the Spirit of him that raised up Jesus from the dead dwell in you, he that raised up Christ from the dead shall also quicken your mortal bodies by his Spirit that dwelleth in you...

For the earnest expectation of the creature waiteth for the manifestation of the sons of God. *For the creature was made subject to vanity, not willingly, but by reason of him who hath subjected the same in hope,*

Because ***the creature itself also shall be delivered from the bondage of corruption into the glorious liberty of the children of God.***

For we know that the whole creation groaneth and travaileth in pain together until now.

And not only they, but ourselves also, which have ***the firstfruits of the Spirit,*** *even we ourselves* groan within ourselves, waiting for the adoption, to wit, **the redemption of our body.**" (Rm 8:11,19-23)

Jesus stated that if men would not praise Him, the rocks would cry out and give Him praise. Both animate and inanimate objects, as well as all demons, know whom the Son of Man, Jesus Christ is. In a way that humans cannot fathom, even the inanimate has a relationship with the Creator. Among the terrestrial creation are foolish men that

26

worship the creation; there are even those who claim that God does not exist. The inanimate objects with the knowledge of the Son of God will be a testimony against the unbelief and atheistic principles of heathen men. Regardless, redemption is at hand, and all of creation is waiting, in great anticipation!

When Christians, because of their spiritual lineage with Christ are quickened back to immortality (Rm 8:11), then the fowls of the air, the trees of the fields, the animals who roam, the fish of the sea, and organic and inorganic matter shall also be changed shortly thereafter. Deliverance shall come to all of creation, when the Sons of God defeat first the Beast kingdom, then the spirit of death. This new earth will be a dwelling place where the Second Adam, Jesus Christ, will fulfill the Jewish feast of Tabernacle and reign on earth for His 1,000 year millennium rule. There will be no presence of Satan, sin, sickness, or disease on earth during this period.

In the last days, Jesus Christ will bring forth out of His bride, the church, a mature man (remnant) who will walk in His shadow, and manifest the greater works of the Holy Ghost. Their collective manifestation will exceed what Christ and all previous prophets have done in His name. These manifested *Sons of God* will come from all four quadrants of the earth, and demonstrate (without measure) to all of earth's inhabitants, the spirit of judgment unto repentance. This remnant will be faceless, nameless Christians representing no church denomination. They will be led by the Spirit of Christ, preach the apostolic Gospel of the Kingdom, dispense the judgments of God upon the Beast and his kingdom, and conclude in grand style with the defeat of death.

When these anointed Sons of God are killed, on the third day they will be raised from the dead, stand upon their feet before the world leaders, and all the dead in Christ will rise with them. This will be the rapture! When these events take place it will help conclude the church age and the temporal age of man, because the eternal will be reestablished and He who is perfect, Jesus Christ, would have returned. The Marriage Feast of the Lamb will follow this great wedding day in the air, when the groom meets His bride in the clouds of heaven, as He returns for His Second Coming. A marriage feast always takes place after the wedding, and likewise will the Christian victory celebration called the Feast of Fat Things, or the Marriage Supper of the Lamb take place. The wife of Christ will be sinless, and found without spot, wrinkle, or blemish.

Christ as the groom, in an ultimate act of love, gave His life for His bride with the desire that the chosen faithful from among them would become His wife. At the rapture, He will gather all Jews and Gentiles who have loved Him with their whole hearts, and who have shown themselves to be disciples and obedient to His Word. This is why the scriptures say *"many are called but few are chosen."* **Many have been *called* to be a part of the bride of Christ, but few in comparison will become members of the chosen, and have the honor of becoming His wife.** The unveiling of the heart affections of the seven churches (Rev 2,3), the purging of the kingdom revealed through the parables of Christ, and the purging of all members of the bride of Christ of their sins through the tribulation will ensure a holy bride. Unbelief will be taken away from the Jewish nation concerning their Messiah, Jesus Christ. All who overcome the Prince of

Darkness during the tribulation, and walk in holiness in this life, shall see Jesus as He is, and shall (in the rapture) be just like Him.

There is only one resurrection for the righteous, consisting of two groups that will be transformed only moments apart from one another. First the dead in Christ shall arise from their sleep. Then those who are alive, having lived through the tribulation period without succumbing to the snares of Mystery Babylon, shall be changed in *"a moment, in the twinkling of an eye"* (I Cor 15:52). This occurs at the last of the seven trumpet judgments, which defeat man's last enemy, the spirit of death. In Adam all die. However, in Christ, the second Adam, all live. When these events transpire according to the prophetic word, demons will also no longer have jurisdiction on earth, and death will lose its stronghold. Hence, the sting of death and the grave will no longer be victorious in the terrestrial realm.

The quickening of the bodies of the saints, the rapture, is not an escape hatch for Christians to avoid the tribulation period. Quite to the contrary, it is the defeat of death, hell, and the grave at the first and only resurrection for the righteous. It is also the marriage of the bride of Christ, the church, to her espoused husband, Jesus Christ. When these things are accomplished, the natural and spiritual realms, the mortal and the immortal, the angelic and the terrestrial, the animate and the inanimate who are all waiting for the manifested sons of God to complete their work will rejoice in victory! Hallelujah! Hallelujah! Amen!

Tribulation? A Biblical Perspective

"I know that, whatsoever God doeth, it shall be for ever: nothing can be put to it, nor any thing taken from it: and God doeth it, that men should fear before him.

That which hath been is now; and that which is to be hath already been; and God requireth that which is past.

And moreover I saw under the sun the place of judgment, that wickedness was there; and the place of righteousness, that iniquity was there.

I said in mine heart, God shall judge the righteous and the wicked: for there is a time there for every purpose and for every work." (Ec 3:14-17)

As the earth rotates on its axis, completing its daily twenty-four hour cycle, **the sun never sets on sin**. The degradation of mankind towards himself, his neighbor, and his Creator is relentless. The eyes of the Lord are fully open to the affairs, deeds, and intent of men. In the *"last days,"* through much tribulation, He will judge all things in heaven and earth perfectly. The Lord has a controversy primarily with the church and natural Israel, and secondly with the heathen. He will resolve, once and for all, the arrogance of those who defy Him, challenge His authority, and pervert holiness and godliness. Listed below are some of the reasons why a holy God will have just cause to terminate the activities of the wicked, and restore the heavens and earth back to its former created glory.

- Preachers, aware of the wrath of God to come, profess to be homosexuals, and endorse the unholy wedlock of same sex marriages.
- Men who prophesy, *"thus saith the Lord;"* however, the Lord has not spoken through them, neither has He sent them.
- Prophets who are for hire, prophesying over those who have money, extorting the hopes of the poor, filling their pockets, and scratching the ears of the simple.
- Preachers taking advantage of the gullible children of the kingdom, in order to build their own religious kingdoms and a family dynasties among men.
- Religious organizations that claim that they are superior to all others and that they are the only ones who have the keys, which grant access to heaven.
- Men in high places (such as presidents and preachers) who cover transgressions, such as commit adultery and lasciviousness.
- Men who reject the love of God and His voice, but who have hearts and "elephant ears" to hear the whispers of the devil, to abuse themselves and commit suicide.
- A deceitful religious jihad whose followers claim to represent God, blowing

themselves up, murdering others, in anticipation of a heavenly whore house to fulfil their lustful fantasies.

- An illegitimate priesthood who forbid their clergy to marry, yet they sexually prey off of the innocence of children and the religious ignorance of their congregates.

- Dictators who murder their underlinks, decapitating the heads and limbs of their opposition, in order to consolidate power and rule by fear.

- Drag Queens who by choice engage in a race to a fiery inferno, and fail to apply the brakes of righteousness, to increase their perverse transgressions.

- Atheistic organizations who believe in sanitizing the commandments of God from the consciousness of men, not knowing that they are controlled by their father, the Prince of Lawlessness. They even seek the removal of the name of Jesus Christ from the work place while other gods are religiously correct. Foolishly, by unbelief they believe they will be exempted from their appointment with divine judgment.

- The mothers, who sacrifice their babies to the god of pleasure, not understanding that their heinous acts of abortion, yoke them together with the kindred Western genocidal spirit of Adolph Hitler and Margaret Sanger

- Men and women who dispose of their spouses and children through divorce in order to scratch the lustful itch of their flesh. Overcome by the toxins of narcissism, they deceitfully look for greener grass elsewhere.

- Parents and relatives who sexually abuse children of their own flesh and blood, spawning confusion, psychological uncleanness, and contempt for the opposite sex.

- Parents, driven by the spirit of insanity, and devils which contort the mind causing to torture and starve their children to death, believing (in a convoluted way) that they love them.

- The voices of those whose blood cry out from the grave for vengeance upon those who have gone after the way of Cain and spilled the blood of the righteous.

- Men, who were created in the image of the Creator, stoop lower than the nature of animals (driven by their gonads rather than their brains) and intoxicate themselves in the hideous act of bestiality.

- The fool that has said in his heart "*there is no God*" and yet he can not add a day to his own life, nor can he guarantee his breath when he sleeps.

- The corporate rich, who exploit the poor, abuse them in sweatshops, and pay their employee's starvation wages.

- Christian denominations that nullify the commandments of God to preserve their religious icons and traditions. They forsake the laws of God and hold themselves not guilty.

- Rebels in the house of God that reject divine order . . . women ruling over men, children oppressing their parents, and effeminate men who reject their divine calling.

- Jews who abide in Talmudic commandments upheld by their esteemed Rabbis thus, nullifying the commandments of the Torah given by Moses. They also reject the New Covenant, which was given by their brother Jesus Christ, who is the author and finisher of the faith.

- Criminals in the house of God, who lie, steal, transgress and even shoot to kill in the sanctuary.
- Homosexuals, who are very flamboyant in the churches of men, flocking to gospel choirs to lift up praises to God with unholy hands, and defiled affections. This to is an abomination!
- Spirit-filled Christians who have power (through the Holy Ghost) to perform miracles, but not enough power to love their brethren, and counteract carnal cultural racism and prejudices.
- Voo doo preachers who cast a spell over their congregations causing their members to seek permission from their pastors concerning all of their earthly decisions.

It should be obvious from the few abominations listed above, that the time for mankind to repent of his sins is rapidly expiring. What once only permeated only an isolated culture, or country, now through technology permeates the globe. God knows the nature of man in his fallen depraved state as a sinner. It was the Lord that gave man this nature after the rebellion of his progenitor, Adam. If men were allowed to continue without God's oversight, limitations, and past interventions in the events of human history (like the tower of Babel episode), mankind would have without question (in his selfish pursuits) destroyed himself. Therefore, sin not only brings death to the transgressors; it is also self-destructive to all that lies in its path. The global flood of Noah's day and the dispersion of the human family after the tower of Babel were two of the most profound methods of delay used by God to postpone man's final judgment. God had to allow time for all prophecies written by the Jewish prophets and apostles, concerning the Messiah, to be fulfilled.

Judgment day is at hand and the prophetic word must be fulfilled. In order to help Christians develop a biblical world-view concerning the end times, the book of Revelation, and the quickening of the church, many scriptures will be used to allow the bible to speak for itself. If Christ is going to deal with sin and stop this global merry-go-round of iniquity, more Christians would need to be born again of the incorruptible seed, the word of God, and become Christ like (I Pet 1:22). When this happens, their hearts and minds will be renewed with God's divine perspective, rather than their own. Then they will understand the prophetic books and their role on earth, declared, in the heavenly script, from the foundation of the world. The word of God can wash and cleanse the human thought process, and can also be a revealer of the intentions and motives of one's heart. The word therefore is a living entity, energized by the spirit, so that it can accomplish the purposes of Christ intended for the salvation of the hearer. Jesus said that His words are "*spirit and life.*" (Jn 6:63)

The Spirit of Life and the prophetic word came together to ordain the methods and covenants whereby God would redeem man back unto Himself. However, the price of redemption was a significant one. Christ paid the ultimate price Himself, as the acceptable Lamb of sacrifice for the sins of man. Those who receive the grace and salvation of

God must also pay a significant price. They must sacrifice their sinful selfish lives in exchange for eternal life. Jesus is the head of His church and the king of His kingdom. The scriptures clearly states that all Christians *"**must through much tribulation enter into the kingdom of God**"* (Acts 14:22). Jesus stated further that **"in the world ye shall have tribulation: but be of good cheer; I have overcome the world"** (Jn 16:33). And the Apostle Paul added an addendum to this thought, announcing that *"For I reckon that the sufferings of this present time are not worthy to be compared with the glory which shall be revealed in us"* (Rm 8:18). Tribulation is an unavoidable consequence of knowing the true and living God.

In the last days those *"who know not God"* will experience Great Tribulation . . . those who *know* their God, shall through tribulation, experience a Great Triumph.

TribulatIon or Triumph?

Tribulation, **persecution**, and **suffering** are three common terms used with practical every day experiences for Christians in third world countries, and where communist and socialistic dictatorships are practiced. However, for most contemporary materialistic American Christians, these terms are foreign concepts and feared like the plague. Their faith has not cost them their lives, or years of incarceration at the hands of governmental authorities, or combatant religions such as militant Islam. Christians are greatly persecuted in many Moslem countries. Catholic and Orthodox dominant nations of Eastern and Western Europe have in the past (and some currently) persecuted Pentecostal churches. Few wars have been fought on America's soil since her inception, and she has never been under the occupation of any foreign power. Even though her minority groups, such as Native Americans and African Americans, were victims of her atrociously hypocritical Western Christian practices, many of their contemporary descendents have not known the depths of their struggles. Racial strife and injustice has been an on going problem, and like an earthquake that periodically rumble to the surface, with one group in denial and the other asserting itself as the victims. However, few in America have been persecuted unto death in the past two generations for their religious faith.

When the topic of the end times is discussed, most Americans have been conditioned to reject any notion of going through the Great Tribulation. Some may even become offended and angry at the slightest mention of the possibility that they may have to suffer for Christ. The worst case scenario for them to imagine would be to be involved in spiritual warfare and contend with the Antichrist. While living a lifestyle of relative ease and comfort, in far contrast to the rest of the world, suffering may be considered disfavor with God. If one receives the message of salvation with joy, but fails to heed the full council of God on other subject matters, he may end up wrestling with unbelief, and become an unstable shallow person with no roots. *"Yet hath he not* *root in himself, but dureth for a while: for **when tribulation or persecution ariseth because of the word, by and by he is offended***" (Mt 13:21). Some Christians do not even believe that demons or the Devil exist, which is quite contrary to the word of God. If there is no Devil then Jesus is a liar and the bible is a lie. If hell was created for the devil and his angels, and it does not exist, there would be no need for salvation, no need for Christ, and definitely no apocalyptic end time message. Apostate Christians, who reject the fact that there is a devil and the literal existence of a hell, destroy by their unbelief the legitimacy for the Christian faith.

The current American anti-suffering or anti-tribulation attitude has not always been the case. Actually, its roots can be traced to early Nineteenth Century England and the American Plymouth Brethren Churches. The recent American materialistic anti tribulation paranoia also has their tentacles imbedded in the Calvinistic doctrine of predestination and the Protestant doctrine "Once Saved, Always Saved." One of the final nails in the coffin that prohibit many from understanding the plight of the church during the tribulation period is the Laodicean type of prosperity gospel. If one were to mix all of these doctrinal stances in a beverage and flavor it with anti-Semitism and European cultural pride, you would have a volatile mixture that can only produce intoxication and doctrinal error.

After over thirty years of research and traveling worldwide, I am fully persuaded that few Christians have thoroughly researched the Old and New Testaments for divine revelations not acquired by the teachings of others. If all who call themselves Christians could hear the voice of the spirit of God, then all Christians would speak the same things (I Cor 1:10). However, the multitude of opinions, personal feelings, cultural paradigms, and private biblical interpretations only makes muddy the water so that few can see clearly in the midst of their apparent doctrinal confusion. Many cherished beliefs are adhered to despite the fact that within every New Testament book, there are countless biblical promises to the effect that, "*all that live godly in Jesus Christ shall suffer persecution*" (II Tim 3:12). In the last days this persecution will come from the heavens and the earth, as both domains are shakened by the mighty hand of God. He will execute justice and judgment in the restitution of all creation. All that can be shakened, will be shakened (Heb 12:25-29)! All whose souls are anchored in Christ will stand in that day, because their foundation cannot be moved. In fact this period at the end of this chapter of human history is called the Great Tribulation. It has been custom designed to exploit the wicked and make the righteous triumph.

The blood of the slain apostles and the millions of Christians, who were martyred at the hands of the Roman government and the Roman Catholic Church for centuries, will cry out as a witness against this contemporary generation of Christians. Their indictment will be charges of neglecting "*so great a salvation*," apostasy, and a lack of desire to live or die for such a precious faith. For the past two thousand years, both Christians and Jews have been killed for their monotheistic testimony of the same God who gave the Old and New Testaments. It is beyond imagination, why so many Christians have placed their soul investment into tradition and wishful thinking, instead of the word of God. In order to preserve their temporal accomplishments and material gain, they would have no burden for the souls of the lost. Consequently, as a friend of the world, they may never open their mouths to proclaim the gospel, for fear of loss. Hence, if there is no preaching or teaching of the gospel of deliverance... then there will be no persecution by the children of darkness or the god of this world. These Christians are no threat to the devil; they are only a threat to themselves. Therefore, the Lord will trouble their waters real soon, to give them an opportunity to sure up their salvation and to bear fruit. If they do not get delivered unto salvation, they will perish without understanding (Jn 15:1-12). Not boasting of his sufferings, the Apostle Paul revealed his crucified life, persecutions, and tribulations for the sake of the gospel,

> *"Are they ministers of Christ?... I am more; in labours more abundant, in **stripes** above measure, in **prisons** more frequent, in **deaths oft**.*
> *Of the Jews five times received I forty stripes save one.*
> *Thrice was **I beaten with rods**, once was **I stoned, thrice I suffered ship-wreck**, a night and a day I have been in the deep;*
> *In journeyings often, in **perils of waters**, in **perils of robbers**, in **perils by mine own countrymen**, in **perils by the heathen**, in **perils in the city**, in **perils in the wilderness**, in **perils in the sea**, in **perils among false brethren**;*
> *In **weariness** and **painfulness**, in watchings often, in **hunger and thirst**, in **fastings** often, in cold and nakedness.*
> *Beside those things that are without, that which cometh upon me daily, the care of all the churches."* (II Cor 11:23-28)

Many Western Christian organizations have billions of dollars secured in their corporate bank accounts. Individual materialistic Christians in pursuit of the American dream often ponder how many cars can they place in their garages or how many bedrooms will they have in their mansions on earth. Unfortunately, all will soon discover that temporal blessings do not mean God's divine favor. On the other hand, Christians in other parts of the world are in diare need of food, drinking water, clothing, shelter, and medicine; and yet they continue to abound in their faith with no shadow of turning back. Christians from prosperous nations and third world countries have some that have sacrificed all to gain a more excellent eternal reward. The selfish have adopted the philosophy, *"out of sight out of mind."* Jesus exposed His disciples to essence Christian love and application in the following manner:

> *"When the Son of man shall come in his glory, and all the holy angels with him, then shall he sit upon the throne of his glory:*
> *And before him shall be gathered all nations: and he shall separate them one from another, as a shepherd divideth his sheep from the goats: And he shall set the sheep on his right hand, but the goats on the left.*
> *Then shall the King say unto them on his right hand, Come, ye blessed of my*

Father, inherit the kingdom prepared for you from the foundation of the world:

For I was an hungred, and ye gave me meat: I was thirsty, and ye gave me drink: I was a stranger, and ye took me in:

Naked, and ye clothed me: I was sick, and ye visited me: I was in prison, and ye came unto me.

Then shall the righteous answer him, saying, Lord, when saw we thee an hungred, and fed thee? or thirsty, and gave thee drink?

When saw we thee a stranger, and took thee in? or naked, and clothed thee?

Or when saw we thee sick, or in prison, and came unto thee?

And the King shall answer and say unto them, Verily I say unto you, Inasmuch as ye have done it unto one of the least of these my brethren, ye have done it unto me.

Then shall he say also unto them on the left hand, Depart from me, ye cursed, into everlasting fire, prepared for the devil and his angels:

For I was an hungred, and ye gave me no meat: I was thirsty, and ye gave me no drink:

I was a stranger, and ye took me not in: naked, and ye clothed me not: sick, and in prison, and ye visited me not.

Then shall they also answer him, saying, Lord, when saw we thee an hungred, or athirst, or a stranger, or naked, or sick, or in prison, and did not minister unto thee?

**Then shall he answer them, saying, Verily I say unto you, Inasmuch as ye did it not to one of the least of these, ye did it not to me.*"* (Mt 25:31-45)

Most First World Christians do not come to the aid of their brothers in other parts of the world nor intercede on their behalf. Does one not think that the Lord of heaven sees the affairs of His children, and their lack of love and compassion for their brothers who are going through great distress? Do they not question the possibility that the Lord will one day reverse the situation, in order that the Western church can know Him and comprehend the greater depths of the gospel (Psa 10:1-18)? Could some perceive God to be their "*sugar daddy*," supplying them with their desires and lust with no strings attached? God forbid! Quite to the contrary, the Apostle Paul explains it this way…

"godliness with contentment is great gain. For we brought nothing into this world, and it is certain we can carry nothing out.

And having food and raiment let us be therewith content. But they that will be rich fall into temptation and a snare, and into many foolish and hurtful lusts, which drown men in destruction and perdition.

For the love of money is the root of all evil: which while some coveted after, they have erred from the faith, *and pierced themselves through with many* *sorrows. But thou, **O man of God, flee these things; and follow after righteousness, godliness, faith, love, patience, meekness.***

***Fight the good fight of faith, lay hold on eternal life,** whereunto thou art also called, and hast professed a good profession before many witnesses."* (I Tim 6:6-12)

Many materialistic faith-based churches use faith not for the winning of souls into the kingdom, nor to overcome the challenges of preaching the gospel in hostile territories, but rather for the acquisition of monetary blessings and materialistic wealth. Even the Old Testament saints, who never received the promises of God in their lifetime, endured faithfully under horrendous circumstances, even succumbing to death. They endured tribulation, persecution, and suffering, with only the hope of the Messiah and a future resurrection. Paul's account of their stance is written in the book of Hebrews.

*"Who through faith **subdued kingdoms, wrought righteousness, obtained promises, stopped the mouths of lions,***

Quenched the violence of fire, escaped the edge of the sword,** out of weakness were **made strong,** waxed **valiant in fight, turned to flight the armies of the aliens.

*Women **received their dead raised to life again**: and others were **tortured,** not accepting deliverance; that they might obtain a better resurrection:*

*And others had **trial of cruel mockings and scourgings,** yea, moreover of **bonds and imprisonment**:*

*They were **stoned,** they were **sawn asunder,** were **tempted,** were **slain with the sword**: they **wandered about in sheepskins and goatskins;** being **destitute, afflicted, tormented;***

*(**Of whom the world was not worthy:**) they **wandered in deserts,** and in **mountains,** and in **dens and caves** of the earth.*

And these all, having obtained a good report through faith, received not the promise:

God having provided some better thing for us, that they without us should not be made perfect." (Heb 11:33-40)

Tribulation, persecution, and suffering bring out the best, and the worst, in an individual. These three are purifiers of the heart and soul, revealing the true issues of the heart under pressure, and one's true standing in God. Through these processes, each individual will have an opportunity to guard his hearts with all diligence by the grace of God or to succumb to *"the lusts of the flesh, the lust of the eyes, and the pride of life."* Many contemporary Christians seek to gain the best of this world and all that it has to offer, but in the process, they loose their souls.

Even Jesus learned *"**obedience by the things which He suffered**."* Consequently, *"**being made perfect, he became the author of eternal salvation unto all them***

36

that obey him" (Heb 5:8,9). If Christ, who was the Word (God) made flesh, suffered and was tempted in all manners that were common to man, yet without sin (Heb 4:15), should His disciples (who walked as He walked, in opposition to the forces of darkness) be exempt from the same persecution? Is the servant greater than His master? The afflictions and suffering of the saints are brought on primarily, because the world loves its own; those who walk in the light are a vexation to the souls of the wicked.

The Apostle Peter was put to the test three times by Jesus when He asked the heart-wrenching question, "Peter do you love me more than these?" Peter's initial response was a quick impetuous "yes," not giving much thought. However, the third time, Peter responded saying, *"thou knoweth."* Peter was put to a test to try his heart, but the Lord knew what his future actions would be. In another account, Peter hastily responded to Christ's question, and Jesus foretold his corresponding actions. *"Peter said unto him, Lord, why cannot I follow thee now? I will lay down my life for thy sake. Jesus answered him, Wilt thou lay down thy life for my sake? Verily, verily, I say unto thee, The cock shall not crow, till thou hast denied me thrice"* (Jn 13:37,38). I'm sure you know the rest of the story, how Peter wept bitterly when this scripture was fulfilled (Mt 26:75). Everyone may say they love Jesus, but the trying of one's faith reveals their internal strengths and weaknesses.

Christians must come to the understanding that all that lives for Christ shall receive tribulation, and that their trials will be validated tokens of their citizenship in His kingdom. The Apostle Paul makes this connection between salvation, persecution, and tribulation, as he prophetically addresses the end time to the First Century church at Thessalonica.

*"So that we ourselves glory in you in the churches of God for **your patience and faith in all your persecutions and tribulations that ye endure:***

Which is <u>a manifest token of the righteous judgment of God, that ye may be counted worthy of the kingdom of God, for which ye also suffer:</u>

*Seeing **it is a righteous thing with God to recompense tribulation to them that trouble you;***

*And to you who are troubled **rest with us, when the Lord Jesus shall be revealed from heaven with his mighty angels, In flaming fire taking vengeance on them that know not God, and that obey not the gospel of our Lord Jesus Christ.***

Who shall be punished with everlasting destruction from the presence of the Lord, and from the glory of his power.

*When **he shall come to be glorified in his saints**, and to be admired in all them that believe (because our testimony among you was believed) in that day.*

*Wherefore also we pray always for you, that our **God would count you worthy of this calling, and fulfil all the good pleasure of his goodness, and the work of faith with power: That the name of our Lord Jesus Christ may be glorified in you**, and ye in him, according to the grace of our God and the Lord*

37

Jesus Christ." (II Thes 1:4-11)

The misconceptions concerning the timing of the rapture and what part, if any, the church will experience during the tribulation is highly contested as the day of reckoning rapidly approaches. Fear, dread, and unbelief on behalf of most **American Christians** have placed them in a very vulnerable position because **their faith has been untried**. Some have even asked the question, "why would a loving God allow His people to suffer at the hands of the Anti-Christ?" If they would thoroughly and objectively study the scriptures for themselves, the answers would come jumping off the pages of the bible, because they are very numerous and quite obvious.

Western scholars and American theologians have seduced their churches to accept the culturally-correct view of a pre-tribulation rapture, which alleges that Christians will not suffer during any of the tribulation period. Eastern European, Asian, communist, and those in African countries, which have suffered harshly from their governments as well as the natural elements of their environment, cannot fathom serving Christ without persecution. Without materialistic distractions, they have maintained their steadfastness under great direst, even the loss of loved ones; yet they count it all joy to be persecuted for the sake of the gospel. These countries have not allowed economic affluence, a materialistic gospel, sexual perversions, narcissistic selfish indulgences, suicidal behavior, nor leisure time (for the most part) to corrupt them. Because they are unmolested by Western thought, they *expect* to go through the Great Tribulation.

With limited resources and limited information, poorer countries abound in the spirit, whereas Westerners with tremendous resources and much knowledge generally have only a shallow cosmetic faith. Eastern and Western European countries are literally worlds apart in their paradigm (world-view) of expectations, application, and understanding of the Christian faith and the end times. One's doctrine, cultural worldview and degree of fellowship with Jesus Christ will determine his ability to understand the Lord's timing and intent of His will. The scriptures declare that,

"Whoso keepeth the commandment shall feel no evil thing: and a wise man's heart discerneth both time and judgment.

Because **to every purpose there is time and judgment**, *therefore the misery of man is great upon him.* **For he knoweth not that which shall be**: *for who can tell him when it shall be?* (Ec 8:5-7)

Protestants and Pentecostal churches in America and Western Europe are in dire need of spiritual brain transplants, to remove the toxins of religious traditions, in order to receive the mind of Christ and understand the scriptures on this subject. Now is the time to understand *"time and judgment."* Unfortunately, Christiandom as a whole, with over 25,000 satellite church doctrines and sects, gravitate towards their own nationalistic experiences and the collective consciousness of their religious leaders.

Unfortunately, many biblical scholars, not knowing the prophetic will of God expressed through the Jewish prophets and apostles presumptuously mislead the people. They instruct the masses, speak as foolish men in the same manner as did the Apostle Peter and Job's wife. The Devil was rebuked sharply by Christ as he spoke through Peter's emotions and caused him to plea with Christ, not to go up to Jerusalem to be slain at the hands of the religious leaders. Peter was quite sincere, and appeared to be pleading a noble cause. However, **those who do not know God, His will, or His timing will always side with the devil, thinking they are doing the right thing. Hence, without an insight into God's prophetic plan, what may seem so right, can also be so wrong.** One can see this fact even more clearly through this account of the incident:

> *"Then charged he his disciples that they should tell no man that he was Jesus the Christ.*
> *From that time forth* **began Jesus to shew unto his disciples, how that he must go unto Jerusalem, and suffer many things of the elders and chief priests and scribes, and be killed, and be raised again the third day.**
> **Then Peter took him, and began to rebuke him, saying, Be it far from thee, Lord:** *this shall not be unto thee.* **But he turned, and said unto Peter, Get thee behind me, Satan:** *thou art an offence unto me:* **for thou savourest not the things that be of God, but those that be of men.** *"* (Mt 16:20-23)

We are told years later, by the Apostle John, that God's will for Christ's crucifixion and resurrection was *"to destroy the works of the devil"* (I Jn 3:8). Peter's compassionate plea to prevent this event from occurring was based on his ignorance of God's prophetic timing and a total disregard of the revelation that he had just received regarding the crucifixion and that Jesus was the Messiah (Mt 16:14-19). **Peter had ears but he could not hear the spirit speaking** on this subject; even though moments earlier, He had heard the voice of the Lord. Such is the case concerning those who believe in a pre- or mid-tribulation rapture theory. They are ignorant of God's redemptive plan for natural and spiritual Israel, and the destruction of Satan's kingdom. They also refuse to accept the counsel of the scriptures that state matters contrary to their opinions.

In the case of Job's wife, after seeing Job go through so much persecution by the hands of the devil and the tribulation allowed by the Lord, she told Job to curse his God and die … thus ending His suffering. Job stated that she *"spoke as a foolish woman."* Job's testimony of victory, faith, and overcoming was summed up in his declaration *"***though he slay me yet will I trust Him** *. . . Naked came I out of my mother's womb, and naked shall I return thither: the LORD gave, and the LORD hath taken away; blessed be the name of the LORD."* (Job 13:15; 1:21)

"In all this Job sinned not, nor charged God foolishly." The same *will not* be said of the shallow materialistic Christians of today, who will go through greater trials than Job and will not be able to stand in the evil day (Eph 6:13), lest they repent. They will be **like Job's wife**, believing they should curse God (receive the mark of the beast)

and die, or **like Lot's wife**, disobediently looking back, desiring the things of this world, and becoming a pillar of salt (Gen 19:26). Many on the other hand may be **like Esau**. Because they do not understand the treasure and reality of their (NEW) birthright as the spirit of adoption has brought them into the eternal family (Rm 8:15), they will for a bowl of food exchange it for their soul. They will sell out and receive the antichrist mark of the beast, in exchange for food and materialistic comfort.

The dilemma that last day Christians will encounter will be that as they seek to increase with goods, they will also be consumed by their own lusts. Will the affections of their hearts be placed on things above or things below? Will their hearts throb for things that are temporal or things that are eternal? Despite the fact that Job lost all that he had, he gained it all back again two-fold. He overcame a tumultuous showdown between the God of heaven and Satan, with Job himself placed in the middle of the conflict (Job 1:6-22). The work that Christ has begun in every Christian, He is able to complete and perfect it until the day of His return, if their hearts' affections are placed in the right directions.

*"Knowing that **he which raised up the Lord Jesus shall raise up us also by Jesus, and shall present us with you** . . .*

*For which cause we faint not; but **though our outward man perish, yet the inward man is renewed day by day**.*

*For **our light affliction**, which is but for a moment, **worketh for us a far more exceeding and eternal weight of glory;***

While we look not at the things which are seen, but at the things which are not seen: for the things which are seen are temporal; but the things which are not seen are eternal. (II Cor 4:14,16-18)

In the last days, Satan will once again appear in the presence of God, as he did with Job. He will seek permission to make unprecedented war against the saints when his kingdom is cast down to earth to be judged (Rev 12:12). As *the accuser of the brethren* he seeks doors which are opened by the sins that Christians permit, and consequently give him lawful permission, to bring havoc into their lives (Rev 12:10). Christians need to wake up and realize that the battle that has raged in the heavenlies will soon be brought to earth! All of the living descendents of Adam, of every race, kindred and tongue, will be in the middle of this final 42-month cosmic showdown. It will take place at the true and only *"Ground Zero,"* planet Earth. This unprecedented display of spiritual warfare will occur during the last three and a half years of the seven-year tribulation period. The Apostle John's prophetic account of these events is as follows:

*"And the **great dragon was cast out, that old serpent, called the Devil, and Satan, which deceiveth the whole world: he was cast out into the earth, and his angels were cast out with him.***

*And I heard a loud voice saying in heaven, Now is come salvation, and strength, and the kingdom of our God, and the power of his Christ: for **the accuser of our brethren is cast down, which accused them before our God day and night.***

*And **they overcame him by the blood of the Lamb, and by the word of their testimony; and they loved not their lives unto the death.***

*Therefore rejoice, ye heavens, and ye that dwell in them. Woe to the inhabiters of the earth and of the sea! **for the devil is come down unto you, having great wrath, because he knoweth that he hath but a short time.***"
(Rev 12:9-12)

The Christian world desperately needs to come out of its comatose, lethargic state, and awaken out of its convoluted darkness. Those who have the mind of Christ know and understand that God does not want to save the Christians' natural body. Instead His purpose in coming was to save mankind's soul, in order that he might receive a heavenly body, fashioned after Christ's likeness. **If one seeks to acquire a heavenly tabernacle that is not subjected to death and decay, then they must be willing to forsake the temporal earthly body,** which was fashioned after the first Adam's. Caught in a cyclical ball of confusion, many want to go to heaven and receive their glorious bodies, but are in direct conflict with the salvation of their souls, because, they also want to preserve themselves in this life. In the gospels, we are told that, *"if one seeks to save his life he will loose it, but if he looses it for Christ's sake, he will find it."* (Mt 16:25). Hence, the earthly tabernacle conceived in the womb of a woman must be prepared to defeat the last enemy, death, to bring forth the resurrected body, which is established in the womb of the resurrected Christ. This is accomplished by the power of the Holy Ghost.

For we know that if our earthly house of this tabernacle were dissolved, we have a building of God, a house not made with hands, eternal in the heavens.

For in this we groan, earnestly desiring to be clothed upon with our house which is from heaven: If so be that being clothed we shall not be found naked.

*For **we that are in this tabernacle do groan**, being burdened: not for that we would be unclothed, but clothed upon, **that mortality might be swallowed up of life.***

Now he that hath wrought us for the selfsame thing is God, who also hath given unto us the earnest of the Spirit.

*Therefore we are always confident, knowing that, **whilst we are at home in the body, we are absent from the Lord:** (For we walk by faith, not by sight:)*

*We are confident, I say, and willing **rather to be absent from the body, and to be present with the Lord.***

Wherefore we labour, that, whether present or absent, we may be accepted of him.

For we must all appear before the judgment seat of Christ; that every one may receive the things done in his body, according to that he hath done, whether it be good or bad.

Knowing therefore the terror of the Lord, we persuade men . . ."
(II Cor 5:1-11)

It is utterly amazing to see how many Christians do not want to walk in total discipleship with Christ. Yet, they want to dwell in heavenly places in the spirit with Him, and expect to receive their "mansions" prepared for them "in the sky" after they die. They want to live carnally on earth but expect to receive a spiritual man's blessings. Man worries and laments over the temporal body even though he knows that it cannot abide forever. Mortality must, and will be swallowed up in victory, when the saints of God are QUICKENED by the Holy Ghost, and changed from mortality to immortality. Like Job, every Christian must place their lives and bodies in the hands of the Lord, and trust Him until the end of their calling. They must complete the work He has called them to do.

"For where your treasure is, there will your heart be also" (Mt 6:21, Lk 12:34). We are warned in the Psalms that, *"if riches increase, set not your heart upon them"* (Psa 62:10). The scriptures commands those who desire to live eternally with Christ, to crucify their flesh, and agree to rise with Christ through water baptism to *"seek those things which are above, where Christ sitteth on the right hand of God.*

Set your affection on things above, not on things on the earth. For ye are dead, and your life is hid with Christ in God. When Christ, who is our life, shall appear, then shall ye also appear with him in glory.

Mortify therefore your members which are upon the earth; fornication, uncleanness, inordinate affection, evil concupiscence, and covetousness, which is idolatry:

For which things' sake the wrath of God cometh on the children of disobedience: In the which ye also walked some time, when ye lived in them. But now ye also put off all these; anger, wrath, malice, blasphemy, filthy communication out of your mouth.

Lie not one to another, seeing that ye have put off the old man with his deeds; And have put on the new man, which is renewed in knowledge after the image of him that created him..." (Col 3:1-10)

The acquisition of wealth, and material prosperity, just before the great end time battle occurs is a snare and an adhesive web cast by the powers of darkness to ensure that most Christians would be caught unprepared and unaware of the final conflict. Most Christians have become affixed with earthly occupations and worldly pursuits that they remain out of tune with the heavenlies and disinterested in spiritual things.

The Apostle Paul set the benchmark of excellence for the church and a warning to the brethren of such natural snares:

*"**I press toward the mark for the prize of the high calling of God in Christ Jesus**. Brethren, be followers together of me, and mark them which walk so as ye have us for an ensample. (For many walk, of whom I have told you often, and now tell you even weeping, **that they are the enemies of the cross of Christ**:*

***Whose end is destruction, whose God is their belly, and whose glory is in their shame, who mind earthly things**.)*

*For our conversation is in heaven; from whence also **we look for the Saviour, the Lord Jesus Christ**.*

***Who shall change our vile body, that it may be fashioned like unto his glorious body**, according to the working whereby he is able even to subdue all things unto himself."* (Phil 3:17-21)

It should be no strange coincidence that the prosperity gospel is being pimped and prostituted worldwide, to appeal to the lust of the hearts of men. The poor are enticed, because they have not, and the rich are snared, because they do not want to be without. Remember, Satan even tried to offer the Creator the kingdoms of this world if Christ would have only bowed down and worshipped him (Mt 4:8,9). Could Satan be using the same tactics that He used on Christ, who overcame His temptations, prior to the beginning of His three-and-a-half years of ministry? If he was bold enough to try and tempt the Lord of heaven, who is man, that he should be mindful of him? King Solomon, who knew all about wealth, noted in his writings that, *"Riches profit not in the day of wrath: but righteousness delivereth from death."* (Prov 11:4)

Serving Christ does not require that one become a pauper or a beggar. God even allows some of His people to be rich, knowing those who will not be corrupted by riches bless the material needs of the kingdom. Christ even promised that,

"there is no man that hath left house, or brethren, or sisters, or father, or mother, or wife, or children, or lands, for my sake, and the gospel's,

But he shall receive an hundredfold now in this time, houses, and brethren, and sisters, and mothers, and children, and lands, with persecutions; and in the world to come eternal life." (Mk 10:29,30)

However, **all can not handle the natural blessings of this world and simultaneously preserve their souls**. We know the story of the rich young ruler all too well. He claimed that he kept all of the commandments, but loved riches more than God. Therefore, he had to walk away from Christ ashamed (Mt 19:21-22). The Prophet Solomon, in his wisdom and much wealth, gives Christians a good guideline to abide by in order to preserve their souls.

*"Remove far from me vanity and lies: **give me neither poverty nor riches**;*

feed me with food convenient for me:

Lest I be full, and deny thee, and say, Who is the LORD? or lest I be poor, and steal, and take the name of my God in vain." (Prov 30:8,9)

The Lord loves to bless His children in every area of their lives. However, the commandment still remains to *"seek ye first the kingdom of God, and his righteousness; and all these things shall be added unto you."* Why? Because, *"your heavenly Father knoweth that ye have need of all these things"* (Mt 6:34,33). Materialistic Christians, like the world, cannot be content having their needs met. They also want a shopping cart to fulfill all of their wants. This too is vexation of spirit! They work night and day to acquire the finances for their earthly dreams, then have no time for their heavenly aspirations. They never have time to read or study the bible to know the will of God for their lives. Perhaps they forgot that *"riches are not forever"* (Prov 27:24). Eventually, at the time of their death, they will see Jesus face to face, and discover that their dreams were merely a mirage, and that their worldly pursuits would become their worst nightmares. The scriptures declare, *"charge them that are rich in this world, that they be not highminded,* **nor trust in uncertain riches, but in the living God, who giveth us richly all things to enjoy.** *That they do good, that they be rich in good works, ready to distribute, willing to communicate; Laying up in store for themselves a good foundation against the time to come, that they may lay hold on eternal life."* (I Tim 6:17-18)

The Apostle Paul exemplified what should be the clarion call of every believing Christian seeking eternal life:

"I count all things but loss for the excellency of the knowledge of Christ Jesus my Lord: *for whom* **I have suffered the loss of all things, and do count them but dung, that I may win Christ,**

And be found in him, not having mine own righteousness, which is of the law, but that which is through the faith of Christ, the righteousness which is of God by faith:

That I may know him, and the power of his resurrection, and the fellowship of his sufferings, being made conformable unto his death . . . " (Phil 3:8-10)

The prosperity gospel found in Western culture could not be preached in a communist country in which the government owns everything . . . that includes all property, houses, food, business profit, and even one's children. Even though many former communist countries are moving to a market-based economy for the sake of economic survival, both systems, communism and capitalism exploit the poor and feed off of their misery. The communist leaders own and control all factors of production.

The capitalist elite controls and manipulates its work force to maximize profits, often times with starvation wages, if they are without government regulations. They also own and control the alleged free press and the media. By manipulating the ignorant masses in opposition to one another, they keep them uninformed through disinformation, to exploit them further. Someone needs to convey to the Christian masses in the prosperous Western countries, that the pursuit of riches, like gambling, is a lustful snare and a bad economic strategy.

Those who understand the biblical principles of salvation realize that all who turn from serving Satan to serve the living God are immediately thrust into spiritual warfare. When they were in the enemy's camp they were aligned with the demonic realm, its destructive fruits of sin, and worldly concepts. However, when they became Christians to walk in the light of truth, they became a threat, and run the risk of exposing satanic darkness and delivering those who are bound from his power. In order for one to resist steadfastly in the faith, they must have the mind of Christ. That mindset that Christians should have both now and during the tribulation period should be to this wise to …

*"**endure hardness, as a good soldier of Jesus Christ. No man that warreth entangleth himself with the affairs of this life; that he may please him who hath chosen him to be a soldier**. And if a man also strive for masteries, yet is he not crowned, except he strive lawfully. . .*

Wherein I suffer trouble, as an evil doer, even unto bonds; but the word of God is not bound.

***Therefore I endure all things for the elect's sakes**, that they may also obtain the salvation which is in Christ Jesus with eternal glory. **It is a faithful saying: For if we be dead with him, we shall also live with him**:*

***If we suffer, we shall also reign with him: if we deny him, he also will deny us**. . . "* (II Tim 2:3-5,9-12)

Tragically, many Christians will become victims of the great slaughter (Zech 11:4,5) rather than overcomers during this period; because they can neither discern the signs of the times, nor are they prepared for total spiritual warfare. They want Christ to return some day, but definitely not in their lifetime. They do not want their goals and plans for the future upset. However, just as in the days of Noah, so shall it also be unto them.

Almost twenty- five years ago, the Lord spoke prophetically in the midst of the congregation in Washington D.C., which I pastored. **The Lord instructed the saints in the congregation to build their arks**. We pondered this prophesy and judged it according to the principles of I Cor 14:29. Knowing that the Lord had stated in His word, that He would not destroy the earth by water again, but by fire the next time, we could not understand the meaning of the prophecy. But thanks be to the Lord, who reveals all things to His people before they happen, the following week, He delivered the elders from this *"cliff hanger prophecy,"* and explained the significance of Christians building their arks in the last days.

The ark was of course, not a physical ark, but a spiritual one. This spiritual ark would bring obedient Christians to a place to hear the voice of God, to deliver them, their families, and their congregations from the judgments to come. The church was instructed to do three things, which would constitute the spiritual ark. They were **to STUDY** to know the will, heart, and mind of Christ; and **to FAST** to get their physical appetites and worldly lusts under subjection to the Holy Ghost. The third component was **to PRAY** at all times, speaking, listening and communing with the Holy Spirit in order to be lead by the spirit of God. These three acts would help every believer become familiar with the voice of the Lord, so he could hear His specific instructions, as He did with Noah. Because Noah heard and obeyed the voice of God, he could make the preparations necessary to endure the cataclysmic deluge that would cover the earth. Study, fasting, and prayer are the only ways to be in position for instruction and discipline by the Spirit of God. *"For as many that are led by the spirit of God, they are the sons of God"* (Rm 8:14).

"I returned, and saw under the sun, that the race is not to the swift, nor the battle to the strong, neither yet bread to the wise, nor yet riches to men of understanding, nor yet favour to men of skill; but time and chance happeneth to them all.

For man also knoweth not his time: as the fishes that are taken in an evil net, and as the birds that are caught in the snare; so are the sons of men snared in an evil time, when it falleth suddenly upon them." (Ec 9:11,12)

Why Tribulation?

The purposes for tribulation are numerous and multifaceted. The Apostle Paul speaking to the saints in the greatest city of Christian persecution, Rome, explains the positive attributes of tribulation:

*"And not only so, but we glory in **tribulations** also: **knowing that tribulation worketh patience;***

*And **patience, experience**; and **experience, hope**:*

And hope maketh not ashamed; because the love of God is shed abroad in our hearts by the Holy Ghost which is given unto us" (Rm 5:3-5). Hitherto, **tribulation is a character builder to perfect the saints in love.**

The sinners and unbelievers will not suffer persecution at the hands of the wicked because they do not represent Christ. No obedience to Christ, no suffering for righteousness sake! No preaching of the gospel of salvation, then they are no threat to Satan's kingdom.

Paul continues instructing the church at Rome concerning tribulation. *"Rejoicing in hope; **patient in tribulation**; continuing instant in prayer; Distributing to the necessity of saints; given to hospitality. Bless them which persecute you: bless,* *and curse not."* (Rm 12:12-14)

Tribulation is also the judgment of God upon His rebellious children in order for them to repent of their iniquity and live. If Christians refuse to turn from their sins, they will receive more severe punishment than that which will be given to the wicked heathen outside of the household of faith.

"But after thy hardness and impenitent heart treasurest up unto thyself wrath against the day of wrath and revelation of the righteous judgment of God...

But unto them that are contentious, and do not obey the truth, but obey unrighteousness, indignation and wrath,

Tribulation and anguish, upon every soul of man that doeth evil, *of the Jew first, and also of the Gentile;*

But glory, honour, and peace, to every man that worketh good, to the Jew first, and also to the Gentile.". (Rm 2:5,8-10)

Tribulation reveals the awesomeness of God, as He delivers His people out of bondage, sin, and the snares of the devil. The greater the tribulation, the greater the deliverance. The greater the deliverance, the more the Lord is magnified. Hard times also give the individual believer a personal opportunity to experience the love of God and discover that He never leaves nor forsakes those that are His.

Who shall separate us from the love of Christ? ***shall tribulation, or distress, or persecution, or famine, or nakedness, or peril, or sword?***

As it is written, ***For thy sake we are killed all the day long; we are accounted as sheep for the slaughter.***

Nay, ***in all these things we are more than conquerors through him that loved us.*** *For I am persuaded, that neither death, nor life, nor angels, nor principalities, nor powers, nor things present, nor things to come,*

Nor height, nor depth, nor any other creature, shall be able to separate us from the love of God, which is in Christ Jesus our Lord." (Rm 8:35-39)

Tribulation is like a pressure cooker for the heart. Once the heat is turned up, it exposes the attitudes of the heart. No man can judge his own heart because it *"is deceitful above all things and desperately wicked"* (Jer 17:9). However, one can be confident that the Lord, who judges not on the outward appearance, but the heart, can reveal to each individual what he has in the deep crevices of his heart. Tribulation also teaches us how to seek and find the way of escape in every form of temptation (I Cor 10:11,12) and personal fear.

"Great is my boldness of speech toward you, great is my glorying of you: I

am filled with comfort, ***I am exceeding joyful in all our tribulation.***

For, when we were come into Macedonia, our flesh had no rest, but we were troubled on every side; without were fightings, within were fears."
(II Cor 7:4,5).

Those who trust in the word of God know from experience, that it is a light unto their path, and a lamp unto their feet. It also restores one's soul after the heat of a battle. Tribulation teaches us how to comfort those who are also afflicted and in need of compassion and consolation. It also gives us the patience needed to trust in Christ, putting no confidence in our own flesh; knowing that He is able to deliver and abound through them in all situations.

Blessed be God, even the Father of our Lord Jesus Christ, the Father of mercies, and *the God of all comfort;*

Who comforteth us in all ***our tribulation, that we may be able to comfort them which are in any trouble,*** *by the comfort wherewith we ourselves are comforted of God.*

For ***as the sufferings of Christ abound*** *in us, so our* ***consolation also aboundeth by Christ.***

And whether we be afflicted, it is for your consolation and salvation, which is effectual in the enduring of the same sufferings which we also suffer: or whether we be comforted, it is for your consolation and salvation.

And our hope of you is stedfast, knowing, that ***as ye are partakers of the sufferings, so shall ye be also of the consolation.***

For we would not, brethren, have you ignorant of our trouble which came to us in Asia, that we were pressed out of measure, above strength, insomuch that we despaired even of life:

But we had the sentence of death in ourselves, ***that we should not trust in ourselves, but in God which raiseth the dead:***

Who delivered us from so great a death, and doth deliver: in whom we trust that he will yet deliver us." (II Cor 1:3-10)

Through tribulation we can also discover if an individual will have a pure heart, seek truth, and abide steadfast in sound doctrine. Those who desire to worship the Lord in spirit and in truth will not be seduced by the spirit of error, nor pervert the way of righteousness. The ignorant and the gullible will succumb to the enticing words of *"the father of lies"* (Satan, Jn 8:44), because the love of the truth is not in them (II Thes 2:11-13). However, the elect of God, will hold the *"towline"* of truth, for they rejoice in the spirit of truth, and will not be deceived during the end times.

" For false Christs and false prophets shall rise, and shall shew signs and wonders, to seduce, if it were possible, even the elect. But take ye heed: behold,

I have foretold you all things.

*But in those days, **after that tribulation**, the sun shall be darkened, and the moon shall not give her light.".*   (Mk 13:22-24).

The Tribulation is also referred to throughout the books of the prophets, as the Day of Judgment and time of Jacob's Trouble. The Lord has custom designed this period to destroy all Christian church denominations and organizations, taking them through the fire to produce one fold. There will be only one church of Jesus Christ and one body. All that are His will follow the voice of the Good Shepherd. He will utterly purge the floor of the temples that host His Holy Spirit and cleanse His kingdom of all that are wicked (Mt 3:11). All religious leaders who have substituted religious traditions for the word of God, and taught the people of God to rebel against His statutes, shall surely be the first to partake of the judgement to come. Unfortunately, the overwhelming majority of Christians worship Christ in vain, following blind guides, who use religion as a cloak for sin. Consequently they all fall into the damnable ditch called heresy and must repent of their sins of their flesh (Gal 5:20). *"Many are called but few are chosen."* (Mt 22:14)

"For the time is come that judgment must begin at the house of God: and if it first begin at us, what shall the end be of them that obey not the gospel of God?

And if the righteous scarcely be saved, where shall the ungodly and the sinner appear?" (I Pet 4:17)

"Ye hypocrites, well did Esaias prophesy of you, saying, This people draweth nigh unto me with their mouth, and honoureth me with their lips; but their heart is far from me.

But in vain they do worship me, teaching for doctrines the command-ments of men. *"* (Mt 15:8,9)

The Great Tribulation is an unprecedented time in human history. The God of Israel will cast the demonic hosts down to earth and destroy them. He will squelch all human rebellion, and prepare the earth's inhabitants for the millennium reign of Christ. Throughout the gospels we are told,

*"For then shall **be great tribulation**, such as was not since the beginning of the world to this time, no, nor ever shall be.*

And except those days should be shortened, there should no flesh be saved: but for the elect's sake those days shall be shortened." (Mt 24:21,22)

Wisdom and explanation is given to the righteous to ensure their triumph during that day. *"Be not afraid of sudden fear, neither of the desolation of the wicked, when it cometh. For the LORD shall be thy confidence, and shall keep thy foot from being taken"* (Prov 3:25,26). The disciples of Jesus Christ will be triumphant during this time and overcome the Beast's kingdom. The Lamb of God will give them robes of righteousness as a covering. *"And one of the elders answered, saying unto me, What are these which are arrayed in white robes? and whence came they?*

And I said unto him, Sir, thou knowest. And he said to me, These are they **which came out of great tribulation**, *and have washed their robes, and made them white in the blood of the Lamb"* (Rev 7:13,14). These Christians overcame the Beast system by the blood of the Lamb and the word of their testimony (Rev 11:11; 20:4).

Throughout the ages, men, who have known Christ walked with Him, and preached the Gospel according to the scriptures, have always received persecution at the hands of the wicked, especially at the hands of the religious who claim to have known God. Before Christ's crucifixion, He strongly admonished His disciples to remember His words when they are persecuted and killed for the sake of the gospel. The following words were true during the First Century concerning the zeal whereby the religious, who think they know God, persecute the righteous, who do. They have also been true throughout church history, and they will continue to be true during the Great Tribulation.

"These things have I spoken unto you, that ye should not be offended. They shall put you out of the synagogues: yea, the time cometh, that whosoever killeth you will think that he doeth God service.

And these things will they do unto you, because they have not known the Father, nor me. But these things have I told you, that when the time shall come, ye may remember that I told you of them. And these things I said not unto you at the beginning, because I was with you." (Jn 16:1-4)

The Apostle Paul, speaking from experience, echoes the same message as Christ concerning his suffering at the hands of evil doers for the sake of the gospel. Biblical Christians, as you will continue to see, had a totally different world-view about tribulation than what you find currently in Christianity. Paul's word to the church concerning their persecution was that *"No man should be moved by these afflictions: for yourselves know that we are appointed thereunto. For verily, when we were with you,* **we told you before that we should suffer tribulation**; *even as it came to pass, and ye know."* (I Thes 3:3,4)

In the book of Revelation, the Lord informs the churches at Smyrna and Thyatira that they would go through the Tribulation for the trying of their faith. **Those who call themselves Christians, but blaspheme the Spirit of Christ, will receive judgment.**

SMYRNA:

*"I know thy works**, and tribulation**, and poverty, (but thou art rich) and I know the blasphemy of them which say they are Jews, and are not, but are the*

synagogue of Satan.

*Fear none of those things which thou shalt suffer: behold, the devil shall cast some of you into prison, that ye may be tried; and ye **shall have tribulation ten days**: be thou faithful unto death, and I will give thee a crown of life."* (Rev 2:9,10)

THYATIRA:

*"And I gave her space to repent of her fornication; and she repented not. Behold, I will cast her into a bed, **and them that commit adultery with her into great tribulation, except they repent of their deeds.***

And I will kill her children with death; and all the churches shall know that I am he which searcheth the reins and hearts: and I will give unto every one of you according to your works." (Rev 2:21-23)

Tribulation is not a curse word for the righteous and those with understanding, because the will of God has been revealed to them. They, as disciples of Christ, have subjected themselves to be obedient, no matter what the cost. They have also been enlightened concerning the mysteries of the kingdom of heaven and rejoice in their fulfillment. Unfortunately, those without understanding resort to fear and dread, and generally prefer the temporal things of this life *more than* the eternal promises of the New Covenant. The end times will declare and manifest all things, including the secret intents of the hearts of Christians. Most importantly, it will show the Lord to be a strong tower and a mighty general in battle. The saints who know their God will perform supernatural feats and walk in heavenly dimensions unprecedented in human history. As a word of comfort, the undefiled in the way of righteousness will heed the following exhortations.

*"**The LORD is my light and my salvation; whom shall I fear? the LORD is the strength of my life; of whom shall I be afraid?***

*When the wicked, even mine enemies and my foes, came upon me to eat up my flesh, **they stumbled and fell**.*

*Though an host should encamp against me, **my heart shall not fear**: though war should rise against me, **in this will I be confident**.*

***One thing have I desired of the LORD, that will I seek after; that I may dwell in the house of the LORD all the days of my life**, to behold the beauty of the LORD, and to enquire in his temple.*

***For in the time of trouble he shall hide me in his pavilion: in the secret of his tabernacle shall he hide me; he shall set me up upon a rock**.*

*And now shall mine head be lifted up above mine enemies round about me: **therefore will I offer in his tabernacle sacrifices of joy; I will sing, yea, I will sing praises unto the LORD**."* (Psa 27:1-6)

Old Testament Roots for New Testament Tribulation

The concept of tribulation is not a New Testament phenomenon. Like all New Testament doctrines, its roots are fully established in the Old Testament. In the Old Testament, the Hebrew word for tribulation is *tsarah* (Strong's Concordance # 6869). The following examples are excerpts from the Old Testament, which refer *to the day of tribulation*, also known as *a day of trouble*, that the world is about to enter into. *A day of trouble* is applicable to every generation whose Christian members have taken a stand for righteousness to overcome the wicked. However, there is coming a day that will be like no other. It will be the ultimate, climatic day of tribulation, appointed by the God of heaven to rid the earth, and the cosmos, of all forms of sin and rebellion. Those who can accept the Lord's wisdom on this matter, even though they may not agree with His methods, must also seek the faith necessary to be an "*overcome*r" in this time of great adversity.

One must not be like the children of Israel, who refused to believe the report of Joshua and Caleb. Their unbelief caused an entire generation to perish in the wilderness. Instead, every Christian must be like Noah . . . after hearing the plans and intentions of God, he was moved by fear, to build an ark that took him almost 100 years to construct (Heb 11:7). Having no concept of rain, he and his household remained faithful to the charge, building a boat that was one and a half football fields long and four stories tall.

If Christians want to survive naturally and spiritually during the coming judgment, then they must agree with the scriptures and believe all of God's word concerning these matters. Faith comes by hearing and believing the spoken word of the Lord. The council of the Old and New Testaments stand sure, and those who agree with it shall live. Those who reject it will discover that the word of God is "*like a hammer*;" it will break the beliefs and philosophies of men into pieces. Jesus will never leave or forsake those that are His. He has promised that He will not leave one without comfort, because **He is the Comforter** (Jn 14:16-18,26,27). The following verses of scripture should help the faithful acquire more faith, to become willing vessels that God can use in the last days for His glory. **They will be used as dispensers for His double-portioned anointing.**

Prov 11:8 "The righteous is **delivered out of trouble**, and the wicked cometh in his stead." The word trouble represents turbulence or tribulation.
Prov 24:10 "If thou faint in **the day of adversity**, thy strength is small."

Isa 33:2 "O LORD, be gracious unto us; we have waited for thee: be thou their arm every morning, our salvation also **in the time of trouble**. At the noise of the tumult the people fled; at the lifting up of thyself the nations were scattered."

During the time of tribulation the righteous will see a greater arm of deliverance.

The greater the tribulation the greater the deliverance.

Dan 12:1 "And at that time shall Michael stand up, the great prince which standeth for the children of thy people: and there shall be **a time of trouble**, such as never was since there was a nation even to that same time: and at that time thy people shall be delivered, every one that shall be found written in the book."

Obed 1:13,14 "Thou shouldest not have entered into the gate of my people in the day of their calamity; yea, thou shouldest not have looked on their affliction in the day of their calamity, nor have laid hands on their substance in the day of their calamity; Neither shouldest thou have stood in the crossway, to cut off those of his that did escape; neither shouldest thou have delivered up those of his that did remain in **the day of distress**."

Nah 1:7 "The LORD is good, a strong hold in **the day of trouble**; and he knoweth them that trust in him."

Hab 3:16 "When I heard, my belly trembled; my lips quivered at the voice: rottenness entered into my bones, and I trembled in myself, that I might rest in **the day of trouble**: when he cometh up unto the people, he will invade them with his troops."

There is a place of rest for the faithful saints of God, where they cease from their own labor, and rest in a secret place of spiritual immunity during times of great tribulation." (Heb 4:3-11)

Psa 46:1-3 "God is our refuge and strength, a very present help in trouble.
Therefore will not we fear, though the earth be removed, and though the mountains be carried into the midst of the sea;
Though the waters thereof roar and be troubled, though the mountains shake with the swelling thereof. Selah."

Tribulation upon the wicked leads to their demise; but tribulation for the righteous brings about their ultimate triumph. The Old Testament also reveals the line of demarcation drawn between the defeated and the triumphant in the day of trouble. Psalm 91 presents this case beautifully, because it was prophesied by King David, and was fulfilled by Christ Himself at His first coming. This time it will be fulfilled by the last day disciples of Christ called the Manchild.

*"And he shall **judge the world in righteousness**, he shall minister judgment to the people in uprightness.*
*The LORD also will **be a refuge for the oppressed, a refuge in times of trouble**. And **they that know thy name will put their trust in thee**: for thou, LORD, hast not forsaken them that seek thee.*

Sing praises to the LORD, which dwelleth in Zion: declare among the people his doings. When he maketh inquisition for blood, he remembereth them: he forgetteth not the cry of the humble.

Have mercy upon me, O LORD; **consider my trouble which I suffer of them that hate me, thou that liftest me up from the gates of death***:*

That I may shew forth all thy praise in the gates of the daughter of Zion: **I will rejoice in thy salvation.**

The heathen are sunk down in the pit that they made*: in the net which they hid is their own foot taken.*

The LORD is known by the judgment which he executeth: the wicked is snared in the work of his own hands. . .

The wicked shall be turned into hell, and all the nations that forget God.

For the needy shall not alway be forgotten: the expectation of the poor shall not perish for ever.

Arise, O LORD; let not man prevail*: let the heathen be judged in thy sight.*

Put them in fear, O LORD: that the nations may know themselves to be but men.*"* (Psa 91:8-20)

In the day of trouble, the Lord will raise up a deliver, out of Zion, the church (Rm 11:25-28) to defend the nation of Israel and remove her current state of blindness. He will also provide supernatural relief to the church during the Great Tribulation. The deliverer will be Jesus Christ, manifesting Himself through an unspecified number of the mature Sons of God. They will walk in the power of His spirit and perform the "*greater works*," exalting the blood-stained banner of Christ, and hallowing the name of the Lord.

Collectively, the Sons of God will serve as the hand of God, touching and judging the affairs of men. Individually, they will be the manifested "finger of God," executing in conjunction with the angels, judgement upon Satan's kingdom. When they speak the word of the Lord and bring on His plagues and judgments, their spoken supernatural acts will be performed instantly! Even though they dwell on earth, they will sit with Christ in the spirit, in heavenly places.

The Lord is about to introduce and impute to His faithful **a new anointing**, which will take them in **a new direction**, as they walk in **new spiritual dimensions**. While most trust in the arm of the flesh (people whom they know, knowledge they have acquired, their material riches, and their natural abilities) the righteous puts no confidence in the flesh. They know that he that puts his trust in the Lord shall never be made ashamed (Psa 25:12-22). These individuals are always abounding in grace, love, and the knowledge of Jesus Christ.

"The LORD hear thee in **the day of trouble***; the* **name of the God of Jacob defend thee; Send thee help from the sanctuary, and strengthen thee out of**

Zion;

We will rejoice in thy salvation, and in the name of our God we will set up our banners: the LORD fulfil all thy petitions.

Now know I that **the LORD saveth his anointed; he will hear him from his holy heaven with the saving strength of his right hand.**

Some trust in chariots, and some in horses: but we will remember the name of the LORD our God.

They are brought down and fallen: but we are risen, and stand upright. Save, LORD: let the king hear us when we call." (Psa 20:1,2,5-9)

The battle is the Lord's! Whenever there is conflict on earth, whether it be of men or of angels, it is first initiated in the heavens, and then carried out through the actions of men. The heathen, without understanding, serves as willing vessels and agents of the prince of darkness, thinking they are actually doing their own will. On the other hand, *"the accuser of the brethren"* (Rev 12:10), Satan, seeks permission from the Lord of heaven to attack the saints; but God has placed a hedge around about them to protect them from unseen forces. His angels are also encamped around the righteous to defend and assist them in times of untold peril. There is also a cloud of fire that goes before them and covers them (Psa 50:1-3). God is a helper, who has enabled the saints to do His will through the power of the Holy Ghost that dwells within each of them. The praises of the saints are another example of mighty weapons in a time of distress (Psa 54:2-70). As a loving father, He hears their every cry and delivers those who fear Him, out of every trial. Hence, the upright always overcome, and remains triumphant over demonic powers and principalities in their day of trouble. The Lord is forever present, standing and interceding on behalf of each Christian, that their faith fail not. He also sends the heavenly hosts to assist them in times of need.

"The angel of the LORD encampeth round about them that fear him, and delivereth them. *O taste and see that the LORD is good: blessed is the man that trusteth in him.*

O fear the LORD, ye his saints: for there is no want to them that fear him . . . The eyes of the LORD are upon the righteous, and his ears are open unto their cry." (Psa 34:7-9,15)

In the Bible, the church is referred to by many terms. Some more common metaphors would be the bride of Christ, wife, temple of God, building, city, and taberncle.

The latter four are dwelling places where the spirit of Christ abides; the Christian, in turn, abides in Him. Jesus is a refuge in times of trouble and a shield surrounding those who trust in Him. He is a God that is at hand and not afar off (Jer 23:23). If there was anyone in the Old Testament who understood God's loving kindness and tender mercies, it was His servant King David (of the tribe of Judah) . . . A man after God's own heart! If God comforted and delivered him out of His many afflictions, how much more shall he deliver the Christian, who abides in a spiritual covenant and dwells with the living Christ in a more excellent way. The Great Tribulation will be the day in which **the absoluteness of the theocracy of God will be fully manifested among men** through His servants and the armies of heaven. The wicked shall be brought down to their knees and confess that Jesus Christ is Lord! There is a secret dwelling place in God where only His disciples can enter, and the righteous shall dwell there in the midst of trouble.

"He that dwelleth in the secret place of the most High shall abide under the shadow of the Almighty.

*I will say of the LORD, **He is my refuge and my fortress: my God; in him will I trust**. Surely he shall deliver thee from the snare of the fowler, and from the noisome pestilence.*

***He shall cover thee with his feathers**, and under his wings shalt thou trust: **his truth shall be thy shield and buckler**.*

***Thou shalt not be afraid** for the terror by night; nor for the arrow that flieth by day; Nor for the pestilence that walketh in darkness; nor for the destruction that wasteth at noonday.*

***A thousand shall fall at thy side, and ten thousand at thy right hand; but it shall not come nigh thee**.*

*Only with thine eyes shalt thou behold and see the reward of the wicked. Because thou hast **made the LORD, which is my refuge, even the most High, thy habitation;***

***There shall no evil befall thee, neither shall any plague come nigh thy dwelling**.*

For he shall give his angels charge over thee, to keep thee in all thy ways. They shall bear thee up in their hands, lest thou dash thy foot against a stone." (Psa 91:1-12)

Understanding How the Doctrine "Once Saved, Always Saved," Closes the Door to Divine End Time Revelation.

Understanding and unraveling the revelations of God's word is similar to unraveling the mysteries and the perpetual surprises found in a Russian doll. Every time one reveals a doll, there is yet another neatly hidden doll; though smaller, yet many more hidden dolls still remain. In this series of unfolding events, one cannot get to the ultimate mystery or insight, until he is able to go through each wrapped package. The doors that guard the mysteries of God remain hidden from mortal men, despite their best and often noble attempts to analyze the secrets of the Lord through human reason, and religious philosophy. One may not be aware that it is only by divine impartation that the mysteries of God are understood, and that He reveals His secrets to those who love Him, fear Him, and obey His will (Psa 25:14). In the New Testament, the spirit of Jesus Christ is also identified as the Spirit of Truth (Jn 14:16,17). In looking at Jesus Christ, the God of light and holiness, we are told that in Him there is no darkness at all (I Jn 1:5). We are also told that it is impossible for God to lie and that no lie is of the truth. After putting God's divine attributes in perspective, we will discover that when men, out of the darkness of their hearts, pervert the nature of God and His word, the doors of revelation remain sealed shut. This human flaw, which was directly attributed to man's ability to choose good or evil, also allows him to believe the truth or believe a lie. Man's freedom to choose may also cause him to error in doctrine and be deceived.

In the past European imperialism (colonial conquest), ethnocentrism (cultural pride and feelings of national superiority), and anti-Semitism (racism towards Jews) has helped formulate doctrines which allowed people of Western culture to justify immorality, racism, Christian denominationalism, and genocide (under a religious cloak). These major cultural padlocks have kept many seemingly "forever learning" about the Christian faith, but perpetually unable to come to the knowledge of the truth. The doctrine *"Once Saved, Always Saved"* created a classic case of deceptive religious immunity, producing **transgressors** (covenant breakers) and **criminals in the house of God**. Many take the scriptures out of context, adding them to their sinking quicksand of delusion, which is then used to produce their own desired theological outcome. Consequently, the results of these misguided hearts will be culturally based doctrinal errors, which lie against the truth. In the last days such practices will come back to haunt those in error and lead to their eventual demise. Furthermore, at the appointed time, **the philosophies and beliefs of men will either condemn, or justify them**, as the divine prophetic word is manifested throughout the earth in the last days.

In order to further mortify themselves behind a wall of doctrinal immunity, supposedly to shield themselves from the scrutiny and chastisement of God's word, the following deceptive methods are employed to excuse their actions. They contort the scriptures, by claiming those sections of the bible that do not agree with their theology were applicable only to the Jews. Others use the deceptive ploy of dispensationalizing the scriptures, claiming that certain selective biblical truths were for a certain time period, and not applicable for today. Another method involving time is used to deceive many is the notion of certain doctrines like the Baptism of the Ghost was only for the First Century church. Many Protestants adhere to the red-letter edition of the bible (the quotes of Jesus in the Gospels), stating that they are to believe the words of Christ, and not His apostles. Unwisely, they pit Jesus and His apostles against each other and create doctrinal confusion. Feminist and men who possess the spirit of Ahab claim that the biblical gender roles are antiquated, and that they must update the commandments of God, to make them relevant for their day. While those who error in their heart continue to study and seemly never acquire the ability to come to the knowledge of the truth, it should be no mystery why they are in that predicament. **They fail to realize that biblical truths have not been placed on an open buffet for ones delight and preferences.** To the contrary one must adhere to the fact that *"All scripture is given by inspiration of God, and is profitable for doctrine, for reproof, for correction, for instruction in righteousness: That the man of God may be perfect, throughly furnished unto all good works"* (II Tim 3:16,17).

One of the main doctrines that have become a cultural snare for many American and European-based Christian denominations has been the gradual development of the Western Protestant Church's teaching, **"Once Saved, Always Saved."** This doctrine has taken on many different forms since the Sixteenth Century Protestant Reformation. It and its splinter counterparts has permeated and perverted biblical doctrines such as **sanctification**, **justification**, and **the grace of God**. This diabolical doctrine was eventually used to misrepresent the writings of the Apostle Paul to the Thessalonians concerning **the wrath of God** and how Christ will correct and judge His church in the last days.

Even to this day, many Christians cannot open the doors of their minds to comprehend end time biblical truths, because of the cultural padlocks prohibiting biblical revelations from becoming obtainable. Claiming that **"God has not appointed us to wrath,"** these biblical scholars, pastors, and their congregations believe they are *unaccountable* for their transgressions. They are the same ones who take the verse in I Thessalonians 5:9 out of context, claim that it guarantees that Christians cannot (and will never) receive wrath from a loving God. They interpret the scriptures, and verses associated with the wrath of God, to be slated only for the heathen (unbeliever) who sins, but not for themselves, who may do the same sinful acts. The erroneous doctrine, "Once Saved Always Saved," and the belief that Christians are not appointed to wrath, blinds an individual from the unsuspecting disastrous consequences for such perversion of biblical truth; therefore, often causing them to remain in their sins. Here is wisdom, if something sounds too good to be true, then one can safely conclude that it is not true. The gullible, and the decidable will always look fall for a scam. In the end times, every doctrine of man will be tried in the bowl of affliction. Their beliefs will either justify them or condemn them.

Many contemporary Christian doctrines are not isolated interpretations of the bible conceived in a vacuum. Rather, they are cultural philosophies and religious traditions mixed with biblical truths, producing a diverse rainbow of interpretations from the biblical text. Just as conquering nations write the history of a newly conquered masses in their biased favor, there is also a psychological tendency by religious leaders to justify their actions. They tend to displace all punishment and judgments of God on other groups (whom they deem inferior), while making themselves appear "*not guilty*," even though they may continue to commit the same sinful acts as the unsaved (heathen). This type of religious delusion was pandemic in Europe by the Roman Catholic Church in Italy, Spain, and France during the crusades and during the Inquisition. If one were to believe that the Christian Jesus of Europe was the same as the biblical Jewish Jesus, one would conclude that Jesus "kills, steals and destroys." However, quite to the contrary, those are the attributes of Satan (Jn 10:10), not the Messianic Jesus Christ. The Jewish Apostle Paul, writer of two-thirds of the New Testament, stated that men would succumb to "**another Jesus**" that is not exemplified in the scriptures, "**another spirit**" that is not reflective of the Holy Spirit, and "**another gospel**" foreign to the apostolic New Testament (II Cor 11:4). America, the home of religious freedom, is also the home of the most pandemic display of biblical rebellion in history. There are thousands of denominational sects which all claim to serve the same God. **In the midst of manifold confusion, there are many gospels, many Jesus', and many religious spirits mimicking The Holy Spirit.**

In the early history of the United States, the doctrine *"Once Saved, Always Saved"* was cherished by many Protestants in order to theologically justify their transgressions in their newly colonized settlements. They embraced the doctrines because they could not restrain themselves from committing multitudes of vial acts in the name of the Western Christian God. Such acts would include murder, genocide, rape, adultery, theft, racism, and confiscation of property committed under the pre-text of a perversion of the biblical doctrine of predestination. History books have only recently began to reflect the atrocities of the doctrine of **Manifest Destiny**, which resulted in the genocide of Native Americans, fraud through cunning illegal treaties, and military campaigns waged against them. This "Christian doctrine," impregnated with the seeds of racism, decreed that the Christian God of Europe had given the American colonist a *divine right* to confiscate the lands of "the heathen" from the Atlantic to the Pacific Oceans. Hence, the slaughter of dehumanized "savages" continued and in the name of the European   Christian God. It has been said that, *"those who are not aware of the past are be doomed to repeat it. "* Like an immanent bad weather forecast, the nature of man (since Adam) has been quite consistent and predictable. It has not changed. The heart of a sinner is also quite consistent. If the sins of the past are never honestly dealt with, and his vices are left uncorrected, then they will hinder the progress of his future, and insure their eternal destruction.

Good religion and truth in the hands of the wicked can only produce bad religion. A controversial issue in America's history, which brings forth a wave of emotions, is the examination of the practices of genocide, racism, lynchings, and injustices against the Negro race. Heinous acts were committed and justified through religion and pseudo-scientific theories (Darwinian Evolution). Accurate examination of these issues would force the conquering group to re-examine its cultural myths and their pseudo-Christian religious beliefs, which have been used to justify their actions for centuries.

For further clarification, consider the following analogy: In order for a wound to heal properly, it must first be cleansed properly. Proper and pure cleansing would prevent infection, and then the wound must be stitched up properly. This would allow the healing process to begin (hopefully with minimal scarring). On the other hand, if spiritual contaminants (such as heresy and false doctrines) enter the bandaged wounds (of past sins), then a life-threatening infection results. If an autopsy is performed on such an individual to determine the cause of death, the examiner would discover that the contaminants (though internally and concealed from view) were actually the cause of death. Unfortunately, it would be too late, and his true cause of death would be determined after his demise. In like manner, many may suffer an agonizing spiritual death caused by unexposed doctrinal cancer, which wars against biblical truths (concealed through culture, and deeply imbedded through religion).

In order to understand the cultural and psychological tendencies, which created the doctrine *"Once Saved, Always Saved,"* we will look at the historical roots of America even further. America's terrorist practices of lynching and reigns of terror by the "Christian" Ku Klux Klan were implemented primarily on people of African descent by individuals, based upon the beliefs of their religious denominations, fraternal organizations, and an institutionalized secular government. After the Civil War, this doctrine was used to create an intellectual bubble of immunity against divine prosecution by a just God. Confronted with the truths of God's word by supporters of the Abolitionist Movement, many American racist and adulterers (though married) used slave women for their own sexual vices; thus, they were faced with many moral dilemmas. Mislead to believe that regardless of what acts they may have committed they would go to heaven, they neither repented of their actions, nor reformed their ways. **Hence, they compounded their problems, by adding more sin, to their sins** (Isa 30:1). These events bring a strong indictment against an apparent hypocritical Christian religion and a psychological history that most would rather forget or deny.

For the most part, America is the rebellious, overseas colony of imperialistic Great Britain. Those Europeans nations who expanded their borders worldwide through imperialism, developing colonies to export their religious doctrines, while importing raw material and precious metals to enhance their own wealth are responsible for this. In the newly formed American Colonies, the Machiavellian scheme of *"by what ever means necessary"*, treachery and brutality were used to Christianize the so-called pagan savages, and commit a form of religious *"justifiable homicide."* If this form of imperialistic conquest had been launched through the atheistic concepts of communism, there would be no conflict of doctrine, because atheistic communist does not prescribe to Christian principles, nor believes in a monotheistic worldview. If these beliefs were espoused by a person who did not claim to believe in the bible, or confess to be a Christian, then one can not expect him to behave as a saint. Hence, certain **European Christians have a psychological and moral dilemma of always having to profess faith in Jesus Christ, while at the same time justifying their ungodly and immoral acts through theology, and pseudo scientific theories**. Evidently, those actions had to be taken in order to appease their conscience and sever any form of guilt or condemnation.

The Roman Catholic Church showed no remorse for her abominable actions throughout her sixteen centuries of history. Through her apostate priestly system, religious extortion and blackmail, was conducted in the worst possible fashion. People who had paid the Catholic Church money and placed their faith in a corrupt church, which promised them salvation and less time in Purgatory, in vain. They were deceived and actually thought that their sins were eradicated. Buying ones way into heaven or paying for ones sins in advance was instituted through the practice known as **indulgences**. Even though the monetary attributes were rejected by the Protestant churches centuries later, it was substituted with the blood of Christ. Hence, the concept that one could continue to sin and still remain saved became a cultural norm, which began first in the Catholic Church and continued through her rebellious children the Protestants.

Five centuries ago the Protestant churches severed their connection with their mother, the Church of Rome, through the Reformation. The catalyst for this movement was the Augustinian Monk, **Martin Luther** of Germany. Luther's adamant stance on the transforming verse, *"the just shall live by faith"* (Rm 1:17), served as a torch to initiate the Protestant Reformation. In his favor, Luther grasped the concepts that one could not be saved by his works, neither could salvation be purchased through monetary means, nor could it be obtained at the authority of Roman Catholic priests. He also deplored the adherence to an illegitimate priestly system of nuns and priests. His full disclosure of complaints and indictments against the Roman Catholic Church resided in his 95 thesis. Luther's list of complaints and doctrinal grievances were nailed to the doors of the Catholic Church in Whittenburg, Germany. Luther realized that penance through the priests, the vain repetitious reciting of religious prayers, chants which venerated the Virgin Mary, and other church traditions would not grant one their salvation. *Faith in Christ alone* permeated Europe through the reformers. Later, Luther and other church leaders in their "back to the bible movement" rediscovered the reality of faith, and the significance of the cross as being more than just an icon and religious jewelry to be worshipped. They began to understand the importance of Christ's shed blood for the atonement for man's sin, as well as the priesthood of every believer in Christ.

Most Christians would agree that faith is an essential ingredient of the New Testament plan of salvation. Faith however, according to the scriptures, is predicated on love (Gal 5:6), and love hinges on obedience (II Jn 5,6, Jn 14:21,23). Therefore, faith cannot stand-alone. It did not in the Old Testament and it does not in the New Testament. If one has biblical faith then he would also have the corresponding works of faith… *"faith without works is dead"* (Jm 2:18-26). If one has faith in Christ, he must

61

also follow through with biblical discipleship, not just religious activities and vain rituals. Faith must be rooted in truth and obedience, if not, it would be damnable faith.

These radical reformers of the European church world began an overhaul of an idolatrist system that was completely foreign to the Jewish biblical Christian faith. Unfortunately, Luther and the Swiss reformer **Ulrich Zwingli** began a series of religious conflicts over the issue of **Consubstantiation verses Transubstantiation**. Transubstantiation is the belief that the bread and wine at Communion turns into the actual blood and body of Christ. Constubstantiation believes that it is merely symbolic. Consequently, as typical of European Christian fashion, Christians began to fight and kill each other over the blood and body of Christ. Doctrines of faith became the dominant issue in Europe, as its many splinter sects began to permeate the world (especially the USA) in the form of denominations, taking on numerous and diverse theological perspectives.

Another doctrinal building block for the doctrine *"Once Saved, Always Saved"* was the teachings of the Protestant French reformer **John Calvin**. Calvin and his followers, who contributed to the theological architectural design of this doctrine, developed a perversion of the biblical doctrine of God's foreknowledge and predestination. The Jewish Apostles, in particular Paul, defined the **Doctrine of Predestination** as the foreknowledge of the omniscient Creator. The Bible clearly states in both the Old and New Testament that God knew from the foundation of the world the choices that all men would make, and could therefore (with-out-flaw), state the events of the end of the world from its beginning (Isa 46:10, Eph 1:3-12). To the contrary, John Calvin's European version basically stated that from birth, one's eternal state was sealed, predestined by God, and could not be altered. Hence, according to this belief, eternal salvation was not a matter of choice of an individual's will, but rather, it was predetermined from above. Perhaps, what they failed to realize was that **if one is protected from the consequences of choice, he has neither choice, nor free will**. Thus according to this worldview, men cannot be free will agents, independent of the creator. He is merely reduced to a robot, programmed by the mind and irreversible will of God.

With many doors of revelation closed to those who prescribe to John Calvin's beliefs, they may be oblivious to the fact that, only the Lord knows who will be saved, and that every man must work out his own salvation with fear and trembling (Phil 2:12). A man can walk with God for a season, and by the choice of his will, choose no longer to do so, returning back to his former lusts. However, we will later see that if during the days of his walk of righteousness he was in covenant with Him, at that time he was considered "saved."

"Salvation" according to the New Testament is a covenant relationship between Christ and the individual members of His Bride. The term salvation can also be used synonymously with the term "deliverance." Through Christ, Christians are **saved from** the consequences of sin: physically, mentally, emotionally, and otherwise. They are also **delivered from** sin, Satan, and the human self-will through the anointing of the Holy Ghost. It is because of the resurrection power of the Holy Ghost, dwelling within Christians, that hell also has no jurisdiction over the Disciples of Christ. Consistently in the Old and New Testament, relationships with the natural and spiritual children of YEHWEH are always classified as a covenant. Most often expressed as the husband and a wife relationship, even the church is identified as the bride of Christ. **If salvation is a contractual covenant relationship, then it is more than by faith and the intellectual contours of one's beliefs.** It is through the knowledge of the covenant, and the fact that it must be maintained, that one does not simply believe they are saved, they can know they are saved. For example, **If one is married to his spouse, he does not wonder from day to day whether he is married or not**, because he is bound by covenant. If we are bound by covenant then it is not based on chance, faith alone, nor ones religious convictions. Furthermore, Eurocentric Christianity, in its generally confused state, teaches that salvation is not based on a covenant (calling it legalism, even though it is called the New Covenant), but rather upon one's beliefs in Christ. Most who prescribe to this unscriptural notion often times say they are concerned about losing their salvation. Unfortunately, using their preferred sections of the bible, they may have *shacked with Christ* (cohabiting or trying to enjoy the benefits of the covenant without entering into covenant), through their denominational errors, but never legally espouse themselves with Him through the New Testament water, spirit, and blood (Acts 2:38). If one was lawfully married, they can not lose their spouse, but can only get out of the relationship by divorce.

In the New Covenant spiritual relationship of fidelity, Christians are the designated bride and Christ is the groom. Once one is in covenant with Christ through the blood, the water, and the spirit (I Jn 5:8, Jn 3:5), he can also break the covenant through rejection or breech of the marriage contract, the end result being divorce. The Western paradigm of salvation must go through a radical shift, from mere "faith" to a marriage relationship (Eph 5:23-33). **If one is lawfully married to an individual, it is never a question of faith as to whether or not they are married. It is a matter of a consensual contract, which lawfully validates their marriage and their appropriate conduct as husband and wife.** Their partnership is recognized by all, whether domestic, foreign, or in heaven. If they are married lawfully, it is not a question of whether they *feel* or *believe* they are married, it is a matter of fact, based on the covenant made. The dubious belief that one simply comes in fellowship with Christ by non-covenant verbal confession is a pure fabrication of Western culture, and is foreign to the biblical standards for a right relationship with YEHWEH. Faith was a starting point for the two parties to agree to engage in holy matrimony and preserve themselves; to love only each other as husband and wife, until the covenant is nullified, through death. **Christ will never leave an individual or forsake him** (Mt 28:20)**; however, an individual by a choice of his will**, can choose to separate himself as a transgressor, creating an irreconcilable breach of contract.

As a final cloak to cover their blindness, many religious denominations have become entangled in **a cyclical reasoning dilemma**. This was accomplished by the claim that *if a person could, or did lose their salvation, they were never saved in the first place*. Such an intellectual response is designed to further justify the doctrine "Once Saved, Always Saved." Their failure to understand the rudiments of salvation, and what is a covenant, becomes quite apparent when one examines such a statement.

Salvation is not an item which you can lose, or find, it is a spiritual relationship with the true and living God established through a covenant, and consummated by spiritual circumcision of the heart (by the baptism of the Holy Ghost, Rm 2:28). **This cyclical reasoning of claiming that if one loses his salvation he was never saved is based on a corrupt understanding of predestination and salvation.** The results of such a   corrupt mental file and self-serving error, closes the door to many revelations that are absolutely necessary to comprehend Jewish New Testament biblical truths. I do not think any one would claim that the Apostle Paul was not saved; however, even he stated that his faithfulness and obedience was absolutely necessary in order to maintain his eternal salvation. *"But I keep under my body, and bring it into subjection: lest that by any means, when I have preached to others, I myself should be a castaway"* (I Cor 9:27).

The European **doctrinal religious house of cards** consisting of predestination and the doctrine "Once Saved, Always Saved," formed a cohesive pair. They gave birth to the belief that*, if one is saved, then he can never lose his salvation because it is predetermined.* According to this doctrine, salvation no longer becomes a covenant between God and man, but an irreversible state of being, predetermined by the Creator at birth. Every biblical covenant that God has had with man, since the creation of Adam, has always had conditions and grounds for default. **Every covenant God has made with man, from Adam to the present was also contingent upon the individual's relationships with God and his conduct with the other descendents of Adam.** The covenants were exemplified by an eternal law; *"Thou must love the Lord thy God with all thy might, with all thy strength, with all thy soul, and thy neighbor as thyself."* We know that God is always faithful, and Christians are told that the Lord Jesus Christ would never leave them, nor forsake them. However, we also know that **man is not faithful**, and throughout human history God's natural children (the Jews), and His spiritual children (the church), has consistently chosen to reject and abandon their relationship with their monotheistic Father in heaven.

Without exception, the Apostle Peter commands all Christians to bear the fruit of the spirit, and **make their calling (salvation) and election (eternal destination) sure** (II Pet 1:10). This concept gives some credence to the fact that **man has much to do in determining his own eternal fate**. The Apostle Paul admonishes all *Christians "to work out [their] own salvation with fear and trembling"* (Phil 2:12). John, the revelator, tells the seven churches of the apocalypse that only those Christians who endure until the end of their life, and remain faithful, shall be saved. Again, both natural Israel and spiritual Israel were both called the wife of God. The Old Covenant law and the New Covenant of the spirit of life gives clear grounds for divorce if the righteous man turns from his righteousness, returns to perdition (wickedness), and plays the harlot.

If one cannot grasp the light established through the foundational truths clearly expressed in the writings of the Jewish apostles and prophets, then the End Time message is totally beyond their reach. If one uses deceitful unjust weights and false measurements to try to establish truth, we are told that it is an abomination to the Lord.

"A False balance is an abomination to the Lord: but a just weight is his delight." (Prov 11:1)

A false balance is a measurement that defrauds an individual of commerce, truth, and due process (justice). According to the Bible, this false balance was conceived in the darkness of the hearts and minds of men. Their doctrinal errors work in conjunction with demonic hosts to deceive as described by the Apostle Paul; *"Now the Spirit speaketh expressly, that in the latter times some shall depart from the faith, **giving heed to seducing spirits, and doctrines of devils**"* (I Tim 4:1). In the context of God's word, this form of deception is enhanced when an individual examines only scriptures that support his doctrinal view and excludes verses contrary to his opinions. His dishonest attempts to establish balance and discover sound doctrine (necessary to understand biblical truth) is inexcusable. Hence, **the willful neglect of the evidence by a deceitful heart results in a deadly combination for error**.

Perhaps the European scholars of the sixteenth century, in their haste to explore the errors of their maternal (mother) religious system (the Roman Catholic Church), did not take the time to explore all of God's counsel on the matter of salvation. However, contemporary theologians are again without excuse. They have the advantage of historical hindsight and the council of the Old and New Testament; therefore we know that it cannot be the spirit of God that causes them to error. The first Century Christian church, consisting of Jews and Gentiles, did not have a New Testament to guide them in doctrinal instructions. They had only the Old Testament. How is it that they, without the New Testament, preached the same gospel and were unanimous in doctrine, and yet men today have both the Old and New Testaments, but can rarely agree upon anything?

It would also be appropriate at this time to give an unbiased biblical definition for the word *saved*. Before we begin we must take into account the fact that there are thousands of Christian sects, each with their own religious interpretation of the requirements for salvation and definition for the word saved. All of these factors collectively make it impossible to develop a universal definition for the term and compounds the problem even further. Since the religious term **saved** seems to be so controversial and is used very loosely by "Christians," it has innumerable meanings and seems to foster much religious miscommunication. There are people who use the same word, but each with their own understanding of the term. The one plausibly accurate definition can be found only in the **divine constitution**, the Bible, as revealed consistently throughout human history by the apostles and prophets. The term **salvation refers to deliverance from the vices of sin, Satan, and the flesh. Once an individual becomes saved, he can then partake in a covenant relationship of love, discipleship, and obedience.** This inclusive definition nullifies the natural and spiritual consequences of sin (which is hell) and the second death (Rev 20:6-15).

A word that is synonymous with *saved* (that could be substituted in its stead) is the term **delivered**. Are you saved? Are you delivered? Deliverance is the bread, meat, and sustenance for the children of the kingdom (Mt 16:19, 15:21-26, Mk 7:27). **If a person is not delivered from sin in this life, the appetites of the flesh: the lust of the eyes, the pride of life, and the powers of darkness, then there will be no salvation in the next life.** A Christian starts off as a babe in Christ, but he must grow up to exercise his senses to discern the difference between good and evil. He must learn to walk victoriously, realizing that Christ, who dwells on the inside of him (by the Holy Spirit), is greater than he himself. New Testament salvation extends beyond the borders of deliverance from eternal judgment or hell. It also includes deliverance from sickness, disease, poverty, demonic deception, spiritual bondage, and mental oppression on this earth. Jesus gives those believers who are in covenant with Him the ability to walk in kingdom power and authority on earth, and to tread upon the demonic hosts (Lk 10:19,20).

Is faith the only key to salvation (as many contemporary Protestant and Charismatic churches suppose)? First, we must make note that the scriptures speak conclusively that "faith" and its twin, "belief" alone does not constitute a proper Christian conversion. James (the half brother of Christ) stated, *"Thou believest that there is one God; thou doest well: the devils also believe, and tremble"* (Jm 2:19). If belief in God alone made one a Christian, then devils would also be saved, because they had a personal encounter with the true and living God from the moment of their creation. Jesus said that He observed Satan being cast out of heaven as lightening (Lk 10:18). Demons speaking through individuals whom they had possessed cried out to Jesus saying, *"What have I to do with thee, Jesus, thou Son of the most high God? I adjure thee by God, that thou torment me not"* (Mk 5:7, Lk 8:28). When the seven sons of Sceva were imitating the Apostle Paul and attempting to exorcise a demon out of a young man, the demons said to them, *"Jesus I know, and Paul I know, but who are you"* (Acts 19:15)? One should be able to clearly see that Satan and his demons believe in both God and Christ, but that does not make them Christians. If one says he believes in Jesus Christ, "big deal." Belief alone is not sufficient. The devils also believe and fear Him. Only temporal men can **believe in God in such a trifling manner and expect to receive the reward of the righteous**. The Christian relationship with Christ is often compared to that of a husband and a wife. Just because a man may see a woman, and then claim her to be his wife, that does not make her his wife. **Their relationship as husband and wife is not based on faith alone, but faithfulness and the marriage covenant.**

Many of the religious leaders of Christ's day heard and believed His words, but would not follow Him because of the social pressure to conform to the religiously correct views of the Pharisees. The biblical account is as follows, *"Nevertheless among the chief rulers also many believed on him; but because of the Pharisees they did not confess him, lest they should be put out of the synagogue: For they loved the praise of men more than the praise of God"* (Jn 12:42,43). Even though the 12 disciples of Christ believed on Him and dwelled with Him, they were not converted into

66

the kingdom Church until Pentecost, when Christ would supernaturally dwell with in them. Jesus told Peter that, *"I have prayed for thee, that thy faith fail not: and when thou art converted, strengthen thy brethren"* (Lk 22:32). It wasn't until Pentecost that their conversion would be internal and completed by Christ. Only then could they experience a **true conversion that would enable them to go beyond the cerebral intellectual realm** to that of a spiritual covenant (Lk 17:22). Before Pentecost, and immediately after Christ's crucifixion, Jesus' disciples could not help themselves (or anyone else for that matter). However, when they were converted into the New Covenant at Pentecost their faith was matched with obedience and truth. It was on that day that they received the spirit of truth (Jn 14:17) after being commanded to go to Jerusalem and wait in the Upper Room to receive the Spirit (Acts 1:8,12-15, Lk 24:46-53). Since Pentecost, those who would know the biblical Jesus would know Him through faith, truth, and obedience. Therefore, salvation was predicated on more than faith to establish a new and better covenant. Most Western scholars find it hard to repent of their cultural religious heritage and allow the Bible to speak for itself. The Apostle Paul summarizes these concepts for the church of the end times: those who will perish and be deceived by the Anti-Christ. The will be ensnared by deception because they refuse to be sanctified by the spirit of obedience and belief of the truth.

"Even him, whose coming is after the working of Satan with all power and signs and lying wonders,
*And with all deceivableness of unrighteousness **in them that perish; because they received not the love of the truth, that they might be saved.***
And for this cause God shall send them strong delusion, that they should believe a lie:
That they all might be damned who believed not the truth, but had pleasure in unrighteousness.
*But we are bound to give thanks alway to God for you, brethren beloved of the Lord, because **God hath from the beginning chosen you to salvation through sanctification of the Spirit and belief of the truth:***
***Whereunto he called you by our gospel**, to the obtaining of the glory of our Lord Jesus Christ.*
*Therefore, brethren, **stand fast, and hold the traditions which ye have been taught, whether by word, or our epistle**."* (II Thes 2:9-15)

The Love of God and Salvation

The ultimate love manifested by the Creator towards man was demonstrated when He allowed freedom of choice to enter into the natural realm of creation. If man was

67

denied by the Creator to express free will, and all of his choices were predestined (like many European and American Calvinists proclaim), then man could not freely receive or freely give his love towards God. Man could neither love God nor could he freely (out of his bowels of compassion) independently love any thing. Man was created with the ability to choose to be obedient to Christ or pay the consequences for disobedience. Based on one's heart (whether selfish or compliant), his fate and destiny would be sealed by his daily choices. **Love is not possessive. It grants liberty to each individual to choose.** It also provides an opportunity for hurt and rejection, directed towards both God and man.

Agape (love) is generally defined as the unconditional love of God towards man. Some Christians, who believe in a perversion of the gospel, fail to believe that it takes at least two to engage in love and abide in a covenant in unison. But the scriptures clearly proclaim how *"can two walk together except they be in agreement?"* In its proper context, the gospel of Jesus Christ can be explained in this manner, that God loved Adam and his descendents, despite the fact that they were sinners and undeserving of His love and mercy. He made the decision to love Adam, his wife, and their children from the foundation of the world. However, with His love came the blessings as well as the consequences of their choices. Taking all these facts into consideration, those who believe that God's love is unconditional are greatly mistaken. Why? Because, the love of God has always had conditions, both for men and angels. That is why He establishes His covenants with mankind, so there would be no misunderstanding by either party.

Love also means conflict. As long as you have at least two people in a relationship, you will have conflict. It was a conflict with Adam that provoked God's judgment upon him. That seed of rebellion has perpetually caused conflicts with men ever since. The Creator established covenants to show His love for Adam and his descendents. The purpose of the covenants with Noah, Abraham, and Moses was to clearly express the bounds of their relationship with Him and establish a means to resolve conflict. What many religious people fail to realize is that the love of God is perfect and that God is Love. It was perfect when he commanded Adam to keep only one commandment… do not eat of the Tree of the Knowledge of Good and Evil. **It was also perfect love that caused the Father to curse Adam and Eve with the penalty of death when they sinned.**

The Lord of heaven is perfect in love and perfect in judgement. **Both love and judgment are connected, and predicated on one's obedience or his choice to sin. If the love of God is rejected, then the judgment of God is sure.** These parameters, which engulf the scope of His love, were established from the foundation of the world. This expression of love was not granted to the angelic hosts. They in turn were baffled by Christ at Calvary (and probably even to this day) that God, in His foreknowledge, was slain from the foundation of the world (Rev 13:8)… knowing He would have to redeem man from his wretched state. Without debate, the love of God was freely given to men in the personification of Jesus Christ. The scriptures state,

68

"He that spared not his own Son, but delivered him up for us all, how shall he not with him also freely give us all things?" (Rm 8:32). In the final analysis, **the love of God is not totally free as some suppose; it requires a covenant relationship based upon the consequences of choice.** *"And the LORD God commanded the man, saying, Of every tree of the garden thou mayest freely eat: But of the tree of the knowledge of good and evil, thou shalt not eat of it: for in the day that thou eatest thereof thou shalt surely die."* (Gen 2:16,17) God did not play with Adam and Eve when they sinned. Neither did he compromise and refuse to judge the millions who perished in the flood. He was not teasing when he destroyed the inhabitants of the cities of Sodom and Gomorrah when he could not find ten who were righteous. It was no joke when He wiped out three million rebellious, stubborn, kicking and screaming Jews in the wilderness. Many contemporary Americans blame and sue others for their own negligence, failures, and lack of self-control. Perhaps they can get away with such actions in the courts of men, but they will not be able to stand and justify themselves in the presence of a Holy God!

If any man will reciprocate the love of God, then he is liberated from Satan, the evil one. The devil, by deceit and lies, connive humans out of their divine blessings and inheritance. Every Old Testament character and New Testament saint, who made decisions out of the issues of his heart, received just recompense for his actions.

"For if the word spoken by angels was stedfast, and every transgression and disobedience received a just recompence of reward;
How shall we escape, if we neglect so great salvation; which at the first began to be spoken by the Lord.". (Heb 2:2,3)

God allows men to choose whom they will serve. He seeks those who, after being liberated by the Holy Ghost, will serve Him in spirit and in truth, with a heart of praise, adoration, and gratitude. For centuries, the major fallacies with Protestant and Catholic doctrines have been the rejection of the Baptism of the Holy Ghost and the biblical manifestation of speaking in unlearned tongues (Acts 2:1-18). Because they lacked the indwelling Spirit of Christ (which exemplified the First Century church), these "brands" of the Christian faith could only abide in half-truths, sin, rituals, vain traditions and cultural self-righteousness.

The Old and New Testaments were authored by the same spirit and the same God. He is "the same, yesterday, today, and forever" and His revealed, congruent nature has proven that God is no respecter of persons. **If He spared not His natural seed Israel, Gentile Christians who were adopted** (by the Holy Ghost, the spirit of adoption, Rm 8:15) **ought to take heed, lest He spare not them,** in the same manner as He spared not the Jewish nation (Rm 11:17-24).

God, the just judge, will never violate the fundamentals of justice, impartiality, and equality. **He is perfect in love and perfect in justice. If one rejects, or desecrates**

69

God's love, he will experience God's perfect Wrath. In the last days, everything shall be judged perfectly according to the number (7) seven. Those who believe in unconditional salvation do not understand impartiality and divine justice. Unfortunately, they have fallen for one of the oldest lies in Satan's book of deception ... *"ye shall not die"*. If one chooses to make judgements concerning God's Word, he must use divine standards of righteous judgment. Otherwise, he forfeits the promises of biblical salvation.

The following are judgment standards of the Lord for natural Israel (the Jews) and spiritual Israel (the church). Each will establish the parameters and criteria for one's salvation with provisionary conditions; thus nullifying the deceptive doctrine "Once Saved, Always Saved" and its supporting network of erroneous doctrinal theories. One should be able to see conclusively, after examining the scriptures, that this doctrine is a theological hoax.

Rm 11:17-24... "And if some of the branches be broken off [natural Jews], and thou, being a wild olive tree [Gentile Christian], wert graffed in among them, and with them partakest of the root and fatness of the olive tree; Boast not against the branches. But if thou boast, thou bearest not the root, but the root thee. Thou wilt say then, The branches were broken off, that I might be graffed in. Well; because of unbelief they were broken off, and thou standest by faith. **Be not highminded, but fear: For if God spared not the natural branches, take heed lest he also spare not thee.** Behold therefore the goodness and severity of God: on them which fell, severity; but toward thee, **goodness, if thou continue in his goodness: otherwise thou also shalt be cut off**. And they also, if they abide not still in unbelief, shall be graffed in: for God is able to graff them in again." (Jn 15:1-11, Lk 8:14, I Cor 10:5-12, Deu 11:26-28)

Heb 2:2,3 ... "For if the word spoken by angels was stedfast, and every transgression and disobedience received a just recompence of reward; **How shall we escape, if we neglect so great salvation**; which at the first began to be spoken by the Lord, and was confirmed unto us by them that heard him."
(Psa 50:22, I Thes 5:1-11, Amos 5:18-20; 9:8-10)

Heb 12:6-29 ... "without holiness no man shall see the Lord... **Looking diligently lest any man fail of the grace of God**... if they escaped not who refused him that spake on earth, much more shall not we escape, if we turn away from him that speaketh from heaven... Our God is a consuming fire."
(II Sam 7:15, Gal 3:1-4)

Gal 6:7,8 ... "**Be not deceived; God is not mocked: for whatsoever a man soweth, that shall he also reap.** For he that soweth to his flesh shall of the flesh reap corruption; but he that soweth to the Spirit shall of the Spirit reap life

70

everlasting." (Jer 32:19; 17:10, Rev 2:23; 22:12, Psa 62:12, Job 4:8; 34:11, Psa 1:4-6, Ecc 3:17, Isa 3:10, II Chron 6:29-30)

I Cor 6:9-10… "Know ye not that the unrighteous shall not inherit the kingdom of God? Be not deceived: neither fornicators, nor idolaters, nor adulterers, nor effeminate, nor abusers of themselves with mankind, Nor thieves, nor covetous, nor drunkards, nor revilers, nor extortioners, shall inherit the kingdom of God." (I Jn 5:18, II Cor 13:5-7, Eph 5:3-8)

II Thes 1:7-9… "And to you who are troubled rest with us, when the Lord Jesus shall be revealed from heaven with his mighty angels, In flaming fire taking vengeance on them that <u>know not</u> God, and that <u>obey not</u> the gospel of our Lord Jesus Christ:
Who shall be punished with everlasting destruction from the presence of the Lord, and from the glory of his power; When he shall come to be glorified in his saints, and to be admired in all them that believe (because our testimony among you was believed) in that day."

Ezek 33:17-20… "Yet the children of thy people say, The way of the Lord is not equal: but as for them, their way is not equal. When the righteous turneth from his righteousness, and committeth iniquity, he shall even die thereby. But if the wicked turn from his wickedness, and do that which is lawful and right, he shall live thereby. Yet ye say, The way of the Lord is not equal. O ye house of Israel, I will judge you, every one after his ways."

I Pet 4:17-19… "For the time is come that judgment must begin at the house of God: and if it first begin at us, what shall the end be of them that obey not the gospel of God? And if the righteous scarcely be saved, where shall the ungodly and the sinner appear? Wherefore let them that suffer according to the will of God commit the keeping of their souls to him in well doing, as unto a faithful Creator." (Isa 30:1)

I Pet 1:16,17… "But as he which hath called you is holy, so be ye holy in all manner of conversation. Because it is written, Be ye holy; for I am holy. And if ye call on the Father, who without respect of persons judgeth according to every man's work, pass the time of your sojourning here in fear."
(Phil 2:12, Lk 13:23-28)

Ezek 18:4-9,19-32… "The soul that sins, it shall die. If the righteous turneth from his righteousness shall he live? If the wicked turns from his wickedness shall he live? Oh house of Israel are not my ways equal? Are not your ways unequal? Therefore I will judge you . . . everyone according to his ways . . . repent .

71

. . so iniquity shall not be your ruin."

[Those who believe in Once Saved, Always Saved, believe that the righteous is saved no matter what, contrary to Old Testament and New Testament scriptures.]

Ezek 9: 2-7... *And the Lord said unto him "Go through the midst of the city, through the midst of Jerusalem, and **set a mark upon the foreheads of the men that sigh and that cry for all the abominations that be done in the midst thereof.** And to the others he said in mine hearing, Go ye after him through the city, and smite: **let not your eye spare, neither have ye pity. Slay utterly old and young, both maids, and little children, and women:** but come not near any man upon whom is the mark; and **begin at my sanctuary. Then they began at the ancient men which were before the house."** (II Tim 2:19, Rev 7:1-4; 9:4; 15:2)*

Heb 10:26-31... *"For if we sin wilfully after that we have received the knowledge of the truth, there remaineth **<u>no more sacrifice for sins,</u>** But a certain fearful looking for of **<u>judgment and fiery indignation</u>**, which shall devour the adversaries.*

*He that despised Moses' law died without mercy under two or three witnesses: **Of how much sorer punishment, suppose ye, shall he be thought worthy, who hath trodden under foot the Son of God, and hath counted the blood of the covenant, wherewith he was sanctified, an unholy thing, and hath done despite unto the Spirit of grace?***

*For we know him that hath said, **<u>Vengeance belongeth unto me, I will recompense, saith the Lord</u>**. And again, The Lord shall judge his people. **<u>It is a fearful thing to fall into the hands of the living God."</u>***

Prov 21:16... *"The man that wandereth out of the way of understanding **shall remain in the congregation of the dead."***
(Mt 7:13,14, I Cor 2: 14, 15, Mt 7:6,7,9, I Jn 3:14, 2:9,10)

Jm 5:19,20... *"Brethren, if any of you do err from the truth, **and one convert him;** Let him know, that **he which converteth the sinner from the error of his way shall save a soul from death**, and shall hide a multitude of sins." (Lk 12:16-20, Ezek 18:4-9, Rm 6:23, II Jn 9, I Tim 4:1,16, I Thes 4:6, II Thes 2:10-15, Gal 1:8,9, Rev 22:18,19, Ex 32:33, Deu 29:19-29, I Jn 4:6, Num 15:22-31)*

II Pet 2:20-22... ***"For if after they have escaped the pollutions of the world through the knowledge of the Lord and Saviour Jesus Christ, they are again entangled therein, and overcome, the latter end is worse with them than the beginning. For it had been better for them not to have known the way of righteousness, than, after they have known it, to turn from the holy commandment delivered unto them.*** *But it is happened unto them according to the true proverb,*

The dog is turned to his own vomit again; and the sow that was washed to her wallowing in the mire." (Prov 26:10,11, Ezek 16:59, Amos 3:2, Jude 4,11-19)

Gal 5:16-21... *"This I say then,* **Walk in the Spirit, and ye shall not fulfil the lust of the flesh.** *For the flesh lusteth against the Spirit, and the Spirit against the flesh: and these are contrary the one to the other: so that ye cannot do the things that ye would. But if ye be led of the Spirit, ye are not under the law.*

Now the works of the flesh are manifest, which are these; Adultery, fornication, uncleanness, lasciviousness, Idolatry, witchcraft, hatred, variance, emulations, wrath, strife, seditions, heresies, Envyings, murders, drunkenness, revellings, and such like: of the which I tell you before, as I have also told you in time past, **that they which do such things shall not inherit the kingdom of God.***"*
(I Jn 3:3-10, 2:29, Mt 6:23, Jn 8:34, 12:48, Mt 10:14, Mk 6:11, Lk 9:5;10:12-15)

Rm 6:6-23... *"**Let not sin therefore reign in your mortal body**, that ye should obey it in the lusts thereof. **Neither yield ye your members as instruments of unrighteousness unto sin**: but yield yourselves unto God, as those that are alive from the dead, and your members as instruments of righteousness unto God. **For sin shall not have dominion over you: for ye are not under the law, but under grace.***

What then? shall we sin, because we are not under the law, but under grace? God forbid. Know ye not, that to whom ye yield yourselves servants to obey, his servants ye are to whom ye obey; *whether of sin unto death, or of obedience unto righteousness?"*
(II Tim 2:26, Eph 4:17-25. Col 3:5, Heb 10:38,39, I Cor 9:27)

Rm 8:13,14... *"**For if ye live after the flesh, ye shall die**: but if ye through the Spirit do mortify the deeds of the body, ye shall live. **For as many as are led by the Spirit of God, they are the sons of God.***"*
(Col 3:5-10, Rm 12:10-14, Eph 4:22-24, Heb 12:1,2)

After surveying this selection of scriptures gathered from the Old and New Testaments, it should be quite apparent that theologians (throughout the ages), who have believed in the doctrine "Once Saved, Always Saved," have purposely only chosen verses for doctrine that would support their theological perspective. Their obvious exclusion of contrary verses would lead one to believe that they wish to remain willfully uninformed. To maintain their doctrinal heresies is to succumb to a deceptive, self-fulfilling prophecy. However, they are without excuse. Whenever contrary verses are read that is not according their religiously correct spin, they through human reason and theology explain the truth away. The previous verses were merely a cross sample of verses that relate to the subject matter of God's judgment of the wicked in and outside of His covenant. These verses are found in all bibles and are not concealed in obscurity.

What are concealed however, are their truths, which are hidden from many who can not receive them because of the conditions of their hearts. If one would examine the whole counsel of God, and systematically study the congruency of the Old and New Testaments, he should not error in these matters. However, those with defiled hearts, regardless of their education and theological training, still cannot figure out the simple phrase, **"THOU SHALT NOT!"** One with a disobedient heart will relentlessly justify his sin. For example, despite all the examples of judgments by God in the Old Testament and the fact that sexual perversion is clearly stated in the New Testament to be an abomination, why do Contemporary Western Christian scholars align themselves with the heathen to justify homosexuality and embrace same sex marriages? The Apostle Paul reveals the answer, as he (through the Holy Ghost) writes his letter to Titus:

*Unto the pure all things are pure: but unto **them that are defiled and unbelieving** is nothing pure; **but even their mind and conscience is defiled. They profess that they know God; but in works they deny him, being abominable, and disobedient, and unto every good work reprobate.*** (Titus 1:15,16)

Their narcissistic attitudes and pleasure-seeking logic, defiles their hearts, and causes them to have no fear of the consequences of their actions. Consequently, they nullify the judgment of God in their minds. However, the judgments of God are sure, and all sinners will have their day in the divine court of heaven (Rev 20:11-15). Shall the selective and willful ignorance of men alter God's divine plan, or judgment? The scriptures emphatically declare:

*"For what if some did not believe? shall their unbelief make the faith of God without effect? **God forbid: yea, let God be true, but every man a liar;** as it is written, That thou mightest be justified in thy sayings, and mightest overcome when thou art judged.*

*But if our unrighteousness commend the righteousness of God, what shall we say? **Is God unrighteous who taketh vengeance?** (I speak as a man). God forbid: for then how shall God judge the world?... **Let us do evil, that good may come? whose damnation is just...***

***They are all gone out of the way,** they are together become unprofitable; there is none that doeth good, no, not one. Their throat is an open sepulchre; with their tongues they have used deceit; the poison of asps is under their lips...Whose mouth is full of cursing and bitterness... Their feet are swift to shed blood:*

Destruction and misery are in their ways: And the way of peace have they not known: There is no fear of God before their eyes." *(Rm 3:3-15)*

Just in case one does not yet understand the biblical mandates concerning the provisions of the New Covenant and God's criteria for judgment, we will examine further the other arguments used to justify the concept "Once Saved Always Saved," also known as unconditional Salvation."The New Covenant can be exemplified through the following statement:

It's not what Christ can do for you, but by the consent of one's own will, what you can do through Christ. Jesus' desired work is to transform individuals into His image . . . holy, perfect, without spot or blemish. However, the doctrine of eternal security, or unconditional salvation, allows compromising believers to be comfortable in sin, thus insuring that they will never be the expressed image of Christ. The New Testament clearly lays down numerous grounds by which **Christians can be dis-inherited** because of breech of covenant if they do not repent and walk in righteousness. The doctrine of eternal security would have one to believe that one **"can make" a covenant with God, that God can not get out of**, regardless of their actions? God forbid! This is utter folly. Some, who believe in the doctrine **"Once Saved, Always Saved," allege that once one believes in Christ, Christ cannot, and will not reject His own children**. They are sadly mistaken. Remember, it took only one sin to cause His children, Adam and Eve, to be thrust out of the Garden. Jesus is the same yesterday, today and forever, and one of His foundational principles is that sin separates all men from God. The following are examples of sins, which if not repented of by Christians would constitute a breech of the New Testament Covenant of salvation:

1. Unforgiveness – Mt 18:21-35, Mk 11:25
2. Holding the truth in unrighteousness – Rm 1:18-32
3. Error – Jm 5:19,20, II Jn 9, Gal 1:8,9
4. Family neglect – I Tim 5:8
5. Hatred of one's brother, the spirit of murder - I Jn 3:14,15, I Jn 4:20
6. Adding to the word of God – Rev 22:18,19, Prov 30:5,6, Ex 32:33, Deu 27:26
7. Adultery, fornication, uncleanness, lasciviousness, idolatry, witchcraft, hatred, variance, emulation, sedition, heresy, envy, drunkenness – Gal 5:19-21
8. Prejudice – Jm 2:1-14
9. Extortion, covetousness, effeminate behavior amongst men, thief – I Cor 6:9,10, Eph 5:3-5, Col 3:5-9
10. Sorcery, whoremonging, murder – Rev 22:14,15
11. Fearfulness, unbelief, abominations, lying – Rev 21:8, Prov 12:22
12. Defiling the spiritual temple – I Cor 3:16,17; 6:19,20
13. Neglect of ones salvation – Heb 2:3
14. Unfruitfulness – Jn 15: 1-10
15. Worldliness – Jm 4:4, I Jn 2:15-17, Mt 6:22,23, II Cor 6:14-18, Lk 17:32; 9:62, Gen 19:17,26

16. The unpardonable sin – Heb 6: 4-8, Mt 12:31, Mk 3:29, Lk 12:10, I Jn 5:16,17
17. Covenant breaking – Prov 21:16, Ezek 18:21-25, II Pet 2:20-22, Transgressors – II Jn 9, Psa 37:37-39, Prov 2:22
18. High-mindedness and no fear of God – Rm 11:18-24, Heb 12:28,29, Deu 4:23,24, Heb 10:26-31
19. Receiving the Mark of the Beast – Rev 14:9; 13:16
20. Denying Christ – Mt 10:33, II Tim 2:11-13
21. Hypocrisy – Lk 13:24-30; 12:45-48, Mt 24:50,51; 23:13-33, 15:7-9, Job 13:15,16; 36:13,14; 27:5-10, Rm 2:1-9
22. Not discerning the Lord's body in communion – I Cor 11:27-31

Despite all of the evidence above, many compromising and contrary religious believers will choose to believe that which opposes truth and biblical sound doctrine. Such actions nail shut the windows of heaven and padlock spiritual revelation from above.

Are Christians Born Again Sinners?

Some denominational religious orders claim that **Christians are simply born again sinners**. Claiming that they will never get victory over the sin in their lives and they have Jesus who will forgive them over and over again, hence, born again sinners. We can thank the evolution of Western European Protestant theology for such an error. Many denominational founders have made such a claim, because their faith was based purely on cerebral human intellect, and was not enlightened, or empowered by the Holy Ghost. They had a form of Godliness, but had denied the supernatural power of the living Christ in their lives for centuries. Consequently, they became engulfed in a quagmire of religious traditions, which could not rid them of their sinful lusts. They became helplessly trapped in perpetual spiritual bondage, with no relief in sight. Henceforth, stuck between a *"theological rock"* and a *"religious hard place,"* Western scholars changed their doctrine to accommodate their personal experiences. However, what they should have done was to seek the Lord to discover how they could change their experiences to line up with the truths of the New Covenant.

European Christianity produced an intellectual version of the Christian faith, which was void of the power of the spirit. Their outward manifestations and substitutes for true spirituality were vain liturgies, traditions, and false religious priestly systems. Consequently, the religious masses became hypocritically bound to endless confessions of sin with no hope of deliverance, in the same manner as the children of Israel who were bound by the law and could not keep it. Without the ability to be delivered from the grips of sin, Western Christians would remain helplessly locked at the cross for mercy (Christ's blood sacrifice at Passover), and could not go to

Pentecost to experience New Testament grace. Because they were ensnared by the sins of their hearts, mighty religious men could not shake off the shackles of religious genocide, greed, sexual lusts, lusts for power, sins of racism, and sins of religious pride. With the reality of being hypocrites facing them in the mirror on a daily basis, it was expedient for them to change their doctrines to appease their religious consciences.

New theological terminology had to be circulated for the masses to justify the ungodly actions of church leaders, and their congregates. The concept of Christians being "**born again sinners**" is a blatant contradiction of the scriptures, which state that Christians are "*new creatures in Christ,*" that their old man is *supposed* to be passed away. "*Therefore if any man be in Christ, he is a new creature: old things are passed away; behold, all things are become new*" (II Cor 5:17). By definition, a new spiritual birth cannot be attained until the death and tenants of the old birth (natural birth, the seed of Adam) have been resolved by the willful death to one's self-will. Chapters 6 and 7 of the book of Romans explain how; "*he that is dead is freed from sin.*" The first man (Adam) brought death into the natural world by transgressing the only forbidden act imposed upon him in the Garden of Eden. The "second Adam," Jesus the Christ, brought life by living without sin, paying the penalty for sin, which was His own death (I Cor 15:45-49). A dead man cannot sin! He cannot lie, murder, hate his brother, fornicate or produce false teachings. Evidently, many Christians throughout the ages never received the Second Adam, the biblical Jesus, because if they had, they never would have committed such dreadful acts in the name of Christ. A scriptural response to this idea can be found and qualified in the writings of the Apostle John, which states;

"*Whosoever **abideth in him** [Christ] sinneth not: whosoever sinneth hath not seen him, neither known him.*

*Little children, **let no man deceive you**: he that doeth righteousness is righteous, even as he is righteous.*

He that committeth sin is of the devil; *for the devil sinneth from the beginning. For this purpose the Son of God was manifested, that he might destroy the works of the devil.*

Whosoever is born of God doth not commit sin; *for his seed remaineth in him: and he cannot sin, because he is born of God.*

In this the children of God are manifest, and the children of the devil: whosoever doeth not righteousness is not of God, *neither he that loveth not his brother.*" (I Jn 3:6-10)

Those who love God will not **abide in sin**, because it would be totally contrary to their new nature, which was miraculously brought about internally by a transforming living Christ (Jn 1:10-12). Unfortunately, Christians from all sectors of the globe have cleaved to nationalism, cultural traditions and ethnic pride, which war against their new spiritual birth experience. Only few have successfully developed sufficient escape velocity to untangle themselves from these traditions. Their carnal, natural thinking has caused them to war against the word of God, thus preventing them from doing the will of God (Rm 8:5-11) and putting on the mind of Christ (Phil 2:5).

"...That ye put off concerning the former conversation the old man, which is corrupt according to the deceitful lusts;
And be renewed in the spirit of your mind; And that ye put on the new man, which after God is created in righteousness and true holiness." (Eph 4:22-24)

The net result is that only a remnant has experienced the true new birth process described in the bible. To prove this statement true, one could simply engage in a controversial issue in which the Bible is contrary to man's culture, racial views, or religious traditions. Then watch and see how their flesh rises up as they justify themselves, in opposition to the word, and they are easily offended. It is at these moments that the latent issues of the heart, and spiritual bondage (anti-Christ and anti-word spirits) will begin to manifest themselves (once challenged). One would see how quickly many "Christians" will become offended because of the word, oppose it, and   vehemently justify their carnal activities and sins.

One may ask the question why do individuals sin? The answer is quite simple. Men love darkness and the temporal lusts of this world more than the eternal light of heaven (Jn 3:17-21). **The irony of this situation is that the religious want salvation, but they want it according to their own carnal religious terms**. Even though the devil tempts men with the pleasures of this life, he can only control them by their willful consent to sin against God, and by agreeing with his philosophies. Furthermore, a man can only sin if he desires the item that is used to seduce him into temptation. The scriptures declare this cycle of bondage in the following manner;

*"Let no man say when he is tempted, I am tempted of God: for God cannot be tempted with evil, neither tempteth he any man: **But every man is tempted, when he is drawn away of his own lust, and enticed.***
Then when lust hath conceived, it bringeth forth sin: and sin, when it is finished, bringeth forth death." (Jm 1:13-15)

The darkness of men does not abide in a vacuum; it is ever present in this present world of ungodliness, violence, and lusts. The world is under the domain of the Prince of Darkness, called Satan, and his followers serve faithfully. He offers to men the temporal world, its lust and materialistic gains, in exchange for their eternal souls. The blind, the unbelieving, and the hypocrites follow him like a pied piper to an eternal inferno. The three areas of human temptation and sin are clearly presented by the Apostle John.

"Love not the world, neither the things that are in the world. If any man love the world, the love of the Father is not in him.
*For all that is in the world, **the lust of the flesh**, and **the lust of the eyes**,*

and the pride of life, is not of the Father, but is of the world.

And the world passeth away, and the lust thereof: but he that doeth the **will of God abideth for ever."** (I Jn 2:15-17)

If one loves the world, he automatically ends up hating God (whether consciously or sub-consciously). Many also begin to devise religious doctrines to appease their guilty consciences. A lack of desire and love for the holy things of God is the root of all sin. The natural affection for the things of this world, human pride, and carnal thinking causes many to forsake righteousness in order to maintain their unscriptural religious beliefs. The Apostle Paul states that the old sinner man, who was alienated from God, is supposed to be dead to sin, buried with Christ through water baptism, and alive unto God for fruitful works. In other words, they should be **sanctified**, or set apart unto God, for His divine purposes. The Apostle Paul tells us that Christians are commanded to make no provisions to fulfill the lust of their flesh. He also qualified the term Christian, by stating that they are Jesus Christ' disciples who hear His voice, and are lead by His Spirit. Paul goes further to say that only these individuals are the true Sons of God (Rm 8:13,14). All Christians may want to go to heaven, but it appears that not all want to obey the prerequisites required for getting there. Christ classifies these individuals as thieves and robbers (Jn 10:7-9) and wolves in sheep's clothing (Jn 10:12, Acts 20:29, Mt 7:15; 10:16). Consequently, *"many are called but few are chosen."* Jesus, their creator, knowing the hearts and nature of man, would give further insight on the exclusiveness caused by human choice on the number of people who would be eventually saved.

*"***Enter ye in at the strait gate***: for wide is the gate, and broad is the way, that leadeth to destruction, and many there be which go in thereat:*

Because strait is the gate, and narrow is the way, which leadeth unto life, and few there be that find it… *Wherefore by their fruits ye shall know them.*

Not every one that saith unto me, Lord, Lord, shall enter into the kingdom of heaven; but he that doeth the will of my Father which is in heaven.

Many will say to me in that day, Lord, Lord, have we not prophesied in thy name? and in thy name have cast out devils? and in thy name done many wonderful works?

And then will I profess unto them, I never knew you: depart from me, ye that work iniquity.

Therefore whosoever heareth these sayings of mine, and doeth them, I will liken him unto a wise man, which built his house upon a rock.".
(Mt 7:13,14, 20-24)

Jesus even asked the question, why do men *"call ye me Lord, Lord, and do not the things which I say* (Lk 6:46)?" The fallacy that has become a stumbling block for many "sincere Christian" organizations (sincerely wrong) is that they receive promises of the covenant without any conditions or mandates attached. Unfortunately, **their unbelief causes them to wrestle with the absolute nature of the scriptures, to their own destruction** (II Pet 3:16). Many overlook the fact that, the Bible is God's Will and Testament, but is commonly called: the Word of God. As with a natural will, one must adhere to all of its content, or he will forfeit his inheritance by default. Historically, all of God's promises, which pertain to eternal salvation, were always conditional. One can be ensured that he will inherit the promises of the Lord's covenants if he chooses to love God, and remain obedient to His will (I Pet 1:8-10). Since Christians have a new and better covenant, it is expressly stated that there are provisionary conditions, just like there were in the Old Covenant. However, **Christians are supposed to have a greater realm of accountability** by a personal Savior, and a greater spiritual capability through the Holy Ghost to fulfill the Old Testament through the spirit of Christ given in the New Testament.

If one walks in Christ he will realize that there is no failure in God. Christ in the Christian, the hope of glory, is greater than the individual that is in the world (I Jn 4:4). **If one wants to be assured of his salvation the biblical formula is as follows:**

"Grace and peace be multiplied unto you through the knowledge of God, and of Jesus our Lord, ***According as his divine power hath given unto us all things that pertain unto life and godliness****, through the knowledge of him that hath called us to glory and virtue:*

Whereby are given unto us exceeding great and precious promises: that by these ye might be partakers of the divine nature, having escaped the corruption that is in the world through lust.

And beside this, ***giving all diligence, add to your faith virtue****; and* ***to virtue knowledge;***

And ***to knowledge temperance****; and* ***to temperance patience****; and* ***to patience godliness;***

And ***to godliness brotherly kindness****; and* ***to brotherly kindness charity.***

For if these things be in you, and abound*, they make you that* ***ye shall neither be barren nor unfruitful*** *in the knowledge of our Lord Jesus Christ.*

But he that lacketh these things is blind, and cannot see afar off, and hath forgotten that he was purged from his old sins.

Wherefore the rather, ***brethren, give diligence to*** <u>***make your calling and***</u> <u>***election sure: for if ye do these things, ye shall never fall:***</u>

For so ***an entrance shall be ministered unto you abundantly into the everlasting kingdom*** *of our Lord and Saviour Jesus Christ.*

Wherefore I will not be negligent to put you always in remembrance of these things." (II Pet 1:2-12)

We can abstract from the above formula that it is the responsibility of every

Christian to "*sure up*," and make their calling and election sure. Again, those who believe in unconditional promises willfully ignore the contrasting counsel of scripture that systematically and clearly lays out man's obligations towards God. **Personal relationships or contracts between two individuals cannot be one sided, neither can God's covenants with man be**. If the promises of God are misconstrued, not adhering to sound doctrine, that will undoubtedly lead to false teachings (as in the case of "*Once Saved, Always Saved)*." When the chief executor of the estates of heaven, the Lord Himself, comes to oversee the execution of His will at judgment, only those who did the will of the father will receive the promises of inheritance (Mk 3:35).

> *"Having therefore these promises, dearly beloved, let us **cleanse ourselves from all filthiness of the flesh and spirit, perfecting holiness in the fear of God**."* (II Cor 7:1)
> *"**Examine yourselves, whether ye be in the faith; prove your own selves**. Know ye not your own selves, how that Jesus Christ is in you, except ye be reprobates?"* (II Cor 13:5)

The Bible is very vulnerable, because of its size and scope of subject matters, to be misrepresented and conveyed in a manner totally contrary to its intent and purpose. One can simply take a verse out of context, because it states partially or similarly what some people want to believe, and use to construct their own private doctrines. One thing we do know is that every one that the New Testament books were written to had received the baptism of the Holy Ghost, and abided in the apostle's doctrines that enabled them to understand the letters of the apostles. The opposite is true concerning the Eurocentric denominational churches, which explain why they can neither, interpret accurately, or adhere to sound biblical doctrine. The following are examples of God's semi-qualifying statements (conditions to maintain the covenant) and blanket promises (general statements of His covenant promises) for the terms **saved**, **eternal life**, and everlasting life that are misappropriated and abused by those who have a shallow and biased understanding of salvation.

Biblical Non-qualifying Statements for Salvation:

Rm 10:9   "confess with your mouth . . . believe in your heart . . . thou shalt be saved."
          [This verse cannot stand alone as a requirement for salvation because it does not even mention repentance, holiness, being born of the water and spirit, etc. Paul is writing to Christians who are already saved in the Church of Rome, which he initially started, not to heathens. Therefore, this verse could not qualify by itself as a standard

for salvation, because these people were already saved, and abiding in the covenant. There is not even a mention of forgiving others as a criteria for salvation, which we know is mandatory (Mt 6:15).]

Rm 10:13   "whosoever, shall call on the name of the Lord shall be saved."
           [If this verse is to be taken literally, alone, and out of context, then anyone can call on the name Jesus, with a loud voice, and pronounce to be saved. The demons also believe in Christ and they know that there is one God, does that make them Christians? (Jm 2:19)]

Acts 2:21   "Whosoever shall **call on** the name of the Lord shall be saved."
           (Joel 2:28-32)

Jn 10:9   "By me if any man **enter in**, he shall be saved."

Acts 16:31 "**Believe** on the Lord…and thou shalt be saved, and thy house."

Rev 3:20   "Behold I stand at the door…if any man **hear my voice**…I will come in.".

Rm 5:8-10 "while we were yet sinners, Christ died for us…now justified by His blood, we shall be saved…we shall be **saved by His life**."

Rm 8:24   "for we are saved **by hope**.".

Eph 2:5,8,9 "**by grace** ye are saved…by grace through faith, not of yourselves; it is the gift of God …not of works.".

Rm 1:17   "the just shall live **by faith**." (Hab 2:4)

Titus 3:5   "not by our righteousness, but according to **His mercy** He saved us."

Qualifying or Conditional Statements for Salvation:

II Thes 2:10-15 "with all, deceivableness of unrighteousness in them that perish, because **they receive not the love of the truth, that they might be saved**…God chose you to **salvation through the sanctification of the spirit and belief of the truth**.".   (I Pet 1:22,24)

Rev 2:10   "Be thou **faithful unto death**, and I will give thee a crown of life." (Mt 10:22;24:13, Mk 13:13)

II Cor 6:1-7:1 "now is the day of salvation… Be not unequally yoked… come out from among them, be ye separate, saith the Lord…Having these promises…let us **cleanse ourselves from all filthiness of the flesh and spirit, perfecting holiness in the fear of God**."

Col 1:22,23 "to present you holy and unblamable and unreprovable in His sight. **If you continue in the faith grounded and settled, and be not moved away from the hope of the gospel**.".

Acts 2:38 "**Repent** and be **baptized** everyone of you **in the name of Jesus Christ** for the remission of your sins and ye shall **receive the gift of the** Holy Ghost."

Mk 12:29-31 "**Love the Lord thy God** with all thine heart. With all thine mind and with all thine soul." (Deu 30:16-19, Jn 12:23,24)

Lk 13:3,5 "except ye **repent**, ye shall like wise perish." (II Cor 7:10)

Jn 3:5 "Except a man is **born of water and of the spirit he cannot enter** into the kingdom of God."

Rev 2:7 "to him that **overcome** will I.". (Rev 2:17,26-29; 3:5,12,21)

Mt 10:22 "He that **endureth to the end** the same shall be saved." (Mt 24:13, Mk 13:13)

Rm 13:11-14 "now is our salvation nearer than when we believed. The night is far spent, the day is at hand: let us therefore **cast off the works of darkness, and let us put on the armour of light**. Let us walk honestly, as in the day; not in rioting and drunkenness, not in chambering and wantonness, not in strife and envying. But **put ye on the Lord Jesus Christ, and make not provision for the flesh**, to fulfil the lusts thereof." (I Thes 5:1-10)

Heb 10:36 "need of patience…after ye have done the will of God, ye might receive the promise." (Heb 6:11,12)

If an individual tells a lie, he often finds himself in an awkward predicament, having to tell more lies to justify the first. Likewise, when one errors in one scriptural interpretation, it often permeates and infects other doctrinal areas. A math problem possessing only one error effects not only the answer, it can also effect every step in the process of solving it. **The Protestant doctrine of eternal security has infected many other doctrinal areas such as Christian sanctification, justification, and the understanding of the grace of God**.

What is Biblical Sanctification?

Sanctification means to **set apart from** the god of this world, the lusts of the flesh, and sin (Jm 4:4, I Jn 3:6-11, II Cor 6:17); to serve the True and Living God. Furthermore, a true Christian is **to be set apart unto** the Lord Jesus Christ for unconditional surrender to His divine purpose and one's calling. The process can be exemplified through the verses in Romans 12:1,2,

"I beseech you therefore, brethren, by the mercies of God, that ye present your bodies a living sacrifice, holy, acceptable unto God, which is your reasonable service.

And be not conformed to this world: but be ye transformed by the renewing of your mind, that ye may prove what is that good, and acceptable, and perfect, will of God."

In the final analysis, the scriptures state that as we prepare to meet the Lord, whether through death, the resurrection, or the translation of the saints at the rapture (at His Second Coming), we are to do the following: *"Abstain from all appearance of evil. And the very God of peace sanctify you wholly; and I pray God your whole spirit and soul and body be preserved blameless unto the coming of our Lord Jesus Christ."* (I Th 5:22,23)

Sanctification is not an experience that takes place in the future. It is a present state of affairs, which is to be maintained by a choice of one's will, accompanied by a supernatural walk in the spirit. The believer is then preserved by the word and his abiding in truth (Acts 20:32; 26:18, I Cor 1:2; 6:11, Jude 1:24). Sanctification also is not a process. It is imputed unto Christians by the one who knew no sin but became sin for us (II Cor 5:21). It is a covenant state, in which a believer enters by matrimony (covenant), and is then solidified with the spirit, the water, and the blood (Act 2:38). The relationship is maintained through obedience, a walk of faith, and a daily choice to be humbly submitted to do the will of Christ. Once Christ has sanctified a Christian, he must maintain his sanctification through discipleship. Without the power of the Holy Ghost, it is impossible to live a sanctified life. When one obeys Acts 2:38, he is thus sanctified, and meets the requirements to enter into the New Testament covenant which is established in heaven and on earth (I Jn 5:8). Many in Christendom are beginning to receive end time apostolic revelations and truths; however, the majority in Western Christianity are astute in cultural pride, which result in ethnocentric blindness, preventing them from seeing afar off.

To be sanctified is to be consecrated unto God, His purity, and His righteousness, thus leading to the perfection of one's character. God also requires those sanctified by an act of His divine will, to set themselves apart for His service, and to reject their old selfish, rebellious, wicked lives. (II Pet 1:2-11, I Tim 4:8; 5:22).

The scriptures speak clearly on the various components and aspects of sanctification involving God and man's responsibility under the New Covenant. Using a biblical standard to define the term sanctification is much wiser than using a theological one. The biblical evidence expressly states that there are basically seven aspects of sanctification which completely set one apart to serve God in his body, soul, and spirit.

This tri-fold sanctification revealed in the scriptures completely liberates man, saving and delivering him from the snares of darkness. They are as follows:

Christians are sanctified through:
1) The Blood – Heb 10:10-14
2) The Spirit – II Thes 2;13, I Pet 1:2, Rm 15:16, I Cor 6:11
3) The Water – I Jn 5:8, I Pet 3:21, Acts 2:38
4) The Word – Jn 15:3; 17:14-17, Eph 5:26,27
5) One's Faith – Acts 26:18
6) The Truth – Jn 17:17-20, II Thes 2:13
7) One's will – II Cor 6:14-18, II Tim 2:19-21

Any definition that does not incorporate these seven components would create an imbalance and would not uphold the biblical standards for sound doctrine. Consequently, many Christians have become disqualified for salvation due to their lack of sanctification and biblical integrity. The Prophet Joel asks the question, "Who can bring a clean thing out of an unclean? Not one." (Job 14:4)
(Jer 13:23; 2:22,29, Prov 20:9, Ecc 7:20, Isa 64:6, Psa 130:3; 143:2)

"For this is the will of God, even your sanctification, that ye should abstain from fornication:
That every one of you should know how to possess his vessel in sanctification and honour; Not in the lust of concupiscence, even as the Gentiles which know not God." (I Thes 4:3-5)

Traditional Protestant theologians declare that we are sanctified in Christ through His redeeming blood. They further claim that at Calvary, the place of His crucifixion, the New Testament was completed. They teach that one is sanctified, and born again, when he accepts Christ as his personal savior. While it is true that Christians are sanctified by the perfect and eternal blood sacrifice of Christ, the blood does not provide the full provisions for salvation. Without the water and the spirit Christians would remain helplessly depraved and still under the bondage of sin. This is the problem with Western Christianity. What good is it to have a perfect sacrifice if one's ungodly habits and sinful nature remains? **Contrary to popular belief, the New Testament was not completed at Calvary as many suppose, because the spiritual components of the New Covenant was not manifested until fifty days later at Pentecost**, as Jesus baptized His disciples with His spirit (Jn 7:37-39, Acts 2:1-19). This sanctifying experience is what the majority of the church leaders from European cultures have been deprived of for almost two millenniums. Even contemporary Charismatics and Pentecostals, which have received the spirit, have embraced these distorted cultural teachings. Like their cultural progenitors, they believe that sanctification is only a once in a life time experience imputed for Christians the moment they believe in Christ. They also claim that believers are *eternally sanctified* from the moment of their confession of their faith.

Shamefully, because of distorted cultural teachings, many believers reject the deliverance (salvation) and power of the baptism of the Holy Ghost, thus remaining enshackeled to their sins and errors of the past. Some use the smokescreen of theology to defend the doctrine of eternal security. **While claiming not to be accountable for their actions, they denounce that any act of righteousness or sanctification expected (or demanded) of them would constitute an act of works, and would be considered a form of legalism.** Perhaps they do not understand that obeying the commandments of the New Testament through Christ (walking in the spirit) **is not legalism, but rather their obligation of the covenant**. All of the works displayed by Christians are not suppose to be independent of Christ, if they are doing His will. Therefore, **the works of a saint are actually the manifestations Jesus Christ's working in the believer, producing the peaceable fruits of righteousness**. The key here is that one must be in Christ and led by His Spirit. It is left up to each individual to yield his heart's desire and body members to whom he will serve. If it were the Lord Jesus Christ, then the Lord will have dominion; if it is Satan, he and his demonic kingdom will rule. Every person has the choice of whom they will sanctify themselves unto ... the Prince of Darkness, or the God of Light (Rm 6:11-23).

What is Biblical Justification?

As previously stated, the "Once Saved, Always Saved" doctrine is referred to by some as **the security of the believer**. As we have seen, this doctrine not only addresses the issues of salvation and sanctification, it also influences the doctrine of justification as well. Using religion as a cloak to cover sin, men array themselves in religious garments of self-righteous that the Lord classifies as iniquity. **Many cannot perceive that most of their cherished religious traditions are religious acts of rebellion to the commandments and nature of Christ**. The net result of such practices as praying to the saints, water baptism by sprinkling, or pouring, and pagan holidays like the celebration of Christmas and Easter is a classic example of Christians **"adding sin to sin"** (Isa 30:1). Shrouded in pagan traditions, and rituals in honor of the sun god and mother earth, Eurocentric Christians conform to the Roman Catholic **Christ Mass** (Christmas) and all of her religious cultural children partake of her iniquity. The Lord in the book of Revelation commanded all of His children who desire to worship Him in spirit and in truth to come out from amongst her (Mystery Babylon) and not partake of her iniquity. *"And I heard another voice from heaven, saying, Come out of her, my people, that ye be not partakers of her sins, and that ye receive not of her plagues"* (Rev 18:4). Those who celebrate the birth of Christ and His resurrection through the traditions of Christmas and Easter, and yet do not allow Him to be the Lord of their lives, will discover that their years of celebration will stand as a witness against them in the Day of Judgment. For they acknowledged that Christ came amongst men and fulfilled His testimony (Isa 9:6), and yet refused to obey His commandments, which were delivered through the writings of His apostles. This stands true for both believers in Christ and non-believers who justify themselves before men, but not before the living God.

The Apostle Luke states that men "**unwisely justify themselves by themselves**." Many Christians, in their corporate delusion, must think they can override the statues of the Lord by collective religious traditions or decrees. Luke goes on to state that "*God knows their hearts, and that that which is highly esteemed among men, is an abomination in the sight of the Lord*" (Lk 16:15). The prophet Hosea sheds more light on this subject by asking and answering the following questions. "*Who is wise, and he shall understand these things? prudent, and he shall know them? For the ways of the LORD are right, and the just shall walk in them: but the transgressors shall fall therein*." (Hos 14:9)

One of the first tendencies for most humans, once they have been caught doing something wrong, is to justify their actions. They then try to alleviate any form of guilt through self-serving religious doctrines. This is one of the first reactions to the knowledge of sin, manifested by the first man Adam, in the Garden of Eden. Adam sought to justify his transgression by displacing the blame for eating of "*the tree of the Knowledge of Good and Evil*" on his wife, Eve. Of course, Adam made his futile argument before the Lord, blaming "the woman" that the Lord had given him for his sin, as though it was the Creator's and Eve's fault for his actions.

Adam sought to cover his iniquity and nakedness by hiding in the garden, and covering himself with woven leaves of his own workmanship. **Men have not learned from the past. They are still trying to stitch together religious systems to cover themselves from their transgressions, in like manner as, Adam did**. Literally, ever since Adam, every man has been "as guilty as sin." David, the Psalmist stated, "*I was shapened in iniquity and in sin did my mother conceive me*" (Psa 51:5). Mankind inherited the nature of his patriarchal progenitor and has been continually wicked ever since. The religious systems of men, though they are numerous, have not, and cannot justify men in the presence of a holy and righteous God. Therefore, only by the methods established by the Father of Adam (through various covenants delivered to his descendents, by the Jewish prophets throughout history, are acceptable in His sight). The only covenant that is valid in heaven and earth is the called the New Covenant. Sin and death was brought into the terrestrial realm of earth by Adam, and through Christ, the Second Adam, eternal life was restored to those who would clothe themselves in His divine nature (I Pet 1:1-10).

However, just as the serpent beguiled Eve, so has he deceived many that believe that a Christian, who has received the baptism of the Holy Ghost (spirit-filled), cannot receive eternal damnation if he chooses to remain in sin. Remember the lie that was conveyed to Eve "***surely you shall not die***." Some have evaded the issue by alleging that Spirit-filled Christians who choose to remain in sin never really received the Spirit of God, because **the Holy Spirit will make one "do right."** However, to the contrary, there are no scriptural grounds for the Holy Ghost (sometimes called the keeping power of the Lord by Pentecostals), to possess an individual, and take over his will, making him do right. Rather, all Christians are required to *yield to the spirit, and submit to the word of God*... **serving God is by choice, not by force**. Even the parable of the sower and the seed reveals that there are men whose hearts receive the word of God with joy, but later become offended and fall away, when they were persecuted for their faith (Mt 13:17-23).

Once one believes and understands the justifying sacrificial act of Christ at Calvary, **he is then commanded to repent of all acts contrary to the ordinances of the Lord**. He is also expected to be crucified like Christ, willingly nailing his flesh and carnality to the cross, in order to live a crucified life in Jesus (Gal 2:20, Lk 9:22-27). Justification is Christ's part in the Christian redemptive process. On the other hand, **discipleship, fellowship, and obedience are the believer's part**. I have often found (more times than not), that the scriptures define its own terms, and gives more than adequate examples for doctrinal issues to be resolved. In the case of justification the same is true.

The biblical criteria for justification includes:
1. by faith – Rm 5:1;1:17,18, Gal 2:16; 3:6,24, Heb 2:4, Phil 3:9, Acts 13:39
2. the blood – Rm 5:9
3. by grace – Rm 3:24, Tit 3:7
4. in the name of the Lord – I Cor 6:11
5. by Christ – Gal 2:17
6. by works – Jm 2:21-26
7. by the Spirit of God – I Cor 6:11

The prophet Job asks the question, *"how then can man be justified with God? Or how can he be clean that is born of a woman"* (Job 25:4-6)? It is through Jesus Christ that Christians stand justified before God; because God Himself shed His blood for the sins of mankind (Acts 20:28). This was an unquestionable act of love that even baffled the angels. It was an open display of undeserved compassion for the descendents of Adam freely given by divine favor. Christians will remain justified if they continue to walk in Christ. **If they sin and repent, *"God is faithful and just to forgive them of their sins, and cleanse them from all unrighteousness"*** (I Jn 1:9). However, if they reject Christ, begin to sin habitually, or become apostate, they prevent themselves from being justified by Christ (Heb 10:26). A scriptural analysis of the previous statements can be summed up in the following verses:

For he hath made him to be sin for us, who knew no sin; that we might be

89

made the righteousness of God in him. (II Cor 5:21)

Therefore being justified by faith, *we have peace with God through our Lord Jesus Christ...*

Nevertheless death reigned from Adam to Moses, even over them that had not sinned after the similitude of Adam's transgression, who is the figure of him that was to come. But not as the offence, so also is the free gift. For if through the offence of one many be dead, much more the grace of God, and the gift by grace, which is by one man, Jesus Christ, hath abounded unto many.

And not as it was by one that sinned, so is the gift: for the judgment was by one to condemnation, but the free gift is of many offences unto justification.

For if by one man's offence death reigned by one; much more they which receive abundance of grace and of the gift of righteousness shall reign in life by one, Jesus Christ.

Therefore as by the offence of one judgment came upon all men to condemnation; even so by the righteousness of one **the free gift came upon all men unto justification of life**. *For as by one man's disobedience many were made sinners, so by the obedience of one shall many be made righteous.* (Rm 5:1,14-19)

For those who walk contrary to the New Testament, the scriptures clearly reveal the conditions of their hearts and explain their loss of justification due to unbelief and rebellion. Without debate, it was Jesus Christ that established this method of redemption for all men at a tremendous expense, His own life.

God is not some ogre, waiting for men to fail His grace so He can swat them with a heavenly swatter. Instead, we are told that it is not His will that any man should perish, but that all should come to the knowledge of the truth, and repentance (II Pet 3:9). **The Lord of Heaven is not sadistic nor is He masochistic. He did not create mankind for the sake of torture and torment, for His own thrills.** He does not rejoice at the death of the wicked, but He has established natural and spiritual laws, with consequences, to govern the dimensions of His creation. However, if men reject Christ, then there is no other alternative, than the slippery slope of destruction, the fruits of sin, which causes one to be consumed. **Sin separates the unholy from the holy... habitual sin results in permanent separation** (Isa 59:2).

Protestant theology teaches that eternal justification through Christ's blood occurs instantly when one ACCEPTS Christ as their personal Savior. Those who believe in unconditional salvation also believe that the blood of Christ is applicable for all sins past, present, and future. However, this stance does not balance out in the heavenly scale of truth laid out in the word of God. It is true that Christ is the Christian's advocate and mediator; however, if an individual lives a life that mocks His grace, Christ will surely be their judge. His blood covers all past and present sins if one turns from his evil ways. Future sins, which one may commit, are to be addressed on an on going basis, through personal discipleship with Christ, and repentance whenever necessary. Even though Christ provided an eternal sacrifice, there is no automatic blanket covering of all future sins without repentance. The Apostle Paul puts a dagger into this heretical teaching of unconditional salvation by stating, *"For **if we sin willfully** after that we **have received the knowledge of the truth, there remaineth no more sacrifice for sins**, But a certain fearful looking for of **judgment and fiery indignation**, which shall devour the adversaries."* (Heb 10:26-31)

Future sins (if committed) must also be confessed, and fled from in order to maintain an on going relationship of spiritual communion with the Living God (I Jn I:9, II Cor 7:10).

... *"Being justified freely by His grace through the redemption that is in Christ . . . to be a propitiation through faith in His blood, to declare His righteousness for remission of sins . . . man is justified by faith without the deeds of the law . . . Do we make void the law through faith? God forbid! Yea, we establish the law."* (Rm 3:21-31)

If doctrinal debate and the theological reasoning of men fail to bring a sound conclusion on any scriptural matter, then the best method to employ is to simply find biblical examples to take the scientific approach and test one's theories. When conflicting biblical issues come to a head, the safest solution is to follow biblical examples where the execution of the word is self- evident. The following are examples of rebellious Christians, who received, or will in the future receive, the judgment of God and eternal damnation, unless they repent. This list is provided to create a doctrinal check and balance for biblical justification, with the word of God as our balancing counter weight.

Examples of New Testament Holy Ghost Rebels:

1. Carnal Christians who walk as heathens. I Cor 3:1-5, Jm 3:13-18
2. Christians held in captivity of the devil by their own sin and will. II Tim 2:25,26
3. Damnation to Christian heretics. Jm 5:19,20, Gal 1:8,9; 5:19,20; 6:1-3, Titus 3:10,11, II Thes 3:14,15, I Tim 6:10, I Tim 4:16
4. Ananias and Sapphira – Satan filled their hearts to lie against the Holy Ghost and they dropped dead. Acts 5:1-12
5. Alexander and Hymenaues, reprobate, resist the truth and was delivered unto Satan for blasphemy. I Tim 1:20, II Tim 4:14,15
6. Reprobate Christians. II Pet 2:10-21
7. End Time "great falling away" of Christians. I Tim 4:1, II Thes 2:3,8-14
8. Diotrephes, an evil Christian Brother. III Jn1:11, others; Acts 20:28-32, II Pet 2:1-3, II Tim 3:7-9, Jude 1:4-13.
9. Fornication by a brother with his stepmother . . . delivered unto Satan; hopefully

he will repent. I Tim 1:20, I Cor 5:9-11, II Tim 2:17-19, Mt 18:15-18, Titus 3:10, Rm 6:12-22.

10. Rebels of the seven churches. Smyrna Rev 2:9, Pergmos Rev 2:13-16, Thyatira Rev 2:20-24, Sardis Rev 3:2-4, Laodicea Rev 3:15-19.

11. Hymenaeus and Philetus – erred concerning the resurrection of the saints and caused many to fall away from the faith. II Tim 2:17-19.

12. Judas the Betrayer and transgressor. Jn 17:20;18:1-5, Lk 22:3,19-23, Mt 26:20-25.

The Unpardonable Sin

Upon examination of all the scriptural evidence available to believers, there is no justification for one to commit the unpardonable sin of blasphemy against the Holy Ghost. **This treasonous act entails that one not only draws back unto perdition (sin) by a choice of their will, but that he also turns his back on God, to serve Satan.** The Apostle Paul declares that, the mature sons of God, who eventually become criminals in the house of God, can only commit this treasonous act. They are Christians who have experienced a spiritual walk and have known the depths of the Holy Ghost. They have tasted of the heavenly spiritual gifts, and walked in the supernatural powers of God; then they openly mock Christ as blatant transgressors of the covenant, flaunting their sins, serving devils, and putting Christ who is in them to open shame.

"For it is impossible for those who were once enlightened, and have tasted of the heavenly gift, and were made partakers of the Holy Ghost,
And have tasted the good word of God, and the powers of the world to come,
If they shall fall away, to renew them again unto repentance; seeing they crucify to themselves the Son of God afresh, and put him to an open shame.
For the earth which drinketh in the rain that cometh oft upon it, and bringeth forth herbs meet for them by whom it is dressed, receiveth blessing from God:
*But that which beareth thorns and **briers is rejected**, and is nigh unto cursing; **whose end is to be burned**."* (Heb 6:4-8)

Babes in Christ and the ignorant cannot utterly reject Christ or blaspheme the Holy Ghost in an unpardonable way. Why? It is because they really don't fully know Him or understand whom they are rejecting. They can simply be deceived and as sinners they die as fools. There are those who blasphemed the Holy Ghost in the scriptures but did not commit the unpardonable sin. For example, the Apostle Paul blasphemed the Holy

Ghost when he was a Pharisee, but was forgiven (I Tim 1:11-16). Not knowing Christ intimately, and lacking understanding, Paul says that he sinned ignorantly. If a mature Christian commits the unpardonable sin, it is not that his sin pertaining to the matter can not be forgiven, but rather, it is the Lord's corresponding actions for the consequence of his decision to serve devils, that will not be forgiven. Instead of casting out devils from individuals who are possessed, he becomes a devil. As with Lucifer, God delivers him over to a reprobate mind, since that person despises Him, and is in contempt with His Holy Spirit. The individual's reprobate mind will not allow him to ever come unto repentance, because he can only contemplate evil.

One must realize that blasphemy against the Holy Ghost, by **a mature spirit -filled Christian who has communed with Jesus Christ (spirit to spirit) and walked in divine truth is the ultimate human rejecter of Christ.** If the one that sups and communes with Him betrays Him, his fate is secured unto damnation (Psa 69:25;109:8, Mt 26:20-25, Acts 1:16-21,25). The Holy Ghost is Jesus Christ, working in Christians to do the Father's good pleasure. **One who commits the unpardonable sin will receive the divine judgment of a reprobate mind, can not contemplate repentance, or abide in righteousness ever again.** In the same manner as Satan they can only contemplate evil continuously. These Christians are consumed by evil and can therefore never come unto repentance again, thus committing willful spiritual suicide.

In conclusion, if one's faith in the Bible is based on blanket, non-qualifying promises, with no consideration of the balancing verses of qualifying conditions, he have **a false faith that will fail him**. If this false faith is developed into a doctrine (such as unconditional salvation) it can lead to **an unsuspecting damnable religious trust** (or faith). The human *"heart is deceitful above all things and desperately wicked: who can know it?"* proclaimed the prophet Jeremiah (17:9). One's faith in God **must not** be based on the thoughts and desires of their heart, but rather on the sound word of God. The word of God is a covenant and He is a covenant God. The Lord has maintained and kept His word through all generations. He binds Himself to an oath by revealing His covenants and performing His word. The Bible states that He *"honors His word above His name."* Time did not prevent Him from keeping His words, which He spoke through the mouths of the Jewish prophets, for the past five thousand years.

He that trusteth in his own heart is a fool: but whoso walketh wisely, he shall be delivered [saved]" (Prov 28:26). (Jer 17:5, Mt 15:6-9, Mk 7:6-9,11, Jn 12:44-50, Rm 3:4)

A New Testament Expose' on the Doctrine of Grace

One of the last loose bolts, that has been attached by western theologians to hold their distorted concept of salvation, is a shallow understanding of the grace of God. As usual, taking the scriptures out of context, while ignoring the whole council of God, seems to be the Western cultural norm. The belief that by God's free gift of grace extended towards mankind, **salvation is granted to anyone who simply confesses Christ as his savior, or just admits that Christ died for his sins, is bogus.** Consequently, a large sector of **Christianity has become an intellectual religion** filled with damnable works that lead to murder, hatred, racism, and a host of heresies that produce the unfruitful works of darkness. They further allege that there is nothing one can do to earn or maintain his salvation. However, while it is true that salvation cannot be earned, yet it remains a covenant between man and God, which must be maintained.

Many denominational preachers might want to consider the fact that the **New Testament grace is not uniquely a New Testament phenomena**, but was first applicable in the Old Testament, then perfected in the New one. Grace is usually defined as God's unmerited (unearned) favor towards man. God has on numerous occasions shown his bowels of compassion both to the human race and to the nation of Israel. The first major instance of the grace of God being manifested was through the Prophet Noah. Because of His mercy, the Lord of heaven did not utterly wipe out the descendents of Adam. Noah found GRACE in the sight of the Lord (Gen 6:8). He and his sons, their wives, and his wife were used to repopulate the earth after the flood. The biblical number five is generally denoted as representing grace. It was therefore in the five hundredth year of Noah's life that his three sons, Shem, Ham, and Japheth were born as triplets. Their coinciding births represented the grace of God, which was extended to the human family for preservation, after the flood, and the future messianic redemption though the lineage of Shem. It is through Noah's son Shem that we get Abraham, Isaac, Jacob, Judah, and David of which patriarchal lineage Christ the Messiah came. It is also from these eight souls that the human family was preserved after the flood to continue the lineage. Hence, **the first time that grace came to mankind; it was in the form of salvation through a man (Noah), and his family, who preserved God's word and ultimately fulfilled the prophetic destiny of the human race.**

It was because of the grace of God that Israel was selected, above all nations, to be the Lord's beloved. This was the second time that grace was extended towards mankind. The prophet Ezekiel commented on Israel's conception and selection when He spiritually described her drowning in her own blood, with no one to pity her or show her mercy (Ezek 16:3-6). It would be through the Hebrew lineage that the Lord ordained the coming forth of Christ the Messiah. It was through the lineage of the human family of Abraham that God produced the nation of Israel, which was the chosen lineage, to bring about the Lord's redemptive work. The Jewish Prophet Ezekiel revealed that God's selective process of Israel, choosing from among all human families, was purely an act of love.

"And say, Thus saith the Lord GOD unto Jerusalem; Thy birth and thy

nativity is of the land of Canaan; thy father was an Amorite, and thy mother an Hittite.

And as for thy nativity, in the day thou wast born thy navel was not cut*, neither wast thou washed in water to supple thee; thou wast not salted at all, nor swaddled at all.*

None eye pitied thee*, to do any of these unto thee, to have compassion upon thee; but thou wast cast out in the open field, to the lothing of thy person, in the day that thou wast born.*

*And **when I passed by thee, and saw thee polluted in thine own blood, I said unto thee when thou wast in thy blood**, Live; yea, I said unto thee when thou wast in thy blood, Live.*

*Now when I passed by thee, and looked upon thee, behold, **thy time was the time of love; and I spread my skirt over thee, and covered thy nakedness:** yea, I sware unto thee, and **entered into a covenant with thee, saith the Lord GOD, and thou becamest mine**.*

Then washed I thee with water; yea, I throughly washed away thy blood from thee, and I anointed thee with oil." (Ezek 16:3-9)

A third time that grace came into the affairs of men was through God's servant Joseph, the son of Jacob. Joseph was perfected through the grace he received from his imprisonment and sufferings in Egypt. He was betrayed by his jealous brothers, and left for dead. Under the dominion of an Almighty God, even that which men contrive for evil, the Lord is still able to make good. We are told in the book of Psalms that, *"Until the time that **his word came** [appointed time]: the word of the LORD tried him. The king sent and loosed him; even the ruler of the people, and let him go free* (Psa 105:20,21). Joseph's word came when his appointed time had arrived, and his love and maturity were perfected, so his divine calling could be fulfilled. The God of Abraham, Isaac, and Jacob used Joseph, the dreamer, to deliver his kinsmen from famine, and preserved their lives for their future destiny. It was through Joseph's brother, Judah, that the promised seed (spoken of to Eve in the garden) would come (Gen 3:15). This spoke of Jesus, who would crushed the head of the serpent, and bruised the heel of Satan.

Furthermore, in the Old Testament scriptures, we find that the prophet Moses and his brother Aaron stood in the gap to prevent the utter fury of the Lord from annihilating the children of Israel in the wilderness. Their intercession invoked the grace of God towards the Jewish people. Thereafter, the Lord's long suffering limited His fury and fiery judgment against them. The Psalmist David commented on the historical dialogue between the Lord and his wayward Hebrew children: ***"Therefore he said that he would destroy them, had not Moses his chosen stood before him in the breach, to turn away his wrath, lest he should destroy them.*** *"Yea, they despised the pleasant land, they believed not his word: **But murmured in their tents, and hearkened not unto the voice of the LORD.** Therefore he lifted up his hand*

95

against them, to overthrow them in the wilderness" (Psa 106:23-26). Again and again, the patience of the Lord was challenged until another priest, Phinehas, the son of Aaron, stood in the gap to make intercession for the children of Israel in order to refrain God's judgment upon them. The prophet king David commented further on these historical events by stating:

"*They joined themselves also unto Baal-peor* [Baal], *and ate the sacrifices of the dead. **Thus they provoked him to anger with their inventions: and the plague brake in upon them.***

Then stood up Phinehas, and executed judgment: and so the plague was stayed. And that was counted unto him for righteousness unto all generations forevermore." (Psa 106:28-31)

In the New Testament, we see that the grace of God extended salvation to not only the natural seed of Israel, but also to a new cultivated spiritual seed. This new addition of spiritual Gentiles, and Jews, would constitute the church. Hence, for the first time in human history, a holy union of Jews and Gentiles constituted into one flock (in 41 AD), through Jesus Christ. This was not a haphazard or random event it was a continuation of the divine script to fulfilled the covenants that God made with Adam, Eve, and Abraham. This phenomenal event, made possible by the seed of Abraham, fulfilled one of the major promises God made to him thousands of years earlier (Gen 17:1-7). The unsolicited, unmerited favor of God was extended to the New Testament saints by the Lord Himself, and to all of the descendents of Adam. His loving act of kindness and tender mercy took place while both Jews and Gentiles were helplessly dead in their trespasses and worthy of eternal death. The natural and spiritual death sentence was pronounced, ever since the first man Adam transgressed (Rm 6:23).

Total deliverance from the curses of sin, was brought by the Lord Himself, in the personhood of Jesus Christ, who provided the only way for man to escape an eternal infernal. All other religious routes promising deliverance were demonic counterfeits, inspired by Satan, to deceive the human race. The Devil seduces mankind with an innumerable list of religious and carnal intellectual philosophies to beguile the sons of Adam. **No other religious way, which excludes, or combines Jesus Christ with another savior or religious philosophy, is acceptable in the divine court of heaven.** Why is the Christian method to obtain salvation so exclusive? It is because the Jewish Christian message clearly states that the very God of heaven came to earth in human flesh, to offer Himself as a ransom for the sins of men. Therefore, no religious leader can substitute, or try to counterfeit, what the Creator did to illustrate His love to the world in dramatic fashion before the theatre of angelic hosts. Jesus Christ of Nazareth is the only way to God, the only truth, because God cannot lie. Although it may be offensive for some He is the only means by which mankind can acquire eternal life.

What makes the New Testament grace *distinctively different* from the Old Testament is the indwelling kingdom power given to every true believer; that is the baptism of the Holy Ghost (accompanied by the evidence of speaking in tongues). It is by the power of the victorious Spirit of Christ, that one is transformed into a new creature, a new spiritual man, empowered to live a holy life. **Therefore, New Testament grace is the supernatural ability to do the will of God, and perform his marvelous works.**

"Ye are of God, little children, and have overcome them: because greater is he that is in you, than he that is in the world." (I Jn 4:4)

We are commanded by the Apostle John that, *"here in is our love made perfect, that we may have boldness in the Day of Judgment: **because as he is, so are we in this world.**"* (I Jn 4:17). The Old Testament was weak because it was based on natural commandments that men could not keep. Neither could carnal commandments make rebellious hearts perfect. In contrast, the New Testament is spiritual. It takes the heart and mind of Christ from the pages of a book and transfers it to an individual's new heart. With this, each believer has the capability of supernaturally doing the will of God (if he chooses). The principles of the kingdom of God, the fruit of the spirit (Gal 5:21,22), and gifts of the spirit (I Cor 12:7-10) make their abode in the temple of a Christian's new spirit. The Holy Ghost also endows them with power and authority over Satan, power over the sin in their lives, the anointing to crucify their self-will, and grants effective supernatural powers to minister to the lost.

Perpetual sin however, can cause the grace of God, and the new wine of the Holy Ghost, to fail in them. Men can also frustrate the grace of God by refusing to yield to the spirit. The Apostle Paul comments further on this subject demanding that Christians should

*"Follow peace with all men, and holiness, without which no man shall see the Lord: **Looking diligently lest any man fail of the grace of God**; lest any root of bitterness springing up trouble you, and thereby many be defiled;*

Lest there be any fornicator, or profane person, as Esau, who for one morsel of meat sold his birthright." (Heb:12:14-16)

The Prophet Hosea prophesied concerning the new wine of the Holy Ghost failing Christians because they choose to walk in the flesh and commit idolatry. *"Rejoice not, O Israel, for joy, as other people: for thou hast gone a whoring from thy God, thou hast loved a reward upon every cornfloor. The floor and the winepress shall not feed them, and the new wine shall fail in her." (Hos 9:1,2).*

The Old Testament Law was weak and no one could obey it; however, **ever since Pentecost and the receiving of the Holy Ghost, Christians throughout history have had no excuse to fail the grace of God.** The Apostle Paul states, *"Being confident of this very thing, that he which hath begun a good work in you will perform it until the day of Jesus Christ"* (Phil 1:6). Christ will perfect that which pertains to Him. If Christians would submit themselves to Him wholly, willingly, and with joy, He will manifest Himself in a perfect way. What few fail to realize, because they rarely examine issues independent of their denominational religious party line, is that **they must make two trips to Calvary (the cross) in order to receive the grace of God**. They must go the first time for the atoning blood sacrifice of Christ, which pardons, and cleanses them of their sins (Jn 3:16, Rm 6:1-23). The second trip to the cross necessitates that they willfully chose to die on own their cross through repentance and water baptism (their burial), to serve the living Christ (Rm 6:1-10). **No cross, no crown!** Paul tells Timothy, *"It is a faithful saying: For if we be dead with him, we shall also live with him: If we suffer, we shall also reign with him: if we deny him, he also will deny us"* (II Tim 2:11,12). It is inexcusable that Christians profess to abide in the faith, but never read the content of the covenant (the Bible); they only believe what others have told them. This practice is scandalous and only produces more confusion. Most Protestant denominations have come to believe that they are saved by grace, through faith in Christ (Eph 2:8,9). This is a true biblical statement, but unfortunately, it is only one side of the coin. However, **they cannot abide in grace if they lack the power of the spirit. Neither can they abide in saving faith, because their beliefs pervert the truth, thus creating false hope and an erroneous faith.**

Examples of Old and New Testament Manifestations of the Grace of God.

1) **Saved by grace through faith, found in the Old Testament:**
   Deu 7:6-9… *"For thou art an holy people unto the LORD thy God: the* **LORD thy God hath chosen thee to be a special people unto himself, above all people that are upon the face of the earth.**
       The LORD did not set his love upon you, nor choose you, because ye were more in number than any people; *for ye were the fewest of all people:*
       But **because the LORD loved you, and because he would keep the oath which he had sworn unto your fathers**, *hath the LORD brought you out with a mighty hand, and redeemed you out of the house of bondmen, from the hand of Pharaoh king of Egypt.*
       Know therefore that the LORD thy God, he is God, **the faithful God, which keepeth covenant and mercy with them that love him and keep his commandments** *to a thousand generations."* (Deu 9:4-6)

2) **Saved by grace through faith, found in the New Testament:**
   Eph 2:7-9… *"That in the ages to come* **he might shew the exceeding riches of his grace in his kindness toward us through Christ Jesus.**
       For by grace are ye saved through faith; *and that not of yourselves: it is the gift of God: Not of works, lest any man should boast."*

(Rm 4:4,5,16; 5:2,6-8,16,21; 11:5-8, I Cor 15:10, Eph 1:5-12, Gal 1:15,16,
II Tim 1:1,9. Tit 3:7).

Heb 9:11,14-16... *"But Christ being come an high priest of good things to
come, by a greater and more perfect tabernacle, not made with hands,
that is to say, not of this building...*
How much more shall the blood of Christ, who through the
eternal Spirit offered himself without spot to God, purge your con-
science from dead works to serve the living God?
*And for this cause **he is the mediator of the new testament**, that by*
*means of death, for the redemption of the transgressions that were
under the first testament, they which are called might receive the promise of eternal inheritance.*
***For where a testament is, there must also of necessity be the
death of the testator."***

Criteria to Receive and Maintain the Grace of God

a) In order to maintain the Grace of God one must abide in Christ
II Pet 1:3-10, Eph 5:1-11, Gal 5:22-25, I Cor 6:9-11

b) In order to abide in Christ, one must have the Holy Ghost indwelling:
Jn 14:15-26; 15:26; 16:13,14; 7:37-39, Rm 8:9, I Cor 12:13, Jn 1:12,13; 3:5,
Acts 1:8; 2:1-4, Lk 24:49

c) Once grace has been received, obedience is the key to eternal salvation:
I Pet 1:2 ....   must do righteousness even as He is righteous
I Jn 2:9-11 ......   must love all others and abide in him if you know Him
Lk 6:46-49 ....   "why call me Lord, Lord, and do not the things I say"
I Jn 3:24 ....   they that keep His commandments dwell in Him
I Jn 4:12-16....   ... as Christ is so are we to be in this world
Jn 12:46 .... believers should not abide in darkness
I Sam 15:22,23 .... rebellion is as the sin of witchcraft; stubbornness is as
iniquity and idolatry.

d) The absolute command of discipleship is unconditional for all those who call
themselves Christians. **Total discipleship is not an option; it is mandatory for
all**.
Lk 14:15-35.... . "Whosoever be of you that forsaketh not all that he hath, he
cannot be my disciple.".
Jn 12:24-26.... .. "Except a corn of wheat die, it abideth alone... he that loves
his life shall lose it. He that hateth his life keep it unto eternal

life."

Mt 10:34-39.... . "I came not to send peace but a sword. If one loves anyone more than me he is not fit to be my disciple."

Mt 16:24-28.... . "What profit is it for one to gain the whole world and lose your soul … if one seeks to save his life….. will lose it….must take up your cross and follow Christ."

Mt 21:28-32.... .. Which son did his father's will?

Gal 2:20 .... .. "I am crucified with Christ: nevertheless I live; yet not I, but Christ liveth in me: and the life which I now live in the flesh I live by the faith of the Son of God, who loved me, and gave himself for me."

I Jn 3:14,15…... "We know that we have passed from death unto life, because we love the brethren. He that loveth not his brother abideth in death. Whosoever hateth his brother is a murderer: and ye know that no murderer hath eternal life abiding in him."

Phil 3:3.___. .. "For we are the circumcision, which worship God in the spirit, and rejoice in Christ Jesus, and have no confidence in the flesh."

Jn 10:1-16,27-29… "My sheep hear my voice and a stranger they will not follow."

Jn 4:23,24.... .. "But the hour cometh, and now is, when the true worshippers shall worship the Father in spirit and in truth: for the Father seeketh such to worship him. God is a Spirit: and they that worship him must worship him in spirit and in truth."

Lk 9:57-62.... .. Many desire to follow Christ but their excuses and the cares for this life will prevent them from inheriting the promises of God. (Jn 6:56-66, Lk 17:32;14:26-35)

The death of one's self will is mandatory for all Christians. The worship of self is Idolatry (Ezek 8:4)! Total discipleship is not optional or designated for a few who are faithful and committed. It is done by choice and should be renewed daily. The Apostle Paul stated that he, likewise, had to die daily (I Cor 15:31) … *"According to my earnest expectation and my hope… Christ shall be magnified in my body, whether it be by life, or by death. For to me to live is Christ, and to die is gain"* (Phil 1:20,21). This biblical concept is quite contrary to the popular Christian worldview, which classify special Christian callings only for those who are in ministry, or who serve as missionaries. Believing that discipleship is reserved for the clergy, **the layman often times forfeit their salvation as a result of neglect, or a lack of understanding of the covenant and the will of God for their lives**. Consequently, they never know Him, never follow Him, nor do His will. Their fate and end result is not very promising or hopeful. Ignorance of the law is no justification for breaking the laws of men; neither is it justifiable to break the laws of God through ignorance, whether willfully, or out of neglect. (Num 15:24-29, Acts 17:30)

Just as under the Law, there can be no remission of sin without a life being given in exchange for another's life. Christians are bought with a price by the precious blood of Jesus Christ. The New Testament scriptures declare that **once one becomes a Christian, they no longer have ownership of their own bodies; and if they try to possess and maintain control, they nullify the grace of God designated to perform its perfect work in them** (I Cor 6:19,20). After one agrees to abide in the covenant of Christ and he understands that Christ has purchased his liberty, he is then freed from the grips of sin and set free to choose whom he will serve.

Christians truly need to be advised that the New Covenant demands that they cannot trespass on God's property, their former bodies, purchased by the blood of Christ. Furthermore, they can no longer use their bodies, minds, or hearts to do as they please. Failure to understand this will only create further misunderstandings of the New Covenant and a continued array of religious heretical doctrines. **Christians also need to be advised that when they receive the baptism of the Holy Ghost, and if they continue to commit carnal acts of the flesh (Gal 5:19,20), Jesus Christ (who dwells in their temples) is thrust into their wickedness with them.** Christ, in this context is not merely watching them from above as the God of heaven, but joined with them in their demonic activity. At the Day of Judgment (second resurrection), the Spirit of Christ will be a witness against them, sealing their irrefutable fate. Surely, they will not escape His judgment if they repent not!

The Lord (through His covenant relationship with His people) renews His mercy and grace with them daily, as they present themselves as a living sacrifice. The Apostle Paul petitions the Church at Rome, Italy, *"I beseech you therefore, brethren, by the mercies of God, that ye present your bodies a living sacrifice, holy, acceptable unto God, which is your reasonable service. And **be not conformed to this world: but be ye transformed by the renewing of your mind, that ye may prove what is that good, and acceptable, and perfect, will of God"*** (Rm 12:1,2, also see II Tim 1:13,14).

Unless they repent, mankind will always be slaves to something (to the devil either directly or indirectly) through the lusts and vices of this world. The only other option left for men and women is to willfully submit to the lordship of the living Christ. The scriptures also declare that if any man defiles the temple of God (his body) whether through sin, wickedness, or perpetual lusts, "him shall God destroy" (I Cor 3:16,17). Jesus Christ will eventually remove His Holy Spirit from such a man and make his temple desolate. Failing the grace of God they "draw back unto perdition." (Heb 10:38,39)

In the atmosphere of contemporary Western Christianity, those who promote homosexuality, lesbianism, abortion, same sex marriages and other vile sexual activities have caused hell to enlarge its borders for the "Christian" leaders and the multitudes who follow their ways. These vile individuals call evil good, and good evil. This is an abomination in the sight of the Lord. It is also the psychological weakness hosted by an imperialistic culture that believes it can lead a spiritual *"coup de tat"* (over throw of divine authority) on earth, and control their own destiny in heaven. Their global natural powers and humanistic intellectualism will not nullify the divinely appointed eternal consequences of their sins, which has been established in heaven. This is strong

101

delusion! *"He that justifies the wicked and condemns the just is also an abomination in the sight of the Lord"* (Prov 17:15). The heathen and abominable Christians shall reap the same consequences of their ungodliness. Those who support their activities will not be found without blame. God is not mocked! The parable of the unwise steward illustrates this point:

"And the Lord said, Who then is that faithful and wise steward, whom his lord shall make ruler over his household, to give them their portion of meat in due season?

Blessed is that servant, whom his lord when he cometh shall find so doing.

Of a truth I say unto you, that he will make him ruler over all that he hath.

But and if that servant say in his heart, My lord delayeth his coming; and shall begin to beat the menservants and maidens, and to eat and drink, and to be drunken;

The lord of that servant will come in a day when he looketh not for him, and at an hour when he is not aware, and will cut him in sunder, and will appoint him his portion with the unbelievers.

*And that servant, which knew his lord's will, and prepared not himself, neither did according to his will, **shall be beaten with many stripes**.*

*But he that knew not, and did commit things worthy of stripes, shall be beaten with few stripes. **For unto whomsoever much is given, of him shall be much required**: and to whom men have committed much, of him they will ask the more."* (Lk 12:42-48)

The psychological apathy concerning the judgment of God, acquired by apostate Christians and seminary theologians, has disabled their ability to discern the difference between good and evil. Their senses are dull to the concepts of holiness, preventing them from repenting of the dead works of the flesh. They live to fulfill the desires of their flesh and shall likewise perish with their flesh in hell fire. For those who perish, the Bible is offensive (Prov 1:23-32); for the righteous, it is refreshing and comforting (Jer 15:16-17, Psa 119:11,35,38,105).

It appears that out of all the institutions of men, it is only through the institution of religion that men reject the qualifying standards to be a legitimate participant. This practice of not qualifying credentials for one's faith is not acceptable for any other vocation. Why do Christians adhere to such practices? If one chooses to become an accountant, a doctor, a lawyer, a nurse, an architect, or a pilot, he must give himself to the study of that profession. On the other hand, if one never reads the covenant (the New Testament - God's study manual), never passes the first level of spiritual competency (Acts 2:38, Heb 6:1-3), never studies to show himself approved before God, nor demonstrates the practice of true biblical faith, how can he claim to be a Christian? **Most, who call themselves Christians should be arrested and charged with the unholy crime of "impersonating a Christian".** They confess with their mouths to be Christians, but do not know the biblical requirements. This also is confusion!

It is through **Christian discipleship** that one qualifies himself to be a Christian… *"Ye shall know them by the fruit they bare"* (Mt 7:20, Jn 15:8,16, Mt 12:33). Those who are Christ's unmistakably produce the fruits of righteousness. *"The fruit of the Spirit is love, joy, peace, longsuffering, gentleness, goodness, faith, meekness, temperance: against such there is no law. And **they that are Christ's have crucified the flesh with the affections and lusts**. If we live in the Spirit, let us also walk in the Spirit"* (Gal 5:22-24). During the end times, every alleged Christian will be made to make proof of his calling, and every "Christian devil" will be exposed.

Discipleship is salvation according to the New Testament. Those who are disciples indeed, without exception, inherit the promises of God. *"Then said Jesus to those Jews which believed on him, **If ye continue in my word, then are ye my disciples indeed**; And ye shall know the truth, and the truth shall make you free… Jesus answered them, Verily, verily, I say unto you, **Whosoever committeth sin is the servant of sin**.*

And the servant abideth not in the house for ever: but the Son abideth ever. If the Son therefore shall make you free, ye shall be free indeed." (Jn 8:31-36)

The prophets of old prophesied of the day of the Christian, but they did not understand their prophetic utterances. The prophet Isaiah spoke of a day when the true disciples would appear and understand the covenant of the Lord. *"**Bind up the testimony, seal the law among my disciples**. Behold, I and the children whom the LORD hath given me are for signs and for wonders in Israel from the LORD of hosts, which dwelleth in mount Zion."* (Isa 8:16-18, Heb 2:13,14)

Thus far, we have examined the doctrine "Once Saved, Always Saved" (also known as the security of the believer), biblical sanctification, biblical justification, and grace. In order for a jury to properly perform its sworn responsibility, it must hear all of the evidence surrounding the case first, and get its instructions from the judge before rendering a verdict. If one wants be fair to himself and not seal his fate with an unjust verdict, he must (without partiality) hear all of the evidence posted by the divine constitution (the Bible) against him. Moreover, it is incumbent upon every individual to read and study the entire counsel of Jesus Christ, which consists of both the Old and New Testament. Jesus Christ *"is the same yesterday, today, and forever."* Unbelief and the willful doctrinal perversions of the biblical text by men, does not nullify the word of His counsel.

Jesus Christ and the prophets of old throughout the ages have declared that "heaven and earth shall pass away, but the word of God shall never fail." All religious leaders and their followers will have their day of justice; and if their names are not found in the Lamb's Book of Life, they will experience the second death (Rev 20:6-15). They will join the devil (who seduced them) and all of his angels in the eternal hell (Mt 25:41).

103

This horrendous location is identified as "**the Lake of Fire and Brimstone**." Such will be the case at the white throne judgment where all of the wicked will be summoned up from hell to hear the cases against them, and they will have an opportunity to give their defense. Unfortunately, all of the lying devils that deceived them will not be able to come to their aid. Of course they will have no legitimate defense for rejecting Christ, other than the fact that they loved darkness more than they loved light. The place commonly referred to as hell is a place of confinement until their trial at the end of the 1,000 year (millennium) reign of Christ (Rev 20:15-20). In that day, those who walk in doctrinal error, and all apostate Christians, shall suffer greater condemnation than those who were heathen, and never knew Christ. (II Pet 2:20-22, Lk 12:45-48)

Even though humans tend to want to have heaven as their final goal, Jesus knowing the hearts of men, mentioned heaven only a few times in scripture. However, He greatly commented on the topic of hell. The permanent Hell, the Lake of Fire and Brimstone, is describe as a place where the fire burns the body, but yet the body it is not consumed. It is where the worms devour the flesh, but it is also not consumed. *"And if thy hand offend thee, cut it off: it is better for thee to enter into life maimed, than having two hands to go into hell, into the fire that never shall be quenched: Where their worm dieth not, and the fire is not quenched."* (Mark 9: 43,44)

A few Christian religious groups, and the contemporary Post Modern Christian Movement, even have the audacity to claim that there is no such place as a hell, **hence, calling Jesus a liar**. They utterly reject the idea that humans can be brought into a place of eternal torment. The Jehovah Witnesses for example (like many liberal Christians) cannot accept the fact that a loving God can bring harsh and eternal judgment upon the wicked. They also deny the reality of an eternal hell, claiming that hell is nothing more than an ancient garbage dump, located outside the city of Jerusalem. In the final analysis all religious theories, beliefs, and philosophies of men will be weighed in the balance and judged in the last days. Before they experience the eternal hell, the Lake of Fire and Brimstone, they will experience hell on earth when their father the Devil is cast down to join them and be judged (Rev 12:7-12).

Have Christians been appointed to the Wrath of God?

So far we have looked at the history and doctrines associated with the teaching "Once Saved Always Saved." It is also necessary to examine the commonly held myth rooted in "Once Saved, Always Saved," that **the Wrath of God cannot come upon Christians**. This belief stems from the former doctrine "security of the believers" and will place many Christians in grave trouble in the last days. Why? Because the majority in Protestant Christendom adhere to this doctrine, and they do not believe that wicked saints will be judged with the wicked heathen for their sins in the last day. They tread in shallow waters for a lack of study of God's counsel and conclude that the church will not go through the seven-year tribulation period that shall come upon all the earth. However, they neither understand the internal dynamics of the Lord's body, the scope of His redemptive plan, nor do they grasp the galactic plan to bring a restitution of all things in heavens and in the earth, in the last days right here on planet Earth.

The answer to the question whether or not Christians are appointed to wrath is quite simple, but the explanation is quite difficult for most Christians to receive. **When biblical truth conflicts with cultural traditions, and the doctrines which appease the flesh of men, more times than not, the truth will lose out**. Like the doctrine of unconditional salvation, fraud is perpetrated when there is an absence of a just balance in the presentation of the weight of scripture. This imbalance cannot yield truth, or sound doctrine; it can only produce a perversion of the truth. If the foundation of a structure is not sound, then the entire structure is off-kilter. One should not want to play Russian Roulette with his soul; unfortunately, it appears that many carelessly do.

The verse that is used to construct the theory mentioned above is found in First Thessalonians 5:9, which states: "***For God hath not appointed us to wrath, but to obtain salvation by our Lord Jesus Christ***." Isolated alone, this verse makes a blanket non-qualifying promise for salvation. However, as we have seen concerning the doctrine "Once Saved, Always Saved," those who use selective scriptures consistently take biblical doctrines out of context (from the preceding and following verses) to support their preconceived biases, and willful deceit. Such actions only reveal the error of their hearts and lead to erroneous doctrines. Again, a statement taken out of context can easily become a pre-text for something totally contrary to its original intended meaning.

For the sake of argument, we will look at I Thes 5:9 in its context. First, we must understand that approximately four hundred years ago, the Bible was divided into chapters and verse to make it easy for reference purposes. Therefore, the reader of the New Testament epistles must take into account the fact that each of the epistles were originally written as one continuous letter. Sometimes the chapter breaks occur in the middle of a thought pattern, such was the case concerning the first book to the Thessalonians in the European country of Greece.

In the fourth division (chapter four), Paul admonishes the Christians in this city to obey Apostolic commandments, telling them not to deny their Christian brothers the love of God. He also demanded that they walk in holiness in order to enjoy the fruit of eternal life. After addressing issues related to New Covenant Commandments, he then conveyed a mystery concerning the rapture (or quickening) of the church, its sequence, and the manner of events that would follow thereafter (verse 13). We are told that the dead in Christ (those who are asleep) will be raised first, and those who are alive at His coming shall be supernaturally translated, to meet Christ in the air. Finally, Christians are then told that they should comfort themselves with these words (end of chapter).

I Thes 4:6 That no man go beyond and defraud his brother in any matter: because **that the Lord is the avenger of all such**, as we also have forewarned you and testified.

7 For **God hath not called us unto uncleanness, but unto holiness**.

8 He therefore that despiseth, despiseth not man, but God, who hath also given unto us his Holy Spirit.

9 But as touching brotherly love ye need not that I write unto you: **for ye yourselves are taught of God to love one another**.

10 And indeed ye do it toward all the brethren which are in all Macedonia: but we beseech you, brethren, that ye increase more and more;

11 And that ye study to be quiet, and to do your own business, and to work with your own hands, **as we commanded you**;

12 That ye may walk honestly toward them that are without, and that ye may have lack of nothing.

13 **But I would not have you to be ignorant, brethren, concerning them which are asleep**, that ye sorrow not, even as others which have no hope.

14 For if we believe that Jesus died and rose again, even so them also which sleep in Jesus will God bring with him.

15 For this we say unto you by the word of the Lord, **that we which are alive and remain unto the coming of the Lord shall not prevent them which are asleep**.

16 For the **Lord himself shall descend from heaven with a shout, with the voice of the archangel, and with the trump of God: and the dead in Christ shall rise first**:

17 **Then we which are alive and remain shall be caught up together with them in the clouds, to meet the Lord in the air**: and so shall we ever be with the Lord.

18 Wherefore comfort one another with these words.

At the beginning of I Thessalonians chapter five, Paul continues, with caution, stating that Christians should take note that the time and season for these events were not to be revealed; however, he did state that *"the day of the Lord will come as a thief in the night.*" This statement gives us a time frame, referring to the same Old Testament phrase **the Day of the Lord**. In the New Testament, this day of the Lord occurs at the end of our current world system. That is, *during* the reign of the Anti-christ and *before* the Millennium reign of Christ. Referring to the end of the world, Paul uses a contrasting analogy between those who walk in darkness and perish (rebellious saints), and those who walk in light and live (righteous saints). Paul also addresses the deceitfulness of those who promise *peace and safety* through such doctrines as the eternal security of the believer. We are told that when destruction and judgment come upon them, it will be unexpected, swift, and sudden. The analogy of a woman travailing in pain is used to illustrate his point even further. Sadly, even though we know that birth pains intensify and increase in frequency, **these misguided Christians who walk in darkness will not be able to recognize the contractual changes which will lead to their own destruction**. In other words, their state of sinful living, will not allow them to discern the signs of the times.

The Apostle Paul admonished these Christians again, as he did in the previous chapter, to walk in holiness. He referred to those who walked in holiness as those who are of the day; verses the wicked, who walk and abide in the darkness of night. **Paul then commands the saints in verses five and six, to be children of the day and not of the night.** He also commands them to watch (the day of Christ as the thief) and to be sober, not drunken, caught asleep, or again walking in darkness. It is proper to mention here that the Apostle John writes to the church of Sardis in the apocalypse, warning them also that **if these Christians would not repent of their darkness and sin, then the Lord will come unto them as a thief in the night**. John utters the voice of the Lord again on this subject in chapter sixteen of Revelations to the Christian churches stating, *"Behold, I come as a thief. Blessed is he that watcheth, and keepeth his garments, lest he walk naked, and they see his shame."* (Rev 3:3; 16:15)

I Thes 5:1 **But of the times and the seasons, brethren, ye have no need that I write unto you.**

2 For yourselves know perfectly that **the day of the Lord so cometh as a thief in the night.**

3 For when they shall say, **Peace and safety; then sudden destruction cometh upon them, as travail upon a woman with child; and they shall not escape.**

4 **But ye, brethren, are not in darkness,** *that that day should overtake you as a thief.*

5 **Ye are all the children of light,** *and the children of the day: we are not of the night, nor of darkness.*

6 **Therefore let us not sleep,** *as do others;* **but let us watch and be sober.**

7 For they that sleep, sleep in the night; and they that be drunken are drunken in the night.

In verse eight of I Thessalonians, Paul continues and challenges every Christian to be sober, and to be full of the spirit of Christ (Eph 5:18). He then commands them to put on the weapons of warfare by putting on the breastplate of faith and love, and the helmet of salvation to be acquired through hope and steadfastness.

After all these admonishments and directives were given, Paul then concludes with the statement, **God has not appointed us unto wrath. It should be without controversy that the wrath of God would be withheld only from Christians who walk in the day. On the other hand those who walk in darkness are assured to be recipients of His wrath.** We are also told that, without holiness no man shall see the Lord (Heb 12:14); nor will they inherit His promises (Gal 5:19-21). However, like always in the Old and New Testaments all that walk in darkness are promised to receive the wrath of God; therefore, wicked Christians are not exempt from His wrath. God is no respecter of persons! **The righteous God of heaven has not destined His obedient children unto the wrath, but to obtain salvation and partake of the resurrection and translation of saints at his coming.** This is the proper, sound, and balanced interpretation of Hebrews five verse nine and ten. One can verify, with the following full texts of chapters 4 and 5, the accuracy of these explanations and let every man judge for himself. One's destiny may depend upon it.

I Thes 5:8: ***But let us, who are of the day, be sober, putting on the breastplate of faith and love; and for an helmet, the hope of salvation.***
      9 ***For God hath not appointed us to wrath***, ***but to obtain salvation*** *by our Lord Jesus Christ,*
      10 Who died for us, that, ***whether we wake or sleep, we should live together with him.***

On the heels of this scriptural discourse, we will continue to dissect this subject matter even further; hopefully, to resolve all contrary opinions, and dispel doctrines of darkness. The approach we will use will be to examine whether or not the Apostle Paul addressed these same issues, using the identical analogies, with other churches in his epistles. Amazingly, Paul did address these exact same concerns of light and darkness to the Christians in the city of Rome. He started off with the issue of not defrauding one's brother of the love of Christ, in the same manner that he addressed the Christians in Thessalonica. He tells them if they love their neighbor as themselves, they would not break the Mosaic Law, but rather fulfill it. The Roman Christians are then commanded to awaken out of their sleep, and come out of their darkness, warning that their salvation was closer than it was when they first believed. They, like the Thessalonians, are commanded to *"cast off the works of darkness and...put on the armour of light*

[His righteousness and holiness]." Finally they are commanded to walk in the day (holiness), putting on the Lord Jesus Christ, making no provisions for the flesh or the fulfillment of its lusts. (Rm 13:8-14)

To the Ephesian Christians, the same dialogue is pursued with greater clarity and detail, as to remove any doubt or confusion. Paul again initiates the fifth chapter compelling them to walk in love, as Christ has loved them. He then, in no uncertain terms, lets them know that no Christian who is a fornicator, sexually unclean, covetous, filthy, a foolish talker, or jester can consider himself to be a saint. He further stated that those who walk in this manner of **darkness,** and are whoremongers and idolaters, **would not inherit the Kingdom of Christ**. Inheritance is an element of a covenant expressed through one's will. The New Covenant is the will that one must abide in to receive the promises. Paul's audience (of course) is only Christians, and he emphatically decrees, ***"Let no man deceive you with vain words: for because of these things cometh the wrath of God upon the children of disobedience. Be not ye therefore partakers with them"*** (Eph 5:6,7). In Paul's second letter to the Thessalonians he conveyed an all telling message that at Christ's Second Coming He will pour out His wrath upon all who know not God (the heathen) and those Christians who obey not the gospel of the kingdom (II Thes 1:7,8).

The doctrine Once Saved, Always Saved, and its out of context counterpart, **"God has not appointed Christians to wrath," are both deceptive and vain beliefs**. In I Thes 5:8, Paul brings up (what should be by now) a familiar subject. Not to appear redundant, but only to illustrate the consistency of the biblical text, he commands them to walk as children of light and not in darkness. Since all saints have the ability to choose whom they will serve, they can either choose to walk in the light of God's word, or walk in the darkness of this world. Either way, there are consequences for their choices. He then reminds them that the manifestation of the fruit of the spirit in the believer's life is the only guarantee of the hope of salvation. The Apostle Peter concurred totally with this statement in his epistle, declaring that if one abounds in the fruit of the Spirit, they shall never fail the grace of God (II Pet 1:2-10).

In Eph 5:11, **Paul commands that those who walk in light are to have no fellowship with their Christian brothers who walk in darkness, "but rather reprove them."** In verse fourteen he commands those who sleep and walk in darkness to **awaken out of their drunken stupor** and arise from the dead, that Christ might give them light. He considered them dead because, as long as they abide in their iniquity, they are children slated for wrath and destruction (Verse 6). Paul compels them to no longer walk as fools, without understanding, but rather redeem the time *"because the days are evil."* He then tells them not to be drunk with the intoxicating deceit of sin, but rather choose to be filled with the spirit. The following is the scriptural discourse:

*"**Be ye therefore followers of God**, as dear children; **And walk in love, as Christ also hath loved us**, and hath given himself for us an offering and a sacrifice to God for a sweet smelling savior.*

*But **fornication**, and **all uncleanness, or covetousness**, let it not be once named among you, as becometh saints; Neither **filthiness, nor foolish talking, nor jesting**, which are not convenient: but rather giving of thanks.*

*For this ye know, that **no whoremonger, nor unclean person, nor covetous man, who is an idolater, hath any inheritance in the kingdom of Christ and of God.***

Let no man deceive you with vain words: for because of these things cometh the wrath of God upon the children of disobedience. Be not ye therefore partakers with them.

For ye were sometimes darkness,** but now are ye light in the Lord: walk as children of light: (**For** the fruit of the Spirit is in all goodness and righteousness and truth) **Proving what is acceptable unto the Lord.

*And **have no fellowship with the unfruitful works of darkness,** but rather reprove them. For it is a shame even to speak of those things which are done of them in secret. But all things that are reproved are made manifest by the light: for whatsoever doth make manifest is light.*

*Wherefore he saith, **Awake thou that sleepest, and arise from the dead, and Christ shall give thee light.***

*See then that ye **walk circumspectly, not as fools, but as wise, Redeeming the time, because the days are evil.***

*Wherefore be ye not unwise, but understanding what the will of the Lord is. And **be not drunk with wine, wherein is excess; but be filled with the Spirit…** "* (Eph 5:1-18)

The final indictment and confession of guilt by disobedient, perverted, heretical, and apostate Christians is found in the first and second chapter of the epistle to the Romans. **The Lord, through the apostle Paul, lays out their indictment and eternal punishment designated for the criminals in His house,** who choose not to walk in the power of the Holy Ghost, but become the servants of sin. In this discourse, I will change the format and comment after each verse. At this point, hopefully, only in the minds of a few, the question still remains, "has God appointed Christians unto wrath?" The answer is that the wrath of God is reserved especially for the Christians, who walk contrary to Him, and refuse to repent of their wicked ways. Addressing the Christians in Rome, Paul answers this questions directly starting in chapter one, verse eighteen:

Rm 1:18 **For the <u>wrath of God is revealed from heaven</u> against all ungodliness and unrighteousness <u>of men, who hold the truth in unrighteousness</u>**;

It should be quite apparent that this verse expressly states the wrath of God is specifically designed for unrighteous Christians. Those who hold and know the truth, but choose to abide in unrighteousness. They are in contempt with the spirit of grace and are as criminals in the house of God, because they

110

know the judgments and truths of God's word, but choose to violate the covenant and remain in willful unrighteousness.

"For, behold, the LORD commandeth, and he will smite the great house with breaches, and the little house with clefts.

Shall horses run upon the rock? will one plow there with oxen? for ye have **turned judgment into gall**, *and* **the fruit of righteousness into hemlock**..."

(Amos 6:11,12)

Rm 1:19 Because that **which may be known of <u>God is manifest in them</u>**; for <u>**God hath shewed it unto them**</u>.

God has manifested Himself in them, showed them the knowledge and power of His kingdom, and they have experienced the indwelling presence of the Godhead through the baptism of the Holy Ghost Jn 14:17-26. We are told that the Godhead has manifested Himself in them in John 17, *"That they all may be one; as thou, Father, art in me, and I in thee, that they also may be one in us: that the world may believe that thou hast sent me."* The kingdom of God was manifested in them as born again Christians (Lk 17:20, Jn 3:5,7). These individuals commit the unpardonable sin, blaspheme against the Holy Ghost, and no longer reverence the spirit of grace.

"This know also, that in the last days perilous times shall come. For men shall be lovers of their own selves, covetous, boasters, proud, blasphemers, disobedient to parents, unthankful, unholy, Without natural affection, trucebreakers, false accusers, incontinent, fierce, despisers of those that are good,

Traitors, heady, highminded, lovers of pleasures more than lovers of God; Having a form of godliness, but denying the power thereof: from such turn away." (II Tim 3:1-5)

These sinful attributes are common place amongst the heathen ever since the fall of Adam. However, these Christians are mature transgressors. They obviously knew many of the mysteries of the kingdom, and walked in revelation knowledge of the Spirit of Christ. God had fully manifested Himself in them by power, anointing, and revelation yet and they still rejected all this to serve devils.

Rm 1:20 For the invisible things of him from the creation of the world are clearly seen, **being understood by the things that are made**, even **his eternal power and Godhead**; *<u>so that they are without excuse</u>*:

These transgressors (covenant breakers) have understood the mysteries of creation, understanding how God brought into existence things that now

111

appear out of things that did not appear (Heb 11:3). They also understand the mysteries of the Godhead. Although packed with all of this intimate knowledge, they still rejected the holiness of the Lord and choose to become the servants of sin. Therefore, they are without excuse and will have no defense at their Day of Judgment, when they shall experience the wrath of God and eventual eternal damnation at the second resurrection.

The Apostle Peter prophesies concerning these individuals:

"That ye may be mindful of the words which were spoken before by the holy prophets, and of the commandment of us the apostles of the Lord and Saviour:

Knowing this first, **that there shall come in the last days scoffers, walking after their own lusts,**

And saying, **Where is the promise of his coming?** *for since the fathers fell asleep, all things continue as they were from the beginning of the creation.*

For this they willingly are ignorant of, that by the word of God the heavens were of old, and the earth standing out of the water and in the water:

Whereby the world that then was, being overflowed with water, perished:

But the heavens and the earth, which are now, by the same word are kept in store, reserved unto fire against the day of judgment and perdition of ungodly men.

But, beloved, be not ignorant of this one thing, that one day is with the Lord as a thousand years, and a thousand years as one day.

The Lord is not slack concerning his promise, *as some men count slackness; but is longsuffering to us-ward, not willing that any should perish, but that all should come to repentance.*

But the day of the Lord will come as a thief in the night; in the which the heavens shall pass away with a great noise, *and the elements shall melt with fervent heat, the earth also and the works that are therein shall be burned up.*

Seeing then that all these things shall be dissolved, what manner of persons ought ye to be in all holy conversation and godliness,

Looking for and hasting unto the coming of the day of God, *wherein the heavens being on fire shall be dissolved, and the elements shall melt with fervent heat?*

Nevertheless we, according to his promise, look for new heavens and a new earth, wherein dwelleth righteousness.

Wherefore, beloved, seeing that ye look for such things, **be diligent that ye may be found of him in peace, without spot, and blameless.**
(II Pet 3:2-14)

Rm 1:21 Because that, **when they knew God, they glorified him not as God**, **neither were thankful**; but **became vain in their imaginations**, and **their foolish heart was darkened**.

Revealing the intent of the hearts of men, Jesus stated in John (3:17-19), that men love darkness more than light. *King Solomon wrote, "the way of the wicked is as darkness: they know not at what they stumble" (Prov 4:19).* These individuals sought light at one juncture in their life (probably only to escape the consequences of hell), but they really never wanted to serve or obey Christ until the end. Consequently, after escaping the wickedness of the world, they lusted to reenter its snares, and become re-entangled. They most likely began to error concerning the judgment of God, seeing that divine judgment was not immediate, they began to manipulate the scriptures to their own end. Infested with liberal Christian doctrines, which have no negative eternal consequences for Christians who sin, they deluded themselves in their own doctrinal religious cocktails of error. We also know that these are not unbelieving Gentile sinners as some theologians suppose, because these individuals "**knew**" God.

In the words of the Lord, *"he that sinneth against me wrongeth his own soul: all they that hate me love death."* (Prov 8:36)

Rm 1:22 **Professing themselves to be wise, they became fools**,

Caught in their own dogmatic deception, embracing doctrines such as "Once Saved, Always Saved," they became fools. While walking in darkness and fulfilling the lusts of their flesh, they thought they could make themselves immune to the wrath of God and His statutes will abide forever. They have become fools, because the Holy Ghost has declared the oracles of God. Even though men may change their doctrines on earth, the word of the Lord is established in heaven, and it will not change. One that lacks wisdom, or is contentious with the spiritual things of the Lord also may not understand the following proverb:

"As a thorn goeth up into the hand of a drunkard, so is a parable in the mouth of fools. The great God that formed all things both rewardeth the fool, and rewardeth transgressors" (Prov 26:9,10).

Prior to their change of actions and folly, these Christians must have been wise. The council of the Lord is sure concerning those who follow the spiritually suicidal path of self-destruction. In the book of proverbs, we are told that *"the man that wandereth out of the way of understanding **shall remain** in the congregation of the dead"* (Prov 21:16).

Rm 1:23 And **changed the glory of the uncorruptible God into an image** made like to corruptible man, and to birds, and fourfooted beasts, and creeping things.

113

Rm 1:24 **Wherefore <u>God also gave them up to uncleanness</u> through the lusts of their own hearts**, to <u>dishonour their own bodies</u> **between themselves**:

These Christians began to construct doctrines and create deities from the inspirations of their vain imaginations. They began to fashion their own gods that could not save. With nothing being held as sacred any more, they would be given over to the lust of their flesh, and engage in vial transgender perversions, mass orgies, lesbianism, homosexuality, bestiality and any other erotic sexual perversion contemplated by their vile imaginations. To their own demise, these Christians have acquired a fatal dose of narcissism. Narcissism is the acute love of one's self, with the pursuit of vice and pleasure, often time enhanced with wealth, leisure, and idle time. The scriptures indicate that these individuals understood the glory of the man, who was created in the image of god, as well as the glory of the woman (I Cor 11:1-16). However, their perverted minds could only mock and defame the holiness of God and the purpose of man's gender and sexual roles. Satan would now use these decadent vessels to mock God the Father, who created man in His image. The Apostle Paul stated in his writings to Timothy that, " *the Spirit speaketh expressly,* ***that in the latter times*** *some shall depart from the faith,* ***giving heed to seducing spirits, and doctrines of devils;*** *Speaking lies in hypocrisy; having their conscience seared with a hot iron.".* (I Tim 4:1,2)

Rm 1:25 Who **<u>changed the truth of God into a lie</u>**, and **worshipped and served the creature more than the Creator**, who is blessed for ever. Amen.
Rm 1:26 **For this cause <u>God gave them up unto vile affections</u>**: for even **their <u>women did change the natural use into that which is against nature</u>**:
Rm 1:27 And **likewise also <u>the men, leaving the natural use of the woman,</u> burned in their lust one toward another**; men with men working that which is unseemly, and **receiving in themselves that recompence of their error** which was meet.

Depravity amongst the heathen is expected but it should not exist among those who abide in the Lord's temple? Jesus said that if the inhabitants of the city of Sodom had seen the miracles he performed, they would have repented of their homosexual activities in sackcloth and ashes, and their cities would have remained until his day (Mt 11:20-24). It is quite obvious that these rebellious Christians are **willfully ignorant** of the fact that the Lord judged the cities of Sodom and Gomorrah for their vile sinful lusts, yet they have the audacity to think that they will not suffer any consequences? If there were no consequences for such actions, then the Lord would have to apologize to the inhabitants of Sodom and Gomorrah for His harsh judgment upon them.

If wicked Christians commit the same sinful acts as an unregenerate unbeliever, but He judges only the unbelievers, then the Lord's ways would not be just. God forbid (Ezek 33:7-20)! The Apostle Paul tells the Corinthian church that, *"if any man defile the temple of God, **him shall God destroy**; for the temple of God is holy, which temple ye are.* (I Cor 3:16,17)

The perversions that existed in Sodom and Gomorrah were the results of the following sins, which were stated by the Prophet Ezekiel.

*"Behold, this was the iniquity of thy sister Sodom, **pride, fulness of bread, and abundance of idleness** was in her and in her daughters, **neither did she strengthen the hand of the poor and needy**.*

*And they were **haughty, and committed abomination before me**: therefore I took them away as I saw good."* (Ezek 16:49,50)

Rm 1:28: And even as <u>**they did not like to retain God in their knowledge**</u>, **God gave them over to <u>a reprobate mind</u>**, to do those things which are not convenient;

By their own choice, they rejected the knowledge of God and choose to believe their own lies. They had become bankrupt concerning truth and decided to serve Satan, the father of lies (Jn 8:44). Consequently, **the LORD WOULD REMOVE HIS SPIRIT FROM THEM, MAKING THEIR TEMPLES DESOLATE** (void of the presence of God). Darkness would consume their heart and mind, and the Lord would turn them over, to a reprobate spirit. Christ, through the Prophet Daniel, prophesied these futuristic events. The apostles referred to these events of the last days as "the great falling away" (II Thes 2:3), in which the tares (**SONS OF PERDITION**) are revealed, exposed, and eradicated out of the body of Christ. The **CHIEF TARE** among them will be the Antichrist, who emerges out of discipleship (like Judas), and goes into perdition. This mystery, which few Christians can grasp because of erroneous doctrines, is called **the MYSTERY OF INIQUITY**.

In the Old Testament, this type of precedent by which demonic spirits tormented an individual after the anointing departed from him, occurred with Israel's first King, Saul (I Sam 16:14). Lying demons were also sent into the false prophets of Israel to prophesy lies to them, because they refused to believe the truth (I Kin 22:22-23, II Chron 18:20-22). We are also told that this will happen again, to selected Christians, in the last days. Paul reveals this truth to the Thessalonians in his second epistle to them:

"Even him, whose coming is after the working of Satan with all power and signs and lying wonders,

*And with **<u>all deceivableness of unrighteousness in them that</u>***

perish; because they received not the love of the truth, that they might be saved. And for this cause God shall send them strong delusion, that they should believe a lie. That they all might be damned who believed not the truth, but had pleasure in unrighteousness."
(II Thes 2:9-12)

Rm 1:29 Being **filled with all unrighteousness, fornication, wickedness, covetousness, maliciousness; full of envy, murder, debate, deceit, malignity; whisperers,**
Rm 1:30 **Backbiters, haters of God, despiteful, proud, boasters, inventors of evil things, disobedient to parents,**
Rm 1:31 **Without understanding, <u>covenant breakers</u>, without natural affection, implacable, unmerciful:**
Rm 1:32 **Who <u>knowing the judgment of God</u>, that they which commit such things are worthy of death, not only do the same, but have pleasure in them that do them**.

"Hell and destruction are never full; so the eyes [lust] of man are never satisfied" (Prov 27:20). Again, as in all previous examples, the offenses committed are the result of a carnal fixation with the sins of the flesh. The temples of the wicked are cohabited with legions of devils that affix themselves to the rebellious Christians, in order to fulfill their symbiotic (mutual partnership) lustful relationship. The Holy Ghost identifies these individuals as covenant breakers. Daniel classifies them as transgressors (Dan 8:23); the terms are synonymous. They have lost the fear of God and take pleasure in taunting with spiritual death. *"All the ways of a man are clean in his own eyes; **but the LORD weigheth the spirits**"* (Prov 16:2).

Jude, the brother of Christ classifies these individuals and places them in their historical context.

"Beloved, when I gave all diligence to write unto you of the common salvation, it was needful for me to write unto you, and exhort you that ye should earnestly contend for the faith which was once delivered unto the saints.

For there are certain men crept in unawares, who were before of old ordained to this condemnation, ungodly men, turning the grace of our God into lasciviousness, and denying the only Lord God, and our Lord Jesus Christ.

I will therefore put you in remembrance, though ye once knew this, how that the Lord, having saved the people out of the land of Egypt, afterward destroyed them that believed not.

116

Even as Sodom and Gomorrha, and the cities about them in like manner, giving themselves over to fornication, and going after strange flesh, are set forth for an example, suffering the vengeance of eternal fire...

Likewise also these filthy dreamers defile the flesh, despise dominion, and speak evil of dignities...

But these speak evil of those things which they know not: but what they know naturally, as brute beasts, in those things they corrupt themselves.

Woe unto them! for they have gone in the way of Cain, and ran greedily after the error of Balaam for reward, and perished in the gainsaying of Core.

These are spots in your feasts of charity, when they feast with you, feeding themselves without fear: clouds they are without water, carried about of winds; trees whose fruit withereth, without fruit, twice dead, plucked up by the roots;

Raging waves of the sea, foaming out their own shame; wandering stars, to whom is reserved the blackness of darkness for ever.

And Enoch also, the seventh from Adam, prophesied of these, saying, Behold, the Lord cometh with ten thousands of his saints,

To execute judgment upon all, and to convince all that are ungodly among them of all their ungodly deeds which they have ungodly committed, and of all their hard speeches which ungodly sinners have spoken against him.

These are murmurers, complainers, walking after their own lusts; and their mouth speaketh great swelling words, having men's persons in admiration because of advantage.

But, beloved, remember ye the words which were spoken before of the apostles of our Lord Jesus Christ;

How that they told you there should be mockers in the last time, who should walk after their own ungodly lusts." (Jude 1:3-8,10-18)

Rm 2:1 Therefore thou art inexcusable, O man, **whosoever thou art that judgest: for wherein thou judgest another, thou condemnest thyself; for thou that judgest doest the same things.**

Rm 2:2 But **we are sure that the judgment of God is according to truth against them which commit such things**.

Regardless of the theological beliefs and philosophical concepts men may devise, *"Be not deceived; God is not mocked! whatsoever a man sow, that shall he also reap"* (Gal 6:7). The proverb of Solomon is true, which states

117

that *"the Lord made the wicked for the day of evil"* (Prov 16:3). In the New Testament, all true Christians are admonished to take a firm stand for righteousness in the evil day… exercising their spiritual senses, equipping themselves with spiritual weapons, and standing steadfastly in the faith (Eph 6:13). One truth that can be abstracted from these character defects is that *"evil men understand not the judgment"* (Prov 28:5). *"Whoso walketh uprightly shall be saved: but he that is perverse in his ways shall fall at once."* (Prov 28:18)

Rm 2:3 And thinkest thou this, O man, that judgest them which do such things, and doest the same, that thou shalt escape the judgment of God?

If one hypocritically judges others for sins committed, he must acknowledge that he will be judged by the same measurement. Every man must give an account for the deeds done in his own body; therefore, those who walk in the flesh, and fulfill the lusts of their flesh, shall perish. They and their flesh are one. If every man will judge himself, there would be no need for any other to judge him; however, the nature of man causes him to justify himself in his own eyes. Even the righteous are admonished to avenge all disobedience, only after their obedience is fulfilled. (II Cor 10:6)

Rm 2:4 Or despisest thou the riches of <u>his goodness and forbearance and longsuffering</u>; not knowing that <u>the goodness of God leadeth thee to repentance</u>?

So often, many take the longsuffering and patience of the Lord to be a sign of weakness (or neglect) on His part. Actually, his extended period of withholding discipline is granted to allow more people an opportunity to repent and turn from their evil ways. However, the wicked cease the moment to increase their folly and create a greater snare for themselves. The Apostle Peter amplified this concept for the last days in the following manner:

*"**The Lord is not slack concerning his promise**, as some men count slackness; but **is longsuffering to us-ward, not willing that any should perish, but that all should come to repentance.***

__But the day of the Lord will come as a thief in the night__; in the which the heavens shall pass away with a great noise, and the elements shall melt with fervent heat, the earth also and the works that are therein shall be burned up.

__Seeing then that all these things shall be dissolved, what manner of persons ought ye to be in all holy conversation and godliness,__

Looking for and hasting unto the coming of the day of God, wherein the heavens being on fire shall be dissolved, and the elements shall melt with fervent heat?

Nevertheless we, according to his promise, look for new heavens and a new earth, wherein dwelleth righteousness.

*Wherefore, beloved, seeing that ye look for such things, **be diligent that ye may be found of him in peace, without spot, and blameless. And account that the longsuffering of our Lord is salvation;** even as our beloved brother Paul also according to the wisdom given unto him hath written unto you."* (II Pet 3:9-14)

Rm 2:5 But **after thy hardness and impenitent heart treasurest up unto thyself <u>wrath against the day of wrath</u> and <u>revelation of the righteous judgment of God</u>;**
Rm 2:6 **Who will render to every man according to his deeds:**

The arrogance manifested by worldly Christian leaders and their followers in their blatant disobedience to the commandments of a holy God, will be annihilated at their appointment when His divine wrath over takes them like a flood. The prophet Daniel stated that the Transgressors must come to their full (climax) in synch with their father the Devil, during the days of the Anti-Christ (Dan 8:23). They will serve the dragon, and by flatteries and deception, initially deceive most Christians, who are only one verse thick in their knowledge of the word.

Christians who believe in the doctrine "*Once Saved, Always Saved*" are unsuspectingly flaunting with death. Quite contrary to popular belief, if one transgresses and lives in sin, the Old and New Testament promises that for them damnation will be sure. Jesus is the heavenly door unto salvation. He is the very God of both the Old and New Testaments, and the Father of Adam. As the God of Abraham, Isaac, and Jacob, He overthrew His natural seed in the wilderness, telling the Hebrew people that their carcasses would rot in the wilderness, because of their rebellion. Roughly three million of them perished and did not make it into the Promise Land. His spiritual children are warned not to be high-minded, because if He corrected and rejected the natural, how much more the spiritual?

*"As truly as I live, saith the LORD, as ye have spoken in mine ears, so will I do to you: **Your carcases shall fall in this wilderness**; and all that were numbered of you, according to your whole number, from twenty years old and upward, which have murmured against me... But as for you, your carcases, they shall fall in this wilderness"* (Num 14:28,29,32).

How much more will He consume puny Gentile Christians, who have no control over the souls or the longevity of their lives after death?

119

Rm 2:7 To them who <u>by patient continuance in well doing</u> seek for glory and honour and <u>immortality, eternal life</u>:

Those who abide in righteousness shall run the race with patience and posses their soul unto life eternal. A sure recipe for salvation is as follows:

> *"For God, who commanded the light to shine out of darkness, hath shined in our hearts, to give the light of the knowledge of the glory of God in the face of Jesus Christ.*
> *But **we have this treasure in earthen vessels**, that the excellency of the power may be of God, and not of us.*
> ***We are troubled on every side, yet not distressed; we are perplexed, but not in despair;***
> ***Persecuted, but not forsaken; cast down, but not destroyed;***
> *Always bearing about in the body the dying of the Lord Jesus, that the life also of Jesus might be made manifest in our body.*
> *For we which live are alway delivered unto death for Jesus' sake, that the life also of Jesus might be made manifest in our mortal flesh.*
> *So then death worketh in us, but life in you. We having the same spirit of faith, according as it is written, I believed, and therefore have I spoken; we also believe, and therefore speak;*
> *Knowing that he which raised up the Lord Jesus shall raise up us also by Jesus, and shall present us with you.*
> *For all things are for your sakes, that the abundant grace might through the thanksgiving of many redound to the glory of God.*
> ***For which cause we faint not; but though our outward man perish, yet the inward man is renewed day by day.***
> ***For our light affliction, which is but for a moment, worketh for us a far more exceeding and eternal weight of glory;***
> *While we look not at the things which are seen, but at the things which are not seen: for the things which are seen are temporal; but the things which are not seen are eternal." (II Cor 4:6-18)*

In conclusion, those who walk in darkness shall never inherit the rewards of the righteous. The righteous walks in faith, hope, and charity and inherits the blessings of the Almighty… making themselves worthy to enter into His rest and eternal glory.

Rm 2:8 But unto **them that are contentious, and do not obey the truth, but obey unrighteousness, <u>indignation</u> and <u>wrath,</u>**

Without question, stating from chapter one, Paul is writing to the church at Rome and condemns those who reject Christ, and those who obey not the truth. One can not get any more explicit than these strong words for the destruction of wicked and unrighteous Christians during the day of His visitation. He over threw the natural children in the wilderness and poured out His judgments upon them because of their evil hearts. Paul also warns the Christians in the book of Hebrews, that they should not provoke the Lord to wrath, lest a similar fate will happen to them.

"But Christ as a son over his own house; whose house are we, if we hold fast the confidence and the rejoicing of the hope firm unto the end.

*Wherefore (as the Holy Ghost saith, **Today if ye will hear his voice, Harden not your hearts, as in the provocation, in the day of temptation in the wilderness:***

When your fathers tempted me, proved me, and saw my works forty years.

*Wherefore I was grieved with that generation, and said, They do alway err in their heart; and they have not known my way. **So I sware in my wrath, They shall not enter into my rest.***

Take heed, brethren, lest there be in any of you an evil heart of unbelief, in departing from the living God.

But exhort one another daily, while it is called To day; lest any of you be hardened through the deceitfulness of sin.

For we are made partakers of Christ, if we hold the beginning of our confidence stedfast unto the end;

While it is said, To day if ye will hear his voice, harden not your hearts, as in the provocation.

For some, when they had heard, did provoke: howbeit not all that came out of Egypt by Moses.

*But with whom was he grieved forty years? was it not with them that had sinned, **whose carcases fell in the wilderness?***

And to whom sware he that they should not enter into his rest, but to them that believed not? So we see that they could not enter in because of unbelief.

Let us therefore fear, lest, a promise being left us of entering into his rest, any of you should seem to come short of it.

For unto us was the gospel preached, as well as unto them: but the word preached did not profit them, not being mixed with faith in them that heard it.

*For we which have believed do enter into rest, as he said, **As I have sworn in my wrath, if they shall enter into my rest:** although the works were finished from the foundation of the world."* (Heb 3:6-4:3)

Rm 2:9 <u>Tribulation</u> and <u>anguish</u>, upon every soul of man that doeth evil, of the Jew first, and also of the Gentile;

INDIGNATION...WRATH...TRIBULATION... ANGUISH, these words are quite explicit and should be without dispute, but the ignorant, and the disobedient will always justify their present state of darkness. However, the word of God states in many of the parables that there shall be weeping and gnashing of teeth when they are thrust out of God's kingdom.

The prophet Zephaniah spoke much on this topic concerning God's ability to judge righteously, to utterly cleanse his temple, and cut off the wicked.

"*And it shall come to pass in the day of the LORD's sacrifice, that I will punish the princes, and the king's children, and **all such as are clothed with strange apparel.***

In the same day also will I punish all those that leap on the threshold, which fill their masters' houses with violence and deceit.

*And it shall come to pass in that day, saith the LORD, that **there shall be the noise of a cry** from the fish gate, **and an howling** from the second, and a great crashing from the hills . . .*

*And it shall come to pass at that time, that **I will search Jerusalem with candles, and punish the men that are settled on their lees: <u>that say in their heart, The LORD will not do good, neither will he do evil.</u>***

*Therefore their goods shall become a booty, **and their houses a desolation**: they shall also build houses, but not inhabit them; and they shall plant vineyards, but not drink the wine thereof.*

The great day of the LORD is near,** it is near, and hasteth greatly, even the voice of the day of the LORD: **the mighty man shall cry there bitterly.

<u>That day is a day of wrath, a day of trouble and distress, a day of wasteness and desolation, a day of darkness and gloominess, a day of clouds and thick darkness,</u>

***<u>A day of the trumpet</u>** and alarm against the fenced cities, and against the high towers.*

*And **I will bring distress upon men, that they shall walk like blind men, because they have sinned against the LORD: and their blood shall be poured out as dust, and their flesh as the dung.***

*Neither their silver nor their gold shall be able to deliver them in the day of **the LORD's wrath**; but the whole **land shall be devoured by the fire of his jealousy** [the image of jealousy- Ezek 8:4-*

18]: for he shall make even a speedy riddance of all them that dwell in the land. (Zeph 1:8-18)

Rm 2:10 But **glory, honour, and peace, to every man that worketh good,** to the **Jew first, and also to the Gentile**:
Rm 2:11 **For there is no respect of persons with God**.

     In the final analysis the Lord will execute judgment upon the criminals in His house, who have no fear of God, and who whose hearts are still in Sodom. The Apostle Peter prophesied concerning the state of affairs of the wicked Christians in the last days in the following manner:

*"But there were false prophets also among the people, even as **there shall be false teachers among you, who privily shall bring in damnable heresies**, even denying the Lord that bought them, and bring upon themselves swift destruction.*

*And many shall follow their pernicious ways; by reason of whom **the way of truth shall be evil spoken of**.*

*And through covetousness shall they with feigned words make merchandise of you: **whose judgment now of a long time lingereth not, and their damnation slumbereth not**.*

For if God spared not the angels that sinned, but cast them down to hell, and delivered them into chains of darkness, to be reserved unto judgment;

And spared not the old world, but saved Noah the eighth person, *a preacher of righteousness, bringing in the flood upon the world of the ungodly;*

*And **turning the cities of Sodom and Gomorrha into ashes** condemned them with an overthrow, **making them an ensample unto those that after should live ungodly;***

And delivered just Lot, vexed with the filthy conversation of the wicked:

*(**For that righteous man dwelling among them, in seeing and hearing,** vexed his righteous soul from day to day **with their unlawful deeds;**)*

The Lord knoweth how to deliver the godly out of temptations, and to reserve the unjust unto the day of judgment to be punished:

*But chiefly them that **walk after the flesh in the lust of uncleanness, and despise government**. Presumptuous are they, selfwilled, they are not afraid to speak evil of dignities.*

Whereas angels, which are greater in power and might, bring not railing accusation against them before the Lord.

*But these, **as natural brute beasts, made to be taken and destroyed, speak evil of the things that they understand not; and shall utterly perish in their own corruption;***

And shall receive the reward of unrighteousness, *as they that count it* *pleasure to riot in the day time. **Spots they are and blemishes, sporting themselves with their own deceivings while they feast with you;***

Having** eyes full of adultery, and that cannot cease from sin; **beguiling unstable souls: an heart they have exercised with covetous practices; cursed children:

*Which **have forsaken the right way, and are gone astray, following the way of Balaam** the son of Bosor, who loved the wages of unrighteousness;*

But was rebuked for his iniquity: the dumb ass speaking with man's voice forbad the madness of the prophet.

*These are **wells without water**, clouds that are carried with a tempest; **to whom the mist of darkness is reserved for ever.***

*For when they speak great swelling words of vanity, they allure through the lusts of the flesh, through much wantonness, **those that were clean escaped from them who live in error.***

While they promise them liberty, they themselves are the servants of corruption: for of whom a man is overcome, of the same is he brought in bondage.

*<u>**For if after they have escaped the pollutions of the world through the knowledge of the Lord and Saviour Jesus Christ, they are again entangled therein, and overcome, the latter end is worse with them than the beginning.**</u>*

*For **it had been better for them not to have known the way of righteousness, than, after they have known it, to turn from the holy commandment delivered unto them.***

But it is happened unto them according to the true proverb, The dog is turned to his own vomit again; and the sow that was washed to her wallowing in the mire. (II Pet 2:1-22)

What About the Thief on the Cross?

Another popular Protestant doctrine used as a last defense to justify a lack of adherence to ordinances of a biblical covenant is "**salvation by a death bed confession.**" This doctrine is based upon the death confession and salvation of the thief that was crucified next to Christ. The Eurocentric churches have passionately used this example found in the book of Luke to justify their claims that water and spirit baptism are not necessary components for New Testament salvation. The biblical account is as follows:

"And the people stood beholding. And the rulers also with them derided him, saying, He saved others; let him save himself, if he be Christ, the chosen

of God.

And the soldiers also mocked him, coming to him, and offering him vinegar,
And saying, If thou be the king of the Jews, save thyself.

And a superscription also was written over him in letters of Greek, and Latin,
and Hebrew, THIS IS THE KING OF THE JEWS.

*And **one of the malefactors [thieves] which were hanged railed on him**,*
saying, If thou be Christ, save thyself and us.

But the other answering rebuked him, saying, Dost not thou fear God,
seeing thou art in the same condemnation?

And we indeed justly; for we receive the due reward of our deeds: but this
man hath done nothing amiss.

And he said unto Jesus, Lord, remember me when thou comest into thy
kingdom.

And Jesus said unto him, Verily I say unto thee, To day shalt thou be with
me in paradise. " (Lk 23:35-43)

Shamefully, like a mirage in the desert, people will always see what they want to see in a dry and religious land. Unfortunately, this doctrine has gaping holes in it that are so large that one can practically drive a "Mac Truck" through them. First we must put these scriptures in their proper context before one can render a verdict. In this account, **we must realize that the thief was not an unregenerate Gentile, or unbelieving Jew, pleading for salvation** through Christ. To the contrary, he was a righteous Jew with a repentant heart (Prov 24:16), who was already in covenant with the Lord, but had violated a natural law of the Roman state and consequently received the death penalty. However, the **deathbed confession by one who is an unbeliever (or heathen) seeking salvation is not within the context of these scriptures.** Therefore, this example cannot be used to discredit or nullify New Testament commandments found in Jn 3:5 and Acts 2:38.

Furthermore, the repentant thief was actually executed and died under the Old Testament Covenant. Jesus, as God in the flesh, had the authority and power to forgive individuals of their sins (Mk 2:5-10, Lk 7:47-50). However, theologians have negated the fact that **the blood of Christ given as a ransom for the sins of men and could not be applied to the thief on the cross** (or anyone else for that matter) until after His actual death. A will or testament cannot be enforced until the death of the testator. Christ was not yet dead. He was still alive and was fully engaged in dialogue with this remorseful Jewish brother.

"And for this cause he is the mediator of the new testament, that by means
of death, for the redemption of the transgressions that were under the first
testament, they which are called might receive the promise of eternal inherit-
ance.

For where a testament is, there must also of necessity be the death of the
testator.

125

For a testament is of force after men are dead: otherwise it is of no strength at all **while the testator liveth**." *(Heb 9:15-17)*

The fact that a will, or Testament, cannot be enforced until the death of the testator is both a natural and a spiritual law. It is amazing how scholars who perpetrate such heretical teachings can be so learned in the scriptures, yet "strain at gnats," and swallow such a camel. Clearly, **this Jewish brother died under the Old Covenant and did not have to comply with the New Covenant mandates**. Anyone with a pure heart, who researches this topic systematically, should come to this same conclusion without much fanfare.

A similar transition episode concerning salvation occurred during the short time span between the New and the Old Covenants in the book of Acts chapter 19. The Apostle Paul met several disciples of John the Baptist, years after John's death, who only knowing the law, and John's Gospel of the Kingdom, had not heard that Christ had come. Paul preached to them Jesus and the baptism of the Holy Ghost. They received his message and were re-baptized in the name of Jesus Christ and then received the Holy Ghost (Acts 19:5-7). **Paul brought them into compliance with the New Testament Covenant**. If the thief who was on the cross with Christ had lived after Pentecost he would also of had to come through the New Testament blood, water, and spirit.

The repentant thief was not only a Jew; he also recognized that Jesus was the Messiah, and even acknowledged that Christ had a kingdom. This thief called on Jesus to save his soul in the afterlife by requesting that Jesus remember him when He entered into His eternal kingdom. When the wicked thief mocked and railed on Christ, the repented thief rebuked him sharply (despite his own personal pain and suffering) to defend Christ, as being innocent of the charges brought against Him. He also knew that Jesus was a just man and rebuked the wicked thief for not having a fear of God. **The repentant thief also called Jesus "Lord,"** which is quite profound. This revealed that he was not an unbelieving Jew, like the multitude who had arranged to have Him crucified at the hands of the Romans. He understood the Messianic text and knew that Jesus was more than just a prophet sent from God.

After looking at the evidence, one should get an answer to the question *"who was the thief on the cross?"* Was he an unclean Gentile seeking salvation in a desperation act out of fear, seeking the grace and mercy of God? Was he an unbeliever, who suddenly became a believer on his deathbed, realizing that Christ was the Savior? **As previously stated, the text clearly indicates that he was already a believer, a Jew, and already in covenant with God. He even revered God and had a genuine fear of Him.** Unfortunately, he had also committed a civil crime of which he was to receive the Roman death penalty *of crucifixion*. **He knew who Jesus was, recognized him as the Messiah, and sought forgiveness of his sins.** *He* knew that **Jesus had an eternal kingdom** while all the other Jews were looking for the Messiah that would have an earthly kingdom.

It would clearly require a stretch of the imagination continued in a deceitful heart, for Protestant theologians to continue to assert that they could nullify the essential components of salvation and slide one into the "back door" in an act of desperation on their deathbed. **God will honor His word above His name**, and He cannot lie. The three components of the water, the spirit and the blood all agree in one, and are the required elements of the New Testament Covenant. If a person is on his deathbed and wants at that time to be saved, he should pray that the Lord raises him up and gives him one last chance to get in covenant with Him. Because, if the righteous are scarcely saved, what chance have the sinners and the ungodly (I Pet 4:17)? **God does not respond to time or a crisis in the manner as men do.** Men are finite and cannot control their eternal destiny, but with God all things are in His hands and within His control. He is not destitute, nor is He hard-pressed for souls. From the foundation of the world the God of creation has known every man that has ever lived. Hence, He knew them before they were even conceived in their mothers' wombs. He also knew the choices every individual would make. Therefore, before men reach their deathbeds, God knows them, and He also knows if more time was granted unto them to serve Him, what their choices would be.

The reality of emanate death for mortal men on their beds of affliction does not force God to respond to their desperate acts of fear. God is still God, and no man can force Him to make exceptions regarding salvation when they choose to serve Him only as a last resort (having no other options). If they are genuine and are sincere, the Lord, who knows each heart, is able to raise them up again and bring them into compliance with His covenant. **The Lord says that He "is the door" and that all that ever came before Him are "thieves and robbers" desiring to come into His kingdom through a method other than the strait and narrow way** (Jn 10:8).

The root of such beliefs pertaining to salvation can be found in the historical development of the Protestant church. Its numerous denominations protested and rebelled against the Roman Catholic doctrines that pertained to salvation. However, their over emphasis upon the blood of Christ, even at the expense of negating spiritual and water baptisms, has caused their doctrinal dilemma. To skirt the truth, they use the thief on the cross incident to justify their false teachings on salvation. Jesus said that He was the door and that any desire to be His sheep must enter only through the way that He had established (Jn 10:9). He said that one must, *"**Enter ye in at the strait gate**: for wide is the gate, and broad is the way, that leadeth to destruction, and many there be which go in thereat: **Because strait is the gate, and narrow is the way, which leadeth unto life, and few there be that find it**"* (Mt 7:13,14). Few have acquired the revelation and adhered to Jesus' statement, *Verily, verily, I say unto thee, Except a man be born of water and of the Spirit, he cannot enter into the kingdom of God"* (Jn 3:5). The answer is found in Acts 2:38 in which the Apostle Peter commanded all Christians to: repent, be baptized (by full immersion) in the name of Jesus Christ, and receive the baptism of the Holy Ghost.

One may have rational arguments for why they might feel that the Lord should accept them in to His kingdom. They even challenge the goodness of God, claiming that Christ should as an act of mercy, do the greater good, and let them into His kingdom. However, many theologians might want to consider the fact that they have His word (the Bible) and the testimony of the apostles and prophets, if they refuse to hear them, then Christ will not hear their plea. This was the same response the Lord gave the rich man who was in the midst of hell fire, as he pleaded with the Lord to send an angel back to minister to his brothers about the reality of hell.

"And it came to pass, that the beggar died, and was carried by the angels into Abraham's bosom: the rich man also died, and was buried;

***And in hell he lift up his eyes, being in torments**, and seeth Abraham afar off, and Lazarus in his bosom.*

*And he cried and said, **Father Abraham, have mercy on me, and send Lazarus, that he may dip the tip of his finger in water, and cool my tongue; for I am tormented in this flame.***

But Abraham said, Son, remember that thou in thy lifetime receivedst thy good things, and likewise Lazarus evil things: but now he is comforted, and thou art tormented.

And beside all this, between us and you there is a great gulf fixed: so that they which would pass from hence to you cannot; neither can they pass to us, that would come from thence.

*Then he said, **I pray thee therefore, father, that thou wouldest send him to my father's house:***

For I have five brethren; that he may testify unto them, lest they also come into this place of torment.

*Abraham saith unto him, **They have Moses and the prophets; let them hear them.***

*And he said, Nay, father Abraham: **but if one went unto them from the dead, they will repent.***

*And he said unto him, **If they hear not Moses and the prophets, neither will they be persuaded, though one rose from the dead.***" (Lk 16:19-31)

In the religious world, it seems like everyone wants to go to heaven, but only a few are willing to do what is necessary to get there. Is God cruel? Is He moved by human tears? He is not cruel, nor does He lack compassion; however, **God is also not a fool**. He knows the heart of every man! If a person sincerely desires to serve Him, he will seek His face, study God's word, and apply his heart to know Him "in spirit and in truth." Perhaps then he will find Him. The disciples asked Jesus a similar question about the number of people that will be saved. Christ's response to them *was as follows:*

"Lord, are there few that be saved? And he said unto them,

Strive to enter in at the strait gate: for many, I say unto you, will seek to enter in, and shall not be able.

When once the master of the house is risen up, and hath shut to the door, and ye begin to stand without, and to knock at the door, saying, **Lord, Lord, open unto us***; and he shall answer and say unto you,* **I know you not whence ye are:**

Then shall ye begin to say, **We have eaten and drunk in thy presence, and thou hast taught in our streets.**

But he shall say, **I tell you, I know you not whence ye are; depart from me, all ye workers of iniquity.**

There shall be weeping and gnashing of teeth, when ye shall see Abraham, and Isaac, and Jacob, and all the prophets, in the kingdom of God, and you yourselves thrust out.

There shall be weeping and gnashing of teeth, *when ye shall see Abraham, and Isaac, and Jacob, and all the prophets, in the kingdom of God, and you yourselves* **thrust out.** " (Lk 13:23-28)

After taking the time to look at the account of the thief on the cross theology and examining its counterpart, the deathbed confession doctrine one would have to reject the current Eurocentric interpretation of these teachings. On the other hand, there would be scriptural support for the following scenario: If one is on his deathbed and is already in covenant with Christ, but confess that he has been living in sin; if he sincerely repents, he can at that time be restored in covenant and saved. This is the only lesson that we can abstract from this account of Christ's crucifixion that can be considered sound doctrine.

Brethren, if any of you do err from the truth, and one convert him;
Let him know, that **he which converteth the sinner from the error of his way shall save a soul from death***, and shall hide a multitude of sins.*
(Jm 5:19,20)

Can a Christian be Oppressed or Possessed by a Devil?

The first biblical principle that addresses this question is rooted in the mandate of water baptism. Scripturally speaking, **water baptism is not** ones testimony to others, symbolizing their new found faith, as taught by many Protestants. Neither is it an act to bring one into a religious institution, a sort of religious fraternal initiation, as you would find in the Roman Catholic Church. Actually, the scriptures clearly establishes the fact that Christians are baptized in water, in the name of Jesus Christ, in the likeness of His burial, to come up out the water (the grave) in the likeness of Christ's resurrection. In short, water baptism is the funeral of the believer in Christ. It is his death to the old man, and former attitudes, lusts, and lifestyle that allows him to become a new creature in Christ. The Apostle Paul describes this spiritual transition in this manner:

*"For if we have been planted together in the likeness of his death, we shall be also in the likeness of his resurrection: Knowing this, that our old man is crucified with him, that the body of sin might be destroyed, that henceforth we should not serve sin. **For he that is dead is freed from sin**"* (Rm 6:5-7). A dead man cannot sin or give place to the devil. A dead man cannot be tempted or seduced to sin, neither can he be provoked with evil. A dead man resides in the grave and cannot be used as a vessel to do Satan's bidding.

Paul comments further stating *"For in that he* [Christ] *died, he died unto sin once: but in that he liveth, he liveth unto God. Likewise reckon ye also your-selves to be dead indeed unto sin, but alive unto God through Jesus Christ our Lord.*

Let not sin *therefore reign in your mortal body, that ye should obey it in the lusts thereof. **Neither yield ye** your members as instruments of unrighteousness unto sin: but **yield yourselves unto God**, as those that are alive from the dead, and your members as instruments of righteousness unto God. **For sin shall not have dominion over you**"* (Rm 6:10-14).

The key here is that the Christian is commanded to exercise **a choice** of their will, to be crucified with Christ (Gal 2:20) and die to the old man of sin. I repeat, a dead man cannot sin nor give place to the devil, especially if he is walking in the newness of life granted to him by Christ. Therefore, whosoever the Son of Man has made free, is free indeed, to no longer serve sin, the devil, or the lusts of his flesh (Jn 8:36, Gal 5:1).

The key to understanding this issue of whether a Christian can have a devil can be found in Roman 6:16. The Holy Ghost, reveals in Paul's writings, *"Know ye not, **that to whom ye yield yourselves servants to obey, his servants ye are to whom ye obey; whether of sin unto death, or of obedience unto righteousness?**"* Here we can clearly see that **whomsoever an individual yields his body, soul, and spirit to, that is whom he serves**. One can have the Spirit of Christ, but be led by devils in their day to day attitudes, actions, and beliefs. Christ's liberating power allows one to choose freely between good and evil. A Christian, by the power given to him by Jesus Christ (the Holy Ghost), has the ability to walk without sin *if he chooses to*. Jesus never committed sin because he never yielded His members to sin, nor gave he place to the devil. Devils do not have natural bodies to exercise their lusts and desires, so they seek humans who will yield to their influence and control. They can cause physical abnor-malities, diseases, mental illness, addictions, and give supernatural demonic powers. The Bible lists the names of many demons as they have influenced the human race since the fall of Adam. Examples would be: familiar spirits (I Sam 28:3,7), jealousy (Num 5:14), lying (II Chron 18:21), perverse (Prov 15:4), haughty (Prov 16:18), lust (Jm 4:2-4), deep sleep (Isa 29:10), heaviness (Isa 61:3), whoredom (Hos 4:12), unclean (Mt 12:43), dumb (Mk 9:17), deaf (Mk 9:25), divination (Acts 16:16), slumber (Rm 11:8), worldly (I Cor 2:12), fear (II Tim 1:7), seduction (I Tim 4:1), and antichrist (I Jn 4:3).

Christian denominations that reject the baptism of the Holy Ghost, with the evidence of speaking in tongues, cannot experience the liberation power of the Holy Ghost. Because they are bound by the sins of their flesh, their culture, unnatural appetites, heresies, and strong demonic influences, they have changed biblical spiritual realities to accommodate their carnal religious helplessness. Unfortunately it is this massive group, the religious sects of Western civilization, that have walked in denial of spiritual oppression and possession of Christians, not realizing that many of their doctrines were also given to them by devils (I Tim 4:1).

So, *can a Christian be oppressed or possessed by a devil?* We will first define the terms oppression and possession. Oppression refers to influences by demonic spirits in a particular area of one's life, but leaving the individual in control of the dominant aspects of his daily activities. For example, a person may have reoccurring battles with certain spirits such as fear, unbelief, diverse lust, erroneous doctrines, unnatural cravings, sexual perversions, phobias, mental disorders, occult bondage or depression. If not "brought in check," spiritual oppression can lead to spiritual possession. Demonic possession occurs when an area of oppression dominates the individual's daily activities and thoughts in one or more areas of his life. It can become totally consuming. **The carnally-minded does not understand that much of what is diagnosed in the realm of mental illness is simply the fruit of sin**. Whichever spiritual forces one serve they will bare the fruit of the seed that is within them. It can be unconfessed sin or sins of the family. The wages of sin is not only death (Rm 6:23), it also gives Satan and his kingdom the legal right to oppress those who rebel against God's word. This should not be an enigma, because Satan is the father of all rebels who disobey and reject the word of God. They do the works of their father (the devil) and reap the fruit of their actions (Jn 8:44).

The Lord also allows the devil (by permission) to buffet (oppress) the righteous for correction of character defects, as in the case of Job (Job 1:6-22) and the Apostle Paul (II Cor 12:1-10). Job's flesh was afflicted with boils, his possessions were taken, and his children were killed at the hands of the devil. Paul was oppressed by a spirit of infirmity that caused him to have a physical illness. Paul prophesied that demons would speak, seduce, and imbed themselves in the minds of many Christians, giving place to false doctrines and a defiled conscience. *"Now the Spirit speaketh expressly, that in the latter times some shall depart from the faith, giving heed to seducing spirits, and **doctrines of devils**; Speaking lies in hypocrisy; having their conscience seared with a hot iron."* (I Tim 4:1,2) The Apostle John exposes the religious demons that work in the church producing all manners of false doctrines. He declared that, *"we* [the apostles] *are of God: he that knoweth God heareth us; he that is not of God heareth not us. **Hereby know we the spirit of truth, and the <u>spirit of error</u>***"

131

(I Jn 4:6,). (also see I Cor 4:3,4, Jn 8:47).

Every Christian denomination has its unique spirits of error, which pervert the truth, and crystallize their identity. The Roman Catholic Church is the best example of a "Christian" organization that has virtually no biblical foundation, but uses biblical names to mask its pagan doctrines of demons. Her denominational offspring, found in Western European and American denominations, vary tremendously with an admixture of truth and error. One may become offended by such statements, if they have not studied these issues, nor compared or contrasted the bible with "Christian" pagan doctrines. The Holy Spirit that authored the Bible, and led the New Testament apostles, is not the author of pagan denominational doctrines. The following examples show that standard Roman Catholic doctrines are not biblical, nor Christian.

1. The Roman Catholic Church's teaching of celibacy for the priests, forbidding them to marry, giving themselves solely to Christ in religious service, and devotion to the church. The Apostle Paul prophetically stated hundreds of years earlier that this teaching would be a doctrine propagated by a devil. *"Now the Spirit speaketh expressly, that in the latter times some shall depart from the faith, giving heed to seducing spirits, and doctrines of devils . . . Forbidding to marry, and commanding to abstain from meats, which God hath created to be received with thanksgiving of them which believe and know the truth"* (I Tim 4:1-3). Even the Apostle Peter, whom the Catholic Church claims to be the first Pope, was married (Mk 1:29-31); Hence, there is no biblical basis for this doctrine. This may also explain why homosexuality has been a vexation to the Catholic Church for centuries.

2. The teaching that the Virgin Mary is a mediator and co-Savior with Christ refutes biblical Christian doctrine. Roman Catholicism also uses dead saints, statues, angels, and priests as mediators between man and God. However, the bible states that there is only *"one mediator between God and man, the man Christ Jesus"* (I Tim 2:5).

3. According to Catholic teachings, the Pope is the head of the church of Jesus Christ and holds the keys of the kingdom to heaven. However, the Bible states that Jesus Christ is the living God that resides as the head of His supernatural church and the savior of His body. *"And **he is the head of the body, the church**: who is the beginning, the firstborn from the dead; that in all things he might have the preeminence. For it pleased the Father that in him should all fulness dwell... Who now rejoice in my sufferings for you, and fill up that which is behind of the afflictions of Christ in my flesh **for his body's sake, which is the church**:* (Col 1:18-24)

4. The Catholic doctrine of Apostolic Succession asserts that the power of the church

was transferred from the Apostle Peter (the alleged first pope) to Gentile popes to head the Kingdom of Christ. Roman church officials fabricated this doctrine to try to legitimize their claims in an attempt to overthrow the Jewish apostles and replace their doctrines with the pagan attributes of Rome… a spiritual "coup de tat!" The term *Pope* did not surface until three hundred years after the early church's inception and was used to replace the biblical supernatural offices established by Jesus Christ (*"apostles, prophets, evangelist, pastors, and teachers"*) (Eph 4:11-13). The Apostle Paul was the apostle to the Gentiles not Peter. Paul in his epistle to the Galatians stated,

"*But contrariwise, when they saw that **the gospel of the uncircumcision [Gentiles] was committed unto me, as the gospel of the circumcision [Jews] was unto Peter;***
(For he that wrought effectually in Peter to the apostleship of the circumcision, the same was mighty in me toward the Gentiles:)
*And when James, Cephas, and John, who seemed to be pillars, perceived the grace that was given unto me, they gave to me and Barnabas the right hands of fellowship; **that we should go unto the heathen, and they unto the circumcision**.*" (Gal 2:7-9)

If the doctrine of Apostolic Succession was true and the popes acquired the power and authority of Peter then why has no Pope ever received the baptism of the Holy Ghost and cast devils out of people by the presence of their shadow like Peter did?

"***And by the hands of the apostles were many signs and wonders wrought among the people***; *(and they were all with one accord in Solomon's porch.*
And of the rest durst no man join himself to them: but the people magnified them.
And believers were the more added to the Lord, multitudes both of men and women.)
Insomuch that they brought forth the sick into the streets, and laid them on beds and couches, that at the least the shadow of Peter passing by might overshadow some of them. *There came also a multitude out of the cities round about unto Jerusalem, bringing sick folks, and them which were vexed with unclean spirits: and they were healed every one.*" (Acts 5:13-16)
Peter's shadow had more power than the powers of all of the Popes in history combined!

5. Papal Bulls and catholic teachings are given greater weight than biblical scriptures. This is extremely unfortunate for the followers of Roman church leadership, because the apostle Paul stated that, "*If any man think himself to be a prophet, or spiritual, let him acknowledge that the things that I write unto you are the*

commandments of the Lord . . . But though we, or an angel from heaven, preach any other gospel unto you than that which we have preached unto you, let him be **accursed** *[damned]. As we said before, so say I now again, If any man preach any other gospel unto you than that ye have received, let him be accursed."* (I Cor 14:37, Gal 1:8,9) The word of God is established in heaven, spoken by the prophetic Spirit of Christ, and delivered by His apostles and prophets (Acts 1:2, Jn 17:20).

6. The doctrine of the Immaculate Conception teaches that the Virgin Mary was born without sin. However, the scriptures state that *"all have sinned, and come short of the glory of God"* (Rm 3:23). This is why Mary, the mother of Jesus, had to bring her sin sacrifice of turtle doves and offer them to the priest on the eight day, according to the Law... (Lk 2:21-24, Lev 15:13-15)

7. The doctrine of Perpetual Virginity claims that Mary remained a virgin after she gave birth to Christ. The scriptures however reveal a different Mary who had at least seven children. The inhabitants of the city of Nazareth asked the question concerning Jesus, and His brothers and sisters, *"Is not this the carpenter's son? is not his mother called Mary? and his brethren, James, and Joses, and Simon, and Judas? And his sisters, are they not all with us? Whence then hath this man all these things?"* (Mt 13:55,56)

8. The doctrine of The Ascension teaches that Mary never died, but rather ascended into heaven, in the same manner as Christ. The Bible clearly states that, since Elijah the prophet, *"no man hath ascended up to heaven, but he that came down from heaven, even the Son of man which is in heaven."* (Jn 3:13)

9. Roman Catholicism claims that the priesthood of Christ on earth consists of the Pope (the Vicar of Christ or the Holy See), Cardinals, ArchBishops, priests and nuns. However, biblically, the priesthood of Jesus Christ consists of all believers, because they all have direct access to the throne of God, through Jesus Christ alone. who is their high priest. *"For we have not an high priest which cannot be touched with the feeling of our infirmities; but was in all points tempted like as we are, yet without sin.* **Let us therefore come boldly unto the throne of grace**, *that we may obtain mercy, and find grace to help in time of need . . . Ye also, as lively stones, are built up a spiritual house,* **an holy priesthood**, *to offer up spiritual sacrifices, acceptable to God by Jesus Christ. . . But ye are a chosen generation,* **a royal priesthood**, *an holy nation, a peculiar people; that ye should shew forth the praises of him who hath called you out of darkness into his marvellous light."* (Heb 4:15,16, I Pet 2:5,9)

In Romans chapter one, we were told that the Lord himself would make the temples of the tares desolate (void of His spirit) and turn them over to reprobate minds in order that they may be consumed by their evil devices (Rm 1:18-32, I Cor 3:16,17). In the book of Revelation the Lord rebukes several of the seven churches for allowing Satan to have a seat in their hearts, minds, and doctrines. The church of Smyrna walked in blasphemies and was considered the "synagogue (church) of Satan" (Rev 2:9). Could there have been devils in their midst, causing them to deviate from the truth and become a cesspool of wickedness? Without question!

At Pergamos, Satan had seats of authority and spiritual control. Some of its members even prescribed to the doctrine of Balaam, and others to the doctrine of the Nicolaitanes (which Jesus hates, Rev 2: 13-15). Thyatira walked in the spirit of Jezebel, fornication, sorcery, and "the depths of Satan" (Rev 2:20-24). It was the Apostle John who identified the spirit of Antichrist which worked in the church among rebellious Christians (I Jn 2:18,22; II Jn 7). Recently, the heresy of Hymenaeus and Philetus of the First Century church has resurfaced, in the form of the **Preterist Doctrine** ... *"And their word will eat as doth a canker: of whom is Hymenaeus and Philetus; Who concerning the truth have erred, saying that the resurrection is past already; and overthrow the faith of some. Nevertheless the foundation of God standeth sure, having this seal, The Lord knoweth them that are his. And, Let every one that nameth the name of Christ depart from iniquity"(II Tim 2:17-19).* In short, this heretical teaching to the early church espoused the idea that the resurrection of the saints had already taken place, and that there would be no future rapture, or resurrection of the saints.

Judas, the son of perdition, walked in the anointing of Christ with the other disciples for over three years before he became possessed by Satan (Lk 22:3). On the other hand, the Apostle Peter (before Christ's crucifixion), while walking in the flesh, yielded to Satan and the Lord rebuked the Devil that spoke through him.

"From that time forth began Jesus to shew unto his disciples, how that he must go unto Jerusalem, and suffer many things of the elders and chief priests and scribes, and be killed, and be raised again the third day.

Then Peter took him, and began to rebuke him, saying, Be it far from thee, Lord: this shall not be unto thee.

*But he turned, and said unto Peter, **Get thee behind me, Satan**: thou art an offence unto me: for thou savourest not the things that be of God, but those that be of men." (Mt 16:21-23)*

Carnally minded Christians will also think in agreement with the prince of darkness. They side with the devil because they cannot receive the things of the Spirit of God (Rm 8:6-8, I Cor 3:1-3, Jm 3:8-18). Plagued with the spirit of intellectualism, most European scholars and American theologians have given place to every devil imaginable in order to come up with over 25,000 denominational sects. One would need only to look at the manifestations of spiritual darkness among the members of the church, to realize the magnitude of demonic influence (**racism, homosexuality, adultery, unforgiveness, incest, worldliness, fornication, the practice of same sex marriages, witchcraft, drug additions, abortions, etc.**) practiced by members in the church. The goal of Satan is to steal, kill, and destroy every human, especially Christians who may pose a threat (Jn 10: 10). Again, demons do not have natural bodies and need human hosts to manifest their perversions and devilish desires through. If humans do not resist temptations, or the devil, by default, they leave themselves vulnerable to demonic attacks, which may result in oppression and possession.

Can a Christian be oppressed or possessed by a devil? We must conclude that, whomsoever, one yields their body, soul, and spirit to that is whom they serve (I Thes 5:23, Rm 6:12-18). Men will always be a slave to something, either enslaved by the material world, its vices and its prince, or yielded to the true and living God. If one wants to alter their eternal destiny then **they must choose their master wisely**. Every Christian that call on the name of the Lord must depart from iniquity (II Tim 2:19). If they truly believe in Christ (the bible way) they can sure up their faith and make their calling and election sure. The biblical spiritual examination for eternal security is as follows:

And hereby we do know that we know him, if we keep his commandments. He that saith, I know him, and keepeth not his commandments, is a liar, and the truth is not in him.

But whoso keepeth his word, in him verily is the love of God perfected: hereby know we that we are in him.

He that saith he abideth in him ought himself also so to walk, even as he walked.

Brethren, I write no new commandment unto you, but an old commandment which ye had from the beginning. The old commandment is the word which ye have heard from the beginning.

Again, a new commandment I write unto you, which thing is true in him and in you: because the darkness is past, and the true light now shineth.

He that saith he is in the light, and hateth his brother, is in darkness even until now.

He that loveth his brother abideth in the light, and there is none occasion of stumbling in him.

But he that hateth his brother is in darkness, and walketh in darkness, and knoweth not whither he goeth, because that darkness hath blinded his eyes.

I write unto you, little children, because your sins are forgiven you for his name's sake.

I write unto you, fathers, because ye have known him that is from the beginning. I write unto you, young men, because ye have overcome the wicked one. I write unto you, little children, because ye have known the Father.

I have written unto you, fathers, because ye have known him that is from the beginning. I have written unto you, young men, because ye are strong, and the word of God abideth in you, and ye have overcome the wicked one.

Love not the world, neither the things that are in the world. If any man love the world, the love of the Father is not in him.

For all that is in the world, the lust of the flesh, and the lust of the eyes, and the pride of life, is not of the Father, but is of the world.

And the world passeth away, and the lust thereof: but he that doeth the will of God abideth for ever.

Little children, it is the last time: and as ye have heard that antichrist shall come, even now are there." (I Jn 2:3-17)

The Timing of the Rapture and the Great Tribulation

The Bible is an enigma. It is a book shrouded in layers of prophetic mysteries declared by an omnipotent God who used men, moved by His Holy Spirit, to write facts and in codes. Thousands of individuals, scholars, and theologians have made an attempt to decode and unravel the divine mysteries to no avail; rather, human reasoning and natural intelligence has only produced more confusion, yielding over 25,000 denominational sects and Christian religious orders. The God of Israel has historically revealed Himself as the Spirit of Truth. The scriptures declare it is impossible for Him to lie; therefore, all ministers who claim to be spokespersons for Jesus Christ, likewise will not lie nor teach doctrines that war against truth. If these preachers, or alleged ambassadors of Christ, have heard from Christ concerning His Second Coming and the rapture of the church, they would be with one accord and declare identical truths.

Those who have heard from heaven and have received divine revelation concerning the end times would understand the following objectives for the rapture. The two primary purposes for the rapture are first and foremost, the wedding of the Lamb as He presents His holy bride, the church, to Himself. Second, the rapture of the church is the fulfillment of Isaiah 25:8 which is the collective defeat of the spirit of death by all of the righteous and faithful saints of Christ. The Apostle Paul, in the resurrection chapter to the Corinthians (chapter 15) stated it in this manner:

*"For as in Adam all die, even so **in Christ shall all be made alive**. But every man in his own order: **Christ the firstfruits; afterward they that are Christ's at his coming**.*

***Then cometh the end, when he shall have delivered up the kingdom [church] to God**, even the Father; when he shall have put down all rule and all authority and power.*

*For he must reign, till he hath put all enemies under his feet. **The last enemy that shall be destroyed is death.***

For he hath put all things under his feet. But when he saith all things are put under him, it is manifest that he is excepted, which did put all things under him.

***And when all things shall be subdued unto him, then shall the Son also himself be subject unto him that put all things under him, that God may be all in all**."* (I Cor 15:22-28)

In exploring this issue, we must determine which of the following views accurately states the timing of the rapture of the Church: the Pre-tribulation rapture theory, the Mid-tribulation, the Post-tribulation, the A-millennium, or the Preterist view?

The most popular and religiously correct view in the Western Christian world is the Pre-Tribulation Rapture Theory. The Pre-Tribulation Rapture Theory began in England in the 1830's by Presbyterian Pastor Edward Irvin, and was espoused throughout Europe and North America by Nelson Darby. A few of the American theologians who helped to popularize this view would include Clarence Larkin, Charles Scoffield, Hal Lindsey, and Tim Lahaye. In support of their theories developed from their Eurocentric worldview, these scholars apparently have not examined the biblical and historical facts from a non-western perspective, nor allowed their cherished beliefs to be challenged under the close scrutiny of the word of God. It is impossible for one to understand the word of God, be lead by the Spirit of Truth, and hear the Lord's voice without confronting one's own cultural biases. The Bible is a divine historical account of the past and the present, while also providing a prophetic look into the future. Those who hear God's voice will believe His report, deplore lying-traditions, obey His word, and keep themselves un-spotted from the world. However, many Christians have prescribed to the notion, *"do not bore me with the facts because my mind is already made up,"* closing their ears from hearing what the Spirit is saying to the churches.

It is also impossible for many to receive biblical truths if these truths war against their traditions. They will love one and hate the other. Many seek at all cost to defend their traditions, oftentimes even substituting tradition for truth. This (perhaps unintended) seduction takes place when *a lie is repeated often enough, and kept in circulation long enough, becoming tomorrow's prevailing truth.* Such is the case concerning the Pre-Tribulation Rapture Theory, one of the most cherished views in the Western Christian World today. Regardless of what one's view on the end times is, the divine script, which was written from the foundation of the world, shall be fulfilled. We are currently living in the last days, and all religious theories will be proven to be either true or false; hence, one's beliefs concerning the end times will either deliver him or condemn him in the last days.

The prophet Jeremiah's words were prophesied into the air of human destiny over 2600 years ago, and were not spoken idly to the wind. These same words (Rev 19:10), delivered through the eternal spirit of Christ are for today, to fulfill their prophetic declaration. Jeremiah prophesied:

"I have seen also in the prophets of Jerusalem an horrible thing: they commit adultery, and walk in lies: they strengthen also the hands of evildoers, that none doth return from his wickedness: they are all of them unto me as Sodom, and the inhabitants thereof as Gomorrah.

Therefore thus saith the LORD of hosts concerning the prophets; Behold, I will feed them with wormwood, and make them drink the water of gall: for from the prophets of Jerusalem is profaneness gone forth into all the land.

Thus saith the LORD of hosts, Hearken not unto the words of the proph-ets that prophesy unto you: they make you vain: they speak a vision of their own heart, and not out of the mouth of the LORD. They say still unto them that despise me, The LORD hath said, Ye shall have peace; and they say unto every one that walketh after the imagination of his own heart, No evil

shall come upon you.

For who hath stood in the counsel of the LORD, and hath perceived and heard his word? who hath marked his word, and heard it? Behold, a whirl-wind of the LORD is gone forth in fury, even a grievous whirlwind: it shall fall grievously upon the head of the wicked.

The anger of the LORD shall not return, until he have executed, and till he have performed the thoughts of his heart: in the latter days ye shall consider it perfectly.

I have not sent these prophets, yet they ran: I have not spoken to them, yet they prophesied.

But if they had stood in my counsel, and had caused my people to hear my words, then they should have turned them from their evil way, and from the evil of their doings. " (Jer 23:14-22)

Relatively few preachers would dare to preach from the book of Revelation with absolute certainty. Probably because, if questioned on its content, it would become obvious that they could not explain the concealed mysteries found therein. Conse-quently, many choose simply to quote what other theologians have said throughout the ages, and repeat diverse opinions, not knowing the truths of Christ themselves. **Hence, we have several generations of preachers regurgitating what they were fed but never feeding off the words of life themselves.** What many individuals fail to realize is that part of the problem with understanding the Bible is that for centuries, anti-Semitic European biblical scholars threw away the keys necessary to interpret the prophetic books. This is unfortunate for the religious masses, which place the responsibility for their biblical knowledge in the hands of their chosen clergy. They have been seduced by apathy and a false sense of security produced by their denominational doctrinal snares. Unknowingly, they will be utterly unprepared for that which is shortly to come. Due to a lack of indepth study of end time issues, most layman claim that they are not con-cerned with which view of the rapture is correct, believing with confidence, that they will be ready for either. However, their concept of readiness is a paradox, because it is impossible for one to prepare for something if he does not know how or what to prepare for, especially, if he is admonished to endure until the end! He that hath an ear, let him hear . . . *"Just as in the days of Noah, so shall also be the coming of the Son of Man."*

There is no way, that the inhabitants of the earth, prior to the flood, could have prepared themselves for the cataclysmic events that would soon follow, except they received specific instructions from the Lord of Judgment, concerning how to build an ark. Mankind, prior to the flood, had never experienced rain, thunder, or lighting. In like manner, the current inhabitants of earth are unprepared for that which lay before them. The next promised round of judgments at the end of this age would also be unprec-edented (never before experienced by mankind). If Christians could honestly hear from heaven in the same manner as Noah did, there would be no guessing, or diversity of

140

opinions concerning the subject matter of the end times. If they could hear from the Spirit of God they would all believe, know, and speak the same message.

If one seriously desires to know the truth concerning the rapture of the church to prepare himself and his family, then understanding the following mysteries is mandatory.

1. The mystery of Iniquity, the Anti-Christ (II Thes 2:5-14, Jn 17:12;6:70,Lk 22:3, Rm 1:18-28)
2. The mystery of the Godhead (I Jn 5:7, I Tim 3:16, Col 2:9, Jn 1:1-12)
3. The spirit, the water, and the blood (I Jn 5:8, Acts 2:38, Jn 3:5)
4. The Incarnation (Isa 9:6, Lk 1:26-56, Rev 13:8)
5. The kingdom of heaven, kingdom of God (Jn 3:3-8, Lk 17:20, Rm 14:17, Mk 1:14, Mt 24:14
6. The parable of the tares and wheat (Mt 13:30,36-43, Rm 1:18-2:10)
7. The Jews and the Gentiles becoming natural and spiritual Israel (Rm 2:28,29;9:2-33;10:19-11:36;11:25,26, Gal 3:27-29)
8. The Jewish prophetic feast days (Lev 23:4-44)
9. The wrath of God upon the disobedient (II Thes 1:7-9, Rm 1:18-28, Mk 9:2-8)
10. The mystery of the resurrection / translation of the saints (I Cor 15:50-56, I Thes 4:13-18, II Thes 1:3-2:17, Rev 10:7;11:7-13;20:4-15, Jn 5:25-29, Rm 8:9,11,18-23)
11. The church - Christ's bride – the early and latter rain of the Holy Ghost (Jm 5:7-9)
12. The mystery of the Image of Jealousy (Ezek 8:5-18, Rev 2,3)
13. Mystery Babylon, the harlot (Rev 17:1-8; 18:1-16)
14. The mystery of the New Jerusalem, the city of God, and the number 144,000.
15. The mystery of Israel's blindness and engrafting (Rm 11:1-36)
16. The mystery of the first and second Adam (I Cor 15:45-51, Gen 1:27;3:15, Acts 2:22-36)
17. The restitution of all things (Acts 3:21)
18. The mystery of creation, the Sabbath, and the prophetic weeks of scripture (Heb 11:3, Gen 1:1-31, II Pet 3:8, Lev 23:15-21,25:1-17)
19. The mystery of the mature sons of God and the Manchild (Zech 4:3,11-14, Rev 11:12-18, 12:5,13, Rm 8:18-23)
20. The mystery of Melchadec, the priesthood and the temple
21. The new birth and divine indwelling (Jn 3:3-8, I Cor 12:12, Acts 2:38, Lk 17:20)
22. The fullness of the Gentiles (Rm 11:25-36)
24. The manifold wisdom of God (Eph 3:3-21; 13-23, I Pet 1: 10-14, I Cor 1:17-2:16, Rm 11:8-36)
25. The mystery of the twin polar cities - Mystery Jerusalem and Mystery Babylon (Heb 11:10,16;12:22, II Cor 5:1-5, Rev 21:9-27)
26. Biblical prophetic numerology - the numbers 7, 12, 24, 144,000.

Those who desire truth and understanding of the timing of the rapture should appreciate the following sound biblical evidence, presented without an anti-Semitic

Western bias. This book also has a complementary counterpart entitled "A Divine Paradigm of the End Times." It also depicts the prophetic writings from a First Century Jewish Christian perspective. Hopefully, after examining the historical and biblical evidence concerning the timing of the rapture, contradictions found in contemporary theories should be fully exposed.

There are two primary reasons for the quickening (Rm 8:11) or rapture of the church. **The first is that it is the marriage of the bride of Christ to Christ, the bridegroom.** After receiving the early and latter rain of the Holy Ghost, the bride will be made ready for its holy groom. Jesus' method to accomplish this great task will be through the purifying fire of the Great Tribulation, purging the church of its idolatry, iniquity, and all false Christians (tares) prior to His Second Coming (II Thes 2:1). In the book of Revelation, chapter 19, this biblical sequence is revealed and clearly laid out for all to see. It begins with the wedding of Christ and the church as He gathers the faithful saints of God, both dead and alive, to meet the Lord in the air. When this wedding sequence begins, it will be followed immediately by the battle of Armageddon and conclude with the marriage supper of the Lamb.

The Wedding Sequence of the Lamb

The Marriage or Rapture:
Rev 19:6 …and I heard as it were the voice of a great multitude, and as the voice of many waters, and as the voice of mighty thunderings, saying, Alleluia: for the Lord God omnipotent reigneth.
Rev 19:7 Let us be glad and rejoice, and give honour to him: **for the marriage of the Lamb is come, and his wife hath made herself ready.**
Rev 19:8 And to her was granted that she should be arrayed in fine linen, clean and white: **for the fine linen is the righteousness of saints.**
Rev 19:9 And he saith unto me, Write, **Blessed are they which are called unto the marriage supper of the Lamb**. And he saith unto me, These are the true sayings of God.
Rev 19:10 And I fell at his feet to worship him. And he said unto me, See thou do it not: I am thy fellowservant, and of thy brethren that have the testimony of Jesus: worship God: for the testimony of Jesus is the spirit of prophecy."
 (also read the parable of the Great supper - Lk 14:15-24, The Drag net -Mt 13:47-50)

In Revelation chapter 21:9-22 we have a combination of metaphors and typologies, which reveal the wife of Jesus Christ, describing her as a city, but yet **she** is also the **measurement of a man** (Rev 21:17). For the unenlightened there appears to be a gender confusion here. However, the angel tells John, *"come hither, I will shew thee* *the bride, the Lamb's wife. And he carried me away in the spirit to a great and high mountain, and shewed me that great city, the holy Jerusalem, descending out of heaven from God" (Rev 21:9,10).* How can His bride, who becomes his wife, and have the measurement of a man, also be of the male gender? Quite easily, Christ is male, and so is His body of which He is its head. In essence, for those who can receive this revelation, it is an awesome picture of Christ and His spiritual body, presenting Himself to Himself, as the bridegroom. This multiplicity of deliverance roles in the redemption of mankind is not unique. Scripture oftentimes portray Him in many roles. Each name or title is a key indicator of His love and man's eventual salvation. Jesus Christ is a judge, an advocate, and a lamb of sacrifice for those who obey Him. We are told that at the end of the Tribulation the bride will be made ready, and counted faithful, to marry the King of Kings.

The Second Coming
Rev 19:11 And I saw heaven opened, and **behold a white horse; and he that sat upon him was called Faithful and True, and in righteousness he doth judge and make war**.

Rev 19:12 His eyes were as a flame of fire, and on his head were many crowns; and he had a name written, that no man knew, but he himself.

Rev 19:13 And he was clothed with a vesture dipped in blood: and his name is called The Word of God.

Rev 19:14 **And the armies which were in heaven followed him upon white horses, clothed in fine linen, white and clean.**

Rev 19:15 And out of his mouth goeth a sharp sword, that with it he should smite the nations: and he shall rule them with a rod of iron: and he treadeth the winepress of the fierceness and wrath of Almighty God.

Rev 19:16 And he hath on his vesture and on his thigh a name written, **KING OF KINGS, AND LORD OF LORDS.**

The Marriage Supper of the Lamb
Rev 19:17 **And I saw an angel standing in the sun; and he cried with a loud voice, saying to all the fowls that fly in the midst of heaven, Come and gather yourselves together unto the supper of the great God;**

Rev 19:18 **That ye may eat the flesh of kings, and the flesh of captains, and the flesh of mighty men, and the flesh of horses, and of them that sit on them, and the flesh of all men, both free and bond, both small and great.**

And I saw the beast, and the kings of the earth, and their armies, gathered together to make war against him that sat on the horse, and against his army.

Rev 19:20 And **the beast was taken, and with him the false prophet that wrought miracles before him, with which he deceived them that had received the mark of the beast**, and them that worshipped his image. These both were cast alive into a lake of fire burning with brimstone.

143

Rev 19:21 **And the remnant were slain with the sword of him that sat upon the horse, which sword proceeded out of his mouth: and all the fowls were filled with their flesh.**

(Also see Mt 24:27,28, The marriage feast is also called -The Feast of Fat Things Isa 25:6)

Ezek 39:1 …Thus saith the Lord GOD; Behold, I am against thee, O Gog, the chief prince of Meshech and Tubal:

Ezek 39:2 And I will turn thee back, and leave but the sixth part of thee, and will cause thee to come up from the north parts, and will bring thee upon the mountains of Israel:

Ezek 39:3 And I will smite thy bow out of thy left hand, and will cause thine arrows to fall out of thy right hand.

Ezek 39:4 **Thou shalt fall upon the mountains of Israel, thou, and all thy bands, and the people that is with thee: I will give thee unto the ravenous birds of every sort, and to the beasts of the field to be devoured.**

Eze 39:5 Thou shalt fall upon the open field: for I have spoken it, saith the Lord GOD. . .

Ezek 39:17 And, thou son of man, thus saith the Lord GOD; **Speak unto every feathered fowl, and to every beast of the field, Assemble yourselves, and come; gather yourselves on every side to my sacrifice that I do sacrifice for you, even a great sacrifice upon the mountains of Israel, that ye may eat flesh, and drink blood.**

Ezek 39:18 **Ye shall eat the flesh of the mighty, and drink the blood of the princes of the earth,** of rams, of lambs, and of goats, of bullocks, all of them fatlings of Bashan.

Ezek 39:19 And ye shall eat fat till ye be full, and drink blood till ye be drunken, of my sacrifice which I have sacrificed for you.

Ezek 39:20 **Thus ye shall be filled at my table with horses and chariots, with mighty men, and with all men of war, saith the Lord GOD.**

Ezek 39:21 And I will set my glory among the heathen, and all the heathen shall see my judgment that I have executed, and my hand that I have laid upon them.

Ezek 39:22 So the house of Israel shall know that I am the LORD their God from that day and forward.

The second reason for the quickening of the saints into the realm of immortality is to allow all Christians to collectively defeat the spirit of death. This will happen for all of the dead in Christ only once, thus fulfilling Isaiah 25:8. If Revelation chapter 19 did not answer the question sufficiently as to the sequence of events concerning the rapture, the wedding, the Second Coming of Christ and the marriage feast of the Lamb, then a closer examination of the timing and sequence of the rapture would be necessary. Hence,

144

the following full examination of the evidence should be helpful for those who desire more evidence and an understanding of the truth.

1. The Rapture shall take place at the Last Trump

The only scriptures in the entire Bible that emphatically state when the rapture will take place are found in I Cor 15:51,52. We are told by the Holy Ghost (through the Apostle Paul) that,

"Behold I show you a mystery; We shall not all sleep, but we shall be changed,

In a moment, in the twinkling of an eye, at the Last Trump: for the trump shall sound, and the dead shall be raised incorruptible, and we shall be changed."

The change from mortality to immortality occurs at the last trump. The pre-tribulation rapture theory is an intellectual and mathematical oxymoron. The last trump is exactly that . . . the last of the seven trumpets clearly stated in the book of Revelation. How can the Pre-Tribulationist conclude that the rapture takes place before any of the trumpets are blown, when we are told in the scriptures, that it occurs at the last trumpet? Surely, this is an example of pure intellectual dishonesty?

Mathematical sequencing should clearly reveal that the *last trump* could not take place before the *first trump* is blown. The primary key needed to unlock the secrets concerning the timing of the rapture of the church can be easily established by determining the timing of the last trump. In the book of Revelation we are told that there are seven trumps, which are judgments, that shall be inflicted upon the inhabitants of the earth. The Apostle John tells us that at the last, or seventh trump, the mystery of God will be fulfilled (Rev 10:7). The pre-tribulation rapture doctrine totally ignores the seven-trumpet indicator because it places the mystery of the fulfillment before the first trumpet is blown. However, we will see beyond any shadow of doubt, that **the last trump takes place at the end of the tribulation period,** thus fulfilling all Messianic prophesies. Again, if there is logic in proper sequence, how can the last trump take place before the first (Rev 8:3-11:16)? This is what would have to occur in order to support the pre- or mid- tribulation rapture theories.

In the eleventh chapter of the book of Revelation, we are told that a voice from heaven will call up the dead, beginning with the slain Manchild witnesses of Christ. They will hear the voice of the Lord beckoning them to "come up hither" (Rev 11:11-15). After the Manchild finishes their testimony (ministry) and are killed, three and a half days will elapse before they rise to their feet in the presence of world leaders. All of the dead in Christ will rise with them (Rev 11:7-11). Immediately thereafter, the saints who are alive at this time shall be changed from mortality to immortality, and together they shall meet the Lord in the air. They shall meet Christ because it is His Second Coming (I Thes 2:2-7;1:7-9). The resurrection of the dead and the translation of the living **take**

place only once and **at the same time**. This is the rapture. Their resurrection from the dead will be the corporate defeat of death by Christ through the saints. The defeat of death by Jesus Christ was a typology of that which was to come (Heb 2:12-16). The fact of the matter is that the last trump takes place only once, and it **occurs at the end of the tribulation**.

Again, it is impossible for the rapture to occur before the tribulation begins. A biblical check and balance can be found as the Apostle Paul addresses this issue by quoting the Prophet Isaiah (Isa 25:8). He expounds with greater revelation by the Holy Ghost to the Greek church at Corinth.

For this corruptible must put on incorruption, and this mortal must put on immortality.

So when this corruptible shall have put on incorruption, and this mortal shall have put on immortality, ***then shall be brought to pass the saying that is written, Death is swallowed up in victory.***

O death, where is thy sting? O grave, where is thy victory?
(I Cor 15:53-55)

The Apostle Paul sheds more light on this subject when he informs the church at Thessalonica that,

I would not have you to be ignorant, brethren, concerning them which are asleep, that ye sorrow not, even as others which have no hope.

For if we believe that Jesus died and rose again, even so them also which are asleep in Jesus will God ***bring with him***.

For this we say unto you by the word of the Lord, that we which are alive and remain unto the coming of the Lord shall not prevent them which are asleep.

For the ***Lord Himself shall descend from heaven with a shout, with the voice of the archangel, and with the trump of God:*** *and the dead in Christ shall rise first:*

Then ***we which are alive and remain shall be caught up together with them in the clouds, to meet the Lord in the air:*** *and so shall we ever be with the Lord.* (I Thes 4:13-17)

Again, **the rapture takes place only once**, fulfilling the prophecy of Isaiah, and it occurs at the end of the tribulation. To state, or continue to believe otherwise, after examining this fixed time marker (the last trump) could be classified as willful ignorance and intellectual dishonesty.

Could there be another biblical check and balance that can further verify these facts? We are told by the Apostle John that the Manchild witnesses will have a ministry that last 1260 days (or 42 months, which is three and a-half years according to the Jewish calendar) before they are killed. Their ministry will mirror that of Christ's . . .

146

three and a half years of preaching the kingdom of God (Mk 1:14), then after they finish their testimonies they will be slain (Rev 11:7, also as Christ was). Jesus was raised from the dead on the third day, and they will likewise be raised on the third day (Rev 11:11), to corporately defeat death (with the resurrected and translated saints).

The ministry of the Manchild will be to judge the kingdom of the Dragon (Satan) with signs and wonders. Satan will also be granted three and a half years to reign over the rebellious inhabitants of earth and persecute the saints (Rev 11:6,14; 13:5,7,10; 12:10,11,13,14; 7:7-17; 14:11-13; 15:1-3; 20:4). He will try the hearts of the wicked, he will cause a falling away amongst members in the church, and lead an insurrection uniting those who are his tares in Christ's kingdom/church (Mt 13:38-41, II Thes 2:3-13).

The Prophet Daniel goes even further and reveals to us the name of the archangel that will **blow the last trump**, ushering in the rapture of the church (Dan 12:1,2). He is identified as **Michael**, the prince of the Lord's people. What few fail to realize is that the rapture of the church is actually the wedding of the bride of Christ. The wedding takes place after the church has been purified of her sins and made without spot, wrinkle, or blemish during the wash cycle of the tribulation period (I Jn 3:2-16, Eph 5:27-32, I Cor 11:3, Heb 12:5-29). The Apostle John speaks to this issue by stating, *"we are the sons of God, and it does not yet appear what we shall be: but we know that, when he shall appear, we shall be like him; for we shall see him as he is. And every man that hath this hope in him purifieth himself, even as he is pure."* (I Jn 3:2,3)

Jesus' bride, the church, shall **meet Him at His Second Coming (in the air)**, at His Holy alter in the clouds of heaven (I Thes 4:17, II Thes 2:1). Christ will not be returning simply to take His church back to heaven as most Western theological theories suppose, but rather, to bring them with Him to avenge their deaths at the Battle of Armageddon. The **Marriage Feast of the Lamb** will take place after this great slaughter of vengeance at His Second Coming. The Lord of Host will gather from the four corners of the earth, the birds of prey and all manner of scavenger birds, to feast on the carcasses of the wicked (Rev 19:17-19, Isa 25:6). In fact, the saints slain during the tribulation (who overcame the Anti-Christ by the blood of the Lamb and the word of their testimony, Rev 7:9-17;13:7;12:9-17) are told by the Lord to wait until their fellow brethren (the Manchild) is slain; then their deaths will be avenged (Rev 6:9-11).

2. The Tares are gathered before the Wheat.

The two primary coordinates necessary to determine when the rapture takes place is its exact timing and the sequence of events that lead up to it. The proponents of the Pre-Tribulation Rapture theory would go to great lengths to justify their theology, even discrediting Christ. The noted theologian, **Charles Schoffield, in defense of the Pre-Tribulation Theory, actually claimed that Jesus made a mistake (lied)** when He gave the parable of the sower and the seed. In order to justify his theological stance,

Schoffield claimed in his study notes, that Jesus should have stated in this parable that **He would gather the wheat first**, **then the tares** (reversing the order). Schoffield had to make such a false statement in order to make his theory work.

Ever since the early eighteenth century, up until now, Western theologians such as Irvin, Darby, Larkin, Hal Lindsey, and Tim La Hay have propagated this blatant doctrinal error. The scriptures clearly state that the wheat represents the righteous saints and the tares are the saints (Christians, who are actually children of the devil, just like Judas, Jn 6:70). The tares were sown in the kingdom of God, and destined to be separated from the wheat, and destroyed at the end of the world.

Again, the popular Pre-Tribulation Rapture Theory alleges that the church (wheat) must be gathered first, then the tares (wicked) in order to justify their theory. However, to the contrary Jesus stated that,

"Nay; lest while ye gather up the tares, ye root up also the wheat with them. Let both grow together until the harvest: and in the time of harvest I will say to the reapers, ***Gather ye together first the tares****, and bind them in bundles to burn them: but gather the wheat into my barn. (Mt 13:29,30)*

The field is the world; the good seed are the children of the kingdom; but the tares are the children of the wicked one;
The enemy that sowed them is the devil; the harvest is the end of the world*; and the reapers are the angels.*
As therefore the ***tares are gathered and burned in the fire; so shall it be in the end of the world.***
The Son of man shall send forth his angels, and ***they shall gather out of his kingdom all things that offend, and them that do iniquity;***
And shall cast them into a furnace of fire: there shall be wailing and gnashing of teeth.
Then shall the righteous shine forth as the sun in the kingdom of their Father. Who hath ears to hear, let him hear." (Mt 13:38-43)

The sequence of events preceding the rapture should not be in dispute; however, those who have hearts not to receive truth can not hear what the spirit is saying to the church. According to Jesus the tares would be gathered **before** the wheat in the last days. This gathering of those who abide in sin, out of His kingdom (the church) at the end of the world, is for judgment and the purification of his temple (I Cor 3:16,17). If we are to be biblically correct, we must accept the fact that the gathering of the tares will precede the gathering (or rapture) of the church. This would nullify the primary assumption upon which most end time prophetic theories are based. Hence, the wicked in Christ's church, and the righteous in His kingdom, must both be present at the same time throughout the tribulation in order for the Lord to complete His purposes.

We have been told by the Apostle Peter that **judgment will first take place in the**

House of God (I Pet 4:17). It will not begin with the world, as many have deluded themselves to believe with self-fulfilling prophecies that will never materialize. We are told by the Apostle John that this world is already judged (Jn 3:17-21). Again, **the rapture of the church takes place at the end of the tribulation**, at the last trump, and after the gathering of the tares out of the kingdom.

All of the parables of the kingdom speak to the same end with absolute consistency: **The Leaven** Lk 13:20,21, **The Drag Net** Mt 13:47-50, **The Talents** Mt 25:14-30, **The Pounds** Lk 19:11-27, **The Great Supper** Lk 14:155-24, **The Ten Virgins** Mt 25:1-13, **The Strait Gate** (Lk 13:24-30, **The Unfaithful Servant** Lk 12:42-48, **The Watchful Porter** Mt 24:45-51, **The Master of the House** Lk 12:35-40, **The Husbandman** Mt 21:33-46, **The Separation of the Sheep and the Goat**.

In short, it should be quite obvious that Jesus did not make a mistake as Scoffield and others have chosen to believe; but rather, men have contorted the scriptures in their minds to their own destruction, in order to fit their self-serving doctrines (II Pet 3:16, Tit 1:15,16). The church's rebellious tares, which from their outward appearance appear to be identical to the righteous, will be exposed in the heat of tribulation. The Lord will cleanse His temple of those who do wickedness, and those who obey not the gospel of the kingdom (I Thes 1:7-9, Gal 1:8,9). Ezekiel states that the judgment of God will begin in the Lord's sanctuary, starting with church elders (Ezek 9:4-11).

3. The Lord will gather (rapture) His elect immediately after the tribulation of those days.

Another key location found in scripture that specifically states the timing of the rapture is found in the book of Matthew. Unfortunately, there are many that view the scriptures through the eyes of their own knowledge filters, which may not allow them to see and understand verses, which may be contrary to their biblical worldview. This selective process causes them to be willfully ignorant of biblical truths. Hopefully, without allowing biased knowledge filters constructed in the minds of men let us now examine what Jesus said about the timing of the rapture in the following verses.

" *Immediately after the tribulation of those days shall the sun be darkened, and the moon shall not give her light, and the stars shall fall from the heaven, and the powers of the heavens shall be shaken:*
And then shall appear the sign of the Son of man in heaven: and then shall all the tribes of the earth mourn, **and they shall see the Son of man coming in the clouds of heaven** *with power and great glory.*
And **he shall send his angels with a great sound of a trumpet, and they shall gather together his elect** *from the four winds, from one end of heaven to the other.*" (Mt 24:29-31)

It should be without controversy, that the statement "*immediately after the tribulation*" would mean anything other than what is stated. However, many choose to be contrary. Again we are clearly told by the Lord Himself that He will send His angels to gather His elect, His bride (the church), with the sound of a trumpet. And as we have seen previously in Paul's letter to the Corinthians, it will occur **at the last trump**. The last trump occurs at the end of the tribulation, at Christ's Second Coming. It is when all the inhabitants of the earth shall mourn when they see the King of Glory coming with His saints in their glorified bodies. This occurs after the Manchild and kingdom church has defeated death (the first resurrection).

Unfortunately, **it appears that when there is no persecution, the church becomes infested with the weeds of false growth, heresies, and the religious pride of men stunting its growth**. For the sake of the righteous, the Lord has given them grace, knowing that there "*shall be great tribulation, such as was not since the beginning of the world to this time, no, nor ever shall be. And except those days should be shortened, there should no flesh be saved: but for the elect's sake those days shall be shortened.*" (Mt 24:21,22)

4. The prophet Joel and the Apostle Peter identify the events that begin and conclude the Church Age.

Another very important clue is given to establish a time frame for the rapture: the atmospheric signs concerning the moon and the sun, as was first given by the Prophet Joel in approximately 700 BC. Then in 31 AD, the prophecy was repeated by the Apostle Peter, on the Day of Pentecost, when the church initially began. **In four verses Joel and Peter stated the events which would begin the church age and the events that would conclude it**.

In other words, Joel and Peter (Joel 2:28-30, Acts 2:17,18) stated the event that would birth the kingdom church into existence. This supernatural spiritual kingdom/church was established by Christ on the Jewish Feast Day of Pentecost and was miraculously signified by the evidence of speaking in other tongues.

"*But this is that which was spoken by the prophet Joel;*
And it shall come to pass in the last days, saith God, I will pour out of my Spirit upon all flesh: and your sons and your daughters shall prophesy, and your young men shall see visions, and your old men shall dream dreams:
And on my servants and on my handmaidens I will pour out in those days of my Spirit; and they shall prophesy:" (Acts 2:16-18)

In reference to the conclusion of the church age we are told by Jesus (Mt 24:30), Joel (Joel 2:31-32), and by the Apostle Peter (Acts 2:19,20) that there would be atmospheric signs in the heavens. These signs would follow immediately after the tribulation of those days, or in other words, at the end of the tribulation. The Arch Angel Michael will at that time, blow the trump of God to gather God's elect, and all saints shall meet Christ in the air.

" *And I will shew wonders in heaven above, and signs in the earth beneath;* **blood, and fire, and vapour of smoke: The sun shall be turned into darkness, and the moon into blood**, *before that notable day of the Lord come.*" (Acts 2:19,20)

Also notice that the last two verses are associated with the day of the Lord (His day of wrath and judgment) which culminates at the end of the age (the notable day of the Lord). The Apostle Paul calls this day of wrath, "**the Evil Day**" (Eph 6:13). Also see Rev 6:12-17, Joel 3:10-17;2:2-10, Mk 13:24-26.

In the Book of Revelation, the Apostle John states the exact same atmospheric wonders as: "the 6th seal" (Rev 6:12-17). If one would simply allow the scriptures to speak for themselves, instead of trying to prove a pre-conceived bias, the truth of a matter can be easily obtained. If one's interpretation of the scriptures does not bare witness with the testimony of Jesus, the prophets, and the Jewish apostles, then it is likely that his revelations came from another spirit, contrary to the spirit of Christ (II Cor 11:4,11-13, Eph 2:20, II Cor 4:3,4).

5. There is only one rapture appointed for the righteous . . . not multiple raptures or multiple resurrections.

The pre-tribulation rapture theory has a major mathematical flaw, of which basic elementary math would prove it to be incorrect. Theologians who profess their belief in a pre-tribulation rapture theory claim that there will be a rapture at the beginning of the tribulation, perhaps one midway through the tribulation, and another rapture at the end of the tribulation for those who are "left behind." Thus we would have at least two and perhaps three raptures for the living. This belief is totally contradictory to what Jesus stated in the Gospel of John. Jesus states that there will **be only two resurrections appointed for mankind**. There is **only one resurrection for the living** and **one resurrection for the dead**. These resurrections also happen only once.

Verily, verily, I say unto you, The hour is coming, and now is, **when the dead shall hear the voice of the Son of God: and they that hear shall live** . . .
Marvel not at this: for the hour is coming, in the which all that are in the graves shall hear his voice,
And shall come forth; **they that have done good, onto the resurrection of life; and they that have evil, unto the resurrection of damnation**. (Jn 5:25-29)

Jesus, as the Lord of the resurrection, established definitive parameters for the rapture. If anyone should know, it should be Him, since it will be at His command through the archangel that these events will occur. He states that there will be **only one resurrection** for the living and **one resurrection for the dead** (damned). Not two or three resurrections for the living, followed by single or multiple resurrections for the damned. In the book of Revelation, the Apostle John (by Revelation of the Holy Ghost) expounded on this matter with further insight, by giving a specific timeline for these events to be fulfilled. He reveals that the **first resurrection** takes place at the end of the tribulation period. It is for all righteous saints who have died in Christ throughout the ages. He also mentions that the overcomers would get their victory over the Antichrist, by the blood of the Lamb and the Word of their testimony (Rev 20:4; 7:9-17; 6:9-11; 14:11-13; 15:1-3, Dan 7:21,25; 8:23,24).

John also speaks of the **second resurrection** that will take place at the end of the 1,000-year Millennium reign of Christ. It is at this time that the wicked, not found in the book of Life, shall be brought before the throne of judgment and be judged according to their works. After their divine trial, they will be cast into the eternal hell, the Lake of Fire and Brimstone, which burns forever (Rev 20:4-15). To teach contrary to these expressly established guidelines would be a tremendous error and (according to the scriptures) will result in grave consequences (Rev 22:18,19).

Many may choose not to study these issues because they may be confusing to them; however, the Bible commands Christians to work out their own salvation with fear and trembling (Phil 2:12). If the Christian masses continue to follow Christian celebrities and blind leaders, they shall all fall into the ditch of destruction (Mt 15:14). Those who choose not to study and show themselves approved unto God cannot blame theologians for their eternal fate (II Tim 2:15). Therefore, being deceived, unprepared, and lost, many shall depart from the faith during the tribulation, which will constitute the great falling away spoken of by the Apostle Paul (II Thes 2:3).

6. **The Jewish feast days also give an exact sequence and timeframe for the rapture of the church.**

Another Jewish prophetic key to establish the timing of the rapture is securely anchored in the seven Jewish feast days. These seven Jewish holy days take place over a seven-month period, and were prophetic declarations of the redemptive work of the Jewish Messiah. Moses recorded these divinely established holidays of the Law in the twenty-third chapter of the Book of Leviticus. **The first four feast days, Passover, Unleaven Bread, First Fruit, and Pentecost were all fulfilled on the exact day of their Jewish observance by Jesus Christ**, in 31 AD. For example, Jesus was the Passover Lamb (April 14, Lev 23:5), and He fulfilled the feast of Unleaven Bread being without sin (April 15, Lev 23:6, I Pet 2:22). He also fulfilled the feast of First Fruit by being the first to defeat death by the resurrection from the grave (April 16, Lev 23:10, I Cor 15:20). The fourth feast day was fulfilled exactly on the day of Pentecost (June 6, Lev 23:15,16, Act 2:1-42). It was on this day, fifty days after the Passover that Christ poured out His Spirit on the Day of Pentecost, baptizing over 120 believers with His Spirit in Jerusalem. This event birthed individuals into His kingdom and baptized them into His church. **If the first four feast days were fulfilled exactly on the day established by the Law of Moses, we could safely conclude that the last three will not break the prophetic pattern.**

The last three feast days are **Trumpets** (Oct 1, Lev 23:24), **Atonement** (Oct 10th, Lev 23:27), and **Tabernacle** (Oct 15, Lev 23:34) and they will be fulfilled in the following manner. The fulfillment of the Feast of Trumpets occurs at the rapture of the church (with the last trump), at the end of the tribulation period. The last of the seven feasts, **Tabernacle, will be fulfilled only two weeks after the last trumpet**. The significance of this is quite profound, because the Feast of Tabernacle ushers in the establishment of the Millennial Kingdom of Christ, **only two weeks after the rapture of the church takes place, not seven years later**. The Pre-Tribulation Rapture Theory teaches that there will be a seven-year gap between the rapture and the 1,000-year reign of Christ. This Eurocentric model does not fit the Jewish prophetic biblical pattern. Between the feasts of Trumpets and Tabernacle is the Feast of Atonement, which signifies the deliverance of both natural Israel (the Jews) and spiritual Israel (the church) from their sins. They become one in Christ through the tribulation. Together they will join Christ in marriage at His Second Coming.

In conclusion, **the Jewish Feast days are a precise and accurate prophetic testimony of the fact that the rapture of the Church, and the millennial reign of Christ are separated by only two weeks, not seven years** (thus nullifying any contrary view).

7. **The Gospel of the Kingdom must be preached until the end of the Church Age and then the end will come.**

And this gospel of the kingdom shall be preached in all the world for a witness unto all nations; and then shall the end come. (Mt 24:14)

In order to justify eighteen hundred years of theology associated with Christianity, and rooted in pagan Greek and Roman culture, contemporary Christian scholars continue to dominate the world's seminaries and church doctrines. In conjunction with the media, and the control methods of corporate literature distribution, they further propagate their errors and consistently misrepresent sound biblical truths. The net result is a multitude of European based churches with over 25,000 Christian sects worldwide. These numbers are absolutely ludicrous. How is it possible that so many religious groups be established from one book, the Bible? Surely all those who call themselves Christians do not know the God of Israel. They must not be cognizant of the fact that *"it is a fearful thing to fall into the hands of the living God"* of Israel (Heb 10:31;12:29); therefore, they believe, and do whatsoever they choose, without fear.

153

We are told in scripture that God is not the author of confusion (I Cor 14:33), yet there are over 25,000 religious sects, all claiming to be Christians. This paradox has caused mega-confusion. Many have forgotten (or have not come to realize) that Jesus Christ is also the God of the Old Testament. European Christianity accepts the love of God through Christ in the New Testament, but it negates the fact that Christ is both perfect love and perfect judgement. If one does not obey Him, or the words of the prophets, he will surely discover His wrath. God is no respecter of persons (Rm 2:11, Acts 10:34).

The Western world, through many wars and acts of genocide over doctrinal issues, developed the concept of Christianity to allow for many denominations to exist within their respective national borders. However, at the beginning of the church age this confusion did not exist. The widely accepted concept of denominationalism is foreign to the Bible, and only clouds the issue in discussing end time events, and discovering biblical truths. For example, since no denomination is found in the Bible, which denomination will Christ return for? Which racial, ethnic, or national church will be raptured? In the beginning, such carnal division did not exist in the church. For the first ten years of church history, it was a Jewish phenomena, then later the Gentiles were granted salvation (Acts10:1-11:18). Eventually, after the death of the Jewish apostles the Gentiles took over the church and perverted many of its doctrines.

In the Bible the Jewish Christian church, headed by the apostles of Jesus Christ, all preached the exact same thing. In fact, **the term Christian was initially applicable only to those who abided in the Apostles' doctrines** (Acts 11:26, 2:42). Since Christianity does not support the apostles' doctrines, it should not be considered a strange thing, that its leaders cannot decipher the prophetic word. If there are divisions in the church, then there must be heresies amongst its leaders' denominational doctrines contrary to the commandments delivered by the Jewish apostles (I Cor 1:10; 14:37, Acts 1:2; Jn 17:20; I Jn 4:6, Acts 20:28,29).

Regardless of whether the Apostle Paul sent a letter to the Corinthians, the Galatians, the Romans, or the Christians at Ephesus; throughout the Roman Empire, there was only one gospel, and it was called the Gospel of the Kingdom. It consisted of three components to establish the covenant: the spirit, the water, and the blood (I Jn 5:8, Jn 3:5). The gospel of the kingdom was first preached on the day of Pentecost. The Apostle Peter preached to Jews throughout the Roman Empire, commanding them to repent, and be baptized by immersion in water, in the name of Jesus Christ, and receive the baptism of the Holy Ghost with the evidence of speaking in other tongues (Acts 2:38-42; 8:12-14; 10:44-48; 19:1-7; 11:1-18). If one can not understand, but chooses to refute and disobey the basic doctrines of the apostles, then how can they comprehend the deeper things of the spirit? **Perhaps the reason why few can understand the prophetic books is because the Bible was not written to denominational Christians, Catholics, Orthodox, or Protestants. It was written only to those who abided in the First Century apostles' doctrines.**

John the Baptist, Jesus, and the New Testament disciples all preached the kingdom gospel established by the blood, the water, and the spirit (I Jn 5:8, Acts 2:38,8:12, Mk 1:14, Mt 3:11). They preached the same message in content, but it was not fulfilled until the day of Pentecost when the power of the kingdom and the Lord's presence indwelled them. Their message also caused them their lives as they prophesied to their accusers of their future fate. In the last days, many shall be brought before world leaders to be a testimony against them at the Day of Judgment and prophesy against them concerning the glorious works of Christ. Jesus connected the end time preaching of the gospel of the kingdom with the persecution of the saints and the antichrist kingdom. Jesus instructed the Christians during the tribulation to do the following when these events occur:

*"But take heed to yourselves: **for they shall deliver you up to councils; and in the synagogues ye shall be beaten: and ye shall be brought before rulers and kings for my sake, for a testimony against them.***

And the gospel must first be published among all nations. But when they shall lead you, and deliver you up, take no thought beforehand what ye shall speak, neither do ye premeditate: but whatsoever shall be given you in that hour, that speak ye: for it is not ye that speak, but the Holy Ghost.

Now the brother shall betray the brother to death, and the father the son; and children shall rise up against their parents, and shall cause them to be put to death.

And ye shall be hated of all men for my name's sake: but he that shall endure unto the end, the same shall be saved.

But when ye shall see the abomination of desolation, spoken of by Daniel the prophet, standing where it ought not.". (Mk 13:9-14)

There should be no dispute after reading these verses that Jesus connects the tribulation period with the persecution, the betrayal, and prophesying of the saints before the global government of the Antichrist. If Gentile denominational Christians were led by the same spirit that gave these revelations, inspiration, and authority to the apostles, they would no doubt confirm their teachings. Instead, they establish their own gospels, doctrines, and crystallizing religious movements. Moreover, cultural traditions, racism, ethnocentrism, and pagan practices have misguided most religious leaders. Apparently these leaders have heard the voice of another Jesus, and not that of the biblical Christ. Of course, this substitution with another Jesus and change of authority can only produce interpretations and explanations not declared by the Jewish apostles and prophets. These gospels are authored by another sprit that wars against the Spirit of Truth (II Cor 11:4,13,14). Even though Jesus is preached throughout the world, the question still remains, which Jesus do most Christians believe? Will it be the Jesus of Roman Catholicism, Mormonism, the Ku Klux Klan, the Jehovah Witnesses, the Freemasons, or Islam.

In God's preordained knowledge, He knew from the foundation of the world,

155

the state of affairs the church would be in prior to His Second Coming. He knew that men would heap disciples after themselves, **hirelings,** who would scatter and segregate the sheep for their own selfish exploits (Rm 16:17,18, II Tim 3:1-7; 4:2-4). Therefore, the Spirit of Truth has ordained that doctrinal purity must be restored in His church, purging it of its present darkness, lies, apostasies and iniquity. Then will their blindness be abated and men will know and experience the truth concerning the end times.

Two thousand years ago, the Apostle Peter prophesied concerning the end times, that deceitful men would try and take over the church and speak evil of the commandments and foundations that they had laid (II Pet 2:1,2). The Apostle Paul wrote to Timothy stating that in the latter days, *"many shall depart from the faith giving heed to seducing spirits and doctrines of devils"* (I Tim 4:1).

The rapture of the church will not take place until Western Christianity repents of its doctrinal errors and obey the commandments delivered initially on the Day of Pentecost by the Apostle Peter (Acts 2:38-42). In conclusion, **it was the gospel of the kingdom that began the church age and it shall also conclude it**. The Jews first delivered the gospel of salvation, then the grace of God extended it to the Gentiles (Acts 11:1-18). In the last days it will be the Gentiles who will restore this same gospel to natural Israel.

8. The Manchild remnant and the Philadelphian church will judge the world and the angels.

The Apostle Paul informs the church at Corinth that *"ye shall judge the world. Know ye not that ye shall judge the angels?"* (I Cor 6:2,3)

From the foundation of the world God chose the planet earth to be the location whereby He would judge the natural and spiritual realms of existence. It is His appointed time to destroy all forms of rebellion and disobedience in the cosmos. Satan and his kingdom of darkness have been destined by the Creator to be cast down to earth (Rev 12:12), for three and a half years, during the tribulation to be judged. Most of the inhabitants of the earth are totally unaware that they, and their souls, are in the middle of this great conflict between heaven and hell. The prophesied divine solution to this spiritual and galactic conflict is the unveiling of the mature remnant of the church. These individuals will collectively manifest the Spirit of Christ without measure, and will for 42 months, systematically destroy Satan's kingdom. The Apostle John reveals to us that these mature sons of God will follow the voice of the Lamb, and bring on the judgments of God as often as they will, to torment the inhabitants of the whole earth (Rev 11:10). The first century apostles did the works of Jesus, and many thereafter have done the same; however, "the greater works" (Jn 14:12) promised by Christ has been reserved for the end times.

The supernatural showdown between the Manchild, the Philadelphian Church, the

Archangel Michael, and the heavenly hosts against Satan and his demonic kingdom, will soon commence. The church has a high calling but it has been seduced through fear, carnality, ignorance, and tradition, into a comatose state right before its greatest moment of triumph. This result is most likely due to its acceptance of the Pre-Tribulation Rapture Theory.

The following disclosure by Jesus Christ concerning the end times states that the saints of God would testify and prophesy under the unction of the Holy Ghost, during the tribulation period. **According to Christ, true Christians will be a testimony against leaders of the world government false religious systems, and the Antichrist, to solidify their pending demise and eternal judgment.** The gospel of the kingdom will be preached to evangelize the world during this time and brother will betray brother during this day of great turmoil. Its present thick darkness will give the righteous an opportunity to shine as the sun in a dark world.

And when ye shall hear of wars and rumours of wars, be ye not troubled: for such things must needs be; but the end shall not be yet.

For nation shall rise against nation, and kingdom against kingdom: and there shall be earthquakes in divers places, and there shall be famines and troubles: these are the beginnings of sorrows.

*But take heed to yourselves: **for they shall deliver you up to councils; and in the synagogues ye shall be beaten: and ye shall be brought before rulers and kings for my sake, for a testimony against them.***

*And the gospel must first be published among all nations. **But when they shall lead you, and deliver you up, <u>take no thought beforehand what ye shall speak, neither do ye premeditate: but whatsoever shall be given you in that hour, that speak ye: for it is not ye that speak, but the Holy Ghost.</u>***

*Now the brother shall betray the brother to death, and the father the son; and children shall rise up against their parents, **and shall cause them to be put to death**.*

And ye shall be hated of all men for my name's sake: but he that shall endure unto the end, the same shall be saved." (Mk 13:7-13)

The First Century Christian church was a supernatural church until Western Christianity transformed it into the powerless hierarchical churches of apostate men. Their religious and doctrinal errors have played directly into the hands of Satan. He is the author of all deviant religions contrary to the truths of the God of Israel. Satan counterfeits the truth and substitutes religion for a relationship with the true and living God (Gal 1:8,9, I Cor 14:37, II Cor 4:3,4).

The first thing Satan inspired the religious European churches to do was to reject the baptism of the Holy Ghost and the supernatural gifts of the spirit, as part of the New Testament Covenant. If he were going to be successful at attacking the church, he would first have to join it and then cut it off from its supernatural power base.

The Holy Ghost is Jesus Christ after His resurrection, dwelling supernaturally within His church, circumcising their hearts through spiritual baptism (Rm 2:28,29). Only Jesus Christ can baptize one with His Spirit; therefore, many men have created churches without His spirit, because they could not control the supernatural. Tragically, Christianity has divorced the Spirit of Christ from His power and changed church theologies to fit their experiences; because they have not the Spirit of Christ the Bible way (Rm 8:9). This would explain why men cannot understand the writings of the Jewish prophets and apostles. They lack the Spirit of Truth, which prophesied through the holy men of God (I Pet 1:10-12). We are told in the book of Revelation that **the testimony of Jesus is the Spirit of Prophecy** (Rev 19:10). He who lacks this anointing cannot understand nor receive the true knowledge of Christ (I Cor 2:5).

Since **Satan could not defeat the head of the church, Jesus Christ, he decided to join the church in the fourth century**. This historical event occurred when the Roman Emperor Constantine made himself the head of the church and the subsequent Emperors of Rome changed their title to Pope. Again, not able to control Jesus Christ (or the supernatural) they would seek to control the layman for the next seventeen hundred years. Since then, Christianity has been plagued with churches which have a form of godliness but deny the power of the Living Christ (II Tim 3:5). Unfortunately, denominational preachers are forever learning but never able to come to the knowledge of the truth (II Tim 3:7).

Until recently, Christianity also rejected the five-fold ministry of apostle, prophet, evangelist, pastor, and teacher. The biblical criteria to function in these offices all required the recipient to receive the baptism of the Holy Ghost. The problem that is presented here is that we have men who do not have the Spirit of Christ, trying to reveal the concealed mysteries of God with only intellectual carnal insights. The biblical five-fold theocracy of Jesus Christ was replaced by the illegitimate religious institutions of men, and illegitimate priesthoods, which exercised a nicolaitan control (Rev 2:6,15) over the uninformed Christian layman.

Void of spiritual understanding, many spiritless Protestant theologians have even proposed the idea that the Spirit of Christ would be removed from the earth during the tribulation period. Such teachings merely prove that they know not the apostles' doctrines, nor are they lead by the same spirit that led the Old Testament prophets and New Testament apostles. What we have are fearful, powerless theologians who dread the idea that Satan would be coming to earth, knowing they are defenseless with their religious institutional dogmas. They can see no purpose in the church going through the seven years of great tribulation. However, the prophet Daniel states that those who know their God will do exploits in the last days (Dan 11:32).

Who is the Anti-Christ that the saints of the Living God should fear Him? **God has never taken His people out of a battle**; He has always taken them through in triumph, spoiling all principalities and powers! We are told by a concert of prophets that the Lord will invoke **the Goshen of God** for the righteous in the last days. In the Old Testament, when divine judgments came upon Egypt they did not come unto the

158

Jewish ghetto called Goshen. In like manner, so shall it be in the last days when the Lord will put a mark in the foreheads of all true Christians, just before the tribulation begins (Rev 7:4, 9:4, Ezek 9:4). When Satan's Mystery Babylonian kingdom is destroyed, the saints of God will sing the updated victory song of Moses (once sung by Miriam after their victory over Pharaoh and deliverance through the Red Sea). The overcoming bride of Christ shall sing the new song, and entitle it the **"song of Moses and the Lamb"** (Rev 15:3).

The purpose of the five-fold ministry is to help the body of Christ mature so that it could develop and measure up to the fullness of the stature of Christ (Eph 4:11-13). Ultimately, a remnant will be groomed by Christ to walk in the supernatural anointing of Moses, Elijah, and John the Baptist in the last days. Just as Moses systematically defeated Pharaoh openly, so shall the Manchild break the stronghold of Satan on the Jewish nation and Gentile Christians ordained unto eternal life. The Manchild shall also deliver the church (spiritual Israel) and natural Israel from their unbelief, sin, and rebellion. Their ministry shall actually bring on the latter rain of the Holy Ghost, producing the greatest revival the world has ever experienced (Jm 5:7,8).

It should be no strange thing that the Protestants and Eurocentric Pentecostals are blinded from these truths. It has taken Catholics almost 1,800 years and Protestants hundreds of years to open their hearts to receive the baptism of the Holy Ghost. When they finally adhere to the doctrines of the Jewish apostles, and reject the doctrines they have substituted from their European church fathers, only then will their blindness to many prophetic truths be unveiled.

9. The Mystery of Iniquity must be revealed and the Transgressors temples are made desolate.

"For the mystery of iniquity doth already work: only he who now letteth will let, until he be taken out of the way.

And then shall that Wicked be revealed, whom the Lord shall consume with the spirit of his mouth, and shall destroy with the brightness of his coming:" (II Thes 2:7,8)

The most difficult aspect of the end times for many to receive is **the Mystery of Iniquity**. It is virtually impossible for those who believe in the doctrine *"once saved always saved"* to comprehend this mystery. The doctrine, "once saved, always saved" was created by Protestant theologians, in order to justify their iniquity, racism, ethnocentrism, and global imperialistic rule. Unfortunately, they deceive themselves by claiming to be exempted from the judgment and wrath of God.

The Mystery of Iniquity will be fully manifested midway through the tribulation period, when the Lord will expose "those who hold the truth in unrighteousness," and draw back unto Perdition, like the disciple Judas. Because they commit the unpardon-

159

able sin of blasphemy against the Holy Ghost, their temples (Holy Ghost spirit filled) will become desolate and be occupied by devils (Heb 6:4-7). Judas (Jn 17:12) and the Antichrist (II Thes 2:3) are the only two individuals identified in the scriptures as the **sons of perdition;** and these reprobate despisers of truth shall join their ranks. The Apostle Paul also speaks of Christians who draw back unto perdition becoming transgressors of the everlasting covenant and vessels of iniquity (Heb 10:38,39).

The biblical typology for this behavior is characterized by the disciple Judas, who for three and a half years, he walked in the anointing, and fellowshipped with Christ and the other disciples. Judas also went out as Jesus instructed them (by two's) healing the sick, and casting out devils. However, at the appointed time he became a transgressor, betraying Christ, and opening the door for Satan to enter into him (Lk 22:3). It should be pointed out that Satan did not possess Judas, until after the moment of his betrayal. The prophet Daniel spoke of the sons of perdition several times stating that the transgressors will come to their full (Dan 8:10-14, 23), and God will make their spiritual temples desolate by removing His spirit from them. He would then pour His wrath upon them. The tribulation period has been custom designed to deal with the transgressors, apostates, and betrayers in the church who forsake the light of God's holiness in order to walk in darkness (II Thes 2:10-12).

The Apostle Paul expands on this subject to the Christians in the city of Rome, stating that Christ would give those who once knew Him (but rejected Him), over to a reprobate mind (Rm 1: 24,28). After reading the following text, there should be no debate as to whom it is addressed. The answer is unequivocally, to spirit-filled Christians who knew Christ personally and understood the mysteries of the kingdom of heaven.

*"For **the wrath of God is revealed from heaven against all** ungodliness and unrighteousness of men, **who hold the truth in unrighteousness;***

*Because **that which may be known of God is manifest in them; for God hath shewed it unto them.***

*For the invisible things of him from the creation of the world are clearly seen, being understood by the things that are made, even his eternal power and Godhead; **so they are without excuse:***

*Because **when they knew God, they glorified him not as God** . . . their foolish hearts was darkened.*

*Wherefore **God also gave them up to uncleanness** . . . For this cause **God gave them up unto vile affections** . . . And even **as they did not like to retain God in their knowledge, God gave them over to a reprobate mind** . . .*

*But unto them that are contentious, and do not obey the truth, but obey unrighteousness, **indignation and wrath,***

***Tribulation and anguish, upon every soul of man that doeth evil,** of the Jew first, and also of the Gentiles. For **there is no respect of persons with God.** "* (Rm 1:18-2:11)

Many Christians who are unlearned in the scriptures and the ways of the God of Israel, take the verse found in I Thes 5:9 out of context; they claim that God does not bring His wrath upon His people. It is true that God has not appointed those who walk in the light unto wrath; on the other hand, Christians who walk in darkness have a promise, they shall receive not only His wrath, but even greater judgments than those who never knew Him (Lk 12:45-48). God has not appointed obedient Christians unto wrath but he commands (in the same chapter) that every Christian should have his body, soul, and spirit preserved blameless at the coming of the Lord (I Thes 5:23).

It would be wise for one to examine all of the scriptural evidence in order to render a balanced and sound verdict on this subject (Eph 5:5-11, II Pet 2:9-22, Ezek 18:19-32, II Thes 1:7-9; 2:8-12, Heb 3:6-4:3, Rm 9:22; 12:9; 13:4,5, Heb 10:37,38; 12:29, I Cor 10:5-12, Rev 14:14-20; 16:15, Col 3:5-10). Christians who walk in darkness and fulfill the lust of their flesh, do not have immunity from the wrath of God. They are called to repent of their evil works. Any one that calls on the "name of the Lord must depart from iniquity" (II Tim 2:19-22). God did not spare His natural children, the Jews, when they transgressed. Throughout the Old and New Testament we are consistently told that the Lord is no respecter of persons (Ezek 33:6-22, Gal 6:7,8, Rm 2:11). Therefore, as Gentiles (who are mere stepchildren grafted into the promises of Abraham), we are told not to be *"high-minded lest he spare not thee"* (Rm 11:11-26).

The Western Church world has deceived itself, claiming a special rapture for it self while the Jews, the unsaved, and disobedient Christians, are left behind for subsequent raptures. Apparently they have never read, nor understood, the Prophet Amos who spoke of them stating, ***"Woe unto them who desire the day of the Lord!"*** **The day of the Lord shall be darkness and not light**. It shall be very dark with no light in it (Amos 5:12-20). They will be expecting to be raptured, but instead they shall be judged, with hopes that they would repent.

Cultural prejudices towards Jews have ensnared many that see only the Jews when they interpret the book of Revelation. **What they fail to realize is that no one in the church will be raptured until the church accomplishes it's primary purpose, which is to provoke the Jews to jealousy and conversion** (Rm 11:11; 26-28). The primary reason why the Gentile world was granted salvation in the first place, was so that they could exemplify the love and power of Christ, and reveal that He is indeed their prophesied Messiah.

Many Protestant, Pentecostal, and Charismatic theologians are not aware of their cultural anti-Semitic biases that still linger in their understanding of Daniel's (and Jesus') statement of the desolation of the temple (Mt 24:15, Dan 9:27;11:31;12:11). They claim that the tribulation period is for the Jews, and believe that the Jews will construct a natural temple in Israel. According to this understanding, the Antichrist will allegedly make the temple abominable when he sacrifices unclean animals in the Holy of Holies.

This carnal interpretation of the prophetic books has misguided many Bible scholars for almost two centuries. The first reason for their error is that they fail to realize that when it comes to fulfilling Bible prophecies, the Lord always *progresses*, He never *regresses.* We are constantly told in the New Testament that each individual Christian is a temple of God (I Cor 3:16,17; 6:19,20). In fact, the Apostle Paul settles the issues when he states that "**God does not dwell in temples made with hands**" (Acts 17:26). **An irrefutable and sound biblical principle is that once Christ has fulfilled the natural with the spiritual, He does not resort back to the natural.** This applies to the temple, His blood, and His indwelling spirit. Even if the Jews were to rebuild a temple it would not matter if attempts were made to defile or make it abominable, because the Spirit of God would not dwell there. God does not dwell in temples made by men; therefore, a natural structure made of wood or stone could not be made unholy.

The accurate interpretation of Daniel's "**abomination of desolation**," was that the temples of the tares in the Kingdom of God would be made desolate. They will become occupied by devils, in the same manner as the disciple Judas was. Contrary to what most would probably think, the Antichrist shall be a mature spirit-filled Christian who would no longer abide in the truth. He will betray the saints of God, become a reprobate, and unify all apostasies to form a new one-world religious system. Virtually all of the parables of the kingdom taught by Christ conveyed this consistent theme, that the wicked would be thrust out of Christ's kingdom (church) in the last days, and that there would be "weeping and gnashing of teeth."

In conclusion, whatever belief one may have about the rapture of the church, his belief will either deliver him or condemn him in the last day. It can also be a matter of life and death, naturally, and spiritually. To be ignorant of the end times and the issues that God must resolve with His church and Israel, may not only cause one to lose his life, but also his soul. Many Christians today believe that it does not matter which view is correct, because they think they will be ready when Christ returns. However, to make such a statement is like having a sprinter line up at the starting line to run a race, not knowing that the race is a marathon. It is also like living in the days of Noah, believing all is well, yet ignorant of why God told Noah to build the Ark. The Prophet Hosea warns spiritual Israel (the church), when he echoes the same words he delivered unto natural Israel:

"My People are destroyed for lack of knowledge; because thou hast rejected knowledge, I will also reject thee, that thou shalt be no priest to me" (Hosea 4:6). This is why they always fail to hear the voice of God.

The book, **A Divine Paradigm of the End Times** is "a must" for those who would like to further examine the mysteries of the kingdom of God. It provides a study of the book of Revelation from a First Century Jewish Christian perspective, using Old Testament typologies and progressive repetitious revelations. The subtitle to the book is "**The Top Thirty Reasons Why the Church Must Go Through the Great Tribulation**." I would highly recommend it as required reading for all (prior to the return of Jesus Christ).

The Mystery of the Natural and Spiritual Temples And the Priesthood

Most European biblical scholars and those who adhere to their interpretations of the book of Revelation, do error in their understanding of end time in the same manner as they do most of the other scriptures. Truth is an unswerving constant. It does not fluctuate because of circumstances or human beliefs. Like a snowball rolling down a hill with increasing momentum, adherence to anti-Semitic theology, ethnocentrism, and imperialistic doctrines, such as *"Once Save, Always Saved,"* produces an intoxicating cocktail of religious delusion. Unfortunately, self serving doctrines blind the eyes, and prohibit the understanding of the commandments found in the Hebraic roots of the Christian faith. Consequently, it becomes impossible to properly interpret the truths concealed in the Jewish scriptures.

If one is spiritually blind, then assistance from Greek, Hebrew, or Aramaic texts will not shed any more light into the paradigms of darkness. The ability to receive truth comes from the type of soil that cultivates one's heart. Understanding of the word of God starts with the fear of God. *"Only the pure in heart shall see God"* and only His sheep will hear His voice. Education can make one literate, but knowledge of the Holy One allows him to receive revelation. Who will hear the voice of the Lord in these last day and be able to discern times and judgements?

Despite Western culture's tumultuous historical legacy of imperialistic conquest over the indigenous masses of the earth, God is giving grace to its descendents (of Italy, Germany, England, Spain, France, and America) and those who have a love for the Jewish people and the Hebraic roots of the Christian faith. Descendents of slave owners and the great-grand children of former slaves are becoming one through the Jewish Messiah, Jesus Christ. A remnant within all racial groups are forsaking the lineage established through their natural birth, and uniting as spiritual Jews to receive the blessings and promises God gave to Abraham. Many have realized that obedience to apostolic commandments, and adherence to New Testament covenants, have opened the windows of heaven to end time prophetic revelations. On the other hand, there are common doctrinal errors, which have caused the door of divine revelation to be closed.

The following are examples of common doctrinal errors that have resulted in the misinterpretation of end time prophecy.

1. **A Jewish temple on the Temple Mount in Jerusalem will be rebuilt.**
2. Many theologians are seemingly religiously salivating over the prospects of a red heifer being found to allegedly **re-establish the Levitical Priesthood with a blood sacrifice in order to fulfill the previously mentioned temple.**
3. Not knowing the hidden wisdom of God, which was concealed from the foundation of the world, many prescribe to **the belief that Daniel's prophecy of the**

163

temple of God being made desolate by the Antichrist is supposed to be done in the restored natural temple.

4. The misinterpretation of "the 144,000" (Rev 7:4-8) as being **Jewish evangelists** from each of the twelve tribes of Israel, **who will be raised up to preach the gospel during the tribulation period**; they claim the church will not be on earth during that time.

With each of these doctrines, scholars have tried to unlock the mysteries of God through the mindset of their denominational doctrines with little success. Without knowing Him personally, and viewing the scriptures from a biblical Jewish paradigm, they have failed to enter into the veil of secrecy. Their rebellious traditions and dogmas have caused them to perpetually error in their understanding, and yield only theological speculation rather than divine revelation. God is a living God and a reigning king. None can come into His secret chambers unless He allows them. All who approach His throne must do so according to proper biblical protocol and through a covenant relationship. Others also try to know him through human philosophy and reason, but they are not successful. Their unbelief in many biblical doctrines prohibits them from receiving revelation knowledge from the Holy Ghost. The Lord speaks through *"progressive repetitious revelations"* and Old and New Testament typologies. **Those who misinterpret the scriptures concerning the natural temple restoration, the reinstitution of the Levitical priesthood and animal sacrifice, and the 144,000 of the tribes of Israel, must realize that Christ does not regress in prophetic fulfillment; He always progresses on to perfection.**

Only those who desire to know truth, and worship God in spirit and in truth, will He grant enlightenment of the mysteries of heaven. The key to unlocking the priesthood and the temple of God's revelations in the last days is based upon the progressive redemptive work of Christ, established in 31 AD. This work can be expressed by boasting of how great are the wondrous works of God, which He kept secret from the ears of men, from the foundation of the world; but He is now making known unto the righteous (Eph 3:2-11; 1:9-11). These mysteries were partially manifested through His son Jesus Christ at His first appearance in human history. Once Christ fulfilled and perfected the priesthood as an eternal priest and by making Himself a living eternal sacrifice for the sins of men at Calvary, there can be no turning back of the hands of time. He then established the priesthood of believers at Pentecost, making Christians partakers of His eternal kingdom.

Upon completion of this process, Jesus Christ also established a new temple which would be manifested as the church and called the invisible (but yet visible) body of Christ. The New Testament defines the new temple in the following manner:

"Know ye not that ye are the temple of God, and that the Spirit of God dwelleth in you?

If any man defile the temple of God, him shall God destroy; for the temple

164

of God is holy, which temple ye are." (I Cor 3:16, 17)

"Every sin that a man doeth is without the body; but he that committeth fornication sinneth against his own body.

What? know ye not that your body is the temple of the Holy Ghost which is in you, which ye have of God, and ye are not your own?

For ye are bought with a price: therefore glorify God in your body, and in your spirit, which are God's." (I Cor 6:19,20)

Christ perfected all things concerning the Law, because only He was worthy and acceptable unto God for such a task. Why? Because He was God Himself, manifested in the flesh! He established a better tabernacle wherein He might dwell and perfected the priestly functions that were ordained under the Law of Moses. Because Christ established all things by His mighty power, it will be futile for one to argue with Him on the Day of Judgment concerning His preeminence in all aspects of the restoration of mankind. He is the first partaker of all things (to demonstrate His love to all). He is the Judge, the Advocate, the Savior, the High Priest, the Deliverer, the Chief Apostle, the Comforter, the Anointed, the Holy One, the Mediator, and the Lord. Consequently, He has earned the titles *"the author and finisher"* and *"the beginning and the end"* of the faith.

After fulfilling His prophetic word and declaring His mighty works, Jesus will never regress in prophetic revelations and allow His sacrifice to be mocked by neither Jew nor Gentile. The religious try to resort to the carnal imperfect elements of the Law, the Levitical Priesthood, the Sabbath, and other aspects of the Torah, to allegedly fulfill the scripture. **However, it is an established biblical fact and New Covenant truth, that God no longer dwells in buildings made of hands; therefore it would not matter if an attempt was made by man or the Antichrist to defile an earthly structure, temple, or tabernacle. Furthermore, no natural temple could be considered Holy, because God's Spirit does not dwell in such structures**. Thus, the end time revelations of Eurocentric scholars in the study of the Jewish temple being rebuilt are at best, wishful thinking. Its tragic outcome will be a grand cultural deception that will insure that those who adhere to such teachings will never understand Christ's deliverance plan in the last days.

Surprisingly, many of those who expect to receive Jesus Christ at His coming may in fact receive the Antichrist instead. While men lacking divine insight remain stagnant in the past, dwelling on the **types** and practices of old in order to interpret the future, the Spirit of Prophecy always moves on to the next level of divine **shadows** and dark sayings (Psa 78:2). Such is the case concerning the abomination and desolation of the temple spoken of by Daniel the prophet (Dan 8:10-14). For example, when the religious authorities heard Jesus early in His ministry say,

*" **Destroy this temple, and in three days I will raise it up**. Then said the*

165

*Jews, Forty and six years was this temple in building, **and wilt thou rear it up in three days?" But he spake of the temple of his body**"* (Jn 2:19-21).

The Jewish leaders thought Jesus was referring to the natural temple in Jerusalem; however, **the Lord was about to bring forth a <u>new revelation</u>, by taking the Old Covenant in a <u>new direction,</u> and pouring out a <u>new anointing</u>** that was foreign to them. The unveiling of a better and perfect temple, called the eternal body of Christ, with its perfect priest and an everlasting King, was inconceivable to them at that time. In like manner, the carnally-minded Christians are looking for a natural temple, even though the spiritual temple has already come.

If there is to be a reconstruction of the temple, then the Sabbath day laws and all other elements of the Law must be re-established with it. *However, God always progresses; He does not regress!* If the Law is re-established with Christ's blessings in the end time, then His redemptive work would have been in vain and rendered null and void. The simultaneous operations of two mutually exclusive covenants would be a violation in a court of law and a contradiction of jurist prudence (justice). The Apostle Paul warned that those who try to abide under the Law negate the grace of the New Testament (Gal 5:4). We will see conclusively that the concept of natural and spiritual temples being compatible simultaneously in the same covenant is without question a major doctrinal error.

First, **Jesus Christ destroyed the temple of the Jews in 31 AD, thirty-nine years before the Romans did it naturally in 70 AD.** The Shekinah Glory, and the Old Covenant, which was fulfilled through Him was removed from the natural temple at His crucifixion. Then, **the Lord allowed the Romans to disassemble the natural temple brick by brick and burn it, in order to destroy it forever; thus making obsolete all structures that had been made with human hands.**

The words of Christ concerning the destruction of the temple were brought back to the minds of His disciples after His resurrection. *"When therefore he was risen from the dead, his disciples remembered that he had said this unto them; and they believed the scripture, and the word which Jesus had said"* (Jn 2:22). However, just prior to Christ's conviction by the Sanhedrin for claiming to be the Messiah (and before His eventual crucifixion), false witnesses were brought in who tried to use Christ's words against Him. In the Gospel of Mark, he gives his account of these proceedings as follows:

"And the chief priests and all the council sought for witness against Jesus to put him to death; and found none. For many bare false witness against him, but their witness agreed not together.

*And there arose certain, and bare false witness against him, saying, **We heard him say, I will destroy this temple that is made with hands, and within three days I will build another made without hands.***"* (Mk 14:55-58, 11:14-18)

166

Even the false witnesses at His trial quoted Jesus without understanding and gave clues of the eternal temple that would not be made with human hands. Ever since **Christ's** crucifixion and outpouring of His spirit at Pentecost, God has not, and will not, dwell in temples made by human hands (Acts 17:24). **Those who are waiting for the re-establishment of the natural have misunderstood Christ's purpose, strategy, and divine plan for His Second Coming**. Jesus' natural minded, unenlightened Jewish brethren, who had Him crucified at the hands of the Romans, also did not understand the purpose of His first coming. *Again, God does not regress; He always progresses.* The key to understanding the end times is that one must accept the fact that Christ and **the Antichrist will not contend for a natural temple in Jerusalem, but with the spiritual temples** of Jesus' church. **Kingdom shall be against kingdom. The Antichrist himself (as we will later see) will be a former spiritual temple of the household of faith that will be made desolate by Christ.**

The biblical precedent for the temple being defiled occurred at the beginning of the Passover week, only days before Christ's crucifixion. Jesus began to shed more light on the spiritual house when He cleansed the Jewish Temple with a whipcord by beating the moneychangers, and casting them out of its chambers. The natural temple that was identified by Christ as His father's house was a shadow of the temple, which was to come. Neither the natural nor the spiritual temples of God are to be defiled by men. With intense zeal and anger, Christ declared to the merchants and priests of the natural temple, that they had perverted His Father's house with their diabolical schemes. He further stated that they fulfilled the scriptures, "And said unto them, It is written, My house shall be called the house of prayer; but ye have made it a den of thieves" (Mt 21:13). Just as Christ cleansed the natural temple two thousand years ago, He shall also cleanse the spiritual temples, his church, in the last days of their iniquity (I Cor 3:16,17).

In Christ's body, both Jews and Gentiles become one. Through one priest, Jesus Christ, they all share in the same blood sacrifice, dwell in the same kingdom, walk in the same covenant, and receive the same Holy Ghost. In Christ, every day is a Sabbath day, and all that are in Him partake of the priesthood of believers. In the last days, all these things will be perfected when the Father of Adam brings all of the children (which came from the lineage of Adam) back into His everlasting presence. He shall quicken their mortal bodies from mortality to immortality and reestablish their perfect state of existence. In order to help one understand the end of temporal time, it is needful to take a look at the big picture, which was prophetically portrayed by Jesus Christ through His Old Testament prophets (I Pet 1:10-12). From this vantage view, one should be able to look at His unfolding plan established before the dawn of humanity.

Under the framework of the restitution of all things back to its eternal glory (in particular the terrestrial world) **the divine instructions given to King David and constructed by Solomon to build an earthly tabernacle was merely a shadow of the heavenly**. Everything that appears in the natural, and is seen by men, was first taken from the mind of God and then spoken into existence. All spiritual principles and natural manifestations were first conceived out of the invisible realm of eternity.

167

However, when human sin entered into the picture, the terrestrial was transformed into the temporal. The God of Abraham, Isaac, and Jacob revealed the pattern of the tabernacle of Moses, which was given to Him in the wilderness from the blueprint of the heavenly model. After Christ's death and resurrection, He ascended to heaven to present His own blood sacrifice before the heavenly *Mercy Seat*. It was for the sins of all men, to reestablish man's eternal reconnection to the heavenly Father.

As we know, Adam was created immortal. He was more than just a custodian of the earth. His earthly body or tabernacle was fashioned after the eternal. It was indestructible until he entered into the forbidden zone and became a transgressor, sinning against His heavenly Father and Creator. Adam was a priest unto his Creator, created in His Father's likeness, and communed with God continuously in a father-to-son relationship. Adam had no mother because he was the original of His kind. His female counterpart would later come from him as "*bone of his bone and flesh of his flesh,*" whereby he named her Eve, meaning "*the mother of all living*" (Gen 3:20). She was called woman because she came from man. Adam was the king of the earth, and his Father was the King of Kings. Adam was given the rule over all of earth's inhabitants. As a lord, he reigned and named all of the inhabitants of the earth. **Man started off perfect, but because he was given free will, he was susceptible to corruption, rebellion, and mortality**.

Knowing their vulnerability and weakness, God had placed in each of His created beings (the angels and men) a prescribed method to deal with their rebellion. The rebellious fallen angelic hosts remained eternal beings after their insurrection; however, they were not given the ability to procreate (reproduce by gender specification), like mankind. They exist unto this day as eternally judged demons led by their leader and deceiver, Satan. As far as man is concerned, God established a redemption plan to restore him before the foundation of the world. The consequence of man's sin would be that he would no longer be an eternal being, but become subjected to death, and abide in a state of temporal existence. **Even though Adam's offspring, though his wife Eve, were not participants in the original sin, they also inherited his temporal state of existence and his rebellious nature**. For in Adam all men die. (I Cor 15:22)

Adam's father was God. Man's seed and likeness was after their father, Adam. On the other hand, Jesus Christ, thousands of years after the fall of Adam, appeared in human history as **the Second Adam**. He came to break the curse of death, change the nature of man, and reestablish the eternal back to those who had become temporal (I Cor 15:45-50). Now all men can partake of the genealogy of a new seed and be engrafted into the spiritual and eternal genealogy of Christ. In short, **Christ, an eternal High Priest, made Himself the eternal progenitor and father of a new seed, that He might have the preeminence in all things.**

We are told that Jesus Christ was even crucified in the spirit realm before the foundation of the world (Rev 13:8), making Himself the only possible Savior before the heavens were created. The role of the priest is to be an intercessor, and to commune with the Divine on behalf of himself, and / or others. Again, Christ, the Divine

One who came in human flesh, is the only one that can bridge the gap between man and God, because He is God.

The divine pattern of the eternal becoming temporal and then resorting back to the eternal can be called **the life, death, and life cycle**; it governs creation today. It can also be expressed as **a one revolution** (rotation) **eternal, temporal, and eternal cycle**. We have a three-hundred and sixty (360) degree rotation in this cycle of redemption. God's ultimate goal is to restore all things that are natural back to the realm of the eternal with a glory that exceeds the former. Hence, the Bible in dramatic fashion, reveals how over the process of thousands of years, the curse of rebellion is removed and an eternal priesthood, kingdom, tabernacle is restored.

To exemplify this cycle through the history of man and his knowledge of the Creator, we must realize that early man understood and abided under the theocracy of God. **Their knowledge of God paralleled with the conditions of their hearts and their state of being**. They knew the Creator as a monotheistic Lord, having no co-partners or lessor gods in the Divine picture. After man's rebellion, the floodgates of his heart caused him to be plagued with the vain imaginations of his mind. Man, having an innate desire to worship (though with a rebellious heart) contemplated that there were many gods. He even began to fashion them with his hands, in the form of dumb idols that could not speak. Man began to worship gods that he could control, giving homage to the creation, rather than the Creator. At the end of God's divine prophetic timeframe, the **monotheistic Creator** will destroy the idolatrous individuals who pride themselves in **polytheistic deities**. They trust in deities that can neither save nor deliver them from the grips of death. At the conclusion of the process of restoration of all things, Jesus Christ will return and reign on earth. All of those who are partakers of His kingdom shall rule with Him as kings and priests in their glorified eternal bodies. Like a wheel within a wheel, we **have the cycle, which started off with man in perfection and the knowledge of the holy monotheistic Creator, who regressed to a fallen state of polytheism, but will eventually (according to God's prophetic clock) return back to monotheism**. Within this sin and death cycle, we have the transformation of eternal bodies to temporal bodies, and then back to eternal again. The righteous shall receive eternal bodies; the wicked shall also receive theirs, when they are raised at the second resurrection, judged, and cast into the Lake of Fire and Brimstone.

This cycle is also quite vivid when we examine the priesthood. It starts off with the Creator as the High Priest standing in the gap for His beloved son, Adam. He reveals Himself to the descendents of Adam (Enoch, Methuselah, Lamech, and Noah). He would also appear unto the Hebrew patriarch Abraham, in the form of a theophany, in the personhood of one called Melchisedec. In essence, the Lord of heaven manifested Himself amongst men to fulfill His prophetic word and continue the cyclic pattern of spiritual, natural and spiritual restoration. God had promised Abraham that through His seed all nations would be blessed, and that **He would make a covenant with him that would eventually lead to a perfect city, a tabernacle, and a kingdom that**

would have no end. This promised and prophesied city / kingdom would not be constructed by the hands of man, but its builder and maker would be the Lord Himself (Heb 11:10,16). Abraham encountered a special priest, sent from God, whose priestly order was not of the earth (Heb 7:1-12). This priest is identified by name as **Melchisedec**. The Apostle Paul elaborates in regards to this eternal, mystery priest, in the following manner:

*"Wherein God, willing more abundantly **to shew unto the heirs of promise the immutability of his counsel,** confirmed it by an oath:*

*That by two immutable things, in which it was impossible for God to lie, we might have a strong consolation, who have fled for refuge to lay hold upon the hope set before us: Which hope we have as an anchor of the soul, both sure and stedfast, **and which entereth into that within the veil;***

*Whither the forerunner is for us entered, even **Jesus, made an high priest for ever after the order of Melchisedec.***

For this Melchisedec, king of Salem, priest of the most high God, who met Abraham returning from the slaughter of the kings, and blessed him;

To whom also Abraham gave a tenth part of all;** first being by interpreta-tion **King of righteousness, and after that also King of Salem, which is, King of peace;

Without father, without mother, without descent, having neither begin-ning of days, nor end of life; but made like unto the Son of God; abideth a priest continually." (Heb 6:17-7:3)

Who was this Melchisedec, a man who had no beginning or end . . . the priest of the Most High God? Obviously he could not have been a mortal man. Furthermore, He was not of the seed of Adam, because Adam's seed had a beginning and a definitive end of his life by the process of death. Adam himself did not have a rival family on earth, nor was there another lineage of humans, that was either superior or inferior to him. Luke reveals that God *"hath made of one blood all nations of men for to dwell on all the face of the earth"* (Acts 17:26). Therefore, this person had to come from heaven. This man Melchisedec was unmistakably Jesus Christ, manifesting Himself before He was declared the Son of God, thousands of years prior to His incarnation. Jesus, the Word of God in flesh, is the Eternal One who holds the preeminence over all things that pertain to the redemption of mankind.

"In the beginning was the Word, and the Word was with God, and the Word was God. The same was in the beginning with God.

All things were made by him; and without him was not any thing made that was made. In him was life; and the life was the light of men." (Jn 1:1-4)

While the natural affairs of the universe are running their predestined course, *the eternal* is also functioning in conjunction, to accomplish God's ultimate purpose. The perfect and eternal Melchisedec, met the temporal, Abraham. Abraham knew intuitively (by the uniqueness of Melchisedec's appearance) that He was a messenger from God, and was not like unto any mortal man. A similar situation occurs in Lk 24: 28-35, when Christ encounters two of His disciples on the road to Emmaus. The Bible states that their hearts burned within them when Christ appeared unto them in His resurrected, glorified body. In like manner so was it with Abraham and Melchisedec. Abraham was so overwhelmed by the presence of Melchisedec that he was compelled to give this High Priest a freewill love offering of a tenth of his spoil of battle. Prior to Abraham, there was no earthly priesthood established by His God who was later known as YEHWEH. Melchisedec had neither mother, nor father, but appeared as a man. The Lord came as a priest to ordain this pattern of the spiritual first, in order to lay a foundation for the temporal priesthood that was to follow through Levi, the son of Israel.

This natural order would be categorized later as a schoolmaster under the Mosaic Covenant and the Levitical Priesthood (Gal 3:24). The Apostle Paul reveals that the carnal priesthoods of Levi and Aaron gave homage to this eternal priest, while they were still in the future (gene pool) ancestral line of Abraham. They gave their tithes and offering to the eternal high priest, Melchisedec, before they were even born, spiritually through the loins of their father Abraham. The spiritual priesthood from heaven, being superior, dispensed a blessing upon Abraham and his seed, until Jesus Christ would reestablish the spiritual seed.

*"**Now consider how great this man was, unto whom even the patriarch Abraham gave the tenth of the spoils**.*

And verily they that are of the sons of Levi, who receive the office of the priesthood, have a commandment to take tithes of the people according to the law, that is, of their brethren, though they come out of the loins of Abraham:

*But **he whose descent is not counted from them received tithes of Abraham, and blessed him that had the promises**.*

And without all contradiction the less is blessed of the better. And here men that die receive tithes; but there he receiveth them, of whom it is witnessed that he liveth.

*And as I may so say, **<u>Levi also, who receiveth tithes, payed tithes in Abraham. For he was yet in the loins of his father, when Melchisedec met him</u>**." (Heb 7:4-10)*

The angel Gabriel revealed to Mary, the mother of Christ the Messiah, *the called name* of Emmanuel, meaning *"God is with us"* (Mt 1:23). However, His name was declared to be Jesus, which means YEHWEH has become our salvation (deliverer). The eternal Christ appeared unto men to reveal the pattern of the heavenly priestly tabernacle unto men.

*"It was therefore necessary that **the patterns of things in the heavens should be purified with these; but the heavenly things themselves with better sacrifices than these.***

For Christ is not entered into the holy places made with hands, which are the figures of the true; but into heaven itself, **now to appear in the presence of God for us:**

Nor yet that he should offer himself often, as the high priest entereth into the holy place every year with blood of others;

For then must he often have suffered since the foundation of the world: but now once in the end of the world hath he appeared to put away sin by the sacrifice of himself." (Heb 9:23-26)

God's masterful plan of redemption was revealed only in part as the drama and the heavenly music of divine fulfillment intensified through the prophetic workings of Christ. Abraham, Moses, and Levi all died, but Christ the Eternal lives forever, making intercession for men. His blood sacrifice was presented once, for all time, for all men, in the tabernacle of heaven **which could not be touched by the hands of men**, even though a natural pattern was ordained on earth. The Jewish leaders of Christ's day were so preoccupied with preserving traditions and keeping the shadow of the heavenly temple, which they could see, that they could not grasp the concept of the eternal temple, which they could not see. Their natural temple in Jerusalem was patterned after the heavenly temple. The temple and priesthood on earth was designed to be a progressive development after original sin was committed in the Garden of Eden. Since then, God's complete restorative method has been missed by the religious, who after receiving only a small portion of revelation from God, fossilized their understanding like a rock, and could not progress on to the next phase of the divine plan.

Christ also revealed His eternal existence to the Pharisees and informed them that Abraham saw His day, received His message as priest and Savior, and rejoiced. He also identified Himself to them as the "**I AM that I AM**" who spoke unto Moses in the wilderness, and was dwelling with them, and speaking to them. The Pharisees and Sadducees understood exactly what Jesus was saying, but rejected His words, and sought on numerous occasions to slay Him. Jesus addressed the Pharisees saying,

"Your father Abraham rejoiced to see my day: and he saw it, and was glad. Then said the Jews unto him, Thou art not yet fifty years old, and hast thou seen Abraham?

Jesus said unto them, Verily, verily, I say unto you, Before Abraham was, I am. Then took they up stones to cast at him: but Jesus hid himself, and went out of the temple, going through the midst of them, and so passed by." (Jn 8:56-59)

The religious always seem to miss the transitional progressive nature of the covenants of God, which systematically and eventually lead back to the eternal.

This is applicable to the Jews in their understanding of the tabernacle of Moses. It seems that they had forgotten that the pattern of the tabernacle and the future temple did not come from Moses nor David, but rather, from God. When John the Baptist came as the prophesied "*voice crying out in the wilderness*" preaching the kingdom of God and preparing the way for the King of Kings (who was also supernaturally without Mother or Father - the divine incarnation) the religious of his day also did not know who He or Jesus was.

The Eurocentric Church world, on the other hand, has regressed back to the Law of Moses in order to interpret the book of Daniel and the book of Revelation. **They have gone backwards, when they should be preparing themselves to advance forward, to receive the full manifestation of the eternal tabernacle that would encompass a better covenant for both Jews and Gentiles in the end times**. Most Jews of Christ's day, and Christian religious leaders today, cannot comprehend in natural terms how God manifested Himself in human form and purchased the church with His own blood (Acts 20:28), becoming its savior, priest, lord, and king. Jesus the Christ could not bring man to heaven in his decadent, temporal, and defiled state to witness the things that exist in His holy dimension; so He gave man a pattern, through Moses, that would be understood by those who move with Him in the spirit. They will understand His covenants and move in "**progressive revelation**" of the spirit.

Jesus Christ stripped Himself of His heavenly glory to live as a man and develop a multifaceted relationship with the hopeless descendents of Adam. The lineage of Adam was in chains of darkness and bondage to the devil until the coming of Christ. For "*without controversy great is the mystery of godliness: God was manifest in the flesh, justified in the Spirit, seen of angels, preached unto the Gentiles, believed on in the world, received up into glory.*" (I Tim 3:16)

He subjected Himself to the same temptations that men encountered to taste, feel, and see the human state of existence.

"*But we see Jesus, who was made a little lower than the angels for the suffering of death, crowned with glory and honour; that he by the grace of God should taste death for every man.*

*For it became him, for whom are all things, and by whom are all things, in bringing many sons unto glory, **to make the captain of their salvation perfect through sufferings**.*" (Heb 2:9,10)

"*Forasmuch then as the children are partakers of flesh and blood, **he also himself likewise took part of the same; that through death he might destroy him that had the power of death, that is, the devil;***

And deliver them who through fear of death were all their lifetime subject to bondage.

For verily he took not on him the nature of angels; but he took on him the seed of Abraham.

*Wherefore in all things it behoved him to be made like unto his brethren, that **he might be a merciful and faithful high priest in things pertaining to God, to make reconciliation for the sins of the people**.*

For in that he himself hath suffered being tempted, he is able to succour them that are tempted." (Heb 2:14-18)

"Seeing then that we have a great high priest, that is passed into the heavens, *Jesus the Son of God, let us hold fast our profession.*

For we have not an high priest which cannot be touched with the feeling of our infirmities; **but was in all points tempted like as we are, yet without sin**.

Let us therefore come boldly unto the throne of grace, that we may obtain mercy, and find grace to help in time of need.*" (Heb 4:14-16)

As the eternal High Priest who suffered and was obedient to His divine plan, Jesus had compassion on the vessels made from the dust of the earth, and became a priest that could relate to all human frailties. **The fact that He did not yield to temptation or sin, made His blood the only exclusive and acceptable sacrifice to break the curse of sin and death for all men**. God made Himself the sacrifice for sins and the only legal way for man to regain eternal life (Acts 20:28) the Messiah of Israel has an exclusive monopoly on salvation. Hence, there is therefore no other doorway to God except that which He has established. No religion or philosophy can destroy the consequences of sin nor open the door to heaven. Even though the religion of **Islam** claims to be the next progression in the phase of Jewish and Christian revelation, it is in gross violation of both covenants. As one of the three so-called *"religions of the book,"* Islam rejects every biblical pattern necessary for salvation, the resurrection, the priesthood, and the deity of Christ. **The claim of Christ to be God in the flesh also nullifies Buddhism, Hinduism, Confuscism, Seikism, Taoism, Freemasonry, Roman Catholicism and every other religion that suggests an alternative way to God**. Christ stated that *"No man can come to me, except the Father which hath sent me draw him: and I will raise him up at the last day"* (Jn 6:44). Christ is all in all, and repetitively in all phases of human salvation, He has the preeminence in all things. What a mighty God! What great wisdom to behold!

"Now of the things which we have spoken this is the sum: *We have such an high priest, who is set on the right hand of the throne of the Majesty in the heavens;*

__A minister of the sanctuary, and of the true tabernacle, which the Lord pitched, and not man.__

For every high priest is ordained to offer gifts and sacrifices: wherefore it is of necessity that this man have somewhat also to offer.

For if he were on earth, he should not be a priest, seeing that there are priests that offer gifts according to the law:

174

Who serve unto the example and shadow of heavenly things, as Moses was admonished of God when he was about to make the tabernacle: for, See, saith he, that thou make all things according to the pattern shewed to thee in the mount." (Heb 8:1-5)

The Law was weak because it was based on the natural elements of the sacrifice of animals and a temporal, imperfect priesthood (Heb 7:11). Hence, the scriptures declare that perfection could not come by the Law of Moses and the priesthood of Aaron. Consequently, the Law and the priesthood had to be *changed*, because they were not designed to abide forever. They were part of the transition and progression towards perfection. *"If therefore perfection were by the Levitical priesthood, (for under it the people received the law,) what further need was there that another priest should rise after the order of Melchisedec, and not be called after the order of Aaron? For the priesthood being changed, there is made of necessity a change also of the law"* (Heb 7: 11,12). Jesus Christ was the eternal priest that was perfected through the things He suffered, and could make intercessions for men accordingly. Christ came not to destroy the Law, but rather through Him, the Law might be fulfilled. The Law was the training wheel to prepare the people of God for that which was to come.

The Apostles of Jesus Christ later received the commandments of the New Testament by spiritual revelation. Jesus Christ established a new indwelling priestly tabernacle officiated by a kingdom priest who would dwell in the hearts of men. The religious refused to relinquish their training wheels, because they preferred the props of religion to hold them up, instead of a pure relationship with accountability to the Lord. In fact, when Christ came, the religious leaders were not even abiding in the commandments of the Torah; instead they commanded the people to obey the traditions and ordinances decreed by their counsels. They had a vested interest in preserving the old order and cherished traditions. The very presence and words of Christ exposed their hypocrisy and transgressions while also revealing their insecurity. Jesus, the author of The Law, threatened their place of prominence that they had amongst the people. Hence, the ministers of God, who were out of fellowship and out of synch with Him, ironically became the enemies of God. Such will be the case with many Christians in the last days, who love their traditions, more than they love the commandments of the New Testament.

Another example of Christ as a priest fulfilling and perfecting the Law in a progressive manner is through the natural commandment of **circumcision**. The natural Law of Moses required a carnal act of the cutting away of the male's foreskin on the eighth day after birth (Lev 12:6-8). This practice was transformed into an essential spiritual component of the New Covenant in a much more perfect way. Paul stated in the book of Romans that **all believers in Christ who receive the baptism of the Holy Ghost were supernaturally circumcised by Jesus Christ** (Rm 2:28,29). In the New Covenant this practice was perfected by spiritual circumcision of the hearts of

Christians, through the Holy Ghost, adding a new dimension that would include males and females, Jews and Gentiles. This progressive divine typology of circumcision transformed both Jews and Gentiles into **spiritual Jews** making them members of the same body of Christ, and citizens of the same kingdom.

"But all these worketh that one and the selfsame Spirit, dividing to every man severally as he will.

For as the body is one, and hath many members, and all the members of that one body, being many, are one body: so also is Christ.

For by one Spirit are we all baptized into one body, whether we be Jews or Gentiles, whether we be bond or free; and have been all made to drink into one Spirit.

For the body is not one member, but many." (I Cor 12:11,14)

This was a revolutionary concept for the natural Jews, who up until this point in their history were commanded by the Law, to keep themselves separate from the unclean heathenistic Gentiles. However, God by His divine power and Holy Spirit consummated a new and better way of salvation, by the eternal priest and Lord, Jesus Christ.

There are not many churches that teach that every male member must resort back to the natural act of flesh circumcision for salvation. The First Century church resolved the issue as to whether Gentiles should be circumcised when they become Christians through the leading of the Holy Spirit. The Holy Ghost gave revelation knowledge to the apostles, prophets, and James, the brother of Christ, at the great Jerusalem Council (Acts 15:5-29). They established that spiritual circumcision was mandatory and was the glue that yoked together both Jews and Gentiles to be one in Christ. It was the baptism of the Holy Ghost that utterly convinced the early Jewish Christians that God had granted salvation to the unclean Gentiles (Acts 11:1-18). The New Testament's progressive fulfillment of circumcision is through spiritual baptism by Jesus Christ, which circumcises the heart of each individual.

When Christ came, He consummated this new and spiritual covenant with His spirit on the Day of Pentecost in 31 AD. **There was a nullification of the Old Covenant, in all aspects, in order to establish the new**. In order for the New Testament to be established, the old had to be done away with. In order for the butterfly to come forth, he must rise out of the shadows of the cocoon stage of development. The Old Testament was the cocoon stage of divinity and the butterfly is the revealed New Covenant, which was concealed in previous generations, but now made known unto the descendents of Adam. *"In that he saith, A new covenant, he hath made the first old. Now that which decayeth and waxeth old is ready to vanish away"* (Heb 8:13).

The Old and new Testaments fit together like a hand and a glove. What was declared in the Old was fulfilled, perfected, or amplified in the New Covenant. In order that there will be no confusion, when it comes to interpreting Daniel's prophecy concerning the destruction and desolation of the temple, we will continue to allow the scriptures to speak for themselves through both Covenants. The Bible is able to explain itself, and God is able to defend Himself. He always progresses, shedding more light on His divine plan! Again, once the New Covenant had been established, **He would not resort back to a Levitical priesthood and a natural temple in the end times,** when everything concerning the church and the world is finally perfected. To their own demise, most churches currently teach that the natural temple and priesthood will be restored in the last day. Unfortunately, they have been greatly deceived. After Christ perfected the blood sacrifice with His own blood, He will not mock Himself by regressing and allowing Jewish priests to sacrifice bulls and goats for human sins in the last days. Because men error in the small things such as this, many other doctrinal errors will begin to intensify among them as the satanic floodgates of deception increases in the last days, because of the Prince of Darkness.

*"And it is yet far more evident: **for that after the similitude of Melchisedec there ariseth another priest,***

*Who is made, not after the law of a carnal commandment, **but after the power of an endless life**.*

For he testifieth, Thou art a priest for ever after the order of Melchisedec.

***For there is verily a disannulling of the commandment** going before for the weakness and unprofitableness thereof.*

***For the law made nothing perfect, but the bringing in of a better hope did**; by the which we draw nigh unto God." (Heb 7:15-19)*

Since the Old Covenant and its **priesthood have been disannulled**, the necessity of priesthood not fashioned after the order of Aaron was established. This priesthood was hidden from Moses as well as the Jewish Sanhedrin of Christ's day. *"**For he of whom these things are spoken pertaineth to another tribe, of which no man gave attendance at the altar. For it is evident that our Lord sprang out of Juda; of which tribe Moses spake nothing concerning priesthood**"* (Heb 7:13,14). This new priesthood came out of the line of Judah, which was the Jewish lineage of Christ. This revolutionary change of priesthoods was a dramatic shift from the lineage of Levi, from which the Law was established. The Jewish King David, who was also of the lineage of Judah, was the prototype of Christ in this role, for he was a priest, a king, and a prophet. To show how congruent the scriptures are, one should be able to see how Christ, being *greater than King David*, mirrored His natural lineage and transformed it into *the eternal*, as a priest, a king, a prophet, and the lord over the house of Abraham. Furthermore, Jesus would also be called the *"Lion out of the tribe of Judah"* whose Kingdom would have no end.

*But now hath he obtained a more excellent ministry, by how much also **he is the mediator of a better covenant, which was established upon better promises**.*

177

For if that first covenant had been faultless, then should no place have been sought for the second.

*For finding fault with them, he saith, Behold, the days come, saith the Lord, when **I will make a new covenant with the house of Israel and with the house of Judah...**"* (Heb 8:6-8)

*"**Wherefore, holy brethren, partakers of the heavenly calling, consider the Apostle and High Priest of our profession, Christ Jesus;***

Who was faithful to him that appointed him, as also Moses was faithful in all his house.

For this man was counted worthy of more glory than Moses, inasmuch as he who hath builded the house hath more honour than the house.

For every house is builded by some man; but he that built all things is God.

And Moses verily was faithful in all his house, as a servant, for a testimony of those things which were to be spoken after;

But Christ as a son over his own house; whose house are we, if we hold fast the confidence and the rejoicing of the hope firm unto the end."
(Heb 3:1-6)

The Jewish house of Judah became the new tribe for the everlasting testament, the foundation for a new priesthood, and yes, a better covenant. Quite contrary to what many Eurocentric Christian denominations teach, the Jewish lineage *has not* been replaced by European church fathers. An example of such a false teaching would be found in the apostate Roman Catholic priesthood, who tried to mimic the Old Testament priestly order and instituted a counterfeit Babylonian order in its stead. Another would be the teachings of the World Wide Church of God; they teach that Great Britain and the United States are the true lost tribes of Israel. Protestant theologians uphold their denominational founders and priestly orders above the five-fold ministry and New Testament Jewish apostolic authority. As long as Jesus Christ is Lord, Savior, and priest over His body in the heavenlies, no priestly system, Roman Papal order, or religious hierarchical structure, will displace or be a substitute for Christ. Jesus is the natural and spiritual head of His church and no temporal, corrupt, sin latent human can take His place.

In the end times all false religious priestly systems will be condemned and destroyed. Neither Pope, priest, preacher or temporal denominational church founder has shed his blood as a perfect sacrifice for the sins of the human race. They are all sinners and must stand before a holy God and give an account for the deeds they have committed in their bodies (Rm 6:23). They are temporal and subjected to death. They are also abominable and without the atoning sacrifice of the perfect Christ, unacceptable to God. Even if the Law of Moss is mimicked or invoked, no Jewish rabbi since the crucifixion of Christ, or at any time in the future, can substitute the blood of animals for the atonement of man's sins. The Antichrist cannot defile a natural temple, because the spirit of God does not dwell in such. Any unauthorized temple constructed by men to contain the spirit of God is a form of idolatry. The Creator of the heavens and earth does not need men to do Him any favors or build Him a temple. However, He does demand that all obey His words. So much for the theories and theologies of men!

God, through Christ authored the covenant, the testament, and the priesthood as He wrote and spoke them at the hands and mouths of the prophets. Therefore, no man has the authority after Calvary and Pentecost to change it. The word of God is established in heaven and the unbelief and rebellion of men cannot make the word of God of none effect. *"God forbid! Let God be true, but every man a liar"* (Rm 3:3,4). Even if an angel should come and proclaim another gospel, discrediting the gospel of the kingdom and the Bible, the scriptures declare that he would also be damned (Gal 1:8,9). Such would be the case concerning the angel named Moroni that appeared unto the founder of the Church of Latter Day Saints, Joseph Smith. Another example would be the angel called Gabriel that appeared unto Muhammad, the founder of Islam. Both angels brought forth messages that contradicted the gospel given to the disciples and apostles of Christ.

Jesus Christ represents an **unchangeable priesthood and a perfect intercessor**. As the Holy Ghost, He also lives supernaturally within each Christian, empowering him to become an individual priest and intercessor, with direct access to heaven. The Holy Ghost governs a direct line from the heart of each Christian (his temple) to the temple in heaven. No mortal man, pastor, or priest can mimic this realm. Paul states that *"Likewise **the Spirit also helpeth our infirmities**: for we know not what we should pray for as we ought: **but the Spirit itself maketh intercession for us with groanings which cannot be uttered**. And he that searcheth the hearts knoweth what is the mind of the Spirit, because **he maketh intercession for the saints according to the will of God**"* (Rm 8:26,27). A saint praying in tongues by the Holy Ghost prays in the mind and knowledge of Christ (Jude 20). One can sometimes receive an interpretation of his tongues and the prayer that he has prayed in the spirit. Paul, speaking to the church at Corinth, gave instructions on church order and prayer in the following manner:

"let him that speaketh in an unknown tongue pray that he may interpret. For if I pray in an unknown tongue, my spirit prayeth, but my understanding is unfruitful.

What is it then? I will pray with the spirit, and I will pray with the understanding also: I will sing with the spirit, and I will sing with the understanding also." (I Cor 14:13-15)

The Apostle Paul continues to explain the uniqueness of Christ's priestly ministry in the New Testament to a supernatural church by stating:
*"By so much was **Jesus made a surety of a better testament. And they***

179

truly were many priests, because they were not suffered to continue by reason of death.

But this man, because he continueth ever, hath an unchangeable priest-hood. Wherefore he is able also to save them to the uttermost that come unto God by him, seeing *he ever liveth to make intercession for them.*

For such an high priest became us, who is holy, harmless, undefiled, separate from sinners, and made higher than the heavens.".   (Heb 7:22-26)

"For every high priest taken from among men is ordained for men in things pertaining to God, that he may offer both gifts and sacrifices for sins...

And no man taketh this honour unto himself, but he that is called of God, as was Aaron. **So also Christ glorified not himself to be made a high priest; but he that said unto him, Thou art my Son, today have I begotten thee.**

As he saith also in another place, For every high priest taken from among men is ordained for men in things pertaining to God, that he may offer both gifts and sacrifices for sins:

As he saith also in another place, Thou art a priest for ever after the order of Melchisedec...

Though he were a Son, yet learned he obedience by the things which he suffered; And being made perfect, he became the author of eternal salvation unto all them that obey him;

Called of God an high priest after the order of Melchisedec."
(Heb 5:1,4,5,6,8-10)

The major weakness of the law was that the **high priest himself was a sinner, subject to death,** and had to be replaced upon his natural demise. However, when the grace of God appeared amongst men, the eternal priest with the eternal spirit was without fault before the heavenly temple. This priest was not subjected to death nor corruption. The Apostle Paul made reference to this issue concerning Christ saying,

"Who needeth not daily, as those high priests, to offer up sacrifice, first for his own sins, and then for the people's: for this he did once, when he offered up himself.

For the law maketh men high priests which have infirmity; but the word of the oath, which was since the law, maketh the Son, who is consecrated for evermore." (Heb 7:27,28)

We know historically, from the witness of scripture, that when Christ was crucified He by His own command gave up His spirit, and allowed His body to experience death. When this occurred, the enormous veil of the temple, which served as the entrance into the Holy of Holies for the High priest, was supernaturally ripped open, exposing its sacred content, the Ark of the Covenant. The scriptures declare that *"Jesus,* when he had cried again with a loud voice, yielded up the ghost. And, behold, *the veil of the temple was rent in twain from the top to the bottom; and the earth did quake, and the rocks rent.*" (Mt 27:50-51). When Jesus uttered His last breath on the cross, even **the sun had to cease to shine** for a period of three hours. Jesus represented the greater light, the Son, which was manifested on the fourth day of human history, 4,000 years since the fall of the First Adam. When He was alive, He shined as light (Jn 8:12) in the darkness of a world controlled by Satan, the prince of darkness. On the cross Jesus defeated Satan and man's greatest enemy, death. *"Now from the sixth hour there was darkness over all the land unto the ninth hour. And about the ninth hour Jesus cried with a loud voice, saying, Eli, Eli, lama sabachthani? that is to say, My God, my God, why hast thou forsaken me"* (Mt 27:45,46)?

When Christ was born, a star shined over Bethlehem. At the time of His death, the sun (which is a star) *did not* shine over Jerusalem, because He was the "**Bright and Morning Star**" that ceased to shine. The light of the world came into a dark and weary planet to press through the veil and bring mankind back into personal communion and fellowship with the Lord of the universe. The mighty hand of God tore the veil of the natural Old Testament Jewish temple, because **Christ, the new High Priest would Himself become the spiritual veil into the eternal, spiritual temples**. *"Having therefore, brethren, boldness to enter into the holiest by the blood of Jesus, <u>by a new and living way</u>, which he hath consecrated for us, through the veil, that is to say, his flesh. And having an high priest over the house of God.*" (Heb 10:19-21). Christ is the first and last for all things that pertain to man's salvation and redemption. Therefore, He exclusively holds the keys of death, hell, and salvation (Rev 1:18).

This new and living way would forever constitute a new building established through a divine blood sacrifice, and the eternal spirit; thus we have a new tabernacle, not made by human hands. The builder of this spiritual tabernacle was also identified by the prophet Zechariah as **THE BRANCH**; we know Him as Jesus Christ.

"Then take silver and gold, and make crowns, and set them upon the head of Joshua the son of Josedech, the high priest;

*And speak unto him, saying, **Thus speaketh the LORD of hosts, saying, Behold the man whose name is The BRANCH; and he shall grow up out of his place, and he shall build the temple of the LORD:***

__Even he shall build the temple of the LORD; and he shall bear the glory, and shall sit and rule upon his throne; and he shall be a priest upon his throne: and the counsel of peace shall be between them both.__" (Zech 6:11-13)

Jesus Christ would erect His spiritual temple to accommodate both Jews and Gentiles into one building, and its cornerstone would be His spirit, the Holy Ghost (Eph 2:20, I Cor 12:12-14). According to the Laws of the Old Covenant, the Jewish temple could not admit the unclean Gentiles. However, God did a *"new thing"* in the earth even though it was prophesied from days of old. At the time, the Jews could not phantom the change in direction the Lord would take, both naturally and spiritually. Even the First Century Jewish church had some initial problems making adjustments to accommodate the Gentiles into the early church. It took the great Jerusalem conference to solve the issues posted by the Judaizers who wanted to require that the Gentiles keep the traditions of the Law. James, the brother of Christ, declared the following words about the Gentiles and the expansion of the borders of the temple of Christ as prophesied by the prophet Amos (9:11,12).

"And after they had held their peace, James answered, saying, Men and brethren, hearken unto me: **Simeon hath declared how God at the first did visit the Gentiles, to take out of them a people for his name.**

And to this agree the words of the prophets; as it is written, **After this I will return, and will build again the tabernacle of David, which is fallen down; and I will build again the ruins thereof, and I will set it up:**

That the residue of men might seek after the Lord, and all the Gentiles, upon whom my name is called, saith the Lord, who doeth all these things.

Known unto God are all his works from the beginning of the world.

Wherefore my sentence is, that we trouble not them, which from among the Gentiles are turned to God." (Acts 15:13-19)

Today, there is a popular belief among the European culturally based Gentile church world that **the tribulation period has been exclusively designed for the Jews. This is most likely based upon anti-Semitic biases, and the belief that the Tribulation is allegedly payback to the Jews for crucifying Christ**. I must state though, that there are a few who believe in the mid-tribulation rapture theory. They claim that those who are left behind after the supposed "first rapture" will be caught away at the end of the first three-and a-half years of the seven-year tribulation period. Either way, this group of Gentiles exclude themselves psychologically from the shakening, wrath, and judgment of God. They support the pre-tribulation rapture theory and **foolishly teach that the church and the spirit of Christ will be removed from the earth during the tribulation period**. This belief is absolutely absurd, because if the spirit of Christ (who is God) is removed from the earth, then earth itself would cease to exist. To further compound their errors, they have taught that the end time temple that will be occupied by the Antichrist, and later made desolate, is a natural building. They have come to this conclusion because it supports their belief that the church and its spiritual temples will be removed from the earth. **Therefore, the only theological option left for these Gentiles, from their anti-Semitic perspective, is to continue to construct their doctrinal house of errors in a regressive manner; thus they conclude that the Jews will rebuild a natural temple again in Jerusalem**.

In many aspects, today's religious leaders are just as blind as the religious leaders of Christ's day. For a multitude of reasons, they could not see that their lack of understanding concerning the Messiah did not permit them to recognize Christ at His first coming. The church world today (as a whole) is just as blind in their preparation for the Second Coming of Christ. They are confused, walk in unbelief, and do not understand the divine script of which they are supposed to be a part.

The progression of scripture, revealed in the New Testament, is that in Christ there is neither Jew, nor Gentile. **Christ does not have a segregated house** like many Westerners would like to think. All believers can press through the veil of His flesh and partake of the same spiritual covenant and promises. **The Jews began the Church age with the preaching of the gospel of the kingdom, and it shall also conclude with them through the mouths of the Gentiles**. All who know Christ shall be of one mind, one spirit, and one pure doctrine, whether they are Jew or Gentile.

*"Wherefore remember, **that ye being in time past Gentiles in the flesh, who are called Uncircumcision by that which is called the Circumcision in the flesh made by hands;***

That at that time ye were without Christ, being aliens from the common-wealth of Israel, and strangers from the covenants of promise, having no hope, and without God in the world:

But now in Christ Jesus ye who sometimes were far off are made nigh by the blood of Christ.

For he is our peace, who hath made both one, and hath broken down the middle wall of partition between us;

Having abolished in his flesh the enmity, even the law of commandments contained in ordinances; for to make in himself of twain one new man, so making peace;

And that he might reconcile both unto God in one body by the cross, having slain the enmity thereby:

And came and preached peace to you which were afar off, and to them that were nigh.

For through him we both have access by one Spirit unto the Father.

Now therefore ye are no more strangers and foreigners, but fellowcitizens with the saints, and of the household of God;

*And are built upon the foundation of the apostles and prophets, **Jesus Christ** **himself being the chief corner stone;***

In whom all the building fitly framed together groweth unto an holy temple in the Lord:

In whom ye also are builded together for an habitation of God through the Spirit." (Eph 2:11-22)

Some Protestant and Pentecostal churches believe that their church buildings are the new temples of God, with their altars, pulpits, and denominational clergy ministering the priestly things of God; however, in the end times, even these religious orders will come to naught, and will be destroyed during the Great Tribulation. Men will learn and understand (even if some know intellectually), but refuse to apply in doctrinal practice that: "**God does not dwell in temples made of hands**" (Acts 17:24). Whether one believes that there will be a Jewish temple rebuilt in Jerusalem, or that his church building is the temple of God, let it be made known unto him that **God does not regress; He always progresses**. In essence, God will prove all things and all those who oppose Him will be made ashamed. For those who choose to be enlightened, they must recognize that:

> *"the times of this ignorance God winked at; but now commandeth all men every where to repent:*
> *Because he hath appointed a day, in the which he will judge the world in righteousness by that man whom he hath ordained; whereof he hath given assurance unto all men, in that he hath raised him from the dead."* (Act 17:30,31)

There are many Christian groups that teach that the Antichrist will desecrate the temple of God. This doctrine is flawed from its very premise. Neither Satan, nor the Antichrist, can defile a temple where God does not dwell! The structure of a natural temple is merely stone and clay. It is the legitimate presence of the true and living God that makes anything holy, whether it is a person, place or thing. The presence of God no longer dwells even in the Holy of Holies because it was destroyed in 70 AD by the Romans. The spirit of the Lord also no longer dwells upon the Ark of the Covenant (whose location is unknown to the religious world) even though it was once located in the Holy of Holies in the Jewish temple. God's presence dwells in the temple of each Holy Ghost baptized, Christian's heart (spirit, Rm 2:28,29). If God no longer dwells in temples made of hands, then it can not be a natural temple that the prophetic scriptures are referring to concerning the Antichrist. Therefore, the question remains, then how will the spiritual temples be made desolate in the last days, and what sequence of events will facilitate this? These questions will be expounded upon further in the chapters addressing the book of Daniel and the doctrine *"Once Saved, Always Saved."*

Contemporary Christians and their denominational leaders should be warned; if they choose to resort back to the Law and compel individuals to regress to the very thing Christ has nullified, they error and become violators of both covenants. Subsequently, they will fall from the grace of the New Covenant (Gal 5:4) and reject the testimony of Jesus Christ. They cannot abide in two covenants simultaneously . . . one natural and one spiritual. Jesus Christ is the Christian's intercessor, spiritual rejuvenator, lord, and testator of the New Covenant. Once the death of an individual has been confirmed, his will and testament can be enforced. No natural commandment, act of human circumcision, or rebuilding of the Jewish temple, can be an acceptable substitute for the divine manifestations of Jesus Christ, the perfect sacrifice and schoolmaster.

> ***"But Christ being come an high priest of good things to come, by a greater and more perfect tabernacle, not made with hands, that is to say, not of this***

building;

Neither by the blood of goats and calves, but by his own blood he entered in once into the holy place, having obtained eternal redemption for us.

For if the blood of bulls and of goats, and the ashes of an heifer sprinkling the unclean, sanctifieth to the purifying of the flesh:

How much more shall the blood of Christ, who through the eternal Spirit offered himself without spot to God, purge your conscience from dead works to serve the living God?

And for this cause he is the mediator of the new testament, that by means of death, for the redemption of the transgressions that were under the first testament, they which are called might receive the promise of eternal inheritance.

For where a testament is, there must also of necessity be the death of the testator. *"* (Heb 9:11-16)

The establishment of a one world religious system will seek to minimize the divisions created by world religions and promote oneness though a common house of worship. This will be accomplished through the Ecumenicalism and the Syncretism Movements by global planners of the New World Order. The construction of a temple fashioned after the one already built by the Baha'i faith in Haifa, Israel (Bahai Gardens) is a prototype of that which is to come. The conclusion of this matter is that in these last days, there will be no Jewish temple built in Jerusalem. However, there will be a natural temple constructed that will promote global peace and religious harmony, sanctioned by the United Nations.

The Global Temple of Peace in Jerusalem

Jerusalem, the city of peace, is the sacred city of three of the world's most influential religions: Judaism, Christianity, and Islam. Historically, these three have been in conflict for almost two thousand years. Even though it is not possible for a Jewish Temple to be rebuilt on the temple mount, nor near the current Muslim Dome of the Rock, there will be a ***common house for all faiths*** constructed in Jerusalem in its stead. If the Jews attempted to build a temple in the place of the Muslin Dome of the Rock, it would immediately lead to a full-fledged war between Muslims and Jews, starting in the Middle East, and possibly causing a ripple effect around the world.

Since the 1950's, many global planners, including former first lady Eleanor Roosevelt, former UN Assistant Secretary General Dr. Robert Mueller, the United Nations (and hundreds of others) have desired to build a *"**Temple of Understanding**."* The original model of this joint religious structure had six wings springing out from a central connecting atrium. Each wing represented the six major religions of the world: **Judaism, Christianity, Islam, Hinduism, Buddhism, and Confucianism**.

185

Historically, it has been the belief of many that religion has been one of the primary causes of world conflict; if mankind is to survive, then the concept of religion must be managed and amalgamated (blended together) to a co-existent level. Of course the moderate and liberal branches of faiths will lead in this global religious transformation. Their philosophies are of a humanistic approach with good intentions; however, they are also spiritual developments orchestrated by the father of global religions, The Dragon, Satan, to create his last day bride of rebellion against all biblical truths. This "benevolent" father of deceit offers to humanity any way to heaven except *"The Way,"* the biblical Jesus Christ.

As the secular world rapidly moves towards its fate with divine destiny, so shall the religious world with its formation of the spiritual bride of the Antichrist. The wife of the Antichrist will be comprised of all of the religions of the earth, united and preaching a gospel that will be universally accommodating . . . many paths to **one world, one religion, and one temple for all**!

The Book of Daniel
The Last Days Witnesses and Judges of Christ

The name of the Prophet Daniel itself gives us a key to his nature, his book, and God's futuristic plans for the end times. The name Daniel means the judge of God. In the Old Testament, Daniel judged the Beast's kingdom, his image, his number, and his king. In the last days the saints of God of the New Covenant will also judge the final Beast's kingdom, his image, his number, and his king. The first Babylonian kingdom of Nebuchadnezzar was natural Babylon. Its typological future counterpart in the book of Revelation, which will be ruled by the Antichrist, is identified as spiritual or Mystery Babylon. The Saints of the Most High shall judge, the world and Satan's antichrist kingdom, in the same manner as Daniel did Nebuchadnezzar's.

In order that one may understand the controversial "**Daniel's 70th week**," found in chapter nine (verses 23-27), it is imperative that one has a telescopic, as well as a microscopic view of this prophetic book. It is a book latent with prophetic dark sentences, dreams, biblical typologies, and historical events which are also shadows of things to come. Daniel addresses the historical events of his day, subsequent conquering kingdoms involving Israel, and the triumph of the Prince of Peace (who will **without hands** supernaturally destroy the Babylonian / Roman god of forces in the last days). Daniel's prophesied antichrist character would be the father of the end time transgressors (Dan 8:33). The Lord shall gather them and they will be allowed to come to a climax as they break covenant with the true and living God to serve devils; consequently, their spiritual temples will be made desolate, and they will be given over unto reprobated minds (II Thes 2:10-12).

Daniel 11:37 and Roman 1:26-29 revel that this man of sin will not have any regard for women, blaspheme the God of heaven, and pervert the sexual orientation of the male gender (who was created in the image of God). He being the chief among homosexuals will seek to pervert the image of the Heavenly (Holy) Father. His bride will be a consortium of consolidated religious antichrist movements to produce a new one-world church. This religious, rebellious harlot church will abide in spiritual fornication, and express every imaginable manner of abominable work, contrary to the God of Israel. Her behavior and religious beliefs will be in contrast to the holy mature man of Christ's body, the church, described in Rev 21:17.

In the prophetic shadowing of Daniel's prophecy he starts with natural Israel in Babylonian captivity then projects to the future with spiritual Israel (the Church) in conflict with Mystery Babylon. This Mystery Babylon would possess the tenants of Persian, Grecian, Roman and Babylonian religious and political ideologies. Daniel then proceeds to conclude human history, as we know it, in chapter 12:1,2 with the rapture of all Israel (Rm 11:25,26), the redeemed bride, the Church. The trump of God, through the Archangel Michael, will utter the announcement of this great event, and the righteous dead shall be partakers of Christ's first resurrection, rising from their graves.

The Historic Gaps in Biblical Prophecy

Many who have studied Daniel's 70 Weeks claim that they can find no creditable evidence for the fulfillment of the last week (or 7 years) of Daniel's prophesy, two thousand years after Calvary. They claim that this interpretation of scripture is disjointed. Even though there are numerous variations of this claim, the general consensus is that Daniel's 70 weeks was a continuous unbroken chain of events ending in the first century. This view is strongly held by the Preterists. They unfortunately ignore the fact that there are three gaps in his prophetic sequence (7 + 62 + 1). Their inability to see a "**gap**" or "**break**" between when Messiah is cut off and the fulfillment of the last week is a snare, prohibiting them from advancing to further insight. They often claim that Daniel's prophecy began with the pronouncement and decree of King Cyrus of Persia and concluded in 70 AD when the Romans destroyed the city of Jerusalem and took the Jews as captives throughout their Empire.

In rejecting the gap concept of Daniel's 70ᵗʰ week, some argue that prophecies, which have precise time periods, must be fulfilled without interruption. For example, they claim Isaiah's 65 years and Jeremiah's 70 years of Jewish captivity were fulfilled exactly as stated. Other examples that are often quoted is the 430 years the Hebrew people resided in the Egypt (Gen 15:13, Ex 12:40-42, Gal 3:17) and their 40 years of wandering in the wilderness (Num 14:34). However, what these individuals fail to realize is that these historical events and prophecies had no divisions of time in their prophetic statements. In Daniel's 70 weeks we have, I repeat, four distinct time periods and purposes assigned to each (7 + 62 + 1 divided in half).

The following should be sufficient evidence to support the fact that there are several prophetic statements, which have prophetic gaps of a 2,000-year time span, which coincides with Daniel's 70ᵗʰ week (last 7 years). These consistencies help establish a check and balance system for sound doctrine.

1. **The dual nature of Messianic prophecy always produces a gap in prophetic history.**

Often in Bible prophecy, there is the immediate natural fulfillment and then later its parallel fulfillment concerning the spiritual. The dual nature of messianic prophecies has caused the nation of Israel to be blinded by the first appearance of Christ, who came as a suffering servant. The Jewish nations, ensnared by the grips of the Roman Empire, were looking for the Messianic Lion out of the tribe of Judah, who would liberate them (like Moses did in Egypt) from Roman bondage.

Such prophetic statements concerning a Messiah who would be the fulfillment of the Passover and serve as the eternal sacrifice for all mankind were just as plentiful in the Old Testament. This non-military Messiah would destroy the works of the devil that men could not see. The suffering Christ was not what they were expecting and He was not religiously correct for their day. This error of their hearts caused them to be totally oblivious to the prophecies concerning Him, even though He was vividly portrayed throughout the prophetic script and manifested before their eyes. In essence, we seemingly have two Christs; however, they are one in the same, serving two roles to fulfill God's divine plan for mankind. The prophet Isaiah revealed Him as a suffering servant in his book (Isa 53:1f). The second Messiah is a reigning king who would inherit the throne of David (Lk 1:32, Zech 6:13, Rev 3:10,21). The problem with many (as exhibited by the religious Pharisees who missed the mark), is that their own pride, self-interest, and a cultural crystallization blinded them. They could not receive the mysteries of the Living Christ, even though He was in their midst, and He clearly identified Himself as the Christ (Messiah).

2. The 2,000-year gap of Joel confirmed by Peter

Few have seemingly pondered the question, *why did the Prophet Joel prophesy in four verses the beginning and end of the church age?* Upon announcing the fulfillment of the first two verses of Joel's prophecy on the Jewish feast Day of Pentecost (Acts 2:16-20, Joel 2:28-32, Lev 23:15-21), the Apostle Peter begins the first two verses as an explanation for the outpouring of the Spirit of God. This spiritual outpouring was accompanied by the evidence of speaking in unlearned tongues. The next two verses concluded with the atmospheric judgments found in the book of Revelation chapter 6 verses 12-17. Peter quoted Joel's utterances as being fulfilled through the circumstances surrounding the Holy Ghost baptism at Pentecost.

But this is that which was spoken by the prophet Joel;
And it shall come to pass in the last days, saith God, I will pour out of my
Spirit upon all flesh: and your sons and your daughters shall prophesy, and
your young men shall see visions, and your old men shall dream dreams:
And on my servants and on my handmaidens I will pour out in those days
of my Spirit; and they shall prophesy:
And I will shew wonders in heaven above, and signs in the earth beneath;
blood, and fire, and vapour of smoke:
The sun shall be turned into darkness, and the moon into blood, before that
great and notable day of the Lord come:
And it shall come to pass, that whosoever shall call on the name of the Lord
shall be saved." (Acts 2:16-19)

When Jesus fulfilled the fourth Jewish feast day of Pentecost, it **marked the beginning of the last days**. Pentecost occurred 50 days after Passover, the day that Christ was cut off from the living. It was on this day that the disciples and many of the followers of Christ (including His mother Mary) began to supernaturally speak in tongues (languages they had never learned), Acts 2:1-15. With the advent of Pentecost, the spiritual temple of the Living God would now be constructed in the hearts of every believing Christian. No longer would the temple of God be constructed by the works of the hands of men (Acts 17:24, I Cor 3:16,17; 6:19,20). This event gave birth to the kingdom of God which would now dwell within the human spirit (Lk 17:20,21) and the establishment of His body, the church. However, the events of Pentecost are summed up in two verses (Acts 2:17,18); on the other hand, the next two verses (19,20) had nothing to do with the events of the Feast of Pentecost (June 6th, 31 AD). Verses 19 and 20 spoke of **the end of the last days**, that notable day of His judgment. Peter did not segment or break up these four verses (Acts 2:17-20, Joel 2:28-32) as he transcended them from the prophetic decrees of antiquity under Joel's inspiration by the Spirit of Christ (I Pet 1:10,11) to bring it into the present tense of his day. These four verses were a prophetic statement of that which had transpired in his day, and that which was to come, in the last days. That which was to come refers to the end of the church age. In essence these four verses reveal an approximate 2,000-year gap between the beginning of the church age and its end.

At the end of this two thousand year gap, at the last trump, and immediately after the atmospheric signs mentioned in Acts 2:18,19, the rapture will take place. Jesus clarified in His Mount of Olives discourse that the conclusion of the church age will be at the end of the tribulation, after the rapture of the church:

"Immediately after the tribulation of those days shall the sun be darkened, and the moon shall not give her light, and the stars shall fall from heaven, and the powers of the heavens shall be shaken:

And then shall appear the sign of the Son of man in heaven: and then shall all the tribes of the earth mourn, and they shall see the Son of man coming in the clouds of heaven with power and great glory.

And he shall send his angels with a great sound of a trumpet, and they shall gather together his elect from the four winds, from one end of heaven to the other." (Mt 24:28-31)

3. The early and latter rain of the Holy Ghost

The prophecy of Joel concerning the outpouring of the spirit of God was unmistakably fulfilled on the Day of Pentecost by the Jewish Messiah Jesus Christ. It was through this event that He poured out His spirit upon over 120 recipients in the Upper Room at Jerusalem. The outpouring of the spirit of God upon the Jews first and then to the Gentiles continued throughout the first century, ushering in the early rain of the Holy Ghost. The latter rain of the Holy Ghost, spoken of by the prophets and the brother of Jesus Christ, James, connected the early rain with the latter rain of the Holy Ghost, which was to occur 2,000 years later, just prior to Christ's Second Coming. James, the pastor at Jerusalem wrote . . .

Be patient therefore, brethren, unto the coming of the Lord. Behold, the husbandman waiteth for the precious fruit of the earth, and **hath long patience for it, until he receive the early and latter rain**.

Be also patient; stablish your hearts: for the **coming of the Lord draweth nigh**. (Jm 5:7,8)

The Early rain began with a deluge and ended the first century with a trickle. The latter rain of the Holy Ghost began as a trickle at the beginning of the 20th Century and will conclude with a deluge during the tribulation period. The Azusa Street Pentecostal movement began in America, but had global ramifications in the rebirth of Pentecostalism in the institutionalized Western churches. It was a catalyst to initiate **the concluding phases of the end of the last days**.

4. The gap between the Feasts of Pentecost and Trumpets

There was also a 2,000-year gap between the prophetic fulfillment of the Feast of Pentecost and the Feast of Trumpets. Again, Pentecost began the church age, and the Feast of Trumpets will culminate its prophetic destiny, as the rapture of the church, at His Second Coming. This gap, or space of time, encompasses the church age and coincides with the early and latter rain of the Holy Ghost. It is also in synchronization with the prophecy of Joel (Joel 2:28-32, Acts 2:17-20) and Daniel's 70th week (Dan 9:24).

The number 7 is used systematically in scripture to denote completion and perfection. When the rapture of the church occurs at the end of Daniel's last week, the Lord would have completed His work with natural and spiritual Israel, and will bring both unto perfection in Christ. One Lord, one faith, one fold in Christ. Both Jews and Gentiles who reject His perfect love will experience His perfect judgment.

5. The Gospel of the Kingdom begins and ends the Church Age.

"But he that shall endure unto the end, the same shall be saved.
And **this gospel of the kingdom shall be preached in all the world for a witness unto all nations; and then shall the end come**.*"* (Mt 24:14)

The Apostle Peter first preached the Gospel of the Kingdom on the Day of Pentecost. Peter's message concluded with the pronouncement of the earthly witness of Christ; the blood, water, and spirit (Acts 2:38, I Jn 5:8). He was the first person ever to preach the newly revealed Gospel of the Kingdom, and it resulted in the salvation of over 3,000 souls. In God's foreordained knowledge, He knew that grievous wolves would creep into the church (Acts 20:28) after the death of the Jewish apostles, and that **the truth concerning the gospel of the kingdom, would be evil spoken of** (II Pet 2:1,2). Biblically sound doctrines would be substituted with all manners of

191

counterfeit religious teachings. For example, Christianity and its thousands of rebellious denominations speak ill of one of the most fundamental apostolic doctrines, water baptism in the name of Jesus Christ. Some even stoop so low as to allege that those who baptize according to the method commanded by the Apostles Peter and Paul were members of a cult. This apostolic commandment of baptism is one of the three components of the gospel pertaining to salvation. Western theologians have rejected the apostolic doctrines for almost two millenniums. The other two components of this gospel include repentance and receiving the baptism of the Holy Ghost (Acts 2:38). The Apostles' gospel was proclaimed in the book of Acts, chapter two, verse 38. It is also called the **Petrine doctrine** (doctrine of Peter and the Apostles); and it began the church age. Jesus tells us in the book of Matthew that this same gospel will bring the church age to a conclusion in the last days, regardless of what men may believe.

6. The priests and the Ark preceded the people (with a gap) into the Promised Land.

"The law came by Moses, but grace and truth, came by Jesus Christ" (Jn 1:14). Moses was prohibited from taking the children of Israel into the Promised Land, but his servant Joshua did. Joshua, a type of Jesus, was given the mantle of taking the Hebrew people into the Promised Land after their 40-year period of purification and separation. The Levitical priests carrying the Ark of the Covenant on their shoulders, stepped into the Jordan River and the waters miraculously parted. The Jewish nation crossed over on dry land. They were commanded to walk behind the priest, **approximately 2,000 cubits**. Joshua led the children of Israel (known as the church in the wilderness) into the Promised Land. **Jesus Christ will lead His church into "the Promised Land"** (millennial reign of Jerusalem) approximately two thousand years after Pentecost.

And they commanded the people, saying, When ye see the Ark of the Covenant of the LORD your God, and the priests the Levites bearing it, then ye shall remove from your place, and go after it.

Yet there shall be a space between you and it, about two thousand cubits by measure: come not near unto it, that ye may know the way by which ye must go: for ye have not passed this way heretofore.

And Joshua said unto the people, Sanctify yourselves: for to morrow the LORD will do wonders among you. (Josh 3:3-5)

A Chapter Breakdown of the Book of Daniel

Chapter 1: The first principle of the book of Daniel is that even though the saints of God may dwell in Babylon, Babylon should not dwell in them. Daniel, under the Babylonian captivity, was given the Babylonian name Belteshazzar. His Hebrew name means "**the judge of God.**" Despite the fact he was renamed did not alter his divine calling and purpose. He judged the kingdoms of the beast. In like manner, so shall the saints of God judge in the last days. The Manchild is the prototype witness of the book of Revelations (Rev 11:4-15; 14:1-6), exemplified through the Jewish teenagers in Daniel chapter three, who received Babylonian names, but would not defile themselves with its idolatrous system. The witnesses anointed in the last days will be exemplified by the Hebrew names of those young men: 1) Hananiah = **Yah has favored** (Shadrack), 2) Mishael = **Who is what God is** (Meshach), 3) Azariah = **Yah has helped** (Abednego).

Be ye sanctified unto the holy things of God. Shadrack, Meshach, and Abednego were **tested ten days** by Babylonian rulers. In the last days the faithful saints of the **church of Sardis** will experience the same; a **ten-day trial** (Rev 2:10). The purpose of this trial of faith is to see which type of meat one would choose to eat . . . whether it would be the meat that perisheth or the eternal meat (to do the will of Him that sent them, Jn 4:31-34) which leads to life everlasting.

Chapter 2: The Babylonian King Nebuchadnezzar receives a divinely inspired prophetic dream that troubled and perplexed him. He then called the soothsayers into his presence, commanding them to tell him what he had dreamed and the interpretation of the dream. If they fail to do this they and they families would suffer the penalty of death. Just as the Chaldean magicians were about to be slain the Jewish Prophet Daniel sought permission to inquirer of the Lord in order to meet and respond correctly to the king's challenge. After a time of prayer and intercession with Hananiah, Mishael, and Azariah Daniel received from the Lord the dream Nebuchadnezzar had and interpreted the dream. King Nebuchadnezzar's dream pertained to four kingdoms (**Babylonian, Medo -Persian, Greek**, and **Roman**) that would arise having an amalgamated combination rule the earth at the appointed end of the age. The Medo-Persian and Babylonian kingdoms were already in operation; however, the Greek and Roman Empires were yet to come.

Chapter 3: The image of King Nebuchadnezzar of Babylon measured **60 cubits** by **6 cubits**. It was a type of image of the beast (whose number and name is **666**), spoken of by the Apostle John in the book of Revelation. Daniel tells us that when certain music was played, the inhabitants of the Babylonian Kingdom were to fall down and worship the image of Nebuchadnezzar. In like manner, demonic spirits will prepare the inhabitants of the earth in the last day to worship the image of the beast through the "anti-music" manifestations of **ROCK**, **RAPP**, **REGGAE** and other synthesizing musical movements. This will be done in the same manner that music was used in the worship the image of the Babylonian king. The sensually enticing and rebellious music, spawned in of the hearts of the ungodly, will prepare the inhabitants of the earth to worship the image of the Beast (and the Antichrist). During the tribulation period, all that will not worship the Dragon or his image will be given the death sentence. They will be expected to participate in vial sexual acts, repeat blasphemous lyrics, perhaps do drugs, perform hideous acts of violence, and seek the delusion of materialistic self-indulgence. Such unseemly behavior is similar to the actions of the Hebrew people at Mt. Sinai (Ex 32:7-29). At the feet of Baal, they indulged themselves in drunkenness, sexual vice and carnage at the sound of seductive music. Sensual music and provocative dancing also led to the beheading of the prophet John the Baptist (Mt 14:1-10). Music will be an instrument used by the forces of darkness to bind the hearts and minds of men, causing them to shun holiness and pursue carnality.

In no uncertain terms, the three Hebrew boys let King Nebuchadnezer know that their God controlled the destiny of all men, especially theirs. The testimony of the last days Witnesses (the Manchild) will be sure; they will, like the three Hebrew boys who passed through the fire and not be burned (Isa 42:2,3). The one, like unto **the Son of God** (Jesus), standing in the midst of the fiery furnace with Shadrack, Meshach, and Abednego now dwells within His witnesses, as the Holy Ghost.

These young men also represent those whom the Lord Jesus Christ will protect from the fiery judgments that shall come upon on the earth, to try the hearts of those who dwell there … those who will be sealed against the wrath of the king of Babylon, the Antichrist.

Refusing to buckle under the enormous pressure of the forces of darkness, the three Hebrew boys were relentlessly committed to upholding the purity of their faith and would not compromise even at the pronouncement of their execution. It appears that judgment and deliverance is perfected in the increment of seven because, the pagan king ordered the fiery furnace heated seven times hotter than normal. The three Hebrew boys boldly proclaimed that **their God was able** to deliver them out of the flames. They did not cast off their faith at that point, rather, they boldly raised the stakes higher and told King Nebuchadnezzar that **their God would deliver them,** as they continued refusing to worship his dumb idol (an idol that could not speak). Finally, they rested their case by stating, even if **He did not deliver them**, *"be it known unto thee, O king, **that we will not serve thy gods, nor worship the golden image** which thou hath set up"* (Dan 3:17, 18).

With the following reassuring words, the Lord will deliver the righteous in the last days again out of the fire of persecution, and the flood of deception.

"Fear not: for I have redeemed thee, I have called thee by thy name; thou art mine.

*When thou **passest through the waters, I will be with thee**; and through the rivers, they shall not overflow thee: **when thou walkest through the fire, thou*** *shalt not be burned; neither shall the flame kindle upon thee.*

For I am the LORD thy God, the Holy One of Israel, thy Saviour..."
(Isa 43:1-3)

Chapter 4: Daniel interprets King Nebuchadnezzar's tree dream and pronounces the end of his kingdom. Nubuchadnezer, like Israel (Lev 26:14 -44) and the church (Rev 2,3) would be judged **7 times** or **7 years** for their sins (Dan 4:16,23, 25,32,34). It was Israel's preoccupation with pagan idolatrous practices that caused the Lord to allow the Northern and Southern kingdoms of Israel to go into captivity by her enemies. His contemporary, spiritual Israel's state of affairs is no different than that of her predecessor. The indulgence in worldliness, courtship with the New Age Movement, acceptance of apostate Christian Freemasonry, and the intoxication with Greco-Roman paganism must be removed from His bride. Daniel's 70th week would also last **7 years** and conclude immediately preceding the millennial kingdom of Christ. Like the revealed prophetic dream of Nebuchadnezzar, Daniel's interpretation of his dream has strong end time prophetic implications. It reveals a final showdown between the Babylonian kingdoms of men, identified as Mystery Babylon (the New World Order) versus the Kingdom of God. In the scriptures Nebuchadnezar is identified by the prophet Jeremiah as "the Lord's servant" (Jer 25:9). He was lifted up with pride (Dan 4:29-34, 37) and as a consequence, he was stricken as a mad man (made abase) for seven years. The spirit of Antichrist and the multitudes in his kingdom (who shall be revealed as tares) shall suffer the same abasement in the last days.

Chapter 5: Nebuchadnezzar's son, Belshazzar, took the holy things of the temple in Jerusalem and defiled them. From a drunken state, he suddenly sobered up in utter terror as he watched a huge handwriting on the wall. We must also not forget the sons of Aaron and Eli (both High Priests of Israel) who also perverted the holy things of God in the Lord's sanctuary and were destroyed for their perverse sacrilegious activities (Lev 10:1-11, I Sam 2:22-36). Daniel interprets the inscription written by the Lord of Host as a judgment from God, which foretold the end of his kingdom. The saints of God will, like Moses, pronounce judgments upon the kings of the earth in the last days (I Cor 6:2,3). Mystery Babylon shall also fall as the Manchild would prophesy against her and pour out the wrath of the Almighty without measure (Rev 11:5,6; 15:2-4).

Chapter 6: A jealousy-inspired conspiracy by the leaders of King Darius' kingdom caused him to sign a decree that caused Daniel to be thrown into a lions' den for praying three times a day. In like manner, the end time deliverers will also be intercessors . . . sighing and weeping for the abominations that take place in Jesus' spiritual temples of apostate Christians (Ezek 8, 9:1-11). The angel of the Lord was sent to shut the mouths of the lions and delivered Daniel out of the pit of raging beasts. Afterwards his accusers and their families were ordered by the king to be thrown in the lions' den, and they were immediately devoured. We are told in the book of Revelation that anyone who attempts to kill the end time witnesses of Jesus Christ will be killed in the same manner (Rev 11:5). **Daniel's testimony as a judge was a witness against his accusers of natural Babylon.**

Chapter 7: Belshazzar continued the prophetic dream sequence of his father, Nebuchadnezzar. He envisioned four kingdoms represented by various beasts: **an eagle winged lion (Babylon), a bear (Medo-Persia), a leopard (Greece)**, and **a ten-horned beast (Rome/Babylon)**. The only person in his kingdom who could interpret Belshazzar's dream was Daniel. The fourth beast, through Greco-Roman conquest, is destined to establish a global government with tenets of the former beast kingdoms. This fourth beast in his dream (in the last days), make war against the saints, the church (Dan 7:21, Rev 13:7). and prevail against them (Rev 12). Daniel then states that the Ancient of Days shall come (Jesus' return), and the saints of God shall utterly destroy the beast's kingdom. Afterwards, Jesus Christ will set up His Millennial Kingdom (Dan 7:22-27, Rev 20:1-3).

Chapter 8: When the final beast's kingdom is fully established, it will **cast down some of the stars** to the ground (saints who are tares, Rev 12:3) and devils shall desecrate their temples (Dan 8:10-14, Rev 12:4-6). It will take **2,300 days** (6 years, 4 months, 20 days) **to cleanse the spiritual temples** of Christ and remove all transgressors and tares from his divine kingdom (I Pet 4:17,18).

> *And it waxed great, even to the host of heaven; and it **cast down some of the host and of the stars to the ground, and stamped upon them**.*
> *Yea, he magnified himself even to the prince of the host, and by him the daily sacrifice was taken away, and the place of his sanctuary was cast down.*
> *And an host was given him against the daily sacrifice by reason of trans- gression, and it cast down the truth to the ground; and it practised, and prospered.*
> *Then I heard one saint speaking, and another saint said unto that certain saint which spake, How long shall be the vision concerning the daily sacrifice, and the transgression of desolation, to give both the sanctuary and the host to be trodden under foot?*
> *And he said unto me, Unto **two thousand and three hundred days; then shall the sanctuary be cleansed**.* (Dan 8:10-14)

These transgressors of the New Covenant (covenant-breaking apostate Christians, Rm 1:18-33) will reach their fullness during this time. Their king knew the truth and deep mysteries of the spirit of God because he understood dark sentences. Psalms 72:8 identifies dark sentences or sayings as the enlightened mysteries of God reserved for His faithful servants. In the end, the Prince of Princes (Jesus Christ) shall destroy the Antichrist without hands.

*"And in the latter time of their kingdom, **when the transgressors are come to the full, a king of fierce countenance, and understanding dark sentences, shall stand up.***

And his power shall be mighty, but not by his own power: and he shall destroy wonderfully, and shall prosper, and practise, and shall destroy the mighty and the holy people.

And through his policy also he shall cause craft to prosper in his hand; and he shall magnify himself in his heart, and by peace shall destroy many: he shall also stand up against the Prince of princes; but he shall be broken without hand." (Dan 8:23-25)

In the New Testament, Christians are required to be living sacrifices (Rm 12:1,2) dying daily (I Cor 15:31) to tenants of the flesh, that we may serve the true and living God. The transgressors will no longer desire to mortify the deeds of their flesh (Rm 8:13) but rather like Cain, become contemptible, and despise the Holy things of God. Consequently, they will walk in the realm of betrayal, carnality, and blasphemy. Hence, the sacrifice of living righteously and yielding their bodies to the spirit of Christ will be shunned. They will choose rather to become reprobates, serving devils, and fulfilling the lusts of their flesh.

Chapter 9: The prophet Daniel offered a prayer with many pleas for forgiveness, intercession, and supplication for the Jewish nation because of their rebellion, iniquity, refusal to obey the prophets, and rejection of the Law (9:2-20). He acknowledged that Israel's transgression of the Law, and their refusal to hear God's voice had caused them to come under the curse of the Law, rather than its blessings, as decreed by Moses (Deu 30). In the midst of Daniel's lamentation, the Angel Gabriel appears unto him to show him the plight of God's holy people and His magnificent redemption plan, for the ultimate restoration of Jerusalem. **Gabriel introduces to Daniel the prophetic 70 weeks determined by God to cover redemption for both natural and spiritual Israel and the city of Jerusalem.** These mysteries are revealed in the controversial, "Daniel's 70th week."

The Prophetic 70 Weeks of Daniel

The prophet Daniel gave a telescopic view of human history concerning the Messiah through his **70 weeks** prophetic timeclock. Ironically, Daniel receives this vision from the **Angel Gabriel** (Dan 9:21), who would also come to Mary and Elizabeth to speak to them concerning their supernatural births and the coming Messiah. From the time that these prophetic utterances were made, God would intervene in human history systematically to bring about a perfect redemption plan over a 70 week period, which spans over 2,600 years. Daniel's divinely inspired writings divided the Messianic prophecy (that would also encompass the tribulation "week" or last 7 years), into three distinct time periods: seven weeks (**7 x 7= 49 years**), 62 weeks (**62 x 7= 434 years**), and 1 week (**1 x 7= 7 years**). Daniel's 70 weeks give us a total span of **490 years**. The Lord uses the term weeks in the prophetic text, to equate with the number **7** denoting completion and perfection.

***Seventy weeks** are determined upon thy people and upon thy holy city, to finish the transgression, and to make an end of sins, and to make reconciliation for iniquity, and to bring in everlasting righteousness, and to seal up the vision and prophesy, and to anoint the most Holy.*

*Know therefore and understand, that from the going forth of the command-ment to restore and to build Jerusalem unto the Messiah the Prince shall be **seven [7] weeks**, and **threescore and two weeks** [62]: the street shall be built again, and the wall, even in troublous times.*

And after threescore and two weeks [62] shall Messiah be cut off, but not for himself: and the people of the prince that shall come forth shall destroy the city and the sanctuary; and the end thereof shall be with a flood, and unto the end of the war desolations are determined.

*And he shall confirm the covenant with many for **one week** [7 years]: **and in the midst of the week** he shall cause the sacrifice and oblation to cease, and for the overspreading of abominations he shall make it desolate, even until the consummation, and that determined shall be poured upon the desolate.* (Dan 9: 24-27)

Daniel 9:24 lists the six objectives that were to be accomplished progressively over a period of 2,600 years. During this time the 490 years will be fulfilled, starting with his writings, and culminating with the return of Christ. They are as follows:

1. **To Finish the Transgression**
   a) Allow the tares and transgressors to come to their fullness and manifest the Mystery of Iniquity (Mt 13:24-30,38-43; II Thes 2:7-13, Dan 8:23)
2. **To Make an End of Sins**
   a) Jesus changes the priesthood from Levi to Judah, from a temporal to an eternal priesthood in the similitude of Melchisedec (Heb 7:1-28). This priesthood shall rule and reign with Him during His Millennial sinless kingdom (Rev 20:1-4).
3. **To Make Reconciliation for Iniquity**
   a) Messiah Jesus, the Lamb of God, became a ransom for the sins of both Jews and Gentiles. (Heb 7:1-28;10:1f;11:1f, Eph 2:7-22)
4. **To Bring in Everlasting Righteousness**
   a) The gospel of the kingdom (known also as the everlasting gospel)

198

preached to eternally save the souls of men was declared by the Jewish apostles and will conclude the church age and perpetuate the kingdom age (Mt 24:14). The church is temporary but the kingdom is eternal (Lk 17:24, Rev 14:6; 19:1-21; 20:1-6, Jn 3:5). The kingdom of Christ, who is the "Lion of the Tribe of Judah," will have no end.

5. **To Seal Up the Vision and Prophecy**

   a) The mysteries concerning the end time have been sealed until the appointed time at the end of the age. The secrets of the Lord are given unto the righteous, that they may know the mysteries of the kingdom, which are to be manifested at the last day. His revelations will be unveiled for the righteous to know what the will of the Lord is: it is to fulfill their prophetic callings. (Amos 3:7, Mt 13:11, I Pet 1:1-13, Isa 46:10, Eph 1:3-23; 3:3-21, Psa 25:14, Dan 8:16-19; 10:14; 11:40; 12:8,9; 12:13, Lk 24:44,45). We are told by Daniel at the end of his letter (chapter 12) that the angel of the Lord revealed to him that the vision and the prophecy must be sealed up until the end of the age. *"But thou, O Daniel, shut up the words, and seal the book, even to the time of the end: many shall run to and fro, and knowledge shall be increased…Go thy way, Daniel: for the words are closed up and sealed till the time of the end."* (Dan 12:4,9)

6. **To Anoint the Most Holy**

   a) Jesus publicly announced before the religious leaders in the synagogue at Jerusalem that the prophecy declared by Isaiah concerning Him was fulfilled before their eyes (Lk 4:16-21,). The prophecy stated, *"The Spirit of the Lord GOD is upon me; because the LORD hath anointed me to preach good tidings unto the meek; he hath sent me to bind up the brokenhearted, to proclaim liberty to the captives, and the opening of the prison to them that are bound: To proclaim the acceptable year of the LORD, and the day of vengeance of our God; to comfort all that mourn."* (Isa 61:1,2) Shortly thereafter, John the Baptist received his confirmation concerning the Messiah (the Lamb) that takes away the sins of the world. The sign given by the spirit to John was to be when he saw the Spirit of God descending on Christ, and resting on Him like a dove (Jn 1:29-34, Mt 3:11-17).

We are told by Daniel that the *"going forth of the commandment to restore and to rebuild Jerusalem unto **Messiah the Prince shall be 7 weeks, and threescore and two weeks**."* This would be the beginning of the dating process previously mentioned. Here we are told that the first week of weeks (49 years) would be for the rebuilding of the temple and the wall of the city. Through the study of Jewish history, we learn that Daniel received his revelation during the time of the Jewish captivity by the Babylonians around 605 BC. **Daniel, Shadrach, Meshach, and Abednego** were all confronted by the natural Babylonian Empire. At the end of the age, spiritual Babylon will confront the end time Christian saints and plummet the earth into great darkness. The mystery of the Jews and Gentiles becoming one in Christ was not revealed to former generations. However, this union was historically manifested ten years after the churches inception on the Jewish feast day of Pentecost, 31 AD. **God will fulfill His ultimate plan for the redemption of both Jews and Gentiles during the last prophetic week**. The end time temple was identified by Christ as not being a natural structure built by human hands, but rather, His spiritual body of saints (Jn 2:18-22). The natural temple in Jerusalem was destroyed in 70 AD by the Romans and it will never be constructed again once it has been perfected and fulfilled by Christ. **After the natural has been replaced by the spiritual, the Lord will not regress, He always progresses**. Therefore, though it may be stunning for some to receive, the natural temple will never be rebuilt again.

Since the Jews were taken into captivity by the Babylonians (and later the Persians), they were without a temple of worship, and their homeland was destroyed. Israel's wickedness had become so great that the "**I Am** that **I Am** " of Israel allowed His own temple, commonly called Solomon's Temple, to be utterly destroyed. It was one of the many consequences prophesied by the prophet Jeremiah against the Southern Kingdom, which lead to their **seventy years** (605 BC - 535 BC) **of Babylonian captivity** (Jer 25:12). The Northern Kingdom, for the same reasons, was brought unto desolation by the Assyrians a century earlier (734 BC – 669 BC). The Prophet Isaiah prophesied their **65 years of captivity** (Isa 7:8). However, in the fullness of time, God put in the hearts of several pagan Persian kings to allow the Jews to return to Jerusalem and rebuild their temple.

The Prophet Isaiah, 200 years before the reign of the Persian King Cyrus prophesied that he would be God's chosen instrument to restore the temple (Isa 44:28-45:7; 45:13). Daniel, one of Israel's most noted prophets, prophesied that it would take the Hebrew people 49 years (or 7 weeks) to rebuild the temple. The first king to grant them the decree to rebuild was Cyrus (a follower of Persian religion Zoroasterism), in approximately 536 BC (II Chron 36:22-23, Isa 44:28; 45:13, Ezra 1:1,2; 5:12,13; 6:13-15, Neh 2:1,3-5). However, during his reign construction came to a halt due to internal problems within his kingdom (Ezra 4:1-6). The sovereignty of the God of Israel is exemplified through Cyrus when He calls this pagan king "*my shepherd*" to accomplish His work concerning Israel.

Cyrus reigned from 538 BC to 529 BC (II Chron 36:22,23). He was followed by Cambyses (529 BC – 522 BC) and Gaumata (also called Smerdis, 522 BC – 521). After the initial decree by Cyrus to rebuild there was an approximate fifteen-year delay on the construction of the temple at Jerusalem.

The second king the Lord would use to allow the Jews to continue building His temple was **Darius** I, in approximately 520 BC (Ezra 6:1-15; 5:1-17). Again the Jews were challenged by the Persian governor Tatnai on their authority to construct the temple at Jerusalem (Ezra 5:6-16). Tatnai requested that Darius, the king, make a ruling on the matter. Darius, referring to the former decree of King Cyrus, reissued a royal decree to continue the temple-building process with haste. It was under Darius' watch that **the temple was completed in 515 BC**. Ezra records this event stating, "*the elders of the Jews builded, and they prospered through the prophesying of Haggai the prophet and Zechariah the son of Iddo. And they builded, and finished it, according to the commandment of the God of Israel, and according to the **commandment of Cyrus, and Darius**, and **Artaxerxes king of Persia**. And this house was finished on the third day of the month Adar, which was in the **sixth year of the reign of Darius the king**"* (Ezra 6:14,15). Darius reigned as king of Persia from 521 BC to 486 BC. He was followed by Xerxes I (Ahasuerus) from 486-465 BC.

The Lord used the prophet Ezra to prepare the heart of the next king to finish the city and the walls of Jerusalem (Ezra 7:1-28). **Artaxerxes** was the third Persian king to give consent, in approximately 458 BC (Ezra 7:11-22). Artaxerxes gave his decree in the **seventh year of his reign** (Ezra 7:11-26). The Jews were making significant progress on the walls and building of the city when Artaxerxes ordered the work to cease. He gave this order after several surrounding tribal leaders conspired against the Jews and falsely claimed that they were planning an insurrection against Persian leadership. A conspiratorial letter was written by Bishlam, Mithredath, Tabeel and Rehum to insight king Artaxerxes to oppose the Hebrew people. This conflict is recorded in the book of Ezra (4:6-23).

There would be a **thirteen-year gap between Artaxerxes' first and second decrees** to rebuild the city. It was the Prophet Nehemiah, the cupbearer of Artaxerxes, who **"in troublous times,"** received the anointing and zeal of the Lord, to see that the house of God was constructed, and the wall protecting the city was rebuilt. The walls and gates had come under attack and were burned. The king's cupbearer was close to the king, because he would taste all drinks put before the king, to make sure the drink did not contain poisons. Nehemiah went forth to accomplished the great task of rebuilding the walls of the city of Jerusalem with much resistance, in only 52 days (Neh 6:15) in approximately 445 BC (Neh 2:1-8). It was in the **twentieth year of his reign** that King Artaxerxes decreed that Nehemiah should return to the place of his father's sepulchres and build the gates and walls of the city, Jerusalem. We are told that the temple was dedicated shortly thereafter, and that the Jews from afar, gathered together to come and build homes in the newly built city (Neh 7:5; 12:27-47).

The first 49 years of Daniel's revelation, given to him by the Angel Gabriel, could not be fulfilled with consecutive years of building the temple and city because, according to the Prophet Ezra, it began with King Cyrus' decree and concluded after the twentieth year reign of King Artaxerxes. This covers a time span of over one hundred years (536 BC-435 BC). In fact, with each there were breaks, intermediate kings, opposition, and cancelled decrees, which led to decades of non-construction. Thus, the 49 years is based on the actual time of construction, during a century of Persian leadership eventually led to the completion of the Jewish temple, wall, and city. We are not told in scripture, how long it took after the celebration of the completion of the wall

201

by Nehemiah for the returning Jews to finish building homes and occupy them within the city of Jerusalem. Nehemiah writes, *"now the city was large and great: but the people were few therein, and the houses were not builded. And my God put into mine heart to gather together the nobles, and the rulers, and the people, that they might be reckoned by genealogy. And I found a register of the genealogy of them which came up at the first, and found written therein.* (Neh 7:4,5; 12:27-47)

The second segment of Daniel's 62 weeks concluded when Messiah, the Prince (Jesus Christ) was cut off for the sins for the whole world (not just for Israel), in approximately 31AD. *"From the going forth of the **commandment to restore and to build Jerusalem unto the Messiah the Prince shall be seven weeks, and threescore and two weeks:** the street shall be built again, and the wall, even in troublous times . . . And **after threescore and two weeks shall Messiah be cut off, but not for himself** . . ."* The scriptures clearly state, that there can only be one reference event used for the Messiah to fit Daniel's prophetic scheme. As we just read that event would be His "**cut off**" (crucifixion). Even though some scholars try to abstract two or more dates during Christ's life to support their analysis of the 70 weeks, we are given **only one** in verses 25 and 26. The six objectives and purposes of the 70 weeks are stated in verse 24, and encompasses the entire period concerning Messiah, the Prince, and His eternal kingdom. Again, they are as follows: **1.** to finish the transgression, **2.** to make an end of sins, **3.** to make reconciliation for iniquity, **4.** to bring in everlasting righteousness, **5.** to seal up the vision and prophecy, and **6.** to anoint the Most Holy. Several of the objectives stated here can only be fulfilled during the tribulation and establishment of the Millennial Kingdom. The angels Michael and Gabriel, appear in Daniel's revelations because the battle against the former and latter Babylonian kingdoms involved spiritual warfare. The fact that Messiah was cut off was also to defeat the spiritual forces of hell and their king. When all is completed through the fulfillment of Daniel's prophetic vision, both the natural and spiritual realms, would be brought under the obedience of Christ. When we count backwards from the date of Christ's crucifixion 434 years (62 weeks), we are placed shortly after the reign of King Artaxerxes, which concluded in 424BC.

If we take the 7 weeks (49 years) that it took to restore Jerusalem and add to it the 62 weeks (434 years), we get a grand total 69 weeks. The Angel Gabriel revealed to Daniel, that the Messiah would be cut off (crucified), thus leaving **one week** (or 7 years) yet to be fulfilled. Daniel stated that the "**Messiah would be cut off, but not for Himself.**" Jesus Christ was the promised Messiah for the nation of Israel, but would be for the Gentile nations as well. It was the same **Angel Gabriel** who would several hundred years in to the future appear and make a declaration to Mary and Elizabeth concerning their supernatural conceptions and deliveries. Even though the first ten years of church history was a Jewish phenomenon, the Gentiles would later receive the gospel of the Kingdom and become one with Israel, through Christ. From that day on, beginning with Cornelius' household (Acts 10:1f, 41AD), the prophetic elements of scripture would refer to both natural and spiritual Israel until the church age concludes.

202

The third part, the last week (or 7 years), of Daniel's 70 weeks deals with the tribulation period. This week is separated from the previous two segments of weeks by the fact after the *"Messiah was cut off."* It produced a prophetic gap of time that would transpire before the prophecy would resume, culminating with the end of the world. The next three chapters in Daniel would substantiate this fact as the time appointed for the end of the age; the Archangel Michael introduced this fact twice (Dan 10:13 and 12:1). The 70th, or last week of his vision, is also subdivided into two periods. It deals specifically with the transgressors and the desolation of the final temple not made by hands. Midway through the tribulation (three and a half years) a prince shall *"cause the sacrifice and oblation to cease, and for the overspreading of abominations he shall make it desolate..."* (Dan 9:27). This prince is of course is the Antichrist who will go into perdition, blaspheme the Holy Ghost within him, and put Christ to an open shame. He will be allowed 42 months (Rev 13:5), which is **1260 days** (Rev 12:6), or **time, times, and half a time** (Dan 7:25; 12:7; Rev 12:14) to go into perdition and persecute the righteous. All of these time spans were used in the scriptures to denote a three and a half-year period. Satan will have his three and a half-year period to create as much havoc as allowed, while the Lord's Manchild witnesses will simultaneously have their three and a half-year (3 ½ year) span to humble him and his antichrist forces (Rev 11:2-6).

The calibration of years, the 30-day month, and 360-day annual cycle

Dating methods used by various cultures have varied tremendously over the past twenty-five hundred years; however, the Lord's dates and times are accurate and consistent. As stated previously, the biblical annual cycle is 360 days and is the standard that the Lord uses for prophetic calibrations. Therefore, if we can agree that Christ was crucified in 31A.D., then we can subtract **483 years** (69 weeks) to discover when Artaxerxes Longimanus' decree to Nehemiah went into effect. That date would be 457 BC.

If one desires to abstract truth from God's word he must allow the Bible to define its own terms, standards, and calibrations. It is only through this method that one can insert variables into prophetic equations to abstract biblical truths.

The concept of weeks in its most rudimentary form is God's time clock for creation and His redemptive work. The divine calibration is expressed in terms of Sabbaths (every seven days), the **feast of Weeks** – Pentecost (seven weeks of seven days), and the **feast of years**-Jubilee (seven weeks of years). If one is to accurately calibrate the duration of time expressed in Daniel's 70 weeks, it is imperative that one uses biblical standards of measurements. There needs to be resolution with Daniel's 69 weeks (483 years) in contrast with the Western Julian calendar, which consists of 365 ¼ days per year verses 360 days to get an accurate time frame.

A standard was established in Genesis by God and revealed to His servant Noah.

We are told that from **the seventeenth day of the <u>second month</u> to the seventeenth day of the <u>seventh month</u> was a hundred and fifty (150) days** (Gen 7:11-24; 8:3-4). From the second to the seventh month we have a span of five (5) months. If one divides the number of months into 150 days, the result is 30 days per month. Thus, a prophetic year cycle consisted of 12 months times 30 days per month, producing a 360-day year. These series of calculations coincide with the time span of the Antichrist's reign and the ministry of the Manchild. Twelve hundred and sixty (1260) days have been given unto both to complete their prophetic destinies, starting midway through Daniel's last week. The exact same length of time (42 months) is also expressed as three and a half (3 ½) years given to cover this time period. The following are examples pertaining to the end times.

To the Manchild: *"But the court which is without the temple leave out, and measure it not; for it is given unto the Gentiles: and the holy city shall they tread under **foot forty and two months**.*

*And I will give power unto my two witnesses, and they shall prophesy **a thousand two hundred and threescore days**, clothed in sackcloth."*
(Rev 11:2,3)

To the Manchild: *"And she brought forth a man child, who was to rule all nations with a rod of iron: and her child was caught up unto God, and to his throne.*

*And the woman fled into the wilderness, where she hath a place prepared of God, that they should feed her **there a thousand two hundred and threescore days**."* (Rev 12:5,6)

To the Antichrist: *"And when the dragon saw that he was cast unto the earth, he persecuted the woman which brought forth the man child.*

*And to the woman were given two wings of a great eagle, that she might fly into the wilderness, into her place, where she is nourished for **a time, and times, and half a time**, from the face of the serpent."* (Rev 12:13,14)

To the Antichrist: *"And one said to the man clothed in linen, which was upon the waters of the river, How long shall it be to the end of these wonders?*

*And I heard the man clothed in linen, which was upon the waters of the river, when he held up his right hand and his left hand unto heaven, and sware by him that liveth for ever that it shall be for **a time, times, and an half**; and when he shall have accomplished to scatter the power of the holy people, all these things shall be finished.*

And I heard, but I understood not: then said I, O my Lord, what shall be the end of these things?

And he said, Go thy way, Daniel: for the words are closed up and sealed till the time of the end.

Many shall be purified, and made white, and tried; but the wicked shall do wickedly: and none of the wicked shall understand; but the wise shall understand.

And from the time that the daily sacrifice shall be taken away, and the abomination that maketh desolate set up, there shall be a thousand two hundred and ninety days. *"* (Dan 12:6-11)

The period of three and a half years also coincides with the middle of the week that the transgressors will come to their fullness (mature wickedness, ripe tares) and the abomination that maketh desolate is established (Mt 24:15). Further light is added to this subject by the Apostle Paul in his letter to the Thessalonians, who calls this abominable sequence of events the Mystery of Iniquity (II Thes 2:7-13).

Chapter 10: In this chapter we catch a glimpse into the heavenlies as the Angel Michael reveals the battle that was waged with the demonic Prince of the Kingdom of Persia. This conflict in the spirit realm delayed the answer to Daniel's prayer for three weeks (21 days, verse 13). When Daniel's answer was delivered by the angel of the Lord, he informed him saying, *"now **I am come to make thee <u>understand what shall befall thy people in the latter days</u>**: for yet the vision is for many days. And when he had spoken such words unto me, I set my face toward the ground, and I became dumb"* (14,15). Michael, in no uncertain terms, informed Daniel that the revelations that had been brought forth pertained to events of the last days which he will usher in with the blowing of the last trump (12:1-4, I Thes 4:13-18, Rev 11:11-13). Michael states that even though their present conflict was with the demonic forces of Persia he reveals that the next spiritual battle would be with the Prince of Grecia (Greece, 10:20). Satan is called the **"Prince of the Power of the Air"** in the New Testament and his kingdom of spirits that rule over the affairs of nations is clearly revealed (Eph 2:2). The Apostle Paul unveils the hierarchy of the demonic realm in the following statement:

"Put on the whole armour of God, that ye may be able to stand against the wiles of the devil.

*For we wrestle not against flesh and blood, but **against principalities**, against **powers**, against **the rulers of the darkness** of this world, against **spiritual wickedness in high places**.*

*Wherefore take unto you the whole armour **that ye may be able to withstand in the evil day**, and having done all, to stand."* (Eph 6:11-13)

Angelic spiritual battles of the past, and future conflicts in the heavens, have already been written in the Holy Scriptures. In the book of Revelation we are told that the Archangel Michael, in concert with the angels of heaven, will do battle with the Dragon (Satan) and cast him out of the heavenlies. He and his demonic hosts will be judged on earth (I Cor 6:3). Coinciding with Daniel's prophecies, he will wage war against the woman (the church, the saints of the Most High), to his own destruction.

*"And there was war in heaven: **Michael and his angels fought against the dragon; and the dragon fought and his angels**,*

And prevailed not; neither was their place found any more in heaven.

*And the great dragon was cast out, that old serpent, called the Devil, and Satan, which deceiveth the whole world: **he was cast out into the earth, and his angels were cast out with him**.*

*And I heard a loud voice saying in heaven, Now is come salvation, and strength, and the kingdom of our God, and the power of his Christ: for **the accuser of our brethren is cast down**, which accused them before our God day and night.*

And they overcame him by the blood of the Lamb, and by the word of their testimony; and they loved not their lives unto the death.

Therefore rejoice, ye heavens, and ye that dwell in them. **Woe to the inhabiters of the earth and of the sea! for the devil is come down unto you, having great wrath, because he knoweth that he hath but a short time.**

And **when the dragon saw that he was cast unto the earth,** *he persecuted* **the woman which brought forth the man child.**

And to the woman were given two wings of a great eagle, that she might fly into the wilderness, into her place, where she is nourished for a time, and times, and half a time, from the face of the serpent.

And the serpent cast out of his mouth water as a flood after the woman, that he might cause her to be carried away of the flood.

And the earth helped the woman, and the earth opened her mouth, and swallowed up the flood which the dragon cast out of his mouth.

And the dragon was wroth with the woman, and went to make war with the remnant of her seed, which keep the commandments of God, and have the testimony of Jesus Christ. *"* (Rev 12:10-17)

Chapter 11: Satan shall deceitfully seize power from amongst the leaders of earth through peace and vain flatteries (11:21). The **Son of Perdition** (the Antichrist) shall forsake the holy covenant of the Lord and draw back unto perdition (sin). He shall corrupt and pervert the Holy Spirit that was placed in him (like Judas). The following verses illustrate his willful, blasphemous rejection of the light that was placed in him (Heb 10:38,39, II Pet 2:10-22).

"And **in his estate shall stand up a vile person,** *to whom they shall not give the honour of the kingdom: but he shall come in peaceably, and obtain the kingdom by flatteries.*

And with the arms of a flood shall they be overflown from before him, and shall be broken; yea, also the prince of the covenant." (Dan 11:22,23)

"And both these kings' hearts shall be to do mischief, and they shall speak lies at one table; but it shall not prosper: for yet the end shall be at the time appointed.

Then shall he return into his land with great riches; and **his heart shall be against the holy covenant;** *and he shall do exploits, and return to his own land.*

At the time appointed he shall return". (Dan 11:28,29)

"For the ships of Chittim shall come against him: therefore he shall be grieved, and return, **and have indignation against the holy covenant:** *so shall*

he do; he shall even return, and have intelligence with them that forsake the holy covenant.

And arms shall stand on his part, and they shall pollute the sanctuary of strength, and shall take away the daily sacrifice, and they shall place the abomination that maketh desolate.

And such as do wickedly against the covenant *shall he corrupt by flatteries:"* (Dan 11:30-32)

The saints who know their God will do exploits during this time; however, many shall fall by the sword and by flames, and go into captivity. This is the **purging of the Lord** to make his bride ready; those that overcome will be given **white garments of righteousness** (11:32-35, Rev 7:13,14; 20:4). The book of Revelation identifies these individuals as the blood washed multitudes who come out of the great tribulation. On the other hand, the transgressors will magnify the **god of forces** (vs-38, the devil), and they shall be destroyed. Consistent with the theme of this book, throughout this chapter Daniel, continuously states that these events are destined for the **time of the end**.

Chapter 12: The **Archangel Michael** blows the trump and the dead shall rise. During the last 3 ½ years of the tribulation the wise will understand the will of God and be made pure (vs-10). *"… From the time that the daily sacrifice shall be taken away, and the abomination that maketh desolate set up* [**Mystery of iniquity revealed**], *there shall be a thousand two hundred and ninety days* [**1290**]. *Blessed is he that waiteth and come to the thousand three hundred and five and thirty days* [**1335**]."* (Dan 12:11,12)

In this chapter Daniel reveals the purpose of the last three and a half years of tribulation. Not surprisingly, they are the same as given by the apostles of Christ. The purpose is to purify, try, and make white the bride of Christ, His church. He expresses this thought in the following manner, *"many shall be purified, and made white, and tried; but the wicked shall do wickedly: and none of the wicked shall understand; but the wise shall understand."* (Dan 12:10)

Where are the Christians (the Church) In the Book of Revelation?

The Jewish leaders of Christ's day, and those today, cannot accept the fact that, there were over one hundred prophesies that pertained to Jesus Christ as the suffering Messiah that He fulfilled at His first appearing. They were looking for a Messiah that would deliver them from the hands of the Romans. Jesus did not fit their perception of a military leader who would overthrow the Roman government, nor did He accommodate their religious worldviews. Even though many members of the Jewish Sanhedrin, and Rabbis had committed the Messianic text to memory (the Law, the prophets, and the Psalms), the prophetic script of God was indeed in their intellect, but not necessarily in their hearts. The deacon Stephen while rebuking the Pharisees testified to this effect shortly before his death,

*"This is that Moses, which said unto the children of Israel, A prophet shall the Lord your God raise up unto you of your brethren, like unto me; him shall ye hear. This is he, **that was in the church in the wilderness** with the angel which spake to him in the mount Sina, and with our fathers: who received the lively oracles to give unto us: To whom our fathers would not obey, but thrust him from them, and in their hearts turned back again into Egypt...*

Ye stiffnecked and uncircumcised in heart and ears, ye do always resist the Holy Ghost: as your fathers did, so do ye. Which of the prophets have not your fathers persecuted? and they have slain them which shewed before of the coming of the Just One; of whom ye have been now the betrayers and murderers: Who have received the law by the disposition of angels, and have not kept it." (Acts 7:37-39,51-53)

These words were some of the last spoken by Stephen, for he was killed for this rebuke of the elders of Israel. Their unbelief, rebellion, religious pride, traditions, and fear of loss of power blinded them from realizing that Jesus Christ was indeed the Messiah. In like manner, Eurocentric Christians since the nineteenth Century have committed themselves to the study of the word, but their doctrinal errors, traditions, and unbelief has blinded their minds so they cannot see the church, and the revelation of Jesus Christ, in the tribulation period. Jesus Christ can be found throughout the Old Testament prophecies for those who have "eyes to see," if the Lord opens up their understanding. The church can likewise be found in virtually every chapter of the book of Revelation for those who have eyes to see, and ears to hear, what the spirit is saying to the churches.

The mystery of the church is revealed through the mysteries of Christ found throughout the book. The church is like a mystery within a mystery, similar to a Russian doll. The mystery of the supernatural glorious church walking in unison with Christ, and giving birth to the manifested Sons of God, is also a mystery. The unveiling of the mysterious Sons of God, within the church of Christ, will be the greatest manifestation of the prophetic anointing of the spirit of Christ ever. Oblivious to God's divine end time plan, the church world today does not follow nor obey the voice of the Good Shepherd. Therefore, spiritual truths concerning the end times are beyond their grasp. If end time revelation was apparent to all denominations, then there would be no need for the Lord to redundantly state to the seven churches, *"he that have an ear let him hear what the spirit is saying to the church."* On the other hand, if one cannot hear or see, then it is probably because they are not His sheep, they are carnal, or they abide in theological heresies.

In the last days, for those who can receive it, one of the great biblical mysteries will be unveiled. Quite to the surprise of many Jesus Christ will be revealed triumphantly through His glorious church during the tribulation period. It's during this time that He will judge the Anti-Christ's kingdom and the kingdoms of men. Collectively, the overcoming church will defeat the hosts of hell, as the supernatural body of Christ extends itself throughout the earth in all out warfare! This truth has been concealed as a great mystery from the traditional Christians who have an escape mentality. **Out of fear, they focus on their individual concerns, rather than the prophetic predestined divine will of God.** The religious world, with all of its divisive denominations, has consistently refused to accept all of God's word as truth and walk in obedience to apostolic commandments. If Western Christians would repent of their unbelief and heresies, then their church leaders may be enlightened concerning the Second Coming of the Messiah. Satan does not want the church to know about their role in his inevitable defeat, to insure that they make no preparation for the great battle. Furthermore, if the church world were spiritually enlightened, then his opposition would be even greater.

This is the same principle that the devil uses to convince the atheist in his mind that he does not exist; that he might manipulate them through their unbelief, intellect, and vain imaginations. He also convinces the agnostic that there is no tangible proof for the existence of God, manipulating them like puppets to do his bidding through their diverse lusts and perversions of the flesh. The cunning ways of the devil are so effective that he even convinces the Satanist that they will rule and reign with him as they "party" in hell; deceiving them that hell is a place of pleasure, not torment. Therefore, it is no strange thing that Satan has convinced religious Christians, who do not know Him in the context of the Word, to believe that they will be resurrected unto Christ in heaven before the tribulation begins. Contemporary Christianity, with all of its wretched doctrinal sins, abominable heresies, and blatant hypocrisies, has the audacity to believe that their church denominations are without spot, wrinkle, or blemish. They think that they are ready to be received as Christ's bride, but apparently they do not see themselves as Christ sees them.

In order to support their cultural ideology, many contemporary theologians claim that in their investigation of the book of Revelation, they can find no evidence beyond the fourth chapter, that Christians are mentioned. They claim that the rapture occurs in chapter 4:1,2 after Christ address the seven churches in chapters two and three.

The account is as follows: *"After this I looked, and, behold, a door was opened in heaven: and the first voice which I heard was as it were of a trumpet talking with me; which said, **Come up hither**, and I will shew thee things which must be here-after. And immediately **I was in the spirit**: and, behold, a throne was set in heaven, and one sat on the throne."* However, it is understandable that they cannot see the church in the remaining chapters of the book. Just as the Jewish Pharisees of old had eyes but could not see Jesus (their Messiah) embellished within the writings of the Old Testament prophets, in the Psalms of David, and in the Mosaic Law (Rm 11:7,8; Lk 24:44,45), the same has happened to Western theologians today. Their blindness, whether willful or spiritual, reflects the nature of their hearts. In both cases, it may be that they simply did not want to see the truth, regardless of the evidence.

Looking again at the fourth chapter of Revelation objectively, we can clearly see that John was caught up in the spirit, in a vision, and revealed further insight concerning the end time prophetic scenario. **There is no indication that the saints were caught up, only John.** In chapter 1, John stated *"I was in the Spirit on the Lord's day, and heard behind me a great voice, as of a trumpet, Saying, I am Alpha and Omega, the first and the last: and, What thou seest, write in a book, and send it unto the seven churches which are in Asia"(Rev 1:10,11).* Since this is the second time John mentions being caught up in the spirit, why don't Western scholars claim the rapture took place in chapter one? Probably, because it would shed further contradiction on their theory. If the rapture took place in the 4th chapter of the book of Revelation, then John himself should have been raptured as well, because he was "caught up." The apostle Paul was also caught up into the third heaven decades before John's revelation, but his experience did not constitute a rapture (II Cor 12:1-6). The resur-rection should have happened at the end of the first century, if this were true. To the contrary, John would later say in the 10th and 11th chapters of Revelation (10:7 and 11:15) that the rapture would take place at the seventh, last trump. A study of the word within proper context reveals that the rapture takes place when the Manchild witnesses complete their ministry, and are slain, then raised by the "spirit of life," after three and a half days at the end of the tribulation period (Rev 11:11).

A second *"come up hither"* is pronounced in Revelation 11, at the last trump. At the seventh trump, the Archangel Michael will command with a shout that all Chris-tians are to *"come up hither"* (Dan 12:1,2, I Thes 4:14-17). This is the summons for all saints to rise from the dead, and ascend up into the clouds, to meet the Lord in the air (Rev 11:12). The question that should be asked is, which *"come up hither"* accurately precedes the rapture of Christ's bride (the church), and can also bare witness with all the other scriptures that pertain to the rapture? Is it the non-sequential random *"come up hither"* found in Revelation chapter 4 at the beginning of John's revelation? Or, is it the sequential seventh or last trump *"come up hither"* of Chapter 11? Unequivocally, the answer is ***the last trump at the end of the tribulation*** in Chapter 11, when the spirit of life enters into the slain Manchild and all Christians who have died in Christ are resurrected. Immediately after they are caught up, those who are alive at His Second

Coming (II Thes 2:1 I Cor 15:23,24) shall be changed from mortality to immortality (I Cor 15:51-56).

There appears to be an obvious attempt to misrepresent the timing and sequence of the resurrection. The same biased error of timing and sequence, due to willful ignorance, can be applied to the Protestant interpretation of Jn 20:22. In this verse Jesus states, *"And when he had said this, he breathed on them, and saith unto them, Receive ye the Holy Ghost."* A large portion of the Western Christian world teaches that when Jesus breathed on His disciples, they received the Holy Ghost at that moment. In order to come to this conclusion, they would have to willfully reject the fact that the disciples did not receive the Holy Ghost until the day of Pentecost (Acts 1:4,5,8-14;2:1-18; Lk 24:47-49). The apostles of Jesus Christ did not receive the Holy Ghost twice (once when Jesus breathed on them, and again on the day of Pentecost). Again, this issue should also be without dispute because the prophecy of Joel 2:28-32 confirms the latter. They receive the Holy Ghost only once, fulfilling the prophetic feast day of Pentecost established in the Law of Moses (Acts 2:1-18). This teaching was erroneously inserted as church doctrine in an attempt to cover up the fact that Western Christianity had not received the Holy Ghost according to the examples of the early church. Their unbelief concerning the issue of tongues would not allow them to receive the spirit of Christ, the bible way. Consequently, they would teach that one receives the spirit of Christ the moment he accepts Jesus as his Savior. Hence, the blindness concerning the timing of the rapture of the church and the receiving of the Holy Ghost, has resulted from hearts of unbelief, and attempts to justify denominational doctrinal errors.

Apparently, a spirit of blindness dominates the Eurocentric church world, concealing the mysteries of God from them because of their unbelief and rebellion. As a result Satan has cleverly set them up to be partakers of **the bride of the Anti-Christ**, instead of being elect members of the bride of Jesus Christ.

The contemporary church world needs the eye salve, that the Lord prescribed to the church of Laodicea, in order to remove their cultural biases and blindness. Then they may be able to hear the voice of the bridegroom calling them unto repentance. If man can be blinded in the natural because of the deceptions of his heart surely he can be blinded spiritually of the hidden things of God. For example, abortionist cannot see that an unborn fetus is a living person. Adolph Hitler and many American Christians did not believe that Jews and Blacks were human. Americans and Europeans scientist have continued to propagate the belief that men evolved from apes. In each of these cases of natural blindness concerning **abortion**, **racism** and **evolution**, even the obvious is concealed from those who walk in darkness. All who believe such things walk in accordance with the character of their spiritual father, the prince of darkness. The Apostle Paul shed light on this subject by stating that, *"if our gospel be hid, it is hid to them that are lost: **In whom the god of this world hath blinded the minds** of them which believe not, lest the light of the glorious gospel of Christ, who is the image of God, should shine unto them"* (II Cor 4:3,4). In the area of spiritual blindness, we have again the Jewish Pharisees and Sadducees for example. They had committed the Torah and many of the prophetic books to memory verbatim. Even though they had the prophetic words concerning the Messiah thoroughly engrained in their memory banks, unfortunately, godly revelation was not in their hearts. They consistently nullified the word of God, and taught the people of God to rebel through their traditions, which despised both the Law of Moses and Christ. However, we are told by the Apostle Paul that if they had known who Jesus was they *"never would have crucified the Lord of Glory"* (I Cor 2:7,8). Many Christians claim that they know Jesus as their Savior, but they will be struck with utter terror, when Christ regretfully informs them that He does not know them as their Lord.

Again, it is with the heart that a man believes unto righteousness. These religious leaders were "forever learning," but were clueless as to who Jesus was. In order to preserve their power and control over the Jewish masses they sought viscously to have Christ killed. The same demonic spirits that were at work amongst the natural Jews in biblical times is also at work today in many that are spiritual Jews (Christians). They promote homosexuality, apostasy, and theological errors of every sort. Christianity's adherence to doctrines such as "**Once Saved, Always Saved**," **Anti-Semitic racial beliefs, and ethnocentric cultural superiority** has also blinded the hearts and minds of many. Though many Christians may be very cerebral or intellectual, yet they are unlearned, and unskilled in the word of righteousness; therefore, their dominant carnal minds cannot understand the revealed mysteries of Christ. They often times abide in perverted gospels, believe in another Jesus contrary to Christ, and are led by another spirit foreign to the biblical Holy Ghost (II Cor 11:4). This deceived body of believers thinks that they are immune from the chastisement and judgments of the Lord. Unfortunately, they have beguiled themselves and relegated the Tribulation to be the day of God's wrath upon the Jews and the anti-Christ kingdom *only*.

Since few claim to be able to see Jesus Christ after Revelation chapter one, many Christians may even say that Christ is not mentioned by name beyond the first chapter of the Book of Revelation. However, He is identified by many of His Old and New Testament names throughout the entire book. Likewise is it with the church. For example, in one verse alone, Revelation 5:6 we see four direct references to Him. The keys to understanding these references are unveiled in both the Old and New Testaments because YEHWEH, the God of Israel is the author of both Testaments. From the inception of the Christian faith, He revealed His mysteries and secrets through the Jewish prophets and apostles and not through Gentile theologians. When one reads the following verse what or whom does this reader invision John saw?

"And I beheld, and, lo, in the midst of the throne and of the four beasts, and in the midst of the elders, stood <u>a Lamb</u> as it had been slain, having <u>seven horns</u> and <u>seven eyes</u>, which are <u>the seven Spirits of God</u> sent forth into all the earth."

Well, what did John see? Did he literally see a hideous monstrous lamb with 7

214

horns, 7 eyes, and 7 spirits? Of course not! The answer is as follows:

1. **A Lamb as it had been slain** - Jesus was the Passover Lamb, and is identified as the Lamb of God. (Jn 1:29,36)

2. **Having seven horns** – Consistently in the scripture horns represent rulership and authority. The biblical use for **the number seven** is for perfection or completion. Jesus is the King of Kings and He is the perfect ruler over all creation.

3. **Seven eyes** - The seven eyes of God are revealed through the prophet Zechariah (Zech 3:9; 4:10). They denote the fact that the number seven represents perfection, and that an omniscient and omnipotent God of heaven knows all things, and sees all the affairs of men, in the past, present, and future.

4. **The seven Spirits of God** – The prophet Isaiah reveals to us that the seven spirits of God which testify of His wisdom, council, character, and criteria for perfect judgment. (Isa 11:1-4)

The sum total of all four descriptions adds up to Jesus. However, the keys to accurate biblical interpretation are hidden within the confines of the Jewish roots, and prophetic utterances of the apostles and prophets. In essence, in this manner, Jesus is revealed throughout the book of Revelation and likewise is the church, for those who have an ear…

If all those who read it could understand the bible, there would be no need for divine revelation or prayer for enlightenment. In fact, if this was true, then the most learned of men should be able to break all biblical codes and understand all mysteries. For such is not the case! However, we are told that the natural mind cannot understand the mysteries of the kingdom of God (I Cor 2:9-14, Mt 13:11). **The bible is written in codes of truth, cemented together by historical facts, and stacked on multiple layers of impenetrable divine revelations**. If one interjects a lie in their doctrinal building process ("no lie is of the truth," I Jn 2:21), it will result in the establishment of error.

Jesus Christ is also not identified by name in the salutations to the seven churches in the Book of Revelation. However, those who can identify His prophetic titles will clearly see Him without the mention of His name. The seemingly mysterious author and His salutation, to each of the seven churches of Asia, is revealed in the following verses:

Ephesus - "These things saith he that holdeth the seven stars in his right hand, who walketh in the midst   of the seven golden candlesticks.". (Rev 2:1, Zech 4:2,11)

Smyrna - "These things saith the first and the last, which was dead, and is alive.". (Rev 2:8) Isa 44:6, Rev 1:18, Jn 11:25.

Pergamos - These things saith he which hath the sharp sword with two edges.". (Rev 2:12) Heb 4:14, Rev 19:14-16.

Thyatira - "These things saith **the Son of God**, who hath his **eyes like unto a flame of fire**, and **his feet are like fine brass** …" (Rev 2:18)

215

Dan 10:6.

Sardis -   "These things saith **he that hath the seven Spirits of God**, and **the seven stars**; I know thy works, that thou hast a name that thou livest, and art dead.".   (Rev 3:1) Isa 11:2-4.

Philadelphia - "These things saith **he that is holy**, **he that is true**, **he that hath the key of David**, he that openeth, and no man shutteth; and shutteth, and no man openeth.".   (Rev 3:7) Isa 22:21-23.

Laodicea -   "These things saith **the Amen, the faithful and true witness, the beginning of the creation of God**…" (Rev 3:14) Eph 1:3-12;3:2-21,Col 1:12-27, Prov 8:4-31.

In the same manner as Christ addressed the church in His prophetic code names, found throughout the Bible, the church itself is referred to throughout the book of Revelation numerous times in one of it's most proper titles … **the saints**. (Rev 5:8; 8:3,4; 11:18; 13:7,10; 14:12; 15:3; 16:6; 17:6; 18:24; 19:8; 20:9). Contemporary Western theologians cannot receive this obvious fact that the church will go through the Tribulation because it wars against their religiously correct paradigms. This biblical worldview contradicts their doctrinal errors, and causes them to either be offended, or reject apostolic truths.

There are twenty-two chapters in the book of Revelation (also referred to as John's book on the Apocalypse and the Revelation of Jesus Christ). If the Church cannot be seen throughout its content, it can only be because of spiritual blindness. The apostle John amplifies and concludes what his predecessors, the Jewish prophets and apostles, had introduced in their prophetic writings. The subject matter was the events that would culminate the end of the world. **Throughout the Book of Revelation, chapter by chapter, there can be found four types of Christians.** They are 1) **the martyred saints** who will be killed, then resurrected; 2) **the translated saints who live through the tribulation** (never experiencing death), but will be translated; 3) **The Manchild**, are the mature sons of God and mature remnant in the body of Christ; 4) **the wicked tares** that also dwell in Christ's kingdom church, but are slated for destruction and burning.

What could cause such a lack of spiritual foresight that would disallow one from seeing the church as Jesus Christ glorifies Himself through His body during the tribulation? The answer lies deeply in the roots of the contemporary Western European and American psyche. The fundamental cultural blinders that have been prohibiting most from seeing the church, and the role that Christians will have during the seven-year tribulation period, are **Anti-Semitism** and **Ethnocentrism**. Anti-Semitism is defined as racism (and sometimes violence) perpetrated against Jews, and it has been a stumbling block for many Gentile church leaders for centuries, that adhered to such ideologies. This concept is an oxymoron for Gentiles who further confuse those in Christianity by denying or ignoring the fact that Jesus Himself was of Jewish birth and the Christian religion was not birth out of European descent, or culture.

Since the advent of the Roman Catholic Church, the Jews have been relegated by many anti-Semitic religious Christian leaders, their denominations, and individuals as **Christ killers**. In his latter years, even Martin Luther, the great Protestant reformer, became very anti-Semitic, and centuries later, a fellow German, Adolph Hitler, would quote his inflammatory anti-Semitic rhetoric in order to justify the Holocaust. This concept branded upon the Jews, by Western Gentile Christians, would become a pretext for the justification of such horrific events as the Russian Pogrom's and the Spanish Inquisition.

Protestants would later apply their inherited beliefs acquired from the Roman Catholic Church that the Jews were Christ-killers, who would receive their judgment in the book of Revelation. This thought began to spread and evolve during the nineteenth Century, starting in England, with the Presbyterian Pastor **Edward Irvin**. Irvin and some of his contemporaries believed that the destructive judgments in the book of Revelation were actually done by Christ, bringing judgment upon the Jewish race for having Him crucified at the hands of the Roman government. Irvin, Nelson Darby, and most Protestant leaders until this day, have made themselves immune to all forms of judgment that might be attributed to the church in the end time. **They began to teach that the Gentile Church would be raptured out of the earth, prior to the beginning of the Great Tribulation, and that all prophesies pertaining to this period are to be interpreted for the Jews only.** This has become the accepted Western cultural delusion as the end times rapidly approaches, and it puts the church in a very vulnerable and dangerous position. We will see, as we examine the book of Revelation chapter by chapter, using the Jewish roots of the Christian faith, that the church is located in all of its content. **This spiritual blindness on behalf of Western churches is identical to the blindness imputed upon the Jewish leaders of Christ's day. The religious scribes knew the Old Testament verbatim, but could not see the prophetic script of Jesus written throughout in the Law of Moses, the prophets, and in the Psalms, concerning Him** (Lk 24:44).

The Bible is quite clear as to the timing of the resurrection of the saints; however, heretical teachings, anti-Semitism, ethnocentrism, and willful ignorance will continue to blind the minds of many. The Apostle Paul emphatically states that the rapture of the church will take place at **the last of the seven trumpets** (I Cor 15:52), which occurs at the end of tribulation period. **He also connects our gathering together unto Christ and His Second Coming as the same event.** Paul states, *"Now we beseech you, brethren, by the coming of our Lord Jesus Christ, and by our gathering together unto him...* (II Thes 2:1). Maybe some have a problem understanding the definition of the word *last*. However, the Gentile church world teaches that it will occur *before* any of the trumpets are even blown (*at the first trump*). Jesus and the apostle John said **there are only two resurrections**, one for the righteous and one for the wicked (Jn 5:25-30, Rev 20:4-15). However, contemporary theologians teach that there will be between three to seven raptures or resurrections. Jesus said that **He would gather the tares out of His kingdom first** and then He would gather His wheat, the righteous bride of His kingdom/church (Mt 13:30,36-43), His holy bride for marriage. The rapture of the church is the wedding of Christ and His spotless bride, the church. However, they say and imply through the pre-tribulation rapture theory that the wheat would be raptured out first, then Christ would later gather the tares. Jesus said he would gather His elect from the Four Corners of the earth "**immediately after the tribulation of those days**" (Mt 24:29-31). Maybe some also have a problem understanding the definition of the word after. In order for one to believe in the doctrine of the pre or mid tribulation rapture theory, the following words must be beyond their scope of comprehension … **last, first, and immediately after.** We have a clear case of intellectual dishonesty and willful ignorance including numerical confusion because Jesus stated there would only be **two** resurrections ordained for mankind. How does one define **the number two**?

In Jesus' discourse on the end of the age, Matthew chapter 24, He gave the prophetic picture of the multitude of Christians who will be deceived, believing in the pre-tribulation rapture. They are portrayed as helplessly confused, running to and fro, and trying to find Christ, or discover where has He gathered the saints. They will come to this realization when they wake up and discover that they are in the midst of hell on earth, the beginning of the seven seal judgments (destruction like no time in human history), and they are not ready. Many will fall away, and their faith will be over thrown like the children of Israel in the wilderness, because they chose to believe a lie (II Thes 2:3,10-13).

"For then shall be great tribulation, such as was not since the beginning of the world to this time, no, nor ever shall be. And except those days should be shortened, there should no flesh be saved: but for the elect's sake those days shall be shortened.

Then if any man shall say unto you, Lo, here is Christ, or there; believe it not. For there shall arise false Christs, and false prophets, and shall shew great signs and wonders; insomuch that, if it were possible, they shall deceive the very elect. Behold, I have told you before.

Wherefore if they shall say unto you, Behold, he is in the desert; go not forth: behold, he is in the secret chambers; believe it not. For as the lightning cometh out of the east, and shineth even unto the west; so shall also the coming of the Son of man be." (Mt 24:21-27)

The elect (the Manchild and the overcoming Christians) will be on earth, not in heaven, as the foolish Christian masses wonder how they missed the rapture (which never happened). The Seventh Day Adventist Church also preaches a secret coming of Christ that occurred in the heavens at the turn of the Twentieth Century in order to cover all of its previous false prophesies. Many Christians will have lying delusions and deceptive apparitions hoping they had not missed the rapture. **When the resurrection does occur, all eyes will see the Saints of**

God rise, starting with the Manchild (Rev 11:7-15). There will be no secret rapture at the beginning of the tribulation. Instead all shall see the Manchild and the saints of God rise and will overcome with great fear (Rev 11:11).

Again, the majority opinion in the contemporary church world is that Christ will gather His elect before the tribulation begins, not after. In the Law of Moses, we find the Jewish feast days, which declare the prophetic script of the Messiah. It clearly states that **there is a gap of a little over a two-week period between the rapture of the church (Feast of Trumpet) and the setting up of the Millennium Kingdom of Christ (Feast of Tabernacle)**. This prophetic pattern is exemplified by the Jewish Feast days of Trumpet and the Feast of Tabernacle (Lev 23:24-44). The European Gentile Christian world teaches primarily that there is a *seven-year gap* between the rapture of the church and the establishment of the Millennium Kingdom of Christ. With these blatant contradictions, it should be quite obvious that someone is deceived, and have, despite the evidence, chosen to believe a lie. I assure you that it is not Jesus Christ or His Jewish Apostles and prophets. Lying is totally contrary to the nature of God. If He did lie to man then that would put Him in the same camp as the deceiver, the Devil, and leave no hope for man to ever know what is truth. Even in the Torah Moses reveals that, *"God is not a man, that he should lie; neither the son of man, that he should repent: hath he said, and shall he not do it? or hath he spoken, and shall he not make it good"* (Num 23:19)? Blindness in the hearts of many has disallowed them from coming to the knowledge of the truth, to the point of even calling Jesus and His apostles liars.

Some may have even neglected the fact that the church is often referred to as **the bride of Christ and she does not become** *the wife* **of Christ until after she has proven herself and made herself ready prior to His Second Coming** (II Thes 2:1, Rev 21:9-17). When the church has prepared and adorned herself for the bridegroom and her wedding, the Apostle John calls her a city, the New Jerusalem (Rev 21:2). In Revelation chapter 19:7, **we are told that the marriage of the Lamb does not take place until after she makes herself ready, through the tribulation**. It should be without debate that only those who overcome the sins of their flesh will inherit the kingdom of God (Gal 5:19-21). It is also worth mentioning that the apostle Paul stated that his greatest desire for the Corinthian church was to present them as a "chaste virgin" to Christ. His desire was also for each individual Christian, to be holy, even as He is holy. Paul also states that, *"they that are led by the spirit of God they are the sons of God"* (Rm 8:14). The Apostle John proclaimed further, *"beloved, now are we the sons of God, **and it doth not yet appear what we shall be: but we know that, when he shall appear, we shall be like him; for we shall see him as he is. And every man that hath this hope in him purifieth himself, even as he is pure**"* (I Jn 3:2,3). The wicked cannot endure such sound doctrine. They will hypocritically expect to receive the reward of the righteous, but refuse to obey the word of God. Jesus asks the question to those of that mindset, *"why call ye me, Lord, Lord, and do not the things which I say"* (Lk 6:46)? Apparently, many may know Christ as His bride in preparation, **but few**, in comparison, **will actually become His wife**. Remember the statement, *"many are called, but few are chosen"* (Mt 20:16; 22:14). The disciples asked Christ the question, *"Lord, are there few that be saved? And he said unto them, Strive to enter in at the strait gate: for many, I say unto you, will seek to enter in, and shall not be able."* (Lk 13:23,24)

The second most common rapture theory in the Western Church world, though substantially smaller in number, but growing in popularity, is the Mid-tribulation rapture theory. This concept is gaining popularity because of accelerating and more frequent recent global events that are causing many to be concerned about the end times. Natural calamities associated with the beginning of sorrows, the advent of the New World Order, global terrorism, and microchip technology, is causing many to question the validity of the pre-tribulation rapture for the first time.

> *"And ye shall hear of wars and rumours of wars: see that ye be not troubled: for all these things must come to pass, but the end is not yet.*
>
> *For nation shall rise against nation, and kingdom against kingdom: and there shall be famines, and pestilences, and earthquakes, in divers places.*
>
> ***All these are the beginning of sorrows.***" (Mt 24:6-8)

Regardless of whether one believes in pre-trib or mid-trib, all prophetic evidence clearly states that there will be a post-tribulation rapture which will purify the bride of Christ for His wedding. The worst rapture theory is **the preterist view.** This view first surfaced in the first century church espousing the idea that the resurrection of the church has already occurred in the First Century (II Tim 2:17,18).

Anti-Semitism and Ethnocentrism has blinded the contemporary Christian Church world because they refuse to receive the truths of a holy God. Consequently, because of a lack of understanding surrounding His return, they have misunderstood His purpose and intent. They will experience a strong hand of divine correction reserved for some 25,000 allegedly Christian denominational sects. He will judge their false doctrines, their heresies, racism, and the vile wickedness they do without godly fear, in the name of Christ. **The tribulation period has been custom-designed by the Lord to allow His *servant for unrighteousness* (Satan) to expose and purge natural Israel** (the Jews by birth) **and spiritual Israel** (the Gentiles Christians who are made Jews by spiritual birth, Rm 2:28,29) **of their abominations and sins.**

Unfortunately, just as with natural Israel, spiritual Israel also nullified the divine Jewish roots of the scriptures through pagan religious practices. Religious substitution became the norm in the Gentile Christian world, unknowingly destroying the prophetic Jewish roots and the true biblical Jewish Christian faith. One will discover that the truths of God's words have been replaced with deceptive Western pagan traditions. These lying cultural religious practices are snares that actually subtly seduce people away from Christ. An example of cultural substitution of Babylonian and Roman pagan practice for biblical standards would be the Roman religion called **Mithraism**, which was fused together with the Christian faith. This **unholy wedlock**, which was and still is the worship of the universal Sun god and his mother (through the holidays of Christmas and Easter), were brought into the church. In 70 AD, Roman armies had ransacked Jerusalem, the Jewish holy city, and taken the Jews captive as inferior slaves throughout their empire. Rome would later, through the Emperor Constantine, try to destroy the Jewish Christian religion by joining it, and making himself its head. Hence, Rome condescended the Jewish race, its culture, and its Bible to put Christian authority in the hands of the pagan Gentile Emperor of Rome. Then they rejected the Bible as the final authority on church teachings and doctrines and placing papal bulls, decreed by the many subsequent Popes, in their stead.

Emperor Constantine was a mighty instrument of Satan, used to substitute virtually all biblical truths and doctrine with pagan practices and ideologies. Hence, **Constantine began to hemorrhage the Christian faith by removing the divine word of life (the Bible). A form of cultural transfusion** took place, which **replaced the bible with Pagan ideologies and vain traditions.** This led to the formation of a parallel counterfeit apostate religion called the Roman Universal Church. The Roman Catholic Church incorporated an illegitimate priest system, rejected the Jewish Sabbath, and in its stead venerated the day of the Sun god (Sunday). They also venerated the Virgin Mary and a host of deified saints, further adding to its numerous idolatrous abominations. The Roman Catholic Church also rejected five of the seven prophetic Jewish feast days and replaced the remaining two of the seven (Passover and First Fruits), with Good Friday and Easter.

Roman Catholicism has been proven, historically and biblically, to be a counterfeit Christian religion. None of its keys that were allegedly granted to the blasphemous office of the Pope were capable of unlocking the mysteries of the kingdom of the God or give one access to heaven. The Roman holidays of Christmas and Easter were used by the newly formed Roman religious system, to unite and transform the collapsing Roman Empire from a secular government to a religious institution. They made efforts to become "Christian" but rejected all Jewish roots. They replaced biblical truths necessary for accurate biblical interpretation with all forms of lies and pagan practices that perverted history and the truth. Ethnocentrism emerged with each European nation and its numerous Protestant denominations holding the banner of its own nationalistic and cultural superiority.

The most devastating substitution for European Christianity was the substitution of the writings and commandments of the Jewish apostles and prophets, in exchange for the European Church fathers. First, the cultural transfusion continued as Christian doctrines were fused with Greek reasoning and Roman philosophies. Second, Emperor Constantine, many Catholic popes, and leaders, such as Francis of Assisi, Thomas Aquinas, Agustine, Martin Luther, John Calvin, John Wesley, and hundreds of others, became the new fathers of the faith. New Testament Jewish Apostolic authority went out the window! However, it is the only biblical authority Christ recognizes. In order for most members of Gentile churches to receive the knowledge of the truth, they must be willing to repent, and acknowledge that the church established by the Jewish Messiah was not built upon the European father's teachings. They must take the next step and admit that their doctrines, even though they contained some truth, were often contrary to the apostolic gospel of the kingdom and biblical holiness (Acts 2:38; 8:7-14) . In other words, they were all in heresy and preached gospels contrary to the Jewish apostles! Could these European roots explain why the church is in such a confused state in trying to interpret the book of Revelation? The answer is unmistakably, yes!

Few, because of their cultural pride, can accept this fact and indictment against the European fathers, but nevertheless it is still true. Not until the European Church world returns back to obedience to **all** of the bible as its final authority will it begin to understand the nature of the God who is the same yesterday, today, and forever. They must return to the revelations and foundational teachings of the First Century apostolic church and the Jewish roots of the Christian faith. They must also fully understand the prophetic word of the Lord; for within these truths are the keys to all end time truths. The Holy Ghost is the Spirit of Truth; He is also the Spirit of Prophesy, Jesus Christ (I Pet 1:10-13) who resides in those that obey His word. If the European church fathers had the same Spirit of Christ that the Jewish apostles had, they would be in agreement with them. However, since they are not in agreement, it should be quite apparent that there is another spirit at work in them that is out of synch with the biblical Christ and His holy scriptures (II Cor 11:4,11-13).

In the bible, the Spirit of God, the word of God, and the prophets of God always agree (Rev 19:10). If one receives a revelation from Jesus Christ, it cannot be a false truth, because it is impossible for God to lie. Therefore, **the ministers of Christ are commissioned to preach only the truth**, by the spirit of truth, or they will surely be damned (Gal 1:8,9). Jesus stated in the Garden of Gethsemane that Christians are to believe on Him through the words of His Apostles (Jn 17:20). The Apostle Paul stated that if any man claimed to be spiritual or a prophet, he must first acknowledge that his writings were the commandments of the Lord. If there is still any confusion as to what foundation the Christian church was established under, the internal biblical evidence found in Ephesians 2:18-22 should bring a final resolution to this matter…

"For through him we both have access by one Spirit unto the Father. Now therefore ye are no more strangers and foreigners, but fellow citizens [Jews and

Gentiles] with the saints, and of the household of God;

And are **built upon the foundation of the apostles and prophets, Jesus Christ himself being the chief corner stone***;*

In whom all the building fitly framed together groweth unto an holy temple in the Lord: In whom ye also are builded together for an habitation of God through the Spirit."

In synch with the spirit of this age, Protestant, and contemporary Pentecostal preachers continue to teach, in a culturally biased fashion, that the book of Revelation expresses both the Lord's revenge on them for the crucifixion of Christ, and the hopeful salvation of some of the Jewish people. They do not realize that the overwhelming majority of those who are in the church world are also not saved. In their minds, they are being justified according to their traditions; but in reality, they are not saved the bible way (which is the only way). **Out of God's mercy and compassion for the ignorant, He will take both Jews and Gentile through the Great tribulation so that** <u>**all Israel**</u> (Rm 11:26-28), **natural and spiritual, can be saved** through His New Testament Gospel of the Kingdom (Mt 24:14). For those who have the audacity to say that God has forsaken the natural Jews and placed in their stead the Gentile Christians as an inheritor of the promises of Abraham are greatly mistaken. The Prophet Isaiah clarifies this issue in this prophetic manner:

"For thy Maker is thine husband; the LORD of hosts is his name; and thy Redeemer the Holy One of Israel; The God of the whole earth shall he be called.

For the LORD hath called thee as a woman forsaken and grieved in spirit, and a wife of youth, when thou wast refused, saith thy God. **For a small moment have I forsaken thee; but with great mercies will I gather thee.**

In a little wrath I hid my face from thee for a moment; but with everlasting kindness will I have mercy on thee, saith the LORD thy Redeemer.

For this is as the waters of Noah unto me: for as I have sworn that the waters of Noah should no more go over the earth; so have I sworn that I would not be wroth with thee, nor rebuke thee. **For the mountains shall depart, and the hills be removed; but my kindness shall not depart from thee, neither shall the covenant of my peace be removed, saith the LORD that hath mercy on thee.***" (Isa 54:5-10)*

It does not matter which historical starting point in Western civilization one may use, it becomes obvious that Europeans have consistently persecuted the Jews. One may start with the Roman Emperor Caligula, Martin Luther during the German Reformation, Russian leaders during the era of the Pogroms, or with Adolph Hitler's Nazi final solution (extermination) for the Jews during the

Holocaust. Their culturally superior attitudes and worldviews have perpetually clouded their judgments, when it comes to accurately interpreting bible prophecy, and obeying the scriptures. The net result is rebellion to biblical mandates and rejection of biblical truths.

There are five doctrinal divorces that spawn error and create an unholy severing of truth from the foundation of the biblical Christian faith. These cultural and pagan twists propagated by Western theologians and church founders actually lay a foundation for the bride of the Anti-Christ. Jesus has been patient for two thousand years to receive the bride He has established by the early and the latter rain of the Holy Ghost (Jm 5:7,8). On the other hand, Satan has espoused, during this same time period, a religious bride of confusion and division, which will be united through ungodly rebellion in the last day. This unholy unification will be accomplished through the New Age, Ecumenical, and syncretistic Movements. These five doctrinal errors have ensured that Western theologians would be blinded from the prophetic truths concealed in the writings of the Jewish apostles and prophets, even though they are essential for end time divine relations. Each of these schisms or doctrinal divorces severs divine truths and has left the religious world with error. Consequently, they have resulted in the preaching of another Jesus, another gospel, another spirit, and multiple resurrections.

The Five Eurocentric Doctrinal Divorces That Produce Error

1. Divorce of the Name of Jesus Christ from Water Baptism

The Catholic Church, under the oversight of Emperor Constantine, **divorced the name of Jesus Christ from water baptism**, a breach of the marriage covenant. If Western Christian denominations were put on trial in the court of heaven for rejecting the biblical command to baptize in the "Name" of the Lord, they would be found guilty and convicted of commandment nullification by tradition (Mk 7:6-10,13). When Christians are baptized in water in the name of Jesus Christ, they take on the name of the one they are betrothed to; they take on His character, His likeness in death and resurrection, and His nature. In the book of Revelation, the Philadelphian church refused to deny His name, His word, and received the kingdom promises of David (Rev 3:8). All Western churches eventually rejected the biblical command to be baptized *in the Name* of the Lord (Mt 28:19) and persecuted unto death those who would obey the scriptures. This left only small pockets of Apostolic Pentecostal churches, which continued to adhere to this biblical teaching until recently. Candidates who were baptized in water, according to the commandments of the apostles and the pattern of the entire First Century church, were always baptized in the name of Jesus Christ. **No one in the Bible or in the Early church history was ever baptized *in the titles*, Father, Son, and Holy Ghost.** If "Christian" leaders cannot understand (by divine revelation) the basis of baptism in the name of Jesus Christ (Acts 2:38; 8:12,16; 9:18; 10:47,48; 19:5), then it would be futile to try to grasp the understanding of the book of Revelation. Needless to say, the Apostles' disclosure of the end times is actually the revelation of Jesus Christ. This unfolding revelation was established by all of the Jewish apostles and prophets in the Old and New Testament. Only those who have a spiritual ear to hear what the spirit of Christ is saying to His bride can hear and understand the mysteries of the book of Revelation.

The Roman Catholic Church and her Trinitarian Protestant and Pentecostal cultural offspring cannot obey this apostolic command, without rebelling against their pagan traditions. They are also bound by the Trinitarian explanation of the Godhead, established by the pagan Emperor Constantine and the heretical Roman church fathers, at the council of Nicea. Despite all the evidence to the contrary, they continue to baptize in the titles, claiming that the apostles actually disobeyed Christ by baptizing in the name of Jesus Christ. In order to justify their position, heresy, and traditions, they pit Jesus against His Apostles claiming they would rather obey the words of Christ rather than the apostles. Obviously, they can not see the pit they have fallen into when they take such a doctrinal and philosophical stance. If the apostles did not obey Christ, whom they knew personally, then none of their writing can be trusted, and the Bible should be destroyed because of the lying testimonies of His disobedient apostles.

Approximately twenty-three years ago, a Baptist pastor in Nashville, Tennessee told me that if the Apostles Paul and Peter baptized in the name of Jesus Christ, it was contrary to Jesus' command in Matthew 28:19, and that they were wrong. I kindly, but firmly, informed this misguided preacher that his beliefs had destroyed both my faith, and his. I told him that if he truly believed that, he might as well take his Bible and use it for toilet tissue because, if the apostles willfully disobeyed Christ, then that would make them false apostles. Without developing his critical thinking skills he negated the fact that the Apostle Paul wrote two thirds of the New Testament. If Paul and the other apostles "were wrong," how could we trust anything that they wrote? If one puts Jesus in opposition to His apostles, because of their lack of understanding of spiritual things, then the bible would be divided against itself. There would therefore be no accurate basis for the Christian faith and all those who called themselves Christians have believed in vain.

2. Divorce of the Baptism of the Holy Ghost from the Gospel of Salvation

The second apostate divorce of the European church was **the divorce of the baptism of the Holy Ghost from the gospel of salvation**. European Christianity, in order to control the clergy and layman, established an illegitimate priestly system, which separated "**the power**" of the spirit from the Spirit of Christ Himself. Their powerless system of beliefs produced a gospel that only had a shell of a form of godliness, because they denied the power thereof (II Tim 3:5). Without exception, there is biblical evidence that everyone in the First Century Church received Jesus Christ by the baptism of the Holy Ghost, with the evidence of speaking in tongues (Acts 2:1-19; 8:11-18; 10:44-48; 19:1-7). The Gentile church world might want to take heed to the fact that the only reason that **the First Century Jewish Christians received the Gentiles into the church, as candidates of salvation**, was because they had received the Holy Ghost with the evidence of speaking in tongues (Acts 10:44-11:18). This occurred ten years after the Jewish encounter in the Upper Room on the Day of Pentecost, at the home of the Roman Gentile soldier, Cornelius. The Apostle Peter preached Jesus Christ to Cornelius' household; the Holy Ghost fell on them, and they began to speak in unlearned tongues (Acts 10:44-11:18) just like the Jews had initially years earlier.

The European churches, without the experience of the baptism of the Holy Ghost by Jesus Christ, were powerless, dead, liturgical institutions riddled with traditions, and vain pagan rituals. The Roman Catholic and Greek Orthodox Churches bound their Jesus up in the form of dumb idols, religious icons, and superstitious relics. However, the God of Abraham, Isaac, and Jacob has always been a living supernatural miracle working God. He was supernatural in the Old Testament, and He was likewise in the First Century Church, which consisted of Jews and Gentiles. The baptism of the Holy Ghost signified Jesus Christ coming as the Comforter (Jn 14:26) to supernaturally empower His church with the gifts of the spirit (I Cor 12:5-9). It was the baptism of the Holy Ghost that brought Christians into His kingdom church where they could drink of the well of salvation (Jn 7:37-39). **Not only was the Baptism of the Holy Ghost a key component of New Covenant Salvation, it is also essential for the quickening power for the dead to rise in the resurrection or the rapture of the church (Rm 8:11). NO HOLY GHOST, NO RESURRECTION, NO RAPTURE! This statement should send shock waves to those who do not abide in the apostle's doctrines or reject the baptism of the Holy Ghost.**

The Pagan church world rejects the baptism of the Holy Ghost because it is a supernatural experience in which mortal men cannot control or duplicate. To no avail, Simon the sorcerer of Samaria desired to be able to lay hands on individuals to receive the Holy Ghost as he had observed the Apostles Peter and John do (Acts 8:14-25). In the First Century Church (and today), the Baptism of the Holy Ghost can fall on an individual or be endowed by the laying on of hands by another Christian (Mk 16:16,17Heb 6:1,2). Men can baptize an individual in water, but only the Living God (Jesus Christ) can baptize one with His Spirit, the Holy Ghost. In the last days the Lord will give a double portion of the Holy Ghost to all who receive Him. This would also enable them to continue to have power and dominion over Satan and his demonic forces, and give them power to perform great miracles.

Unfortunately, multitudes have perished with false hope, expecting to be raised from the dead, in vain. They have been deceived by lying traditions of men (Mt 15:8,9), and the false assurances of counterfeit Christian doctrines (Gal 1:8,9, II Cor 4:3,4). Tragically, they received and believed in an another Christ, not the Jesus Christ personified in scriptures. Receive ye the Holy Ghost . . . the Bible Way . . . it is the only way!

3. Divorce of the Necessity of the Spirit, the Water, and the Blood, from the New Testament Covenant

The third great divorce that opened a gateway to darkness in the churches was the segregation of the covenant components of the New Testament will. This established a ball of confusion, in classic fashion! European denominations **divorced the necessity of the spirit, the water, and the blood, from the New Testament Covenant**. Because this nullified the Gospel of the kingdom, Christianity consequently produced thousands of competing theological gospels that were never established through divine or apostolic authority. Each divisive denominational sect found in Christianity can be classified into various religious categories as they willfully **reject, neglect, or segregate doctrinally, the necessity of three divine covenant witnesses.**

Seventeen hundred years of European Christianity has caused the way of truth to be evil spoken of and labeled as heresy. An indepth study of the word of God would reveal that the three witnesses of *the spirit, the water, and the blood* were all necessary components of every covenant of deliverance that God has made with man, from Adam to Pentecost. These three components of the covenants of God consolidated deliverance or salvation for His people. The apostle John reveals that these witnesses are established in heaven, and are God's seal on the earth...
"And there are three that bear witness in earth, the Spirit, and the water, and the blood: and these three agree in one" (I Jn 5:8).

These three components of spirit, water, and blood agree in one, because the Lord of heaven **does not segregate them into three separate acts, but sees the three as one consolidated complete act**. The three collectively consummates God's New Covenant of deliverance and salvation. For example, in the covenant of deliverance that the Lord made with the children of Israel in Egypt, **it was necessary for them to be delivered by all three components in order to be fully saved from the hands of the Egyptians and the elements in the wilderness.** If the children of Israel had only observed the Passover command, by placing the lamb's blood over their door post, but they neglected to leave Egypt, they would not have been "baptized" in the Red Sea (I Cor 10:1,2); they would have died in

Egypt without salvation. If they had not been lead by the spirit of God with the cloud by day, and the pillar of fire by night, they would have been lost and out of fellowship with their God. In like manner, the lamb's blood in Egypt was a prophetic type and shadow of Christ's blood, which would be shed at Calvary hundreds of years in the future. Therefore, **one should also be able to clearly see that it was through the three witnesses (spirit, water, and blood), that the Hebrew people had been delivered (saved) from the bondage of the Egyptians.**

Many Protestant churches over-emphasize the role of the blood of Christ, which was shed for salvation, creating numerous gospels that have an imbalance. Their over emphasis on the blood of the New Covenant has been a reactionary movement (starting with full steam in the sixteenth Century), to the doctrines of their mother, the Roman Catholic Church. Catholicism has always placed the forgiveness of sins in the hands of apostate priests, a counterfeit Virgin Mary, and her son, the Eurocentric Christ. The Protestant churches rightfully so returned the issue of remissions of sins back to Christ and His blood that was shed at Calvary. Unfortunately, the rebellious churches associated with the Catholic Church also error, by de-emphasizing and segregating water and spirit baptism, from the New Testament Covenant. The net result is a deformed version of the Christian faith foreign to the biblical Christian faith.

The spirit, the water, and the blood were also found in the tabernacle in the wilderness. We find that the Spirit of God resided in the Holy of Holies, where only the High Priest could enter and commune with the true and living God, on behalf of the nation of Israel (I Kings 8:6-11). The blood was found at the brazen alter of sacrifice, which was used to burn the sin offerings, offered up to God, on behalf of the twelve tribes of Israel (Ex 29:35-37). The water was first signified by the laver as the instrument in the outer court designated for the priests to wash themselves, before they could partake of the holy things of the Lord, lest they would die (Ex 30:18-20). The scriptures state that by the mouth of two or three witnesses that everything is established (II Cor 13:1). In the scriptures we have more than three witnesses of the spirit, water and blood in unison collectively representing salvation. First with Adam, then Noah, twice with Moses, then John the Baptist, the apostles of Christ, and Christ Himself.

The cultural delusion for many European-based Christian groups can be quite extreme. Those who claim that one can only gain access to Christ through an eccleseastical religious system consisting of priests, and religious leaders, who are intermediaries between God and men are greatly mistaken. On the other hand, there are those at the other extreme who make each individual a god and a law unto himself; they believe they can have their own private interpretation of the scriptures. As in the days of old, so is it today, every man does right according to his own eyes (Prov 21:2;14:12). The apostle Paul commanded the Corinthian Church to have no divisions among them, and to be of the same mind and the same judgments concerning the doctrines of Christ (I Cor 1:10). After almost two thousand years of rejecting Jewish apostolic authority and their commandments, Eastern (the Orthodox Church) and Western Christianity, has made the three witnesses declared by the First Century Church a major stumbling block for themselves. Adherence to the **"Petrine doctrine" (Acts 2:38)**, repentance through the blood of Christ, water baptism by immersion in the name of Jesus Christ, and baptism of the Holy Ghost with the evidence of speaking in tongues, is considered heresy by most in Christianity. However, the Apostle Peter warned that heretics would come into the church, and **the way of truth would be "evil spoken of."**

*"But there were false prophets also among the people, even as there shall be false teachers among you, **who privily shall bring in damnable heresies, even denying the Lord that bought them, and bring upon themselves swift destruction.***

And many shall follow their pernicious ways; by reason of whom the way of truth shall be evil spoken of.

And through covetousness shall they with feigned words make merchandise of you: whose judgment now of a long time lingereth not, and their damnation slumbereth not." (II Pet 2:1-3)

Having the biblical patterns firmly and unquestionably established in Jewish history, and in biblical typology, it should be no strange thing that Peter, on the Day of Pentecost, echoed the same divine pattern to begin the church age. If one is contentious with Peter's command, to repent, be baptized in the name of Jesus Christ for the remission of their sins, or to receive the baptism of the Holy Ghost, **it is obvious that they are not hearing the same spirit that gave Peter this commandment...** *Until the day in which he was taken up, after that he through the Holy Ghost had given commandments unto the apostles whom he had chosen* (Acts 1:2). He that has an ear, let him hear, what the Spirit of Jesus Christ is saying to His church. If one cannot grasp and obey this concept, then he will not be able to understand why the church will go through the tribulation, nor will he understand why the Gospel of the Kingdom must be preached until *the end* of the tribulation (Mt 24:14). The blood, the water, and the spirit represented salvation the bible way, throughout the ages. It was, and always will be, the only way of deliverance until Jesus Christ returns.

4. Divorce of the Father, the Son, and the Holy Ghost for Belief in a Trinitarian, Tri-theistic, Three-person Godhead

The fourth Eurocentric doctrinal divorce of apostasy incorporated the Babylonian, Egyptian, Hindu, and Masonic explanation of the godhead into the Jewish monotheistic church. One of the great mysteries of the pagan Catholic Church is

229

the **mystery of the Trinity**. Trinitarian doctrine was authorized at the Council at Nicea, Italy in 325 AD, as the official Western church explanation of the Godhead. The unlearned may not be aware that the concept of the Trinity is not uniquely "Christian**." In fact the doctrine of the Trinity predated the Christian era by thousands of years and was found in the ancient religions of Babylon, Egypt, India, and the Freemason.** The Freemasons also laid the foundation for many American Protestant seminaries that taught their graduating preachers, unknowingly, the tenants of the mysteries of ancient pagan godheads. **This new Babylonian church theology divorced the Father, the Son, and the Holy Ghost and substituted a tri-theistic, three-person godhead in its stead.** Allegedly, all members are considered co-equal, but yet *three separate persons*. At the Council of Nicea, the decree was given that anyone who did not believe in the Trinity were not Christian and could be put to death for heresy. Even to this day, the religious children of the Roman Catholic Church and the Protestant denominations vehemently defend this doctrine, even though they may not prescribe to many of her other pagan tenants; these would include praying for the dead, worship of the virgin mother, and praying to saints. The doctrine of the Trinity is universally known in all pagan religions going as far back as the ancient Babylonian kingdom of Nimrod (Gen 10,11). This concept of the godhead is being used in the last days as the rallying cry to unite all Baalist religions, in preparation for the antichrist and his global reign over the New World Order.

The final Trinity will be the **Anti-Christ**, the **False Prophet**, and **the Beast** … three separate persons united for one purpose. Roman Catholic Ecumenicalism, which began in 1963 at the Vatican II Conference, is uniting all Christian denominations under her wings through syncretism social movements and the Love Gospel. She, with the aid of the Black Pope (Jesuit General), also nurtures another movement called syncretism. Syncretism is the uniting of all non-Christian and occultic New Age Religions who also share in the doctrine of the Trinity. It also includes those who desire to promote global peace to create a New One-World Roman / Babylonian Religion (unknowingly for the Anti-Christ). Most Christians today do not know that the term Trinity was a pagan term and its theological development was established three thousand years before the Jewish Christian church came into existence. Many continue to blindly remain steadfast in their pagan traditions as sheep to the slaughter. The Hindu Trinity consists of Brahma, Vishnu, and Shiva. The Egyptian Trinity consisted of Isis, Horus, and Seb. The harlot bride of the anti-Christ will receive the satanic Trinity of the Beast, the False Prophet, and the Anti-Christ.

Only the monotheistic God of Israel can be Father in creation, Son in redemption, and Holy Ghost in His church **simultaneously**, because He is not a created being limited by time or space. **The Shema** is the Hebrew term to describe the Hebrew monotheistic God, *"Hear, O Israel: The LORD our God is one LORD"* (Deu 6:4). This verse also capsualizes the Christian God of the New Testament because He is the same God of the Old Testament. Jesus was not just the Son of God, He was God in the flesh walking in the eternal spirit (I Tim 3:16). He was in the world, and the world was made by Him, but the world knew Him not (Jn 1:10). He can govern things visible and invisible, He can dwell in heaven, in earth, and under the earth; and He can indwell each and every spirit baptized Christian, and still not have any limitations to His ability and presence.

The doctrine of the Trinity is one of a host of theological snares spawned by the ancient religious web of darkness, which blinds the minds of those who reject the Jewish roots of the Christian faith. Jesus was the image and manifestation of the invisible God, who appeared unto Abraham as Melchisedec (Heb 7:1-5). He also appeared as a theophany (divine appearance) in the Babylonian fiery furnace as one like unto the Son of God, before His incarnation in the fiery furnace with Shadrach, Meshach, and Abednego (Dan 3:19-25). Jesus Christ came to earth to fulfill His divine script and to legally overcome sin as the Second Adam (I Cor 15:45-50). He defeated Satan, death, and hell for all men who would place their faith and trust in Him. Is there anything to hard for the God of Israel to do? The mystery of the Godhead is really quite simple to understand, for those who have a heart to receive it. God did not send a substitute or created being to die for the sins of mankind. He came Himself (Acts 20:28) to fulfilled His divine word (Lk 24:44), because none of His creation (having free will) could be trusted to do the impossible. With God all things are possible and He died the death of a sinner, though He knew no sin, in order to demonstrate His love towards man. This incredible divine act astonished and baffled the angelic hosts of heaven!

5. Divorce of the Rapture of the Church from the Second Coming of Christ

The fifth doctrine that presented a bill of divorcement to depart from sound biblical truths was **the divorcing of the rapture of the Church from the Second Coming of Christ.** In order to justify the pre-tribulation rapture theory, and explain the seven-year gap between the rapture and the Second Coming of Christ, European theologians developed another theory (consisting of two parts). They taught that there would be a **secret rapture** called **the Blessed Hope**, which would be a secret appearance of Christ for His church. This would allegedly occur just moments prior to the Great Tribulation. The second part of this theory was labeled **the Blessed Appearing**, which was accompanied by another rapture, to be in synch with the Second Coming. This theory teaches that there would be at least two raptures for the righteous; one for the church (at the beginning of the tribulation), and one at the end of the tribulation for those who were *left behind* (including converted Jews). This fabrication is totally contrary to what Jesus taught. Jesus unequivocally stated that there would be **only one rapture (quickening or resurrection) for all of the righteous** (Jn 5:25-30). He revealed also

231

through the Apostle Paul that it would take place at the last trump (I Cor 15:52) and would thus **fulfill the prophecy that Christ, through the Spirit of Prophecy (I Pet 1:11), gave to Isaiah 25:8,9** (also see I Cor 15:52-55). The rapture of the church and resurrection of the saints would take place **only once, not in multiple successions** (according to sound scriptural doctrines).

The pre-tribulation rapture theology originated in Port Glasgow, England with Edward Irvin in the 1830's. It was espoused by John Nelson Darby, the founder of the Plymouth Brethren, and William Kelly and W. Trotter, who were two of his many of followers. Afterwards, numerous European scholars joined the bandwagon, teaching the pre-tribulation rapture hoax and propagating their cultural deception worldwide... to name only a few, they could include F.W. Grant, James M. Gray, A. C. Gaebelein, and F. C. Ottman. Some of the most influential pre-tribualionist's (besides Darby), were Charles I. Scofield, the author of the *Scofield Reference Bible*; W.E Blackstone (*Jesus is Coming*, 1878); H. A. Ironside (*Not Wrath, But Rapture*); Clarence Larkin (*Dispensational Truth*); Gerald B. Stanton (*Kept From the Hour*, 1956); John F. Walvoord (*The Rapture Question*, 1957); and J. Dwight Pentecost (*Things To Come*, 1958). Tragically, all of these scholars ignored the fact that Christ said He would gather the wicked out of His church/kingdom **before** He gathers His Bride. He clearly stated that this would take place at the end of the tribulation (Mt 13:30,38-42, Rev 14:15-20). If they had put eye salve on their eyes, perhaps they may have seen the error of their way (and their wretched church condition) through the eyes of the Lord.

"Because thou sayest, I am rich, and increased with goods, and have need of nothing; and knowest not that thou art wretched, and miserable, and poor, and blind, and naked:

I counsel thee to buy of me gold tried in the fire, that thou mayest be rich; and white raiment, that thou mayest be clothed, and that the shame of thy naked-ness do not appear; and anoint thine eyes with eyesalve, that thou mayest see." (Rev 3:17,18)

In more recent years, we have the Southern Baptist theologian, **Hal Lindsey**, who popularized this view for the unlearned masses (*The late great Planet Earth*, 1970). Lindsey presented this pre-tribulation rapture view in written book form, and through the film industry in the 1970's. The popular fictional series entitled **"Left Behind," by Tim LaHay**, has become a phenomenal literary and financial success. As people become more and more interested in bible prophecy, because they see the signs of the end times becoming more apparent, books are being marketed to financially capitalize on the demand. The fallacy of many that are religious is that they would rather read a book and gather the opinions of others instead of studying the bible for themselves. However, La Hay continues to perpetrate this cultural hoax in his writings as well. Unfortunately, the Christian masses have been beguiled because they choose not to study the word of God and

232

develop their spiritual senses. They seem to prefer to go along with the religious fads of their day, succumbing to many false beliefs, and naively think that because a biblical view is popular, it is therefore true. The Hellenistic Eurocentric church, as a whole, since the Second Century has never in practice believed the truths of God's word. Therefore, it should not cause one to go into a quandary as to why this subject seems so confusing.

If the same spirit led these men who lead the Jewish apostles and prophets, their understanding of the scripture would be in agreement with the words of the apostles. If they had received divine revelation, they could also use only the Old Testament to teach the timing of the rapture and the events of the end times, because the apostles of Christ did so (using only the Law and the Old Testament prophets). Hence, the First Century Church did not have a written, complete New Testament, and none of the apostles, except for John who wrote it, ever saw the book of Revelation. Contemporary scholars have the Old Testament; they have the New Testament, and supposedly the spirit of Christ, why do they continuously stumble over the prophetic word?

If the truth is told concerning the end times, in the manner in which this book seeks to do, the majority of those who call themselves Christians, and claim to love the Lord, are easily offended. Truth, to the religious and the wicked, is like pouring water into a flour sifter. **They are consumed with the holes of traditions and cannot endure sound doctrine.** When a book is popular and the world highly exalts it, one can rest assuredly that it is highly suspect. Why? Because history has revealed that the church of Jesus Christ and the nation of Israel have never wanted to hear the prophetic word concerning their plight. They have always stoned the prophets and burned the preachers of righteousness at the stake. Christians today are more attracted to religious celebrities and stars that tell them what they want to hear, because they have itching ears the size of an elephant. These gullible souls wait for someone to give them a favorable personal word. They also seek preachers that would tell them the doctrines they want to hear. The Apostle Paul addressed this issue in his writing to Timothy…

*"I charge thee therefore before God, and the Lord Jesus Christ, **who shall judge the quick** [the translated saints] **and the dead** [those who have died in Christ] **at his appearing and his kingdom;***

Preach the word; be instant in season, out of season; reprove, rebuke, exhort with all longsuffering and doctrine.

For the time will come when they will not endure sound doctrine; but after their own lusts shall they heap to themselves teachers, having itching ears;

*And they shall turn away their ears from the truth, **and shall be turned unto fables**. But watch thou in all things…"* (II Tim 4:1-5)

Christ will rapture the dead in Christ first, and quicken those who are alive, to be transformed from mortality to immortality at His Second Coming as stated in II Tim 4:1. This event happens only once, not in multiple occurrences as many choose to believe. Jesus Christ, at the sound of the Archangel Michael's trumpet, will cause the dead to rise incorruptible, by the power of the Holy Ghost that dwells with in them. This event will trigger the rapture. If anyone should know what would happen, it is Jesus Christ, as expressed in the writings of the Apostle Paul. It is not wise to refute or contradict their revelations on this matter. This is the only way…it is the Bible way.

Are the Terms Love and Judgment Compatible?

Many Christians have a perverted concept of love, which is diametrically opposite of the love of God. Their love is weak, wicked, and with out consequence. Can God love His church if He allows her to go through the tribulation? What is the basis and objective of the Lord's taking the church through the tribulation? Is there an Old Testament prototype for such an event? The answer is unequivocally, yes! First, a typology of the church receiving God's perfect judgment and love is found in the Old Testament book of Leviticus. The Lord dealt with His natural children "**seven times**" for their sins, until they were without fault. He is the same "yesterday, today, and forever;" therefore, his character is consistent and His love is balanced." Seven is the number of perfection, and Christ "*will perfect that which concerns Him*" (Psa 138:8). In the book of Revelation there are seven churches (chapters 2 and 3). Each has been, and will be, judged perfectly with a strong hand of correction in order for each of them to repent of their sins. If they choose not to be reformed by the chastening of the Lord, their names will be blotted out of the Lamb's Book of Life and they will perish (Rev 3:5). Natural and spiritual Israel will experience the wrath and judgement of God during the days of tribulation in order to separate the wicked from the righteous in His house. In the book of Revelation Jesus also tells the church of Laodicea, *"As many as I love, I rebuke and chasten: be zealous therefore, and repent" (Rev 3:19)*. In the book of Hebrews, the Apostle Paul adds more light on this subject, **connecting the love of God with the judgment of God…**

*"My son, **despise not thou the chastening of the Lord, nor faint when thou art rebuked of him: For whom the Lord loveth he chasteneth, and scourgeth every son whom he receiveth. If ye endure chastening, God dealeth with you as with sons; for what son is he whom the father chasteneth not?***
*But if ye be without chastisement, whereof all are partakers, then are ye bastards, and not sons. Furthermore we have had fathers of our flesh which corrected us, and we gave them reverence: **shall we not much rather be in***

subjection unto the Father of spirits, and live?" (Heb:12:5-9)

Jesus Christ will have a glorious church at His coming. His bride will be found without spot, wrinkle, or blemish. The tribulation period is "the wash cycle" that will remove all the wickedness, darkness, doctrinal spots, and hellish ways out of the church. In the Old Testament pattern, the Lord systematically broke the pride of Israel and brought every form of chastisement and judgment upon her through four successive rounds of severe reprimands of love. The same is applicable to the church world today. If one can understand the natural correlation between love and chastening, then he should also be able to comprehend the spiritual dynamics and the necessity of the tribulation for the 25,000 rebellious Christian denominational sects. In the book of Leviticus, Moses by the prophetic spirit of Christ, gave a prototype of God's perfect love and judgment on Israel. This event served as a blueprint for the churches in Asia, found in the book of Revelation chapters two and three, of which the book was addressed. The prophetic pattern is as follows:

The First ...... Seven Times (perfect judgment for natural Israel)

Lev 26:14 But **if ye will not hearken unto me**, and **will not do all these commandments**;

15 And **if ye shall despise my statutes**, or **if your soul abhor my judgments**, so that ye **will not do all my commandments**, but **that ye break my covenant**:

16 I also will do this unto you; **I will even appoint over you terror, consumption, and the burning ague**, that shall consume the eyes, and cause sorrow of heart: and ye shall sow your seed in vain, for your enemies shall eat it.

17 And **I will set my face against you**, and ye shall be slain before your enemies: they that hate you shall reign over you; and **ye shall flee when none pursueth you**.

18 And if ye will not yet for all this hearken unto me, then **I will punish you seven times more for your sins.**

The Second ...... Seven Times (perfect judgment for natural Israel)

Lev 26:19 And **I will break the pride of your power**; and I will make your heaven as iron, and your earth as brass:

20 And your strength shall be spent in vain: for your land shall not yield her increase, neither shall the trees of the land yield their fruits.

21 And **if ye walk contrary unto me, and will not hearken unto me; I will bring seven times more plagues upon you according to your sins.**

The Third ...... Seven Times (perfect judgment for natural Israel)

Lev 26:22 **I will also send wild beasts among you**, which shall rob you of your children, and destroy your cattle, and make you few in number; and your highways shall be desolate.

23 And **if ye will not be reformed by me by these things, but will walk contrary unto me**;

24 **Then will I also walk contrary unto you, and <u>will punish you yet seven times for your sins</u>.**

The Fourth …… Seven Times (perfect judgment for natural Israel)

Lev 26:25 And **I will bring a sword upon you, that shall avenge the quarrel of my covenant**: and when ye are gathered together within your cities, **I will send the pestilence among you**; and ye shall be delivered into the hand of the enemy.

26 And when I have broken the staff of your bread, ten women shall bake your bread in one oven, and they shall deliver you your bread again by weight: and ye shall eat, and not be satisfied.

27 **And if ye will not for all this hearken unto me, but walk contrary unto me**;

28 Then **I will walk contrary unto you also in fury; and <u>I, even I, will chastise you seven times for your sins.</u>**

The sequence of events with natural Israel in Leviticus is again, a typology of the chastising love that the Lord will induce upon His church in order to bring her unto repentance, and reduce the rebellious 25,000 Christian denominational sects into one holy cohesive body. In the New Testament, perfect judgment is administered to the seven churches damning those who refuse to repent, but promises of blessings are given to those who overcome. Christ delivered Christians from the spirit of whoredom (Hos 4:12;5:4) that caused them to error and purchased them at a tremendous price, His own blood. Therefore, Jesus Christ will go to great lengths to rescue those who will allow Him to deliver them out of Satan's camp and save their souls.

The **Lord had controversies** with natural Israel that he would not leave unresolved. Through out the ages man-made religions have been a substitute for truth, mercy, and the fear of God. Therefore, in like manner, God shall resolve His controversies with His contemporary bride, the spiritual Israel. The prophet Hosea, in a typological fashion, foretells the work that the Lord will do with the future church.

*Hear the word of the LORD, ye children of Israel: <u>**for the LORD hath a controversy**</u> **with the inhabitants of the land, because there is no truth, nor mercy, nor knowledge of God in the land.**

By swearing, and lying, and killing, and stealing, and committing adultery, they break out, and blood toucheth blood...

My people are destroyed for lack of knowledge: because thou hast rejected knowledge, I will also reject thee, that thou shalt be no priest to me: seeing thou hast forgotten the law of thy God, I will also forget thy children.

As they were increased, so they sinned against me: therefore will I change their glory into shame. They eat up the sin of my people, and they set their heart on their iniquity.

And there shall be, like people, like priest: and I will punish them for their ways, and reward them their doings...

*My people ask counsel at their stocks, and their staff declareth unto them: **for the spirit of whoredoms hath caused them to err**, and they have gone a whoring from under their God.*

***I will not punish your daughters when they commit whoredom**, nor your spouses when they commit adultery: for themselves are separated with whores, and they sacrifice with harlots: **therefore the people that doth not understand shall fall**...*

Though thou, Israel, play the harlot, yet let not Judah offend; and come not ye unto Gilgal, neither go ye up to Beth-aven, nor swear, The LORD liveth.

For Israel slideth back as a backsliding heifer: (Hos 4:1-16)

A third prototype of the church being judged is the Lord's Judgment of the inhabitants of His natural temple in Ezekiel's day. In the last days, God shall also judge the end time spiritual temples for the abominations that occur in the body of Christ (I Cor 3:16,17; 6:19,20). Contemporary abominations would include virtually all of the teachings and idolatrous dogmas of the Roman Catholic Church and many Protestant, Post-Protestant, and Pentecostal teachings. They would also include the infiltration of Masonic, New Age, Liberal Post-Modern Christianity, and Babylonian doctrines in the church. Judgement will also be given for the sins of the flesh, such as homosexuality, divorce, and adultery, amongst church leaders and members. Practices of abortion, spouse and child abuse, murder, occultism, heresies, racism, and the Nicolaitan doctrine are sins festering in the church world like cancerous cells. **One option the Lord has is to kill this wretched "woman" before she destroys herself. A second option would be to take her through a complete wash cycle, called the Great Tribulation, to display His love for her and provoke her unto repentance.** This way, as with natural Israel, He will judge her <u>seven times</u> (seven years) for her sins. Hence, the wicked and the ungodly Christians have a good reason to fear the wrath of God and are warned, "*it is a fearful thing to fall into the hands of the living God.*" We are also told in scripture that the Lord God "*is a consuming fire.*" The God of Israel is a jealous God, and He will not tolerate disobedience or spiritual idolatry of any sort. He is the Lord God that changes not and His name is YESHUA HOMASHEA, Jesus the Christ… the same yesterday, today, and forever!

Perhaps contrary to popular beliefs, the book of Revelation is God's greatest love story since Calvary. However, few can understand it because of their perverted concepts of the love of Christ, their rejection of divine judgment for the church, and their Eurocentric deformed versions of salvation. The cup containing His wrath is filled up to the brim and is about to overflow on the wickedness in His church and then in the world. God revealed to the prophet Ezekiel that there were **THREE GREAT ABOMINATIONS** occurring in the natural temple of Israel that provoked Him to **jealousy and righteous indignation**.

Ezek 8:3 And he put forth the form of an hand, and took me by a lock of mine head; and the spirit lifted me   up between the earth and the heaven, and brought me in the visions of God to Jerusalem, to the door of the inner gate that looketh toward the north; where was the **seat of the image of jealousy, which provoketh to jealousy.**

5 Then said he unto me, Son of man, lift up thine eyes now the way toward the north. So I lifted up mine eyes the way toward the north, and behold northward at the gate of **the altar this image of jealousy in the entry.**

6 He said furthermore unto me, Son of man, seest thou what they do? **even the great abominations that the house of Israel committeth here, that I should go far off from my sanctuary**?
[See Rev 3:19, Christ kicked out of His sanctuary.]

Abomination #1

The senior priests worship idols in darkness in the basement of the temple of the Lord

Ezek 8:9 And he said unto me, Go in, and behold the wicked abominations that they do here.

10 So I went in and saw; and **behold every form of creeping things, and abominable beasts, and all the idols of the house of Israel, pourtrayed upon the wall round about**.

11 And there stood before them **seventy men of the ancients of the house of Israel**, and in the midst of them stood Jaazaniah the son of Shaphan, with every man his censer in his hand; and a thick cloud of incense went up.

12 Then said he unto me, Son of man, **hast thou seen what the ancients of the house of Israel do in the dark, every man in the chambers of his imagery?** for they say, **The LORD seeth us not**; the LORD hath forsaken the earth.

Abomination #2

The women of Israel weeping in the temple of God for the Egyptian god Tammuz

Eze 8:13 He said also unto me, Turn thee yet again, and thou shalt see greater abominations that they do.

14 Then he brought me to **the door of the gate of the LORD's house** which was toward the north; and, **behold, there sat women weeping for Tammuz.**

Abomination #3
The priests facing the East in the Lord's house worshipping the Sun god with their backs to the alter of God

Eze 8:15 Then said he unto me, Hast thou seen this, O son of man? turn thee yet again, and thou shalt see greater abominations than these.

16 **And he brought me into the inner court of the LORD's house**, and, behold, at the door of the temple of the LORD, between the porch and the altar, **were about five and twenty men, with their backs toward the temple of the LORD, and their faces toward the east; and they worshipped the sun toward the east.**

17 Then he said unto me, Hast thou seen this, O son of man? Is it a light thing to the house of Judah that they commit the abominations which they commit here? for **they have filled the land with violence, and have returned to provoke me to anger:** and, lo, they put the branch to their nose.

18 <u>**Therefore will I also deal in fury: mine eye shall not spare, neither will I have pity: and though they cry in mine ears with a loud voice, yet will I not hear them.**</u>

The Lord God is a jealous God, and He will not allow spiritual whoredom to continue in His church. He will deal with these religious leaders who deceitfully comfort each other by saying, *"I'm O.K., you're O.K."* They foolishly believe that the Lord will continue to do them good and that He does not see the iniquity that they do. However, when sudden destruction comes upon them like a whirlwind, they will not know from where it comes, or understand why it is coming. They will be like the atheist who is manipulated intellectually without the knowledge of truth, and like a puppet on a string, controlled by the spirit of rebellion. They falsely believe that their thoughts are their own, because they have been seduced by devils of unbelief. They have contempt for an absolute sovereign God, because they are oblivious to the attached demonic strings, which grip their hearts and

239

minds. In the same manner, for those who believe they will not go through the tribulation period, their hearts and minds provide an open door, allowing them to be subtly controlled by Satan, the Prince of the Powers of the Air (Eph 2:2). At all cost, the devil tries to conceal his inevitable doom by making his thoughts the thoughts of men. The prophet Zephaniah expounds on this further.

> "*And it shall come to pass at that time, that **I will search Jerusalem with candles, and punish the men** that are settled on their lees: **that say in their heart, The LORD will not do good, neither will he do evil.***
>
> ***Therefore their goods shall become a booty, and their houses a desolation****: they shall also build houses, but not inhabit them; and they shall plant vineyards, but not drink the wine thereof.*
>
> ***The great day of the LORD is near****, it is near, and hasteth greatly, **even the voice of the day of the LORD: the mighty man shall cry there bitterly.***
>
> ***That day is a day of wrath, a day of trouble and distress, a day of wasteness and desolation, a day of darkness and gloominess, a day of clouds and thick darkness . . .***" (Zeph 1:12-15)

Man is not wiser than his maker. All of the collective knowledge of men cannot stop the events ordained by God from the foundation of the world. If all humans could gather themselves together to war against the God of heaven, could they alter His prophetic divine decrees or covenant statutes? Absolutely not! *"He hath made every thing beautiful in his time: **also he hath set the world in their heart, so that no man can find out the work that God maketh from the beginning to the end***" (Ec 3:11). *"For man also knoweth not his time: as the fishes that are taken in an evil net, and as the birds that are caught in the snare; **so are the sons of men snared in an evil time, when it falleth suddenly upon them***" (Ec 9:2). The world's religious can never discern the proper signs, or the times, to know God's divine agenda. The unbelieving also do not know that there is a time and a season for everything under the sun. However, the righteous knows that, *"the Lord GOD will do nothing, but he revealeth his secret unto his servants the prophets"(Amos 3:7).*

The day of God's wrath is at hand, but Christianity has been anesthetized by seducing doctrines making it comatosed to the workings of the spirit. We are told by the Prophet Daniel, that those who know their God will "do exploits" in the last days (Dan 11:32). They shall also be shielded by a divine mark placed in their foreheads by the angels of God to protect them from the wrath, indignation, and desolation to come. These types and shadows occurred in the natural and will again happen with the spiritual. The account of Gods' solution to remedy the natural temple of Judah, of the image of jealousy and the three great abominations found in His temple, is characterized as follows: He tells the angel to…

Ezek 9:4 . . . Go through the midst of the city, through the midst of Jerusalem, and **set a mark upon the foreheads** of the men that sigh and that cry for all the abominations that be done in the midst thereof.

5 And to the others he said in mine hearing, Go ye after him through the city, and **smite: let not your eye spare, neither have ye pity:**

6 **Slay utterly old and young, both maids, and little children, and women: but come not near any man upon whom is the mark; and begin at my sanctuary. Then they began at the ancient men which were before the house.**

7 And he said unto them, Defile the house, and fill the courts with the slain: go ye forth. And they went forth, and slew in the city.

8 And it came to pass, while they were slaying them, and I was left, that I fell upon my face, and cried, and said, Ah Lord GOD! **wilt thou destroy all the residue of Israel in thy pouring out of thy fury upon Jerusalem?**

9 Then said he unto me, The iniquity of the house of Israel and Judah is exceeding great, and the land is full of blood, and the city full of perverseness: **for they say, The LORD hath forsaken the earth, and the LORD seeth not.**

10 And as for me also, **mine eye shall not spare, neither will I have pity, but I will recompense their way upon their head.**

Again, from the typology of the natural temple, we can conclude that God will utterly judge His spiritual temples in the same manner as He did with the natural (I Pet 4:17). The Lord cleansed His temple of Israel's three great abominations by sending the angel of wrath to slay His own people, including their children, without pity. So shall it also be with the church, as He purges His floor of its whorish, stubborn, and rebellious ways (Mt 3:12). We are told that before any of the judgments begin, He will command His angel to put **a mark upon the foreheads** of those who have their hearts towards God and intercede for the abominations committed by members of the body of Christ (verse 4).

In the New Covenant, the Holy Ghost is the first seal given to all who walk in accordance with the word of God. "*In whom ye also trusted, after that ye heard the word of truth, the gospel of your salvation: in whom also after that ye believed, ye were sealed with that holy Spirit of promise* [Holy Ghost baptism, Acts 1:8, Lk 24:49], *Which is the earnest of our inheritance until the redemption of the purchased possession, unto the praise of his glory*" (Eph 1:13,14). We also find that in the book of Revelation, before any of the judgments begin, the angels are likewise commanded to seal the foreheads of the righteous who abide in His temple with the number of Jesus Christ (their God).

"*Saying, Hurt not the earth, neither the sea, nor the trees, **till we have sealed the servants of our God in their foreheads.***

*And **I heard the number of them which were sealed**: and there were sealed* *an hundred and forty and four thousand of all the tribes of the children of Israel."* (Rev 7:3,4, also see Rev 9:4)

The divine pattern established from the foundation of the world, for those who can receive it, is that the righteous are sealed first, then the judgments begin for the rebellious. I will emphasize the fact that **the saints are sealed for protection,** *not to be raptured out* of the earth. God has always taken His people *through* the natural and spiritual battles . . . He has never taken them out of their battles. The battles are the Lord's, and He shall never fail. Always, when the battles conclude, both the heathen and the righteous confess that the God of Israel . . . "He is Lord." The escape mentality of the contemporary Christian world goes against the grain of biblical history and the character of God. To make matters even worse, their false belief that they will be raptured out in their present state of spiritual decadence and doctrinal darkness, is a mockery to the holy groom of heaven. Jesus Christ, the Bridegroom, desires to marry a holy and spotless bride. **Only God can take a worldly whorish woman and make her a pure and holy bride.** In order to get Christianity where it needs to be, of one mind and in one accord, He will have to shake the heavens and the earth. He will have to reform her heart to remove her wickedness. This point is clearly illustrated in the book of Hebrews, which speaks of a time of great shaking, that will shake the heavens and the earth.

"And to Jesus the mediator of the new covenant, and to the blood of sprinkling, that speaketh better things than that of Abel.

See that ye refuse not him that speaketh. For if they escaped not who refused him that spake on earth, ***much more shall not we escape, if we turn away from him that speaketh from heaven:***

Whose voice then shook the earth: but now he hath promised, saying, ***Yet once more I shake not the earth only, but also heaven.***

And this word, Yet once more, signifieth ***the removing of those things that are shaken,*** *as of things that are made, that* ***those things which cannot be shaken may remain.***

Wherefore we receiving a kingdom which cannot be moved, let us have grace, whereby <u>***we may serve God acceptably with reverence and godly fear:***</u>
<u>***For our God is a consuming fire.***</u>" (Heb 12:24-29)

Natural Israel tried, tempted, and constantly murmured against the Lord in the wilderness, and He overthrew them there, allowing their carcasses to rot in the wilderness. **The tribulation is a type of wilderness** prepared to try the hearts of all saints who choose to be rebellious. Referring to the church, the prophet Zechariah prophesies that **two thirds** of the church would be rejected by Christ, and only **one third** will He deliver through the fire (Zech 13:8,9). The Apostle

Paul makes a direct parallel with the children of Israel in the wilderness and the church, warning that Christians had better learn from the examples of old, lest they behave in the manner of natural Israel, and get slaughtered. There is coming a great falling away (II Thes 2:3) and a great slaughter (Zech 11:4,5) among the wicked in the Lord's house. Just in case some may still doubt the possibility of the church receiving God's wrath, the Apostle Paul rebuked and warned the church, not to have an evil heart of unbelief and perish.

"But with many of them God was not well pleased: for they were overthrown in the wilderness. ***Now these things were our examples, to the intent we should not lust after evil things, as they also lusted.***

Neither be ye idolaters, as were some of them; as it is written, The people sat down to eat and drink, and rose up to play. Neither let us commit fornication, as some of them committed, and fell in one day three and twenty thousand.

Neither let us tempt Christ, as some of them also tempted, and were destroyed of serpents. Neither murmur ye, as some of them also murmured, and were destroyed of the destroyer.

Now all these things happened unto them for ensamples: and they are written for our admonition, *upon whom the ends of the world are come.*

Wherefore let him that thinketh he standeth take heed lest he fall." (I Cor 10:5-12)

Christians beware, your heavenly Father is coming quickly and He is bringing His "licking stick" for chastisement. Then He will extend His hand in marriage to those who endure His chastening and make themselves ready for the marriage of the Lamb.

The book of Revelation is the greatest love story since Christs' crucifixion at Golgotha, the hill of the skull. At Calvary, Christ died for the sins of the whole world. During the tribulation period, each Christian will have his final opportunity to die to the sins of their flesh (Gal 5:19-21) and false doctrines, to serve the living God. Natural Israel will also have an opportunity to turn from her unbelief and complete her destiny by partaking of the spiritual covenant, which first began at Pentecost. Hence, it should be no strange thing to believe and understand why the church must go through the tribulation. The biblical pattern has always been to take ***the remnant*** to deliver ***the masses***.

The Four Categories of Saints Found in the Book of Revelation

The following legion will be used to decipher the four categories of Christians found throughout the Book of Revelation. The book of Revelation, also referred to as the apocalypse, is entitled the Revelation of Jesus Christ. It can only be unveiled through the symbolism and keys found throughout the Old and New Testaments. Within this book, the church is revealed as the body of Christ, who battles with the kingdom of darkness in types and shadows and prophetic symbolism.

1. **Category 1 Saints are the Martyred Saints** whom the Beast will make war against (Rev 12:11; 13:6; 12:13). Satan will persecute the Christian masses in the church because he cannot touch the mature sons of God, who will come out from the church and judge his kingdom (Rev 12:4-6,13-17). They will overcome the Beast and the Anti-Christ system by the blood of the Lamb and the word of their testimony. They will be a witness against the rulers of this world at the Day of Judgment.

    " *...these are the beginnings of sorrows. **But take heed to yourselves: for they shall deliver you up to councils; and in the synagogues ye shall be beaten: and ye shall be brought before rulers and kings for my sake, for a testimony against them.***

    *And the gospel must first be published among all nations. **But when they shall lead you, and deliver you up, take no thought beforehand what ye shall speak, neither do ye premeditate: but whatsoever shall be given you in that hour, that speak ye: for it is not ye that speak, but the Holy Ghost.***

    *Now the brother shall betray the brother to death, and the father the son; and children shall rise up against their parents, **and shall cause them to be put to death.***

    *And ye shall be hated of all men for my name's sake: **but he that shall endure unto the end, the same shall be saved**" (Mk 13:8-13).* They will be resurrected from the dead at the last trump, and encouraged by the Lord, as He assures them that He will avenge their deaths. (Rev 6:9-11, 20:4) <u>Resurrected Saints</u>!

2. **Category 2 Saints are those who will live throughout the tribulation**, never experiencing death. They will be translated from mortality to immortality, at the last trump, after the resurrected saints are raised from the dead. (Rev 14:12, I Cor 15:51-55, I Thes 4:15-18) <u>Translated Saints</u>!

3. **Category 3 Saints are the mature sons of God called The Manchild**. The will bring forth many of the judgments in the book of Revelation, including the vial judgments. They will be revealed midway through the tribulation (3 ½ years) and will be totally oblivious to the rebellious Christian masses. Their ministry will be in conjunction with that of the Anti-Christ's, lasting 42 months, which is also three and a half years. They will render unto the anti-Christ the same measure as Moses did to buffet Pharaoh and destroy his kingdom. The Manchild will destroy Satan's kingdom, both naturally and spiritually. They shall also walk in the tri-fold anointing of Moses, Elijah, and John the Baptist, to do exploits in the earth. Their ministry will exceed the ministry of Jesus and the apostles, as the "*greater works*" of the Holy Ghost. Collectively, they will move in the Spirit of Christ without measure, preach the apostolic Gospel of the Kingdom, and deliver both natural and spiritual Israel from their sins.

    The Manchild will be invincible, and cannot be killed until their appointed time, just like Christ. At the very end of the tribulation period, the Beast will finally be allowed to kill them (Rev 11:7). However, just like Christ, their deaths will be the doom of Satan, hell, and death. After three days, they will miraculously rise to their feet, and all the dead who has died in Christ will rise with them. This is the RAPTURE of the church, when the Manchild and all of the dead saints in Christ are raised first, and then those who are alive at Jesus' coming shall be changed into immortality to meet Christ in the air. The redemption of the earth and mankind is predicated on the resurrection of the Manchild. In concert the resurrected and translated saints will fulfill the typology of Jesus Christ at the 7th, or last trump (Rev 10:7; 11:7-15; 12:17).

4. **Category 4 Saints are the wicked tares** that currently dwell in Christ's kingdom/ church. They are those who love religion more than they love God, and will not repent to receive the truths of God's word. Their religion shall fail them, and they will hate Jesus Christ the more. Most will become apostate and willingly give their allegiance to the anti-Christ. These religious and false Christians will be exposed in the last days, and shall constitute "the Great falling away" (II Thes 2:3). These individuals will be cut off from the kingdom of God in the manner that Christ spoke of in the parables of His kingdom. **"There shall be weeping and gnashing of teeth" for all criminals in the house of God.** They will be overcome by the flood of false doctrine and lying wonders, because they have not a heart to receive sound doctrine, that they might be saved (II Thes 2:11-13). Many will betray Jesus, like Judas did, and become engrossed in all manner of vial wickedness. They will not repent from their harlotry, apostasy, gross sexual perversions and abominations, but will walk as the heathen, accepting the Mark of Beast.

    For those who cannot locate, or identify these four Christians groups in the book of Revelation, there is a clear indication of spiritual blindness, or willful ignorance of the evidence. The natural man cannot receive the things of the spirit of God, because they must be spiritually discerned (I Cor 2:7-14). Even the saints of God must put on the mind of Christ, and flush away their prejudices and darkness, in order to understand the pure word of God. The appearance of the church throughout the Book of Revelation is so abundant and obvious, that men must intentionally look at this book with a preconceived bias in order to error. Darkness blinds the hearts first, then the mind, causing the religious to always miss the revelations of God. If one studies only to defend his cultural world-view, then any contrary evidence will be overlooked or twisted to fit his desired outcome. Self-deception should not exist, because the book of Revelation is the only Book in the bible that promises a blessing to the reader and the doer. Why should one want to receive its judgments (curses) instead?

The Blessing:

"Blessed is he that readeth, and they that hear the words of this prophecy, and keep those things, which are written therein: for the time is at hand." (Rev 1:3)

The Curse:

"For I testify unto every man that heareth the words of the prophecy of this book, If any man shall add unto these things, God shall add unto him the plagues that are written in this book:

And if any man shall take away from the words of the book of this prophecy, God shall take away his part out of the book of life, and out of the holy city, and from the things which are written in this book." (Rev 22:8,19)

Behold . . . The Revelation of Jesus Christ
His Bride - His Body – His Church

Categories of Christians (Saints) in the Book of Revelation:

1) The Martyred Overcomers
2) The Living Overcomers
3) The Manchild Remnant
4) The Tares

Scriptures	Type of Saint(s)
Rev. 1:1 **The Revelation of Jesus Christ, which God gave unto him, to shew unto his servants things which must shortly come to pass; and he sent and signified it by his angel unto his servant John**: [The book of Revelation is a revelation of the one that seems to be an enigma to mankind. Who is Jesus Christ? The Jehovah Witness claims that He is the Archangel Michael. Eurocentric Christianity embraces the idea that He is the third person of the Trinity. The Freemasons, according to Albert Pike, believe that Jesus and Lucifer were twin brothers. Jews and Muslims believe that Jesus was a prophet, but reject His message. Most members of the Ku Klux Klan do not believe that Jesus was a Jew. Oneness Pentecostals adhere to the revelations taught by the Jewish apostles who believe that Jesus Christ was God manifested in the Flesh. Each of these groups, and thousands of others, have their own private understanding as to who they believe Jesus is. The confusion is quite staggering, even though there is sufficient historical and biblical evidence to dispel the confusion. The book of Revelation is the unveiling of Jesus Christ, declaring His mysteries to those who know Him, and divulging His secrets to His disciples. Jesus is the Creator of the universe manifested in the flesh. John's reveals Him to be Savior, and who is His body, the church. In His kingdom / church there are the *"good, the bad, and the ugly."* The REVELATION OF JESUS CHRIST reveals a line of demarcation drawn between the forces of light and the forces of darkness, as Jesus defeats the hosts of hell through weaker vessels made strong (His spiritual body). Jesus' final solution to all discord in the universe and rebellion in creation shall be put to rest. This is especially true of His church as He purges her and prepares her for her wedding. Jesus spoke of this day through His teachings with the parables of the kingdom and the seven churches found in chapters two and three of the book of Revelation. The Apostle Paul comments on the reality of this need for purification when he spoke of	1, 2, 3, 4

the conflict in the house of God with those vessels appointed unto dishonor. *"Nevertheless the foundation of God standeth sure, having this seal, The Lord knoweth them that are his. And, Let every one that nameth the name of Christ depart from iniquity.* *But in a great house there are not only vessels of gold and of silver, but also of wood and of earth; and some to honour, and some to dishonour.* *If a man therefore purge himself from these, he shall be a vessel unto honour, sanctified, and meet for the master's use, and prepared unto every good work."* (II Tim 2:19-21)]	
Rev. 1:3 Blessed is **he that readeth**, and **they that hear the words of this prophecy, and keep those things, which are written therein**: for the time is at hand. [This end time consolidating prophesy was revealed through the Apostle John and the blessing remains for Christians who will inherit their promises. Rev 22:7]	**1, 2, 3, 4**
Rev. 1:5 And from Jesus Christ, who is the faithful witness, and the first begotten of the dead, and the prince of the kings of the earth. **Unto him that loved us, and washed us from our sins in his own blood,** [Jesus Christ, the God of the universe, came as a man to purchase the church with His own blood. Acts 20:28, Col 1:13-19, Rev 1:8;4:8]	**1, 2, 3, 4**
Rev. 1:6 And hath made **us kings and priests unto God and his Father; to him be glory and dominion for ever and ever. Amen.** [Christians collectively constitute a royal priesthood and a holy nation. I Pet 2:5,9, Rev 2:26; 3:21]	**1, 2, 3**
Rev. 1:7 Behold, **he cometh with clouds**; and every eye shall see him, and they also which pierced him: and all kindreds of the earth shall wail because of him. Even so, Amen. [The Lord will appear at His second coming and all eyes will behold Him with clouds of glory, which are the saints. Jude, the brother of Christ stated, *"...Behold, the Lord cometh with ten thousands of his saints,* *To execute judgment upon all, and to convince all that*	**1, 2, 3**(with Him) **4** (Destroyed)

are ungodly among them of all their ungodly deeds which they have ungodly committed, and of all their hard speeches which ungodly sinners have spoken against him." (Jude 14,15) Mt 23:39, Zech 14:4-9;13:5,6; 12:4, Nation of Israel]	

Rev. 1:16 **And he had in his right hand seven stars**: and out of his mouth went a sharp twoedged sword: and his countenance was as the sun shineth in his strength.
 	
    [Jesus Christ is the word of God made flesh. He will manifest His spoken word through His body in the last days to execute judgment throughout the earth. *"For the word of God is quick, and powerful, and sharper than any two-edged sword, piercing even to the dividing asunder of soul and spirit, and of the joints and marrow, and is a discerner of the thoughts and intents of the heart.*
    Neither is there any creature that is not manifest in his sight: but all things are naked and opened unto the eyes of him with whom we have to do." (Heb 4:12,13, Rev 19:13-15)]
	1, 2, 3, 4

Rev. 1:20 **The mystery of the seven stars** which thou sawest in my right hand, and **the seven golden candlesticks. The seven stars are the angels of the seven churches: and the seven candlesticks which thou sawest are the seven churches.**
 	
    [There were more than seven churches in Asia Minor, but the seven cities chosen by Christ were selected as representative of types of sins in His body. The number seven denoted His perfect judgment upon His bride.
    Often times theologians try to interpret the bible to fit their understanding; however, students of the scriptures know that the bible usually interprets and defines its own terms, as we see in this verse.
The seven stars = The seven angels, The seven candlesticks = The seven churches]
	1, 2, 3, 4

Chapter Two Notice to Four of the Seven Churches Even though European scholars claimed that the seven churches, in chapters two and three of this book pertained to seven distinct chronological church ages, there is no scriptural indication that such is the case. This theory was	

introduced by Western scholars to try and legitimize their chronological cultural developments from the advent of apostate Roman Catholicism to her Protestant European offspring. Rejecting the Jewish roots of the Christian faith, and the Baptism of the Holy Ghost, they have tried to legitimize their illegitimate Eurocentric biased church history. Most of the current Western theologian's charts on the Seven churches are merely fabricated timelines of Western Civilization... The Roman Catholic and Protestant Churches. They exclude the Eastern Orthodox Church and all aspects of Pentecostal movements in church history since the first century, from their chronology.

In its biblical context, the Lord addressed **only the sins** of each of the churches in Asia Minor, calling each of them unto repentance. Failure to repent would cause them to have their names blotted out of the book of life and experience the second death (Rev 2:11; 3:5). Their sins were indicative of wickedness of their day (two thousand years ago), and reflective of common sins found throughout the church age, until Christ returns. With no time frame indicated in the scriptures, the Lord warns the seven churches and the church in general, of their need to repent before His Second coming. Failure to do so would mean that they would not be found without spot, wrinkle, or blemish, and that their candlestick would be removed from His divine presence. Each of the churches was warned of divine judgment unless they repented. This definitely goes contrary to the doctrine *"Once Saved, Always Saved."*

The churches of Smyrna and Thyatira were promised the greatest amount of tribulation in the end times unless they repented of their sins. In the last days Christ will judge His church perfectly, as indicated through His selection of only seven churches. The Lord Jesus Christ is perfect in judgement, perfect in love, and perfect in His wrath. To those with a pure heart, these concepts are easy to understand, but for those with preconceived biases, and doctrinal error, it wars against their carnal spirits (I Cor 2:10-14). After the church has gone through *"the wash cycle"* of tribulation, the more than 25,000 denominations will be transformed into one body, adorned for marriage to the Lamb, to the King of Kings, and Lord of Lords.

1) The Martyred Overcomers
2) The Living Overcomers
3) The Manchild Remnant
4) The Tares

At the end of the tribulation the rapture takes place. The Rapture is the marriage of the bride to the bridegroom at His second coming. To those who can receive this . . . peace.

Rev. 2:4-7	**Ephesus**	1, 2

Ephesus

Rev. 2:4-7

[4] Nevertheless I have somewhat against thee, because **thou hast left thy first love**.
[5] Remember therefore from whence thou art fallen, and repent, and do the first works; or else I will come unto thee quickly, and **will remove thy candlestick out of his place**, except thou repent.
[6] But this thou hast, that thou hatest **the deeds of the Nicolaitanes**, which I also hate.

1, 2

[The church at Ephesus lost her first love! She did not just lose her love, but her *"first love."* A love relationship is a living entity that must be nurtured and maintained in order that it may thrive, and stay alive. One way to lose one's fervor, and kill a loving relationship with Christ is through neglect. Some allow their love to grow cold through the motions of religious service, serving God out of duty, fear, and obligation, without their heart being in it. It is easy to get involved in the religious aspects of one's local assembly, loving the religious activities, but losing sight of the one whom you serve. This happens when one's relationship with Christ becomes routine and he loses his fervor and affections for Christ in the process. To lose one's love is like a man who provides for his family in an exemplary fashion, but spends little or no time in conversation and intimacy with his wife. One cannot live off of yesteryear's experiences. He must sow to spiritual intimacy daily.

The deeds of the Nicolaitanes created a schism in the body of Christ, separating them into religious classes of the clergy and the layman. Rather than having all Christians walk in the New Testament pattern of the priesthood of believers, with each individual having a direct relationship with Christ, a false ecclestical priestly system (similar to the Old Testament Levitical priesthood) was established in Rome. The Roman Catholic priesthood (Popes, Cardinals, nuns and priests) and the Protestant model of the visionary pastors (or liturgical priests), would require the Christian masses to go through the Eurocentric clergy in order to hear from God. The clergy also interpreted the sciptures and heard the voice of God for the dependent believers. Hence, the layman masses became pew-warmers, never knowing, or doing the will of God; consequently, they ignorantly followed the traditions, and precepts of men. The clergy held the layman in captivity, preventing them from knowing, or doing God's will. Unfortunately some laymen are still seemingly content allowing the clergy to blindly lead them. By default they allow their religious accountability to be placed in the hands of the denominational leaders. These laymen remain dependent, immature, deceived, believing that there is safety from God's judgment because of large numbers.

The doctrine of the Nicolaitanes is at the root of why multitudes, who call themselves Christians, will never inherit the kingdom of God. It is identical to what the Pharisees did to prevent the Jewish masses from obeying the word of God. They did not allow any who follow their ways to enter into the Kingdom of Heaven (Mt 23:13). Their traditions nullified the word of God and shut the doorway to heaven from men. Their sins caused the ignorant masses to reject God's commandments and obey the commandments of men (Mt 15:8,9).

The biblical model of the five fold ministry (Eph 4:11), the baptism of the Holy Ghost (Jn 7:37-39, Act 1:8), and gifts of the spirit (I Cor 12:7-10) **for all members** of the body of Christ, was rejected by European Christianity. In its stead, controlling spiritless religious organizations, and many illegal, clerical priesthoods, governed the people. Tragically, few in Christianity have known or done the will of God, because of the snare of the doctrine of the Nicolaitanes. This is why Jesus hates this doctrine with a passion. (Rev 2:5,15)]

[7] **He that hath an ear, let him hear** what the Spirit saith unto the churches; To him that overcometh will I give to eat of the tree of life, which is in the midst of the paradise of God.
   [Gen 2:9; 3:24]

Rev 2:9-11	**Smyrna**

[9] I know thy works, and tribulation, and poverty,

(but thou art rich) and **I know the blasphemy** of them which say they are **Jews** [false Christians], **and are not**, but are the **synagogue** [church] **of Satan**.

4

1, 2

¹⁰ Fear none of those things which **thou shalt suffer**: **behold, the devil shall cast some of you into prison, that ye may be tried; and <u>ye shall have tribulation ten days</u>: be thou faithful unto death, and I will give thee a crown of life.**

[The church of Smyrna <u>would go through tribulation</u> to purge it of the wicked who had given themselves over to Satan. This method of separating the righteous from the tares by taking them through the fire is the Lord's signature of perfection. The Lord used Jewish symbolism, **the synagogue of Satan**, to show how His spiritual children error in heart in the same manner as His natural children. As He has always done countless times to the natural, so shall He also do to the spiritual . . . the false Christians, or those who call themselves spiritual Jews (Rm 2:28,29), will be exposed as tares (Mt 13:30,38-41).]

When there is no persecution, the church becomes infested with the weeds of false growth and heresies. For the sake of the righteous the Lord's grace has been extended, knowing that there *"shall be great tribulation, such as was not since the beginning of the world to this time, no, nor ever shall be. <u>And except those days should be shortened, there should no flesh be saved: but for the elect's sake those days shall be shortened</u>."* (Mt 2:21,22)

The church of Smyrna promised to go through tribulation as the Lord gives Satan permission to try the hearts of those who called themselves Christians. Those who choose to believe that God would not permit such a thing, but rather, rapture His church before any of the seven years of tribulation begins, have to be willfully ignorant of the scriptures and two thousand years of church history. Jesus Christ did not remove the first, second, and third century churches from their days of great trial. They had to overcome Roman persecution in order to inherit eternal life. Neither will He remove the church in the last days from its persecution at the hands of the revived Roman empire (The New World Order). One of the tragedies throughout history has been the unfortunate persecution of the righteous true Christians by false Christians. The same can be said of the Jewish leaders who killed and persecuted their righteous brothers, the prophets. Again, so shall it be in the last days. *"Brother will betray brother and the love of many will wax cold" (Mt 24:12). Jesus stated these facts in this manner, "O Jerusalem, Jerusalem, which killest the prophets, and stonest them that are sent unto thee; how often would I have gathered thy children together, as a hen doth gather her brood under her wings, and ye would not!"* (Lk 13:34)

The overcomers shall receive a crown of life like the Church of Phladelphia. (Rev 3:10,11)]

[11] **He that hath an ear, let him hear** what the Spirit saith unto the churches; He that overcometh shall not be hurt of the second death.

Rev 2:13-17 **Pergamos** [13] I know thy works, and where thou dwellest, even **where Satan's seat is**: and thou holdest fast my name, and hast not denied my faith, even in those days wherein **Antipas was my faithful martyr**, who was slain among you, **where Satan dwelleth**.	**1, 2** **4**

[The tares in the kingdom of God have a stronghold in this church. They murder the righteous, kill the prophets, and reject truth. The righteous will maintain their steadfastness in the faith. They do not reject the name of Jesus Christ in word or deed (Col 3:17) and they also abide in the apostolic baptism in the name of Christ like the Philadelphian church. (Rev 3:8) These Christians abide in and preach the Gospel of the Kingdom proclaimed by the First Century Church (Acts 2:38).]

[14] But I have a few things against thee, because thou hast there them that hold the **doctrine of Balaam, who taught Balac to cast a stumblingblock before the children of Israel, to eat things sacrificed unto idols, and to commit fornication**.

[The church of Pergamos began to abide in the idolatrous practices of Balaam, which was similar to what

255

was practiced in the Roman Catholic and Greek Orthodox churches. They used statues, relics, and cons as images of worship, which is an abomination in the sight of God. These practices were in violation of the basic biblical principles established in the first and second commandments of the Torah (Ex 20:3-6). Roman Catholicism claims to be the church of Jesus Christ; however, it is actually the worship of the sun god through biblical names and is close in form and fashion, to the religion of Freemasonry. (Num 31:16; 25:1,2)]

[15] So hast thou also them that hold the **doctrine of the Nicolaitanes**, which thing I hate.

[As previously stated with the church of Ephesus, Jesus hates the doctrine of the Nicolaitanes. This doctrine leads to the spiritual death of laymen who are controlled and led by a rebellious priesthood called the clergy. Contemporary Christianity and its 25,000 denominations, each have their own Nicolaitan priesthood and religious order, making disciples after themselves, rather than Christ.]

[16] **Repent**; or **else I will come unto thee quickly, and will fight against them with the sword of my mouth.**

[Jesus stated in John 12 that He came in the flesh the first time not to judge but that His words would judge all men in the last day. *"And if any man hear my words, and believe not, I judge him not: for I came not to judge the world, but to save the world.*

He that rejecteth me, and receiveth not my words, hath one that judgeth him: the word that I have spoken, the same shall judge him in the last day. For I have not spoken of myself; but the Father which sent me, he gave me a commandment, what I should say, and what I should speak.

And I know that his commandment is life everlasting: whatsoever I speak therefore, even as the Father said unto me, so I speak." (Jn 12:47-51)

The sword of His mouth is the sword of the spirit, the word of God, and it shall judge perfectly exposing the intentions and thoughts of the hearts of men. *"For the word of God is quick, and powerful, and sharper than any twoedged sword, piercing even to the dividing asunder of soul and spirit, and of the joints and marrow, and is a discerner of the thoughts and intents of the heart. Neither*

is there any creature that is not manifest in his sight: but all things are naked and opened unto the eyes of him with whom we have to do." (Heb 4:12,13) Also see Rev 19:11-15, Jer 23:29] [17] **He that hath an ear**, let him hear what the Spirit saith unto the churches; To him that overcometh will I give to eat of the hidden manna, and will give him a white stone, and in the stone a new name written, which no man knoweth saving he that receiveth it. [Psa 78:23-25; Isa 62:2]	
Rev. 2:20-29 **Thyatira** [20] Notwithstanding I have a few things against thee, because **thou sufferest that woman Jezebel, which calleth herself a prophetess, to teach and to seduce my servants** to commit fornication, and to eat things sacrificed unto idols. [The spirit of Jezebel often times work in conjunction with the spirit of Ahab. Jezebel seeks to control through treachery, sorcery, and seduction. This spirit is an idolatrous spirit that persecutes and intimidates the righteous. When manifested through a female, it will make the male counterpart (husband) subservient to her. The male who operates under the spirit of Ahad prefers to have Jezebel lead the relationship and cowardly allows her to do the treacherous work to acquire power. He would prefer to have the women lead. This manifestation is quite apparent as most churches become increasingly matriarchal and all rebel against divine order and biblical gender roles. The movement to place women in the role of leadership in the five-fold ministry is one example. Rebellion to divine order by males or females opens the floodgates of demonic activities. I Kings 16:31,II Kings 9:22,30)]	1, 2, 4
[21] And I gave her space to repent of her fornication; and she repented not. [22] Behold, I will **cast her into a bed, and them that commit adultery with her into great tribulation**, except they repent of their deeds. [23] And **I will kill her children with death; and**	4

all the churches shall know that I am he which searcheth the reins and hearts: and I will give unto every one of you according to your works.

    [Jeremiah the prophet states this message in this manner: *"The heart is deceitful above all things, and desperately wicked: who can know it? I the LORD search the heart, I try the reins, even to give every man according to his ways, and according to the fruit of his doings."* (Jer 17:9,10)

    This church is promised <u>to go through great tribulation</u> because of her devilish ways. She shall be purged of her iniquity if she endures the chastening of the Lord. The days of Ananias and Sapphira shall return to the church during the tribulation period, to teach the saints not to blaspheme, or mock the spirit of Christ, which He has placed with in them – (Acts 5:1-11). The Lord has promised that <u>he will kill the children of these Christians</u> unless they repent.

    God is no respecter of persons and he shall judge every man according to the fruit of his doings. *"Be not deceived; God is not mocked: for whatsoever a man soweth, that shall he also reap. For he that soweth to his flesh shall of the flesh reap corruption; but he that soweth to the Spirit shall of the Spirit reap life everlasting."* (Gal 6:7,8) Also see Ezek 26:2-6]

[24] But unto you I say, and unto the rest in Thyatira, as many as have not this doctrine, and which have not known **the depths of Satan**, as they speak; I will put upon you none other burden.

[25] But that which ye have already **hold fast till I come**.

[26] And he that overcometh, and keepeth my works unto the end, to him will **I give power over the nations:**

[27] **And he shall rule them with a rod of iron**; as the vessels of a potter shall they be broken to shivers: even as I received of my Father.

[28] And I will give him the morning star.

[29] **He that hath an ear, let him hear** what the Spirit saith unto the churches.

1, 2

	1) The Martyred Overcomers 2) The Living Overcomers 3) The Manchild Remnant 4) The Tares
Sardis Rev. 3:2-6 [2] **Be watchful**, and strengthen the things which remain, that are ready to die: for I have not found thy works perfect before God. [3] Remember therefore how thou hast received and heard, and hold fast, and repent. If therefore **thou shalt not watch, I will come on thee as a thief, and thou shalt not know what hour I will come upon thee.**	**1, 2, 4**
[The righteous have not been appointed unto wrath. They will not be like the unfaithful servants who, when the master of the house comes, will not find them doing the Father's will. The unrighteous in the church will be walking in darkness and the Lord shall come upon them as a thief in the night. Jesus stated this fact in the gospels and Paul in his epistle. (I Thes 5:2-11, Lk 12:42-48, 13:23-30; 21:21-38; Rev 16:15)]	**1, 2**
[4] Thou hast a few names even in Sardis **which have not defiled their garments; and they shall walk with me in white: for they are worthy.** [These Christians walk in white because they are overcomers and have received the victory over the beast and his kingdom. (Rev 7:9,13-17;19:8; 12:11,17; 20:4)] [5] **He that overcometh, the same shall be clothed in white raiment**; and I will not blot out his name out of the book of life, but I will confess his name before my Father, and before his angels. [*"And at that time shall Michael stand up, the great prince which standeth for the children of thy people: and there shall be a time of trouble, such as never was since there was a nation even to that same time: and at that time thy people shall be delivered, every one that shall be found written in the book."* (Dan 12:1), Also see Psa 69:28]	

[6]He that hath an ear, let him hear what the Spirit saith unto the churches.	

Rev. 3:7-13 **Philadelphia** [7] And to the angel of the church in Philadelphia write; These things saith he that is holy, he that is true, he that hath **the key of David,** he that openeth, and no man shutteth; and shutteth, and no man openeth;	**1, 2**

[The church of brotherly love is a sinless church, which walks in the kingdom power of Christ. Jesus is the lion of the tribe of Judah who prophetically inherited the throne of David, in order to set up His everlasting kingdom. *"And I will clothe him with thy robe, and strengthen him with thy girdle, and I will commit thy government into his hand: and he shall be a father to the inhabitants of Jerusalem, and to the house of Judah. And the key of the house of David will I lay upon his shoulder; so he shall open, and none shall shut; and he shall shut, and none shall open."* (Isa 22:21,22). Jesus has given all power to His church to tread upon serpents and devils (Lk 10:17-20).

This kingdom power and authority supernaturally empowered the First Century church to do the works of Christ and turn the Roman Empire upside down. The Philadelphian church walks in apostolic doctrine, authority, and holiness, which makes them distinctively different from all Eurocentric churches and rebellious denominations. Jesus told the Apostle Peter that, *"upon this* rock [Revelation knowledge by the Holy Ghost] *I will build my church; and the gates of hell shall not prevail against it.*

And I will give unto thee the keys of the kingdom of heaven: and whatsoever thou shalt bind on earth shall be bound in heaven: and whatsoever thou shalt loose on earth shall be loosed in heaven. Then charged he his disciples that they should tell no man that he was Jesus the Christ." (Mt 16:18-20, Lk 17:20)]

[8] I know thy works: behold, I have set before thee an open door, and no man can shut it: for thou hast a little strength, and hast **kept my word**, **and hast not denied my name**.	**1, 2**

[These Christians understand and adhere to the doctrines of the first century apostles, which was restored back unto the church during and before the tribulation. They abide in the Jewish roots of the Christian faith and walk the lordship of Jesus Christ. These Christians have not denied His name, as being witnesses of Christ before men; neither have they denied His name in water baptism, which is customary in Eurocentric churches [Acts 2:38, Col 3:17].

⁹ Behold, I will make them of **the synagogue of Satan** [the church], **which say they are Jews** [Christians-spiritual Jews- Rm 2:8], **and are not, but do lie**; behold, **I will make them to come and worship before thy feet, and to know that I have loved thee**.

4

2

[Many Christians who walk in darkness will betray their brethren just as Joseph's brothers, the sons of Jacob (Israel), did when they plotted to kill him. However, after Joseph had gone through his trials in Egypt and the Lord brought him to prominence, he delivered His family from famine and certain death. His brothers, not knowing God's divine plan, would come and worship at Joseph's feet, as the prince of Egypt. Rather than giving retaliation for their wicked deeds, Joseph showed them love, kindness, and mercy. This was as a typology of the church of the apocalypse . . . how love will cover a multitude of sins. Joseph had a dream as a young boy that this event would happen and it provoked his brothers to jealousy and anger (Gen 37:9). The other six churches of the apocalypse will be against the Philadelphian church because they are blinded by their many sins. But the Philadelphian church will help the Manchild bring about the deliverance of all those who will come out of Mystery Babylon, the harlot world religious system.

The Prophet Isaiah prophesied of these end time events by stating that *"the glory of Lebanon shall come unto thee, the fir tree, the pine tree, and the box together, to beautify the place of my sanctuary; and I will make the place of my feet glorious.*

The sons also of them that afflicted thee shall come bending unto thee; and all they that despised thee shall bow themselves down at the soles of thy feet; and they shall call thee, The city of the LORD, The Zion of the Holy One of Israel." (Isa 60:14, 49:22,23)]

[10] Because **thou hast kept the word of my patience, I also will keep thee from the hour of temptation**, which shall come upon all the world, to try them that dwell upon the earth. [The righteous will receive divine protection, sealed with the mark of God in their foreheads (Rev 7:3; 9:4; 21:17; Ezek 9:4-6). This Goshen of God protection will be just like that which the children of Israel received in Egypt during the plagues.]	1, 2
[11] **Behold, I come quickly: hold that fast which thou hast, that no man take thy** crown. [2] Him that overcometh will I make a pillar in the temple of my God, and he shall go no more out: and **I will write upon him the name of my God, and the name of the city of my God, which is new Jerusalem**, which cometh down out of heaven from my God: and I will write upon him my new name. [Rev 21:9-17; 14:1-5] [13] **He that hath an ear, let him hear** what the Spirit saith unto the churches.	1, 2
Rev. 3:15-22 **Laodicea** [15] I know thy works, **that thou art neither cold nor hot**: I would thou wert cold or hot. [16] So then because **thou art lukewarm**, and neither cold nor hot, **I will spue thee out of my mouth.**	1, 2, 4
[17] Because thou sayest, I am rich, and increased with goods, and have need of nothing; and **knowest not that thou art wretched, and miserable, and poor, and blind, and naked:** [18] I counsel thee to buy of me gold **tried in the fire, that thou mayest be rich; and white raiment, that thou mayest be clothed**, and that the shame of thy nakedness do not appear; and **anoint thine eyes with eyesalve, that thou mayest see.** [Jesus Christ will awaken this church out of its' self-	1, 2, 4

induced spiritual coma through great tribulation. The method of trial was prophesied by Zechariah the prophet, *"two parts therein shall be cut off and die; but the third shall be left therein. And I will bring the third part through the fire, and will refine them as silver is refined, and will try them as gold is tried."* (Zech 13:7-9)]

1, 2, 4

[19] As many as **I love, I rebuke and chasten: be zealous therefore, and repent**.

[*"The Lord knoweth how to deliver the godly out of temptations, and to reserve the unjust unto the day of judgment to be punished"* (I Pet 2:9). The love of God is sure and so are His corrections. Paul comments on chastisement from the Lord, that we may understand who He is and why He does what He does:

"if ye endure chastening, God dealeth with you as with sons; for what son is he whom the father chasteneth not? But if ye be without chastisement, whereof all are partakers, then are ye bastards, and not sons.

Furthermore we have had fathers of our flesh which corrected us, and we gave them reverence: shall we not much rather be in subjection unto the Father of spirits, and live?

For they verily for a few days chastened us after their own pleasure; but he for our profit, that we might be partakers of his holiness.

Now no chastening for the present seemeth to be joyous, but grievous: nevertheless afterward it yieldeth the peaceable fruit of righteousness unto them which are exercised thereby." Also see Prov 3:12, Lev 26:14-44, Heb 12:2-11]

1, 2, 4

[20] Behold, **I stand at the door, and knock: if any man hear my voice, and open the door, I will come in to him, and will sup with him, and he with me.**

[Amazingly, Christ has been kicked out of His own Church and the Christians are carrying on without Him. How did He get outside of His own body? We have here, a Christless church, possessing all the trimmings of religion and forms of godliness, *"but denying the power there of."* Multitudes have established churches and formulated their own organizations, but only those who abide in Christ and are built upon His foundation will last.]

²¹ **To him that overcometh** will I grant to sit with me in my throne, even as I also overcame, and am set down with my Father in his throne. ²² He that hath an ear, let him hear what the Spirit saith unto the churches.

Rev. 4:1 After this I looked, and, behold, a door was opened in heaven: and the first voice which I heard was as it were of a trumpet talking with me; which said, **Come up hither**, and I will shew thee things which must be hereafter. 2 And immediately I was in the spirit: and, behold, a throne was set in heaven, and one sat on the throne.

[The great Error! This is one verse, among many, that is a major stumbling block for Western theologians. They falsely claim that the rapture of the church takes place at this juncture when a trumpet is blown and an angel conveys the message and commands John to *"come up hither."* We will clearly see that this trump is not for the rapture of the church. It takes place at the wrong time for the quickening of the saints, and it produced no quickening or single resurrection of the body of Christ. What this verse actually refers to is the fact that John was caught up in the third heaven, like the Apostle Paul had been previously (II Cor 12:1-7), and shown unspeakable things. The same also happened to the prophet Daniel twenty seven hundred years ago. Being caught up in the spirit, in the presence of God, is not the same as being resurrected or translated by the spirit of Christ to receive a new heavenly body.

John was also shown things that would come afterward. There is no indication that the saints were caught up with John (Rev 1:10). **He** was caught up in the spirit, in a trance (in a vision). This was not the rapture of the church as many suppose. If it was, then the rapture would have already taken place at the end of the first century (which is a variation of the heretical Preterist view.)

The apostle Paul revealed almost half a century earlier that the rapture would take place at *"the last trump"* (I Cor 15:52), not the first or any random trumpet as found in this chapter. This trumpet does not qualify as one of the trumpet judgements that would be indicators of the timing of the rapture later in chapters eight through eleven. In order to validate this point, we are told further in the book of Revelation that at the seventh, or last trump, the Archangel will blow his trump and say *"come up hither,"* and the righteous are raised with the Manchild witnesses from the dead (Rev 10:7;11:7-15). The phrase *"come up hither"* is used again. It correlates with all the other scriptures that cross-reference with the accurate timing of the quickening of the saints. At the last trump, which occurs at the end of the tribulation period, the mystery of God that was spoken of by the Apostle Paul will be finished. (I Cor 15:51, I Thes 4:13, Mt 24:29-31)]

	1) The Martyred Overcomers 2) The Living Overcomers 3) The Manchild Remnant 4) The Tares
Rev. 5:5 And one of the elders saith unto me, Weep not: behold, the Lion of the tribe of Judah, the Root of David, hath prevailed to open the book, and to loose the seven seals thereof.	
Rev. 5:8 And when he had taken the book, the four beasts and four and twenty elders fell down before the Lamb, having every one of them harps, and **golden vials full of odours, which are the prayers of saints.**	**1, 2, 3**
Rev. 5:9 And they sung a new song, saying, Thou art worthy to take the book, and to open the seals thereof: for thou wast slain, and **hast redeemed us to God by thy blood** out of every **kindred, and tongue, and people, and nation**;	**1, 2, 3**

[These Christians are the overcoming saints who were victorious over the Beast kingdom. Chapter five is the summation and conclusion of that which is to come in the remaining chapters. This chapter is a victory chapter that coincides with chapter 15 both testifying of the saints of God receiving their victory over the beast kingdom. Also at the end of this chapter the Lord reveals the end of the book in typical prophetic fashion, stating the end from the beginning. The events of this chapter can be over lapped and coincides like the gospels with the victorious accomplishments of chapters 14:1-5; 15:1-5;19:1-10; 21:1-8]	
Rev. 5:10 And **hast made us unto our God kings and priests: and <u>we</u> shall reign on the earth**. [The promise declared in this verse was first stated prophetically in the Law of Moses for natural Israel (Ex 19:6, Isa 61:6) and will be fully manifested during the millennium kingdom of Jesus Christ. During the millennium, the saints of God shall rule and reign with Him.]	**1, 2, 3**
Rev. 6:6 And I heard a voice in the midst of the four beasts say, A measure of wheat for a penny, and three measures of barley for a penny; and see thou **hurt not the oil and the wine.** [Jesus Christ grants divine protection for the true saints of God. The angels of God will already know who the righteous are, because the Father has already given ministering spirits to those who are heirs to salvation (Heb 1:14). They will seal the mark of Christ in the foreheads of the righteous protecting the saints in the same manner as He did in Egypt for the Jewish community.) It is also important to mention that the saints of God are sometimes referred to as wine and oil. (Zech 4:12, Isa 65:8-10; Hosea 9:2, Joel 2:21-25; Ezek 9:4]	**1, 2, 3**
Rev. 6:9 And when he had opened the fifth seal, **I saw under the altar the souls of them that were slain for the word of God, and for the testimony which they held**: [The souls of the martyred saints cry out for vengeance upon those who were killed during the first three and a half years of the tribulation. The Anti-Christ does not take complete control of the world system until	**1**

mid-way through the seventieth week of Daniel, covered earlier. In order to put a definitive time for this event we will follow the biblical indicators. The seventh seal judgement is the beginning of the first trumpet judgment, and the beginning of the last three and a half years of the tribulation. The major conflict between the saints of God and the powers of darkness take place at this same time, with the unveiling of the Manchild, who will judge the Antichrist kingdom. These are saints who will be slain for the sake of the gospel. They are comprised of those who were killed from the beginning of the first century until the tribulation period, by the secular and religious harlot systems of history.]	
Rev. 6:10 And they **cried with a loud voice, saying, How long, O Lord,** holy and true, **dost thou not judge and avenge our blood** on them that dwell on the earth? [The martyred saints are told to wait until the Manchild is slain (verse 11, chapter 11:7-14), then Christ will destroy the wicked and avenge their deaths at His Second Coming. Like the blood of Abel, which cried out from the earth unto the Lord, and was innocent of any wrong doing, the blood of the righteous will cry out for judgment upon the wicked. Abel's brother Cain did the first murder and shedding of innocent blood. Throughout Jewish history, the righteous prophets were always slain at the hands of their fellow brothers and tribesmen of Israel. The sad part about this shedding of innocent blood is that the Antichrist will also be a Christian brother who becomes reprobate. He will betray his brothers and seek to have them killed. The Lord will avenge their deaths and the deaths of all the apostles and prophets who have testified against the wickedness of ungodly men (Rev 18:20; 16:6, II Thes 2:4-6). They shall not only be avenged for their deaths as a witness of Christ, but through their resurrections, they shall also defeat the spirits of death, hell and the grave. Consequently, all those who are in Christ will return with Him in glory, after they meet Him in the air. The vengeance of the Lord will be swift and thorough.]	1
Rev. 6:11 And **white robes were given unto every one of them**; and it was said unto them, that they should rest yet for a little season, until	1 3

their **fellow servants also and their brethren** *[The Manchild]*, **that should be killed as they were, should be fulfilled.** [The statement *"their fellow servants and their brethren"* refers to the Manchild who will be slain after they finish their testimony (Rev 11:7-14). Their ministry lasts three and a half years, just like Christ's, as they bring many judgments upon the earth (Rev 11:6, 16:2-21). The Lord will avenge the death of the righteous at His Second Coming, and it will be followed immediately by the Feast of Fat Things (Isa 25:6), commonly called the Marriage Feast of the Lamb.]	
Rev. 6:17 **For the great day of his wrath is come; and who shall be able to stand?** [Since the fall of Adam, all the days that men have been on earth, there has been evil. However, the Apostle Paul prophetically stated that Christians must stand in the *"evil day."* The evil day is the tribulation period. It is a time of great darkness and Christians must *"put on the whole armor of God"* in order to stand in that day. The greatest display of God's miracles and judgements in human history will occur during this period. (Eph 6:13; Rm 1:18-32; 2:5-11; Joel 2:10,11; I Pet 4:17,18)]	**1, 2, 4**

	`1) The Martyred`
	`Overcomers`
	`2) The Living`
	`Overcomers`
	`3) The Manchild`
	`Remnant`
	`4) The Tares`

Rev. 7:1-3 ¹ And after these things I saw four angels standing on the four corners of the earth, holding the four winds of the earth, that the wind should not blow on the earth, nor on the sea, nor on any tree. ² And I saw another angel ascending from the east, having the seal of the living God: and he cried with a loud voice to the four angels, to whom it was given to hurt the earth and the sea, ³ Saying, **Hurt not the earth, neither the sea, nor the trees, till <u>we have sealed the servants of our God in their foreheads</u>.**	**1, 2, 3**

[Hundreds of years ago, the prophet Ezekiel prophesied of the seal that would be placed in the forehead of the righteous during the scourging of the Lord. His prophecy had, like most prophecies, a double fulfillment. *"And the LORD said unto him, Go through the midst of the city, through the midst of Jerusalem, and* **set a mark upon the foreheads of the men that sigh and that cry for all the abominations that be done in the midst thereof.** *And to the others he said in mine hearing, Go ye after him through the city, and smite: let not your eye spare, neither have ye pity…"* (Ezek 9:4).

Again, God's divine protection will be given to true Christians before any of the judgments begin. They will receive the mark of God in their foreheads, as he instructs the angels, to begin the separation process of the wheat and the tares (Mt 13:30,36-43). An angel was also given specific instructions at the Passover judgement in Egypt not to come near anyone's home to slay their first born who had blood sprinkled over the mantle. Their obedience preserved them from the devastation of God's judgment.

In the next verse, verse 5, John heard their number, the number of them that were slain. The number that he heard was 144,000, which is the dimension of the New Jerusalem and wife of Christ in chapter 21:9-17. This is also the same number given to the Philadelphian church in chapter 3:10-12 representing His name, His city, and His body, which at the quickening of the saints, becomes His wife. All true saints, like the Philadelphian church, will be preserved during the great trial that will permeate all the earth. They shall be used mightily of the Lord.]

Rev. 7:4-8 [4] And **I heard the number of them which were sealed**: and there were sealed **an hundred and forty and four thousand of all the tribes of the children of Israel**. [5] Of the tribe of **Juda** were sealed twelve thousand. Of the tribe of **Reuben** were sealed twelve thousand. Of the tribe of **Gad** were sealed twelve thousand. [6] Of the tribe of **Aser** were sealed twelve thousand. Of the tribe of **Nephthalim** were sealed twelve thousand. Of the tribe of **Manasses** were sealed twelve thousand. [7] Of the tribe of **Simeon** were sealed twelve thousand. Of the tribe of **Levi** were sealed twelve thousand. Of the tribe of **Issachar** were sealed twelve thousand. [8] Of the tribe of **Zabulon** were sealed twelve thousand. Of the tribe of **Joseph** were sealed twelve thousand. Of the tribe of **Benjamin** were sealed twelve thousand. [John **heard the number of them** that **were sealed. He never saw 144,000 individuals** from each tribe. Not to appear redundant, but a emphasis must be placed on the fact that he **heard** their number, and **did not see the number of them**. What he saw was identified in verse 9 as **a great multitude that no man could number (martyred saints)**. John heard, he did not see, a literal count. The significance of this distinction is quite profound. In the Lord's wisdom, He has caused those who are carnal and unbelieving to stumble over this section. Most people without spiritual revelation interpret the number as a literal 144,000 Jews from each of the 12 tribe; however, this is contrary to what John said. He said he heard their number. Denominational doctrinal errors have blinded the Western church world, and caused them to negate the fact that Jesus Christ abolished the Jewish tribal system and its priesthood (Heb 7:7-28). Jesus Christ, in all prophetic revelations of the past and present, always progresses. He does not regress! The tribal system was abolished with the induction of the Gentiles to create a new spiritual compound consisting of both Jews and Gentiles.	1, 2, 3

The book of Revelation is entitled the revelation of Jesus Christ. The mystery of the number 144,000 (the city of God and His wife) is one of the many concealed revelations found in this book. All believers become one in Christ, forming one tribe after the new priestly order of Judah, to reign with Christ on the throne of David. The new priest-king would be from the tribe of Judah, and all members of the church would constitute this priesthood established by the new spiritual Covenant.

"For the priesthood being changed, there is made of necessity a change also of the law. For he of whom these things are spoken pertaineth to another tribe, of which no man gave attendance at the altar. For it is evident that our Lord sprang out of Juda; of which tribe Moses spake nothing concerning priesthood.

And it is yet far more evident: for that after the similitude of Melchisedec there ariseth another priest,

Who is made, not after the law of a carnal commandment, but after the power of an endless life." (Heb 7:12-16)]

Christ established an eternal priesthood after the order of the Melchisedec; thus, making all Christians priests of the eternal kingdom of which He is king and priest. Making all Christians priests many would be astounded to learn that the Apostle Paul identifies faithful Christians as the Israel of God (Gal 6:16). Again, Western scholars must correct their anti-Semitic ideas and accept the fact that there are no longer acceptable Jewish tribes according to the word of God. There are also no legitimate priesthoods since their abolition by Jesus Christ in 31AD, when He rent the veil of the temple. However, Jesus Christ does recognize the individual Jew unless he repents, for he is a sinner, like all other men. The individual Jew must come in covenant with Christ just like the first century Jewish Christians did, who were the first partakers of the faith. In the last days, He will deal with them as a nation as He allows the global forces to try and annihilate the Jewish state with no success.

In Christ, we are neither Jew, nor Gentile; this is the framework of the New Covenant. Jesus is our eternal High priest. All Christians collectively constitute the priesthood of believers and are spiritual Jews by the baptism of the Holy Ghost (Rm 2:8,9). One must also keep in context the

theme of this book (Rev 1:1); it is designated as **the revelation of Jesus Christ**. Later in the book of Revelation, the angel of God shows John the church, **the Lamb's wife** (Rev 21:9-14,18-21). He describes her as having twelve Gates representing the 12 Jewish patriarchs, and 12 precious stones found on the ephod of the High Priest. James the brother of Jesus Christ **addresses the church as the twelve tribes scattered abroad** (Jm 1:1). In order to interpret this book one must use all the clues given in the Jewish scriptures, from both the Old and New Covenant, and then allow it to interpret itself. The use of the number 144,000 is symbolic and introduces again in chapter 14 (verses 1-5) as the number for the Manchild, and Jesus Himself (as his body) in chapter 21:17. The bride coming down out of heaven will help make up the Lord's army at Armageddon. The army of king David was not allowed to be counted by the Lord but David sinned against God and did so any way. Unfortunately, his actions led to thousands being slained by an angel of the Lord (I Chron 21:1f, II Sam 24:1f). **Hence, the army of the Lord in the Last Day can not be numbered but we do have its number.**	
Rev. 7:9 After this I beheld, and, lo, **a great multitude, which no man could number**, of all nations, and kindreds, and people, and tongues, stood before the throne, and before the Lamb, **clothed with white robes**, and palms in their hands;	**1**
Rev. 7:13-17 [13] And one of the elders answered, saying unto me, What are these which **are arrayed in white robes?** and whence came they? [14] And I said unto him, Sir, thou knowest. And he said to me, **These are they which came out of great tribulation, and have washed their robes, and made them white in the blood of the Lamb.** [15] Therefore are **they before the throne of God**,	**1**

and serve him day and night in his temple: and he that sitteth on the throne shall dwell among them.

16 They shall hunger no more, neither thirst any more; neither shall the sun light on them, nor any heat.

17 For the Lamb which is in the midst of the throne shall feed them, and **shall lead them unto living fountains of waters: and God shall wipe away all tears from their eyes.**

[There should be no doubt that these individuals are Christians. It is clearly stated that they are martyred during the Great Tribulation, and overcame their adversaries by the blood of the Lamb. The blood of Jesus can only be applied to believing, repentant Christians who testify and stand as a witness for Christ. If they are believers, they must come through the door of the New Covenant. There is no other, and will be no other means of salvation, except that which was originally preached at Pentecost by the Jewish apostles (Acts 2:38).

This great multitude was given white robes, representing the righteousness of the saints, speaking in reference to the Christians (Rev 19:8). This same group is also identified in Revelation 12:11,17; 20:4; 6:9,10; 15:2,3.

The prophet King David received a harsh judgment upon his army for counting the exact number of each of the twelve tribes that would partake in their natural battle (II Kings 24:1-6, I Chron 21:1-30). Likewise, as with David, the battle with the Anti-Christ is the Lord's and only the Lord knows the number of those that are His. The exact number that will participate in the great end time spiritual battle is insignificant, because *"the battle is the Lord's."* The strength of the victory is not measured in numbers, but rather by whom the Lord is. The one who inherited the throne of David, Jesus Christ, will engage this final battle. It will not be won by power, nor by might, but by the spirit of the Lord reigning and ruling in the hearts of His people.

Again, in this chapter we have a multitude of overcomers that "no man could number." They receive divine protection because they are righteous saints, and are identified as the number 144,000, which is also the measurement of a city, a wife and a man (Rev 21:9-17).]

1) The Martyred Overcomers
2) The Living

273

	Overcomers 3) The Manchild Remnant 4) The Tares
Rev. 8:3 And another angel came and stood at the altar, having a golden censer; and there was given unto him much incense, that he should offer it **with the prayers of all saints** upon the golden altar which was before the throne. [In the New Testament only Christians bare the title saints. They are sanctified and set apart to do the work of the Lord. Only living saints can continue to send their prayers of intercession up to heaven.]	**1, 2, 3**
Rev. 8:4 And the smoke of the incense, which came with **the prayers of the saints**, ascended up before God out of the angel's hand. [Prayers only ascend up by the mouths of the living, not the dead. The dead can only inquire (Rev 6:10) of the Lord. Here again we are told that the Christians are praying. The only prayers that the Lord will entertain will be those of any descendent of Adam who repents and becomes a Christian.]	**1, 2, 3**
Rev 9:4 And it was commanded them that they should not hurt the grass of the earth, neither any green thing, neither any tree; **but only those men which have not the seal of God in their foreheads**. [The majority of the tares will be revealed midway through the tribulation when their father, the Devil and his demonic hosts, indwells the multitude of reprobate Christian for 42 months. The chief of the reprobate tares will become the Anti-Christ, Satan dwelling and possessing him. After the saints are sealed, the tares are gathered out of Christ's kingdom first (Mt 13:30) in order that the Lord may purge His spiritual floor (house, Mt 3:12). The unrepented heathen shall not receive the seal of God; however, those who will become partakers of the latter rain of the Holy Ghost (Jm 5:7-9) and receive the Gospel of the kingdom (Mt 24:14) will be granted sufficient grace to overcome.]	**4**
Rev. 9:20 And the rest of the men which **were not killed by these plagues yet repented not** of the works of their hands, that they should not worship devils, and idols of gold, and silver, and	**4**

brass, and stone, and of wood: which neither can see, nor hear, nor walk: [This multitude would include all heathen, whether Jewish by birth or Gentile, and all apostate Christians, who draw back unto perdition and sin (Heb 10:39, II Thes 2:7-9). This is part of the great separations; the tares from the wheat, the sheep from the goat, the called from the chosen, the great falling away, and the heathen from the elect.]	

Rev. 9:21 **Neither repented they** of their murders, nor of their sorceries, nor of their fornication, nor of their thefts.
 	
    [The apostle Paul warned that Christians who abided in the sins of the flesh would not inherit the kingdom of God (Gal 5:19-21). Those who abide in the sins of the six churches of sin (Ephesus, Smyrna, Pergamos, Thyatira, Sardis, and Laodicea) must repent of their transgressions as well.
 	
    "For men shall be lovers of their own selves, covetous, boasters, proud, blasphemers, disobedient to parents, unthankful, unholy,
 	
    Without natural affection, trucebreakers, false accusers, incontinent, fierce, despisers of those that are good, Traitors, heady, highminded, lovers of pleasures more than lovers of God;
 	
    Having a form of godliness, but denying the power thereof: from such turn away.
 	
    For of this sort are they which creep into houses, and lead captive silly women laden with sins, led away with divers lusts. Ever learning, and never able to come to the knowledge of the truth.
 	
    Now as Jannes and Jambres withstood Moses, so do these also resist the truth: men of corrupt minds, reprobate concerning the faith." (II Tim 3:2-8)]
	4

	1) The Martyred Overcomers 2) The Living Overcomers 3) The Manchild Remnant 4) The Tares
Rev. 10:7 But in the days of the voice of the **seventh angel** [the last trump], when he shall begin to sound, **the mystery of God should be finished**, as he hath declared to his servants the prophets.	**1, 2, 3**

[The mystery of God referred to here is obviously the mystery of the last or seventh trump spoken of by the Apostle Paul. The text clearly states that it is the seventh trump, which is blown by the seventh angel. It is definitively the sound that the Archangel Michael (Dan 12:1,2) will make as he blows his trump to summons the dead from the grave at the great quickening of the bride of Christ, His church. Paul states, *"**Behold, I shew you a mystery**; We shall not all sleep, but we shall all be changed,*

In a moment, in the twinkling of an eye, at the last trump: for the trumpet shall sound, and the dead shall be raised incorruptible, and we shall be changed.

For this corruptible must put on incorruption, and this mortal must put on immortality. So when this corruptible shall have put on incorruption, and this mortal shall have put on immortality, then shall be brought to pass the saying that is written, Death is swallowed up in victory.

O death, where is thy sting? O grave, where is thy victory?" 1 Cor 15:51-55

This mystery of the defeat of death and the grave by all the saints coincides with the resurrection of the Manchild, after they had been slain by the beast from the bottomless pit and raised on the third day (Rev 11:7-15), just like Christ. Their resurrection from the dead shall respond to the voice of the Lord in chapter 11:12 which says, *"come up hither."* We are told repetitively in scripture that the dead in Christ shall rise first (I Thes 4:13-17) and those who are alive at his coming shall be translated from mortality to immortality. This is the great mystery and the defeat of the last enemy, death.

The prophet Isaiah (Isa 25:8) reveals that this mystery will be fulfilled only once, not in multiple successions. Translated saints are not resurrected because they never die (one must experience death to be resurrected) There is only one resurrection for the righteous and one for the wicked (Rev 20:4-15, Jn 5:2-30, Dan 12:2). Those who believe in multiple raptures for the righteous ranging from three to seven do not understand this basic biblical concept. Hence, they fail to pass a biblical test of the definition and numerical value of one.]

Rev. 11:1 And there was given me a reed like unto a rod: and the angel stood, saying, Rise, and measure the temple of God, and the altar, and them that worship therein.	**1, 2, 3**
Rev. 11:2 But the court which is without the temple leave out, and measure it not; for it is given unto the Gentiles: and the holy city shall they tread under foot **forty and two months.**	
Rev. 11:3-7 ³ And I will give **power unto my two witnesses, and they shall prophesy a thousand two hundred and threescore days, clothed in sackcloth**. [These individuals shall judge the world in typical Old Testament fashion, *"sackcloth and ashes,"* denoting repentance, intercession, and judgment. They will judge the kings and kingdoms of this world for 42 months, or three and a half years, which is the exact same time frame as the reign of the Antichrist (Rev 12:6,12-14). ⁴ **These are the two olive trees, and the two candlesticks standing before the God of the earth.** [*These men are first revealed by the prophet Zechariah and we are told that the anointing oil of God will be poured out of them. They will be saturated with the Holy Ghost and collectively possess the spirit of Christ without measure.* *"Then answered I, and said unto him,* **What are these two olive trees upon the right side of the candlestick [church-Rev 1:20] and upon the left side thereof?** *And I answered again, and said unto him, What be these two olive branches which through the <u>two golden pipes empty the golden oil out of themselves</u>?* *And he answered me and said, Knowest thou not what these be? And I said, No, my lord. Then said he, These are* **the two anointed ones***, that stand by the LORD of the whole earth."* (Zech 4:11-14)] ⁵ And **if any man will hurt them, fire proceedeth out of their mouth, and devoureth their enemies: and if any man will hurt them, he must in this manner be killed.**	3 3 3

[The Manchild will be invincible, and like Jesus indestructible, until they finish their testimony of three and a half years of ministry. Even though the Pharisees tried on numerous occasions to put Christ to death, it was impossible for them to do so until the appointed time. That appointed time was without question, on Passover, in order that the scriptures might be fulfilled. Jesus stated that no man could take His life, but rather, He gave His life freely for the ransom of many (Jn 3:16). Jesus stated that He had the power to lay His life down and He had the power to take it up again. This is exactly what He did to deliver man from his sins and to destroy the works of the devil (I Jn 3:8).]

⁶ These **have power to shut heaven, that it rain not in the days of their prophecy:** and have power **over waters to turn them to blood, and to smite the earth with all plagues, as often as they will**.

    3

[Two of the miracles of Moses are listed here (turning water into blood, and smiting the earth with plagues) and as well as two of the miracles of Elijah (calling fire down out of heaven, and stopping the rain from falling). Unfortunately, many theologians teach that Moses and Elijah will return from the dead to judge the earth. However, they cannot be any further from the truth. The bible states that no man returns from the dead for *"it is appointed unto man once to die and then the judgement"* (Heb 9:27). However, we do have a precedent where the spirit of Christ, which was on Elijah was remanifested in the personhood and the anointing of John the Baptist, two thousand years ago (Mal 4:5, Mt 11:13-15). Every Old Testament prophet was empowered by the anointing of the Spirit of Jesus Christ (I Pet 1:10,11) which enabled them to perform signs and wonders, and prophesy of the coming Messiah. Therefore, there will not be a literal return of Moses or Elijah, but rather a return of the anointing that they had. Their anointing will be poured out of the Manchild to judge the Antichrist and kings of the earth.

Nothing God does is done haphazardly or left up to circumstance. It was no coincidence that at the Mount of Transfiguration, Christ transfigured Himself in a vision before Peter, James, and John with a manifestation of Moses and Elijah on both of his sides. The symbolism of

Moses and Elijah was a prophetic declaration representing the two types of saints that would be changed into their immortal bodies in the last day. Moses represents the saints that will be resurrected from the dead and Elijah represented the type of saints that will be translated at the rapture and never see death.]

The number two, which represents *"the witnesses"* is not to be interpreted literally as two individuals. In the mystery of the Manchild there will actually be an outpouring of an anointing of three (for those who have an ear to hear). The scriptures state that *"by two or three witnesses, let everything be established"* (II Cor 13:1). The Lord skillfully hid these mysteries from theologians, the unlearned, and the unbelieving (II Pet 3:16) to confound the wisdom and folly of men.

The mysterious third anointing is an enigma concealed in the anointing of Elijah the prophet. The anointing that was on Elijah was manifested though John the Baptist. John the Baptist was a prophet, Nazzarite, and priest. He did no miracles, yet, according to Jesus, he was the greatest prophet that ever lived prior to the church / kingdom age (Mt 11:11). The Prophet Isaiah declared that John was the prophetic voice crying out in the wilderness to prepare the earth for the coming of the Messiah. He preached the Gospel of the Kingdom, and brought the people under the conviction of sin, commanding them to repent, receive water baptism, and prepare themselves to receive the Holy Ghost. Hence, the Manchild will have the anointing of Moses, Elijah, and John the Baptist. These manifested Sons of God (Rm 8:19), His remnant, will be located on every continent and will fulfill the Apostle Paul's prophecy that the church will judge the world and the fallen angels in the last days (I Cor 12:2,3, Rev 12:13).

[7] And **when they shall have finished their testimony**, the beast that ascendeth out of the bottomless pit **shall make war against them, and shall overcome them, and kill them.**

3

[The Manchild witnesses are the Christians that shall all be killed at the appointed time at the end of their three-and-a-half year timeframe in Jerusalem. This will occur after they finish their ministry to the lost, to the nation of Israel, and their judging of the wicked. This scenario is a classic example of *"progressive repetitious revelation"* where the Lord repeats and duplicates a situation numerous times until it is complete or perfected. We are told in chapter six, at the fifth seal, that the martyred saints were to hold their peace until their brethren, the Manchild, would be slain (Rev 6:9-11).]

Rev. 11:8-12
[8] And **their dead bodies shall lie in the street of the great city**, which spiritually is called Sodom and Egypt, where also our Lord was crucified.
[9] And they of the people and kindreds and tongues and **nations shall see their dead bodies three days and an half, and shall not suffer their dead bodies to be put in graves**.
[10] And they that dwell upon the **earth shall rejoice** over them, and **make merry**, and shall **send gifts** one to another; **because these two prophets tormented them that dwelt on the earth.**

[The demons also rejoiced and celebrated over the crucifixion and death of Christ, because they had finally been granted permission to have Him killed through the hands of men thinking they could rid themselves of the Christ. The hosts of hell incited the mob to have Christ crucified and to release a murderer in His place. When Satan finally had Jesus murdered at the hands of men, He and his demonic council failed to take in account the fact they had just killed a man who had never sinned. Hell was not created for such a man and had no jurisdiction over Him. Consequently, Christ would defeat hell and death (Rev 1:18) and spoil them of their authority and dominion. He put them to open shame (Col 2:15). This scenario is repeated again through the third Manchild, when the mature Sons of God, like Christ, will be killed and subsequently defeat death. Again, in a repetitive fashion, just as the demons in hell and the religious Pharisees prematurely rejoiced at Christ's death, the inhabitants of the earth, the Antichrist, and all of the demonic hosts will again prematurely celebrate their alleged victory over the Manchild.

However, the Manchild will torment the inhabitants of

3

the earth until their appointed time, just as Jesus tormented devils (Mk 5:7, Mt 8:29).]

¹¹ And **after three days and a half the spirit of life from God entered into them**, and **they stood upon their feet**; and great fear fell upon them which saw them.
¹² And **they heard a great voice from heaven saying unto them, Come up hither. And they ascended up to heaven in a cloud**; and their enemies beheld them.

3

1, 2, 3

[**Unmistakable, this is the rapture, or quickening of the church, by the Holy Ghost** (Rm 8:11, I Cor 15:45). It is the only resurrection appointed for the righteous (Jn 5:25-30). In grand style, and with a great climatic finale, at the end of the seven-year tribulation, all saints finally defeat death and the grave cooperatively. The general resurrection of all Christians is directly connected to the death and resurrection of the Manchild. The Manchild will collectively duplicate, many-fold, the ministry of Jesus Christ. The greater works of the Holy Ghost have been reserved for this day, because it is the ultimate showdown between the kingdom of darkness and the kingdom of light. The 7th angel blows the last trump of God, and fulfills the mystery spoken of by the Apostles Paul (I Cor 15:51,52) and John (Rev 10:7). Michael will echo the command to *"come up hither,"* as Christ summons their spirits to be quickened from their graves.
    They will ascended up in the clouds to meet the Lord in the air because He is on His way back to earth to receive His wife and to annihilate the wicked.
    "Now we beseech you, brethren, <u>by the coming of our Lord Jesus Christ, and by our gathering together unto him</u>..." (II Thes 2:1)
    "For this we say unto you by the word of the Lord, that we which are alive and <u>remain unto the coming of the Lord</u> shall not prevent them which are asleep.
    <u>For the Lord himself shall descend from heaven with a shout, with the voice of the archangel, and with the trump of God</u>: and the dead in Christ shall rise first:
    Then <u>we which are alive and remain shall be caught up together with them in the clouds, to meet the Lord in the</u>

air: and so shall we ever be with the Lord." (I Thes 4:15-17)]	
Rev. 11:15 [15] And the **seventh angel sounded** [_the last trump proclamation after the righteous are raised, Rev 10:7_]; and **there were great voices in heaven, saying, The kingdoms of this world are become the kingdoms of our Lord, and of his Christ; and he shall reign for ever and ever.**	**1, 2, 3**
Rev. 11:18 [18] And the nations were angry, and thy wrath is come, and the time of the dead, that they should be judged, and that thou **shouldest give reward unto thy servants the prophets, and to the saints, and them that fear thy name**, small and great; and shouldest destroy them which destroy the earth. [The overcoming saints of God are judged according to their works as stewards of the mysteries of God (I Cor 4:1) and as stewards of His kingdom. All will receive their rewards and crowns (Rev 3:11). 1) The Incorruptible Crown (I Cor 9:2) 2) The Crown of Righteousness (I Tim 4:8) 3) The Crown of Life (Jn 1:12) 4) The Crown of Glory (I Pet 5:4; Rev 2:10)]	**1, 2, 3**
| | ```
1) The Martyred
Overcomers
2) The Living
Overcomers
3) The Manchild
Remnant
4) The Tares
``` |
| Rev. 12:1 And there appeared a great wonder in heaven; **a woman clothed with the sun, and the moon under her feet, and upon her head a crown of twelve stars.** And there appeared another wonder in heaven; and behold **a great red dragon, having seven heads and ten horns, and seven crowns upon his heads.**
    [Great wonders will appear in heaven. The first wonder is a woman and she represents the church. She has the moon (which represents Satan) under her feet. Satan, as the moon, appears to be an angel of light (II Cor 11:13,14). However, he is a deceptive light. The moon has no light | **1, 2, 3** |
```

source of itself; it instead reflects the sun, which causes it to appear to be a light in the midst of darkness. To the wicked, his light is sufficient, because they hate the true light, which exposes their wicked deeds (Jn 3:17-19). The moon shines in the night, producing it's false light. All those who walk in darkness will follow it's light. The saints of God are clothed with the true light, represented by the sun and shine as stars (also true lights) in the night of a perverted apostate generation.

The most common Eurocentric interpretation of *"the woman clothed with the sun"* is that the she represents natural Israel who allegedly will give birth to the end time Jewish evangelists. However, even if the woman is Israel, she cannot produce a Manchild, because *"the nation"* of Israel will remain under the control of the spirit of slumber until her appointed time (Rm 11:8,12-28). If these special Jews from each of the twelve tribes become evangelist, what message, or gospel, will they preach? Biblically, if such were the case, they could only preach the gospel of the kingdom, not the lukewarm heretical doctrines of Western Christianity (Mt 24:14). Jesus Christ will not endorse any other gospel other than that which was preached by the First Century Jewish Christians.

The New Covenant will not be replaced or modified until He that is perfect (Christ) is come (I Cor 13:10). In fact, the Gentile churches ignore the fact that the only reason they were saved in the first place was to bring the natural Jews back unto Christ with their gospel, which was delivered to them at the hands of the Apostles of Christ (Gal 1:8,9). All must enter through the same door… *"one Lord, one faith, one baptism,"* one church, one kingdom, one gospel, one body, and one head. There are no other covenants or means of salvation established on this side of the millennium reign of Christ. <u>Any Jew or Gentile who believes on Christ would become members of the Kingdom church</u>; thus, perpetuating the church throughout the tribulation period. They must come in through the baptism of the Holy Ghost, like the Jews on the day of Pentecost two thousand years ago (Acts 2:16-18,36-38). Hence, Jews and Gentiles who convert and become Christians during this period will help constitute the Latter Rain of the Holy Ghost.

The pre-tribulation rapture theory falsely teaches that the Spirit of Christ would be taken from the earth during

this period, because the Church is supposed to be raptured out. This is preposterous! Is God limited to space and time? Of course not! This biased belief assumes that the spirit of Christ is limited in His scope and operations to the Gentile Church. Perhaps, they have forgotten that the spirit of Christ has operated from the foundation of the world (from Adam and through the Hebrew prophets) and will not flee because Satan comes to earth. Who is the Antichrist . . . a mere servant of God for unrighteousness sake used to fulfill God's word. Furthermore, the spirit of Christ operated before grace was extended to the Gentiles and will continue to do so until the end of the world (Rm 11:11). The Gospel of the kingdom will be preached until the end of the world, because the church will still be here. The Manchild will consist of Gentile and Jewish believers, as one in the body of Christ. Again, they will not appear as Jewish evangelist who are suppose to preach another gospel foreign to the New Covenant. On the other hand, others claim that the woman in Rev 12:1 refers to the Virgin Mary, who gave birth to Christ. What they fail to realize is that the content of the book of Revelation was to be fulfilled after it was written, which was approximately 98 AD. Hence, these events could not apply to Mary and Christ, that interpretation does not fit the historical time frame. Christ was born almost a century prior to the completion of the book of Revelation. Secondly, Mary did not give birth to the church, nor Israel. Those who interpret the woman in this passage to be Mary giving birth to Christ is baseless. The birth of Christ occurred over two thousand years ago. It is not a future event. There is no biblical account of Mary, the mother of Jesus, being engulfed in the sun or standing on the moon. On the other hand, the pagan Mary of the Roman Catholic Church who is known as *"The Queen of Heaven"* is often portrayed in this manner. (Jer 7:18-22; 44:18-22)]	
Rev. 12:2 And **she being with child cried, travailing in birth, and pained to be delivered.** [The church gives birth to the Manchild as *"the elect"* or *"delta force"* of God. It can be restated that the Manchild is comprised of those members of the body of Christ (the church) who have been totally sanctified unto the Lord, and remained unspotted from the world. They set	1, 2

themselves apart as being the manifested Sons of God, His remnant, and end time warriors. Like Giddeon's army, though few in numbers (from the four corners of the earth), they will accomplish a great tactical defeat of the prince of this world. The Manchild's greatest opposition will come from false Christians (tares), and haters of God. The slaughter of the innocent babies during the contemporary "global holocaust"(abortion movement) has been another prophetic fulfillment of Satan's attempt to kill the Manchild after he has been born. This happened with Moses under the rule of Ramses II, as well as with Jesus Christ under the rule of Herod.]	

Rev. 12:4 And **his tail drew the third part of the stars of heaven, and did cast them to the earth**: and **the dragon stood before the woman which was ready to be delivered, for to devour her child as soon as it was born.**
 	
    [Some of the saints who sit in heavenly place, to be tried and purified of their sins, will be overthrown by the dragon, Satan (Rev 13:7). Since Christians are lights who shine in the night in a world that abide in darkness, this verse reveals how many shall fall as part of the great falling away (II Thes 2:3). This is indicative of the 10-day trial of the church of Smyrna (Rev 2:10) and the great tribulation of the church of Thyatira (Rev 2:20-22). In the Old Testament the stars in Joseph's dream represented the twelve sons of Israel (Gen 37:9,10).
 	
    Whether Christians realize it or not, their citizenship is established in heaven, and they can move and operate in the heavenly kingdom powers while dwelling here on earth (Mt 16:19, Heb 6:4,5). The Apostle Paul states that God *"hath raised us up together, and made us sit together in heavenly places in Christ Jesus"* (Eph 2:6). If Christians walk in the spirit, they walk in heavenly dimensions, powers, revelations, and in the miraculous (Lk 17:20, Heb 6:4,5).
	1, 2, 4

Rev. 12:5 And **she brought forth <u>a man child</u>**, who was to rule all nations with a rod of iron: and her child was caught up unto God, and to his throne. [The church will bring forth the Manchild at the appointed time to begin their ministry and judge the world	**1, 2** **3**

of sin (Rev 11:6, I Cor 6:2,3). Like Moses and Jesus, they will arrive on the scene suddenly, and they will be totally unknown to most of the Church world. They are also the restrainers that will buffet and hold back the Man of Sin. Even though they walk on the earth, they shall say and do whatsoever the Lamb says to do, in the same manner that Christ did when he spoke and did as He was instructed by His Father.

The Manchild is identified in Revelation 14:1-5 with the overcoming saints as virgins. They are completely unspotted from the world and blameless. Their mouths are totally in subjection, they speak no guile, and they follow the Lamb wheresoever He leads them. They will have the number of God (144,000), His name, and the city of their God in their foreheads.

Like all the other overcoming saints, the Manchild shall rule and reign with Christ during the Millennium kingdom. This promise is applicable to all of the seven churches whose members overcome. It is stated specifically to Thyratira (Rev 2:24-28), Philadelphia (Rev 3:12), and Laodicea (Rev 3:21).]

Rev. 12:10 And I heard a loud voice saying in heaven, Now is come salvation, and strength, and the kingdom of our God, and the power of his Christ: for **the accuser of our brethren is cast down, which accused them before our God day and night**.	1, 2, 3, 4

[Satan is identified as the accuser of the brethren because he makes accusations against the saints of God. We find him appearing with the heavenly angels before the throne of God in the Book of Job seeking permission from God to do Christians harm as a consequence of their sin. Satan has direct access to the throne of God in the third heaven but he cannot dwell there.

"Now there was a day when the <u>sons of God came to present themselves before the LORD, and Satan came also among them</u>.

And the LORD said unto Satan, Whence comest thou? Then Satan answered the LORD, and said, From going to and fro in the earth, and from walking up and down in it." (Job 1:6,7)

Many may not realize that Satan is the Lord's servant

for the purposes of unrighteousness, whereas Christians and the holy angels are His servants for righteousness sake. Satan greatly desires to kill, steal, and destroy Christians (Jn 10:10); however, just as during the days of Job, Satan cannot do anything without permission. When Satan and his kingdom is cast down to earth by Michael the Archangel to be judged by the saints, he will be furious and seek to take vengence on the children of God. However, what he doesn't realize is that even though Christians may appear harmless, their Good Shepherd dwells within them. He will rise up within them to be a standard against Satan. The Devil's attack upon the righteous is a trap that he cannot resist; however, he will be destroyed as a result of his blind blunder. (Rev 12:7-12)	
Rev. 12:11 And they **overcame him by the blood of the Lamb**, and by **the word of their testimony**; and they **loved not their lives unto the death**. [All of the overcomers who live through the tribulation, those who are martyred, and those who are members of the Manchild will have the victory over Satan, the Antichrist, and the Beast System. Their weapons will not be carnal, but mighty, through God... able to break all of the strongholds of the devil (II Cor 10:3,4). Who is the Antichrist that the saints of the living God should be fearful of Him? Everywhere one looks in the scriptures, Satan loses. Only Christians can overcome the devil by the blood of the Lamb and the word of their testimony; therefore, this group cannot be unconverted Jews or Gentiles as some suppose. If either of these groups become converted, they become Christians, part of the New Testament Covenant, and established into the kingdom / Church. (Also see Rev 12:17;20:4)]	**1, 2, 3**
Rev. 12:12 Therefore rejoice, ye heavens, and ye that dwell in them. **Woe to the inhabiters of the earth and of the sea! for the devil is come down unto you, having great wrath, because he knoweth that he hath but a short time.** [Satan has only 42 months (three-and-a-half years) to create his havoc on the earth. Through intense seduction and deception, he will attempt to destroy as many souls of	**1, 2, 3, 4**

men as possible. (Rev 12:6,14; 13:5)]	

Rev. 12:13   And **when the dragon saw that he was cast unto the earth**, **he persecuted the woman** [the church] which brought forth **the man child**.
 	
[Midway through the tribulation, Satan will repeat what he did to Judas, Cain, and Korah. He will enter into the body of the one chosen from the foundation of the world, as chief of all transgressors (the Antichrist). Possessing the body of this betrayer of Christ, he will mock and blaspheme the God of heaven, and fill this reprobate Christian with utter contempt for the true Christian church. Previously, similar spirits were manifested in the Emperors of Rome and Roman Popes, such as Dicliatian, Nero, Caligula, and Pope Urban II.
    Quite to the surprise of most Christians, he will be one that was used mightily of the Lord, communed with the Holy Ghost, supped with Him, and will without prior indication, betray Him. In great delight, Satan will enter into this individual and persecute the woman (the church) who brings forth the Manchild. The reason he will go after the church is because the Manchild will be judging him and his kingdom. However, he cannot touch the Manchild, because they cannot be injured or killed until they complete their three-and-a-half years of ministry (Rev 11:4-7).
    In the 13th chapter of Revelations, this persecution is identified as war against **the saints** (Rev 13:7,10). The prophet Daniel prophesied the same. *"I beheld, and the same horn <u>made war with **the saints**</u>, and prevailed against them; Until the Ancient of days came, and judgment was <u>given to **the saints**</u> of the most High; and the time came that <u>**the saints**</u> possessed the kingdom. And he shall speak great words against the most High, and shall wear out **the saints** of the most High, and think to change times and laws: and they shall be given into his hand until a time and times and the dividing of time."* (Dan 7:21,22,25)
    Also at this juncture, the Lord will begin, in a more accelerated fashion, to gather the tares out of His kingdom (Mt 13:30, 36-43). He will also give these rebellious Christians (who were planted within the kingdom of God
	1, 2
	3

by the devil) over to demonic spirits of delusion (II Thes 2:10-13). Their hearts will be exposed, they will be despisers of truth, and will refuse to submit to the Holy Ghost which they had received earlier. Therefore, they will be without excuse (Rm 1:18-2:10). The Apostle Paul writes concerning these individuals: *"And with all deceivableness of unrighteousness in them that perish; because they received not the love of the truth, that they might be saved. And for this cause God shall send them strong delusion [devils], that they should believe a lie:* *That they all might be damned who believed not the truth, but had pleasure in unrighteousness."* (II Thes 2:10-13)]	
Rev. 12:14 And to **the woman were given two wings of a great eagle**, that she might fly into the wilderness, into her place, where she is nourished for **a time, and times, and half a time, from the face of the serpent.** [Divine protection is given to the saints during the second half of Daniel's Seventieth week. He bore them on eagle wings (Ex 19:4) and provided for them in the wilderness. Likewise will God provide for the Christian saints in the last days.]	**1, 2**
Rev. 12:15 And **the serpent cast out of his mouth water as a flood after the woman, that he might cause her to be carried away of the flood**. [A flood of deception and persecution is coming. Satan will use every method of guile he has tried over the past 6,000 years to deceive the saints. His deceptive lures will be so enticing that, if it was possible, even the very elect would be deceived (Mt 24:24). However, like Pharaoh, he shall pursue the children of God to his own demise.]	**1, 2**
Rev. 12:16 **And the earth helped the woman, and the earth opened her mouth, and swallowed up the flood which the dragon cast out of his mouth**. [Pharaoh pursued the Hebrew people out of Egypt, but the Lord supernaturally opened the Red Sea and led them out of their enemy's grasp. In the end time the Antichrist (a typology of Pharaoh), will be outraged because of the strong hand of judgement by the Lord against him.]	**1, 2**

Rev. 12:17 And the **dragon was wroth with the woman**, **and went to make war** with **the remnant of her seed**, which **keep the commandments of God, and have the testimony of Jesus Christ.** [The Devil will engage in a futile battle with the Manchild remnant that will relentlessly, in conjunction with the angels, bring havoc on the natural and spiritual kingdoms of darkness. The angels of God will bring on the trumpet judgments (Rev 8:1-10:7). The Manchild will bring on the vial judgments (Rev 16:1-19). Satan's only recourse in this lop-sided battle will be to persecute the woman, the church; but even then He still will be defeated, because they will overcome him by the blood of the Lamb, and by the word of their testimony.]	**1, 2** **3**
	1) The Martyred Overcomers 2) The Living Overcomers 3) The Manchild Remnant 4) The Tares
Rev. 13:4-7 [4] And **they worshipped the dragon which gave power unto the beast**: and they worshipped the beast, saying, Who is like unto the beast? who is able to make war with him? [5] And there was given unto him a mouth speaking great things and **blasphemies**; and power was given unto him to continue **forty and two months**. [6] And he **opened his mouth in blasphemy against God, to blaspheme his name, and his tabernacle, and them that dwell in heaven.**	**4**
[7] *And it was **given unto him to make war with the saints, and to overcome them:** and power was given him over all kindreds, and tongues, and nations.*	**1**

[Satan will make war against the **Saints** and overcome many. Saints can only refer to the New Testament Christians. Only they are sanctified through Christ. The Old Testaments Jews were not referred to as Saints; nor the angels or Gentile nations. However, Daniel prophesied of the grace that would be revealed through the church in the last days, when he spoke of the Messiah, Jesus. The Prophet Daniel testified of the same events over seven hundred years before John received His revelation: *"I beheld, and **the same horn made war with the saints, and prevailed against them;*** *"Until the Ancient of days came, **and judgment was given to the saints of the most High**; and the time came that the saints possessed the kingdom. . .* *And he shall speak great words against the most High, **and shall wear out the saints of the most High**, and think to change times and laws: and they shall be given into his hand until a time and times and the dividing of time [3 ½ years]."* (Dan 7:21,22,25) *"And in the latter time of their kingdom, when **the transgressors** [the tares, Mt 13:30] **are come to the full**, a king of fierce countenance, and understanding dark sentences, shall stand up.* *And his power shall be mighty, but not by his own power: and he shall destroy wonderfully, and shall prosper, and practise, **and shall destroy the mighty and the holy people.*** *And through his policy also he shall cause craft to prosper in his hand; and he shall magnify himself in his heart, and by peace shall destroy many: **he shall also stand up against the Prince of princes; but he shall be broken without hand**."* (Dan 8:23-25)	
Rev. 13:7-10 ⁷ And it was **given unto him to make war with the saints, and to overcome them: and power was given him over all kindreds, and tongues, and nations.** ⁸ And all that dwell upon the earth shall worship him, whose names are not written in the **book of life of the Lamb slain from the foundation**	1 4

of the world. [9] If any man have an ear, let him hear. [10] He that leadeth into captivity shall go into captivity: he that killeth with the sword must be killed with the sword. **Here is the patience and the faith of the saints**.	**1, 2**
Rev. 13:15 And he had power to give life unto the image of the beast, that the image of the beast should both speak, and **cause that as many as would not worship the image of the beast should be killed**. Rev. 13:16 **And he causeth all, both small and great, rich and poor, free and bond, to receive a mark in their right hand, or in their foreheads:** Rev. 13:17 And that **no man might buy or sell, save he that had the mark, or the name of the beast, or the number of his name.** Rev. 13:18 Here is wisdom. Let him that hath understanding count the number of the beast: **for it is the number of a man; and his number is Six hundred threescore and six.** [This kingdom is called Mystery Babylon. It is a typological fulfillment of the natural Babylonian Kingdom of King Nebuchadnezzar, who had an image of himself constructed for the people of his kingdom to worship. When certain music was played all the people were to worship his image or they would be put to death (Dan 3:3-11). The measurement of Nebuchadnezzar's image was 60 cubits by six. The image of spiritual Babylon is the number 666. This number and name is the antithesis of the number of Christ and His wife city, which is 144.000. Both Jesus Christ and the Antichrist have a number that is the measurement of their names and their kingdoms.]	**1, 2, 3** **4**

Rev. 14:1 And I looked, and, lo, a Lamb stood on the mount Sion, and **with him an hundred forty and four thousand, having his Father's name written in their foreheads**. [These saints have gotten the victory over the beast system. Their victory coincides with the events of chapters 5:1-14, 15:1-5, 19:1-10, 21:1-8. As previously mentioned, the number 144,000 is not a literal number (chapter 7:3-8). Remember, John **heard** the number of those that were sealed; **he did not see** 144,000. This number represents the number of the righteous (Rev 3:12), and is their seal for divine protection from God's judgments during the tribulation (Rev 7:3,4; Ezek 9:4). It also represents the city, the New Jerusalem (Rev 21:10-16), the wife of Christ (Rev 21:9-17), and the prophetic city that Abraham sought after *"whose builder and maker was God"* (Heb 11:8-10,16, Rev 21:9-23). Christ's glorious church will return with the Lord in great splendor and glory at the rapture, to execute the final judgment at Armageddon. (Rev 19:11-21)]	1, 2, 3
Rev. 14:3 And **they sung as it were a new song before the throne**, and before the four beasts, and the elders: and **no man could learn that song but the hundred and forty and four thousand, which were redeemed from the earth.** [Again, the number 144,000 is the code name for the faithful and true Christians, who after the defeat of the Harlot city, the bride of the Antichrist, will sing the ultimate victory song … *"**The Song of Moses and the Song of the Lamb**"* (Rev 15:2-4). The Song of Moses (part 1) was sang by the prophetess Miriam and all the women of Israel (Ex 15:1-21) after their defeat of Pharaoh at the Red Sea. The mighty hands of YEHWEH delivered them, their Savior and God. Their prophetic song is updated (part 2) to include *"the Lamb"* because the saints and the Manchild will destroy the kingdom of the Antichrist in the same manner as Moses did to Pharaoh's kingdom and Elijah judged Jezebel and Ahab. They will even perform the same miracles of Moses (Rev 16:1-19). This victorious celebration and course of events is a repeat of what the first Manchild, Moses, did on the natural kingdom of Pharaoh.	1, 2, 3

This time Christ will pour out His wrath on the both the natural and spiritual kingdoms of darkness, through the church, upon the Antichrist.	
Rev. 14:4 These are **they which were not defiled with women; for they are virgins. These are they which follow the Lamb whithersoever he goeth. These were redeemed from among men, being the firstfruits unto God and to the Lamb**. [The overcoming Christians do not commit spiritual fornication or whoredom with the Beast. This is the victorious church consisting of the church of Philadelphia, the Manchild, and the faithful overcomers of Ephesus, Smyrna, Pergamos, Thyatira, Sardis, and Laodicea. At this juncture in Kingdom / church history, the saints have already partaken of the first resurrection and have fulfilled the Jewish feast of First Fruit, in the same manner as Jesus did two thousand years ago (I Cor 15:13-20). Resurrected saints are called the first fruit from the dead in this verse.]	1, 2, 3
Rev. 14:5 **And in their mouth was found no guile: for they are without fault before the throne of God.** [These saints reflect Christ's glory and walks as He walked. The Apostle John tells us that, *"Herein is our love made perfect, that we may have boldness in the day of judgment: because as he is, so are we in this world."* (I Jn 4:17)	1, 2, 3
Rev. 14:9 And the third angel followed them, saying with a loud voice, **If any man worship the beast and his image, and receive his mark in his forehead, or in his hand,**	4
Rev. 14:10 The same **shall drink of the wine of the wrath of God, which is poured out without mixture into the cup of his indignation; and he shall be tormented with fire and brimstone** in the presence of the holy angels, and in the presence of the Lamb:	4
Rev. 14:11 And the smoke of their torment ascendeth up for ever and ever: and they have no rest day nor night, who worship the beast and his image, and **whosoever receiveth the mark of his name.**	4

Rev. 14:12 Here is the **patience of the saints:** here are **they that keep the commandments of God, and the faith of Jesus.** [Consistently, we see the word saints used throughout this book because the witness and testimony of Jesus Christ is to be revealed through His body, the church. They are the only ones who keep the commandments of God and obey His covenant. *"The secret of the LORD is with them that fear him; and he will shew them his covenant" (Psa 25:14).* The Old Testament Commandments are not valid during the kingdom/ church age. There is also no other covenant outside the New Covenant, which was consummated on the day of Pentecost two thousand years ago. There is also no other gospel that men are to obey, other than the gospel of the kingdom, which was declared by the New Covenant. (Acts 2:38, Jn 3:5, Rm 14:17)]	1, 2, 3
Rev. 14:13 And I heard a voice from heaven saying unto me, Write, **Blessed are the dead which die in the Lord from henceforth**: Yea, saith the Spirit, that they may rest from their labours;	1, 3
Rev. 14:16-20 And he that sat on the cloud **thrust in his sickle on the earth; and the earth was reaped.** [17] And another angel came out of the temple which is in heaven, he also having a sharp sickle. [18] And another angel came out from the altar, which had power over fire; and cried with a loud cry to him that had the sharp sickle, saying, **Thrust in thy sharp sickle, and gather the clusters of the vine of the earth; for her grapes are fully ripe.** [19] And the angel thrust in his sickle into the earth, and **gathered the vine of the earth, and cast it into the great winepress of the wrath of God.** [20] And the winepress was trodden without the city, **and blood came out of the winepress, even unto the horse bridles, by the space of a thousand and six hundred furlongs.**	4

[This devastation is done at the valley of decision . . . Armageddon. The angels thrust in their sickles to initiate the great slaughter of the wicked, who had the audacity to slay the righteous, and blaspheme the God of heaven. It is the Second Coming of Christ. The saints and the hosts of heaven are with Him to bring vengeance upon the wicked for the martyr of the saints, who overcame by the blood of the LAMB.

"And to you who are troubled rest with us, when the Lord Jesus shall be revealed from heaven with his mighty angels,

In flaming fire taking vengeance on them that know not God, and that obey not the gospel of our Lord Jesus Christ*:*

Who shall be punished with everlasting destruction from the presence of the Lord, and from the glory of his power;

When he shall come to be glorified in his saints, and to be admired in all them that believe (because our testimony among you was believed) in that day." (II Thes1:7-10) *Also see Rev 19:11-21.*

The winepress represents the final squeezing and immense pressure exhibited upon the Antichrist forces to destroy the kingdoms of men, crushing them in His presence. This occurs just before Satan is bound for the one thousand Millennial years reign of Christ (Rev 20:1-3, also see Mt 13:30,36-43).]

	1) The Martyred Overcomers 2) The Living Overcomers 3) The Manchild Remnant 4) The Tares
Rev. 15:3 And they **sing the song of Moses the servant of God, and the song of the Lamb**, saying, Great and marvellous are thy works, Lord God Almighty; just and true are thy ways, thou **King of saints**. [In this verse the Lord God is identified as the King of saints. The word saints can only refer to Christians, not natural Jews who are not in covenant, nor the heathen who are foreign to Him. In earlier chapters, we are told that Satan made war with the saints in opposition to the King of	1, 2, 3

Kings (Rev 13:7,10; 12:13,4-6,11,17).	
In the book of Revelation, we are told how the angels sing their songs of praise and worship before the throne of God and in the midst of heaven. However, God has given the redeemed of the children of Adam a song that the angels cannot sing.	
The first stanza of their song was sung thousands of years ago by Miriam and the women of Israel. Known as the prophetic Song of Moses, it can be read in its entirety in Exodus 15:1-21. The Song of Moses was sung after the God of Israel delivered the Hebrew children through the Red Sea. The *"I AM, that I AM"* utterly destroyed Pharaoh's army through the hands of His servant Moses. Pharaoh's army drowned in the Red Sea and YEHWEH delivered the Children of Israel out of his grips. Pharaoh was a prototype of the Antichrist. This was the victory song manifested as a result of the first Manchild type, Moses.	
The final Manchild, described in the book of Revelation as the mature Sons of God, will also defeat the Antichrist Kingdom and hold him in captivity until his forty-two months have expired. In like manner, as with Moses, all of the righteous who overcome by the blood of the Lamb and by the word of their testimonies, will partake in the updated Song of Moses. Their new song will be called **the Song of Moses and the Song of the Lamb**.]	
Rev. 15:4 **Who shall not fear thee, O Lord, and glorify thy name? for thou only art holy: for all nations shall come and worship before thee; for thy judgments are made manifest.**	1, 2, ,3
[Here we have the praise of the saints who glorify the name of Jesus Christ. There is no name greater in the heavens or in the earth. In the last days the Lord will judge perfectly the demonic angelic realm and the rebellious inhabitants of the earth. Their folly will be fully manifested and their defeat will be fully assured.]	
Rev. 16:1-9 And I heard a great voice out of the temple saying to the seven angels, Go your ways, and pour out the vials of the wrath of God upon the earth. [2] And the **first** went, and poured out his vial upon the earth; **and there fell a noisome and**	3

grievous sore upon the men which had the mark of the beast, and upon them which worshipped his image.

[The miracles of Moses also consisted of the plague of grievous sores (Ex 9:8-16). The following miracles will be done to combat the unbelief of natural Israel and to make the testimony and witness of the Manchild believable. Many Jews today do not believe that the miracles performed by Moses actually happened. Therefore, the Manchild will duplicate the miracles that were performed at the hands of Moses to quicken their faith and subdue their fears. These miracles also correlate directly with the trumpet judgements of the seventh seal. Hence, the angelic forces, via the trumpet judgments, will unite with the Manchild and their vial judgments, to bring on the judgments for both the natural and spiritual kingdoms. Through the love and miracles extended towards natural Israel, they shall be provoked to jealousy, and turn towards Jesus, their Christ (Rm 11:11). <u>The Apostle Paul reveals that the deliverer (Manchild) will come out of Zion</u> (the church) and turn ungodliness from the natural Israel, so that both natural and spiritual Israel will be saved. This is one of the great mysteries of the church.

"For I would not, brethren, that ye should be ignorant of this mystery, lest ye should be wise in your own conceits; that blindness in part is happened to Israel, until the fulness of the Gentiles be come in.

*<u>And so all Israel shall be saved</u>: as it is written, **<u>There shall come out of Sion the Deliverer, and shall turn away ungodliness from Jacob</u>**: For this is my covenant unto them, when I shall take away their sins.*

As concerning the gospel, they are enemies for your sakes: but as touching the election, they are beloved for the fathers' sakes. For the gifts and calling of God are without repentance.

*For as ye in times past have not believed God, yet have now obtaine*d mercy through their unbelief: *Even so have these also now not believed, that through your mercy they also may obtain mercy.*

<u>For God hath concluded them all in unbelief, that he might have mercy upon all</u>. *O the depth of the riches both of the wisdom and knowledge of God! how unsearchable are his judgments, and his ways past finding out! For who*

3

hath known the mind of the Lord? or who hath been his counsellor?" (Rm 11:25-34)

The Apostle Paul tells the Corinthians that the church would one day judge the world (I Cor 6:2). In the next verse (verse 3) he states that they will also judge the fallen angels. The only church of the seven listed in chapters two and three of Revelation that has the fruit and doctrine needed to work closely with the Manchild, is the Philadelphian Church (3:7-13). These events have been slated in the realm of God's divine plan to be fulfilled during the tribulation period.]

3

And the **second** angel poured out his vial upon the sea; and **it became as the blood of a dead man**: and every living soul died in the sea.

[This was another manifestation of a miracle performed by Moses, Ex 4:9, The sea becomes blood. This judgment also correlates with the angels who bring on the trumpet judgment # 1, Rev 8:7,8]

3

[4] And the **third** angel poured out his vial upon **the rivers and fountains of waters; and they became blood.**

3

[5] And I heard the angel of the waters say, Thou art righteous, O Lord, which art, and wast, and shalt be, because thou hast judged thus.

4

[6] **For they have shed the blood of saints and prophets, and thou hast given them blood to drink; for**

[7] And I heard another out of the altar say, Even so, Lord God Almighty, true and righteous are thy judgments.

[For the sake of the natural children of Israel, in order to counteract their unbelief we have again, another miracle of Moses (Ex 7:17-25). The rivers and waters becomes blood. This judgment also correlates with the angels who bring on the second trumpet judgment (Rev 8:8,9)]

3

[8] And the **fourth** angel poured out his vial upon the sun; and power was given unto him to scorch men with fire.

⁹ And men were scorched with great heat, and blasphemed the name of God, which hath power over these plagues: and they repented not to give him glory. [We have another miracle plague that was performed by Moses (Ex 9:23,24). Men are scorched with fire. This judgment also correlates with the angels who bring on the third trumpet judgment , Rev 8:10:11]	

¹⁰ And the **fifth** angel poured out his vial upon the seat of the beast; and his kingdom was full of darkness; and they gnawed their tongues for pain,
¹¹ And blasphemed the God of heaven because of their pains and their sores, and repented not of their deeds.
 	
    [This vial is also another one of the miraculous plagues and judgments delivered by Moses (Ex 10:21-29), the plague of darkness. As noted above, the Beast's kingdom will be full of darkness also. This judgment will correlate with the angels who bring on the fourth trumpet judgment (Rev 8:12,13)]
 	
¹² And the **sixth** angel poured out his vial upon the great river Euphrates; and the water thereof was dried up, that the way of the kings of the east might be prepared.
¹³ And I saw three unclean spirits like frogs come out of the mouth of the dragon, and out of the mouth of the beast, and out of the mouth of the false prophet.
¹⁴ For they are the spirits of devils, working miracles, which go forth unto the kings of the earth and of the whole world, to gather them to the battle of that great day of God Almighty.
 	
    [Also corresponding with the miracle of Moses (Ex 14:13-31), the armies of the beast will gather for the slaughter, having unclean spirits like frogs.]
	3
	
	3

Rev. 16:15 **Behold, I come as a thief. Blessed is he that watcheth, and keepeth his**	1, 2, 4

garments, lest he walk naked, and they see his shame.

Rev. 16:16 And **he gathered them together** into a place called in the Hebrew tongue **Armageddon**.

[The admonition to keep one's garments pure and to be clothed with righteousness is consistently found in the numerous parables of the kingdom spoken of by Jesus. Without exception, these parables were all in reference to His kingdom / church (Mt 24:43-54, Lk 12:35-40,42-48; 21:31-38). In chapter three, the church of Sardis is told to *"hold fast, and repent. If therefore thou shalt not watch, <u>I</u> <u>will come on thee as a thief</u>, and thou shalt not know what hour I will come upon thee: Thou hast a few names even in Sardis which have not defiled their garments; and they shall walk with me in white: for they are worthy"* (Rev 3:3,4).

In chapter seven, we are told that the saints who kept their garments undefiled came out of the great tribulation. *"These are they which came out of great tribulation, and have washed their robes, and made them white in the blood of the Lamb"* (Rev 7:14).

The Apostle Paul revealed to the church of Thessalonica that all Christians who walk in darkness shall suffer sudden destruction. And they are also admonished *<u>"that the day of the Lord so cometh as a thief in the</u> <u>night</u>. For when they shall say, Peace and safety; <u>then</u> <u>sudden destruction cometh upon them</u>, as travail upon a woman with child; and they shall not escape"* (I Thes 5:3).

Jesus put the church of Laodicea on notice because of their lukewarmness, nakedness, and darkness. *"Because thou sayest, I am rich, and increased with goods, and have need of nothing; and knowest not that thou art wretched, and miserable, and poor, and <u>blind, and naked</u>:*

"I counsel thee to buy of me gold tried in the fire, that thou mayest be rich; <u>and white raiment, that thou mayest</u> <u>be clothed, and that the shame of thy nakedness do not</u> <u>appear; and anoint thine eyes with eyesalve, that thou</u> <u>mayest see.</u>" (Rev 3:17,18)

Jesus also commanded those in His kingdom to watch and pray for they know not when our Master shall come.

4

Rev. 16:17 And the **seventh** angel poured out his vial into the air; and there came a great voice out of the temple of heaven, from the throne, saying, **It is done.** 18 And there were voices, and **thunders, and lightnings; and there was a great earthquake**, such as was not since men were upon the earth, so mighty an earthquake, and so great. 19 And the great city was divided into three parts, **and the cities of the nations fell: and great Babylon came in remembrance before God, to give unto her the cup of the wine of the fierceness of his wrath**. 20 And every island fled away, and the mountains were not found. 21 And there **fell upon men a great hail out of heaven, every stone about the weight of a talent: and men blasphemed God because of the plague of the hail; for the plague thereof was exceeding great.** [Here again, we have another miracle of Moses, thunder, lightening and hail (Ex 9:13-35). This judgment also correlates with the angels who bring on the seventh trumpet judgment (Rev 10:7, 11:7-15). This final judgment (the seventh vial) concludes with the statement ... **IT IS DONE,** and ironically coincides with the seventh (or last) trump, which concludes with the statement ... **IT IS FINISHED**. Simultaneously the vial judgments and the trumpet judgments close the curtain on the world, as we know it today. Both of these judgements also coincide with the rapture of the church and the fulfillment of Jewish feast day of Trumpets.]	3
	1) The Martyred Overcomers 2) The Living Overcomers 3) The Manchild Remnant 4) The Tares
Rev. 17:6 And I saw **the woman drunken with the blood of the saints, and with the blood of the martyrs of Jesus:** and when I saw her, I wondered with great admiration. [Throughout European church history Christianity has	1

shed the blood of the saints, prophets, and the apostles of Jesus Christ. The spirit of anti-Christ operated through the ancient Jewish leaders as they stoned the prophets who spoke the truth and were indeed, led by the spirit of Christ (I Pet 1:10-12). The Roman Empire, both secular and religious, persecuted true Christians without mercy for approximately seventeen hundred years. Her Protestant and Post-Protestant children did the same. In the last days the revived Roman / Babylonian global system will move in fury to attack their only threat... righteous Christians... because their leader, the Antichrist, knows that he has only a short time of 42 months (Rev 12:10-13,17). Also see Rev 18:20,23,24; 16:6]

Rev. 17:8 **The beast** that thou sawest was, and is not; and shall **ascend out of the bottomless pit, and go into perdition: and they that dwell on the earth shall wonder, whose names were not written in the book of life from the foundation of the world, when they behold the beast that was, and is not, and yet is**.	4

[The tares who are gathered first, and thrust out of the kingdom of God (Mt 13:30) shall unite with the heathen wicked because they have the same father, the Devil (Jn 8:44). The Antichrist, who will be chief amongst the tares, will destroy the harlot church which he created, and command absolute worship of himself. Likewise, in reference to Judas, the disciple that betrayed Christ, Jesus told all of His disciples that He had chosen the twelve, yet one of them was a devil (Jn 6:70). Judas was the only disciple of Christ that was not written in the Book of Life. However, no one knew this until after the fact (Lk 10:19,20).

The criminals in the house of God will be exposed midway through the tribulation as the Lord allows them to go into perdition just as He did with Judas (Jn 17:12). Western theologians might want to reconsider their dogmas concerning whether or not a Christian can have a devil, because Judas was possessed by Satan **after** he betrayed Christ.

"Then entered Satan into Judas surnamed Iscariot, being of the number of the twelve. And he went his way, and communed with the chief priests and captains, how he

might betray him unto them." (Lk 22:3,4)

Can a believer in Jesus Christ be possessed by a devil? Judas was not possessed by just any devil, but by Satan himself . . . so shall it also be with the Antichrist (II Thes 2:3,7).

In Revelation chapter 13, the beast consolidates his kingdom, blasphemes the host of heaven, and commands all to worship his image. We are also told in Revelation 13:8 that *"all that dwell upon the earth shall worship him, whose names are not written in the book of life of the Lamb slain from the foundation of the world."*

When the Manchild completes their testimony and finish their 42 months of ministry, we are told that the Antichrist, identified as the beast that came of the bottomless pit, will be given permission to slay them. (Rev 11:7-11)]

Rev. 17:11 And the beast that was, and is not, even he is the eighth, and is of the seven, and **goeth into perdition**. *[The nature of the beast is perdition (sin); that's why he is a devil.]*	**4**
Rev. 18:4 And I heard another voice from heaven, saying, **Come out of her, my people, that ye be not partakers of her sins, and that ye receive not of her plagues.** [The only groups that the Lord considers being *"His people"* are the natural and spiritual Jews. Both have been and are currently partaking of the tenants of Mystery Babylon. Both must come out of her to drink of the well of eternal life. They must wash their garments in the blood of the Lamb or they will perish.]	**1, 2, 4**
Rev. 18:6 **Reward her even as she rewarded you, and double unto her** double according to her works: in the cup which she hath filled, fill to her double. [This revelation is an explanation of what the Apostle Paul stated to the church at Thessalonica. *"Seeing it is a righteous thing with God to recompense tribulation to them that trouble you;* *And to you who are troubled rest with us, when the Lord Jesus shall be revealed from heaven with his mighty angels, In flaming fire taking vengeance on them that know not God, and that obey not the gospel of our Lord Jesus*	**1, 2, 3**

Christ: *Who shall be punished with everlasting destruction from the presence of the Lord, and from the glory of his power; When he shall come to be glorified in his saints, and to be admired in all them that believe (because our testimony among you was believed) in that day."* (II Thes 2:6-10)]	
Rev. 18:20 Rejoice over her, thou heaven, and ye **holy apostles and prophets**; for God hath avenged you on her. [The Lord commanded the Christian Church at Rome not to repay evil with evil. He stated that at the appointed time, vengeance would be His (Rm 13:19). His vengeance, wrath, and judgment upon all those who dared to touch His anointed will be thorough and complete. This is the day of His vengeance, to recompense evil upon all murders. When an individual persecutes a Christian they also persecute God who dwells within them.]	**1, 3**
Rev. 18:23 **And the light of a candle shall shine no more at all in thee; and the voice of the bridegroom and of the bride shall be heard no more at all in thee:** for thy merchants were the great men of the earth; for by thy sorceries were all nations deceived. [These attributes of wickedness were characteristic of the church of Thyatira (Rev 2:18-24).]	**4**

Rev. 18:24 And in her was found **the blood of prophets, and of saints**, and of all that were slain upon the earth.
    The saints of god will be a witness and testimony against the harlot bride of the Antichrist. The Lord told His disciples in the Mount of Olives discourse to *"take heed to yourselves: for they shall deliver you up to councils; and in the synagogues ye shall be beaten: and ye shall be brought before rulers and kings for my sake, for a testimony against them.*
    And the gospel must first be published among all nations. But when they shall lead you, and deliver you up, take no thought beforehand what ye shall speak, neither do ye premeditate: but whatsoever shall be given you in that hour, that speak ye: for it is not ye that speak, but the Holy Ghost.
    Now the brother shall betray the brother to death, and
	4

the father the son; and children shall rise up against their parents, and shall cause them to be put to death. *M'r:13:13: And ye shall be hated of all men for my name's sake: but he that shall endure unto the end, the same shall be saved." (Mk 13:9-13)]*	
	1) The Martyred Overcomers 2) The Living Overcomers 3) The Manchild Remnant 4) The Tares
Rev. 19:2 For true and righteous are his judgments: for he hath judged the great whore, which did corrupt the earth with her fornication, **and hath avenged the blood of his servants at her hand.**	4
Rev. 19:5 And a voice came out of the throne, saying, Praise our God, **all ye his servants**, and ye that fear him, both small and great.	1, 2, 3
Rev. 19:7 Let us be glad and rejoice, and give honour to him: **for the marriage of the Lamb is come, and his wife hath made herself ready**. [The marriage of the Lamb is the rapture of the church; for His bride *"hath made herself read"*. The marriage of the Lamb does not come until after the tribulation of those days. The church is often referred to as the bride of Christ and only those who overcome shall inherit the kingdom of God and be considered His wife. They overcome by the blood of the Lamb and the words of their testimony. The quickening, or rapture of the saints, will unite the bride with the groom and they will become husband and wife.]	1, 2, 3
Rev. 19:8 And to her was granted that **she should be arrayed in fine linen**, clean and white: **for the fine linen is the righteousness of saints**. [The victory of the saints coincides with the events of chapters 5:1-15;14:1-5;15:1-5; 19:1-10; 21:1-8]	1, 2, 3
Rev. 19:10 And I fell at his feet to worship him. And he said unto me, See thou do it not: **I am thy fellow servant, and of thy brethren that have the testimony of Jesus: worship God:** for the testimony of Jesus is the spirit of	1

prophecy.	
Rev. 19:14 And **the armies which were in heaven followed him upon white horses, clothed in fine linen, white and clean**.	1, 2, 3

Rev. 19:14 And **the armies which were in heaven followed him upon white horses, clothed in fine linen, white and clean**.

[Unmistakeably this is Christ's Second Coming. Jesus' brother Jude, the son of Joseph, states that *"Enoch also, the seventh from Adam, prophesied of these, saying, Behold, the Lord cometh with ten thousands of his saints, To execute judgment upon all, and to convince all that are ungodly among them of all their ungodly deeds which they have ungodly committed, and of all their hard speeches which ungodly sinners have spoken against him."* (Jude 1:14,15)

The prophet Joel gives a full account of the saints taking part in the battle of Armageddon. The glorified, resurrected, and translated saints will do battle in their invincible bodies.

*"**Blow ye the trumpet in Zion**, and sound an alarm in my holy mountain: let all the inhabitants of the land tremble: **for the day of the LORD cometh**, for it is nigh at hand;*

A day of darkness and of gloominess, a day of clouds and of thick darkness, as the morning spread upon the mountains: a great people and a strong; there hath not been ever the like, neither shall be any more after it, even to the years of many generations.

A fire devoureth before them; and behind them a flame burneth: the land is as the garden of Eden before them, and behind them a desolate wilderness; yea, and nothing shall escape them.

*The appearance of them is as the appearance of horses; and as horsemen, so shall they run. Like the noise of chariots on the tops of mountains shall they leap, like the noise of a flame of fire that devoureth the stubble, **as a strong people set in battle array. Before their face the people shall be much pained: all faces shall gather blackness.***

They shall run like mighty men; they shall climb the wall like men of war; and they shall march every one on his ways, and they shall not break their ranks: Neither shall one thrust another; they shall walk every one in his path: and when they fall upon the sword, they shall not be wounded.

They shall run to and fro in the city; they shall run upon the wall, they shall climb up upon the houses; they shall enter in at the windows like a thief. The earth shall quake before them; the heavens shall tremble: the sun and the moon shall be dark, and the stars shall withdraw their shining: *And the LORD shall utter his voice before his army: for his camp is very great: for he is strong that executeth his word: for the day of the LORD is great and very terrible; and who can abide it? Therefore also now, saith the LORD, turn ye even to me with all your heart, and with fasting, and with weeping, and with mourning:"* (Joel 2:1-12)]	
Rev. 19:19 And I saw the beast, and the kings of the earth, and their armies, gathered together to make war against him that sat on the horse, **and against his army**.	**1, 2, 3**
Rev. 20:4 And I saw thrones, and they sat upon them, and judgment was given unto them: and **I saw the souls of them that were beheaded for the witness of Jesus, and for the word of God, and which had not worshipped the beast, neither his image, neither had received his mark upon their foreheads, or in their hands; and they lived and reigned with Christ a thousand years.** [Many of these martyred saints share the fate of the prophet / priest, John the Baptist, who was beheaded for his stand against unrighteousness. Christians will serve as witnesses for the condemnation of the wicked, and shall be as Christ for those who walk in darkness. *"And this is the condemnation, that light is come into the world, and men loved darkness rather than light, because their deeds were evil.* *For every one that doeth evil hateth the light, neither cometh to the light, lest his deeds should be reproved"* (Jn 3:19,20). Since they hate the light of Christ, which is exemplified in true Christians, they will persecute the representatives of light. However, because Jesus is the light of the world, light always overcomes darkness. Those who are Christ-like overcome the beast, his system, and his image.	**1**

Jesus Christ taught that persecution was one of the costs of discipleship:

"These things have I spoken unto you, that ye should not be offended. They shall put you out of the synagogues: yea, **the time cometh, that whosoever killeth you will think that he doeth God service. And these things will they do unto you, because they have not known the Father, nor me.**

But these things have I told you, that when the time shall come, ye may remember that I told you of them. And these things I said not unto you at the beginning, because I was with you." (Jn 16:1-4)]

Rev. 20:5 But the rest of the dead lived not again until the thousand years were finished. **This is the first resurrection**. [There are only two resurrections as Jesus emphatically stated in the gospels: one for the living saints of God, and one for the dead in Christ (Jn 5:25-30). The Rapture of the church is the first resurrection. There is only one rapture for the righteous and it consists of two parts, the resurrection of the dead and the translation of those who are alive.]	1, 2, 3
Rev. 20:6 Blessed and holy is he that hath part in **the first resurrection: on such the second death hath no power, but they shall be priests of God and of Christ, and shall reign with him a thousand years.** [The second resurrection is the rapture of the wicked unto damnation after the one thousand year millennium reign of Christ. The Lord promises the churches of Smyrna that if they overcame their trials, they would not be hurt of the second death (Rev 2:11). This warning proves conclusively that not only could one lose his salvation; he can consequently go to hell. The church of Sardis is told that if they overcome and do not succumb to their sins, their names would not be blotted out of the Lamb's book of life. The churches of Philadelphia (3:12) and Laodicea (3:21) are promised that if they overcome, they will reign with the Lord in His kingdom.]	1,2, 3 4

Rev. 20:9 And they went up on the breadth of the earth, and **compassed the camp of the saints about, and the beloved city: and fire came down from God out of heaven, and devoured them.**	1, 2, 3
	1) The Martyred Overcomers 2) The Living Overcomers 3) The Manchild Remnant 4) The Tares

Rev. 21:2 And I John saw **the holy city, new Jerusalem, coming down from God out of heaven, prepared as a bride adorned for her husband.**
    [Many have read the book of Revelation and interpret spiritual things naturally and natural things spiritually, adding to their confusion. Most error by inserting their own definitions or using outdated concepts and inappropriate definitions, resulting in misinterpretation. In this chapter the term city and bride are used interchangeably with significance. The church is described throughout the bible in many metaphoric terms, such as the body (Eph 5:30,31, I Cor 12:12), a temple (I Cor 3:16,17; 6:19,20), a building (Eph 2:20-22), and a bride (Jn 3:29). In this instance, John sees the glorious purified bride of the Lamb, after they have received their resurrected bodies at the rapture, in the form of a city. When the saints are raptured, they will see Christ as He is, and they shall be just like Him (I Jn 3:2).
    The saints of God as a city, is one of the greatest fulfillments of the promises that YEHWEH had made to the Hebrew Patriarch Abraham. You see, we were told that *"he looked for a city which hath foundations, whose builder and maker is God . . . But now they desire a better country, that is, an heavenly: wherefore God is not ashamed to be called their God: for he hath prepared for them a city" (Heb 11:10).* **The bride of Christ will be transformed into the wife of Christ at the rapture** (Rev 19:6-10) <u>and they will constitute that marvelous city which Abraham sought, whose builder and maker was God.</u> One must remember that this supernatural city was not made with human hands, neither is the supernatural body of Christ (even though men often refer to their natural buildings as the church of Christ.)
    This heavenly city is called the New Jerusalem, bearing
	1, 2, 3

the name of Jesus' Holy city on earth. This name is simply another name for His wife, the glorified church. The antithesis of this city is the harlot bride of the Antichrist, which is also identified as a city; her name is Mystery Babylon. Mystery Babylon's number and measurement of is 666; however, the number and measurement of the New Jerusalem is 144,000. The number 144,00 corresponds with the overcomers who are identified as the tribes of Israel in chapter 7, and virgin disciples of the Lamb in chapter 14 (7:3-8; 14:1-5).	
Rev. 21:3　And I heard a great voice out of heaven saying, **Behold, the tabernacle of God is with men, and he will dwell with them, and they shall be his people, and God himself shall be with them, and be their God.** [The tabernacle of God dwells in the righteous as the Spirit of Truth (Jn 14:17). They have overcome the floodgates of lies and deceptions that beguiled the inhabitants of the earth. Those who have experienced fellowship and discipleship with Christ shall tabernacle with Him, as they proceed into the millennium kingdom together.]	1, 2, 3
Rev. 21:4　And **God shall wipe away all tears from their eyes; and there shall be no more death, neither sorrow, nor crying, neither shall there be any more pain**: for the former things are passed away. [The saints of God will no longer have to be concerned about, death, sickness, disease, and war. Their victory coincides with the events of chapters 15:6-10; 14:1-5; 15:1-5; 19:1-10]	1, 2, 3
Rev. 21:7 He that **overcometh shall inherit all things; and I will be his God, and he shall be my son.** [We have gone full circle from chapters two and three which make many eternal promises to those who overcome. The saints of the Most High God will finally and fully experience the hope of their patience. The Apostle Paul wrote to the saints in Rome, *"For I reckon that the sufferings of this present time are not worthy to be compared with the glory which shall be revealed in us."* (Rm 8:18)]	1, 2, 3

Rev. 21:9-13 And there came unto me one of the seven angels which had the seven vials full of the seven last plagues, and talked with me, saying, Come hither,**I will shew thee the bride, the Lamb's wife.**
[10] And he carried me away in the spirit to a great and high mountain, **and shewed me that great city, the holy Jerusalem, descending out of heaven from God,**

[If the angel was going to show John the bride, the Lamb's wife, why does he show him a city? The answer was given previously in verse 2. The New Jerusalem is the glorified church, the city of promise whose builder and maker is God.]

[11] **Having the glory of God: and her light** was like unto a stone most precious, even like a jasper stone, clear as crystal;
[12] And had a wall great and high, and had twelve gates, **and at the gates twelve angels, and names written thereon, which are the names of the twelve tribes of the children of Israel:**
[13] On the east three gates; on the north three gates; on the south three gates; and on the west three gates.

[How is this city (who is female, and a bride) having twelve gates which represents the twelve tribes of Israel, associated with the church? This is another mystery concealed in chapter seven. The number 12,000 was selected figuratively from each of the 12 tribes, totaling 144,000. As we saw earlier, John did not see 144,000, he **heard** their number. The city / bride of Christ is built on Jewish foundations, not European. This is why many Western scholars, consistently studied to no avail and were unable to unravel the mysteries of Christ. Jesus Christ was a Jew, the Old Testament prophets were Jews, and all of the original New Testament apostles were Jews. The Apostle Paul gives us the key to understanding why the kingdom church has Old Testament patriarchs as its gates.

"Now therefore ye are no more strangers and foreigners, but fellowcitizens with the saints, and of the household of God;

1, 2, 3

1, 2, 3

And are built upon the foundation of the apostles [New Testament] and prophets [Old Testament], Jesus Christ himself being the chief corner stone; *In whom all the building fitly framed together groweth unto an holy temple in the Lord: In whom ye also are builded together for an habitation of God through the Spirit."* (Eph 2:19-22)]	
¹⁴ And the wall of the **city had twelve foundations, and in them the names of the twelve apostles of the Lamb.** [The foundations of the city are represented by the Jewish Apostles of the first century. Paul warned all church leaders, "According to the grace of God which is given unto me, as a wise masterbuilder, I have laid the foundation, and another buildeth thereon. But let every man take heed how he buildeth thereupon. For other foundation can no man lay than that is laid, which is Jesus Christ. Now if any man build upon this foundation gold, silver, precious stones, wood, hay, stubble..." (I Cor 3:10-12). Again, the Christian Church is built upon the foundation of the apostles and prophets. Therefore, it should not be out of character for John to use Jewish terms to describe the church. For example, the Lord addressed some of the church of Smyrna as the synagogue of Satan and others who call themselves Jews and are not. Also, referring to the Christians in chapter seven, He identified them as the twelve tribes of Israel ... and in this chapter, as the 12 precious stones of the New Jerusalem representing the ephod. This is also in character with the salutations given to the church by Paul and James. James, the brother of Jesus' addressed the church as the twelve tribes scattered	1, 2, 3

abroad (Jm 1:1). Paul also identifies the church as the Israel of God (Gal 6:18).]	
¹⁵. And he that talked with me had a golden reed to measure the city, and the gates thereof, and the wall there of. ¹⁶ And **the city lieth foursquare, and the length is as large as the breadth: and he measured the city with the reed, twelve thousand furlongs. The length and the breadth and the height of it are equal.** [This: bride, wife, city, built with Old Testament tribal gates and foundations of the 12 apostles of the Lamb, is a perfect cube of equal dimensions. The distance in measurements of furlongs is of no consequence in the interpretation of this verse; the most important component is the number 12,000. Because it also identifies the wife of Jesus Christ, His glorified body, it obviously cannot be a literal city, as many suppose. The carnally minded are looking for a literal city that is roughly fifteen hundred miles (12,000 furlongs) in length, height, and depth. Also, as previously mentioned, the church of Christ is not composed of natural buildings, but is a spiritual body of believers universally filled with the Holy Ghost. How can His bride, who becomes His wife, also be of the male gender? Using the biblical keys, we can conclude that because Christ is male, so is His body, of which He is the head even though it is also His bride. In essence, for those who can receive this revelation, it is an awesome picture of Christ and His spiritual body, presenting Himself (the church –bride) to Himself, as the bridegroom. This multiplicity of roles that Christ occupies as: judge, advocate, and the lamb of sacrifice, to deliver all those who are ordained unto eternal life, is part of the great mysteries that can only be revealed by the Holy Ghost. <u>**The bride must make herself ready to be counted faithful to marry the King of Kings**</u>.]	1, 2, 3
Rev. 21:17 And he measured the wall thereof, **an hundred and forty and four cubits, according to the measure of a man**, that is, of the angel. [The measurements of the wall of the city was 144 cubits (a cubit ranges from 18-22 inches). This measurements, in meters or feet, does not necessarily have	1, 2, 3

to match the previous dimensions in furlongs (4860 ft.). The measurement of the image of Nebuchadnezzar was 60 cubits by 6 cubits (Dan 3:1). The Antichrist's measurement is 666 without any increments of distance. The number of Christ revealed through His body as the number, 144,000 was in the previous verses; it denoted His wife.

The Apostle Paul also revealed this measurement of the city / wife as the primary purpose of the five-fold ministry necessary to prepare the church, as a virgin, for the fullness of Christ.

"He that descended is the same also that ascended up far above all heavens, that he might fill all things.)

And he gave some, apostles; and some, prophets; and some, evangelists; and some, pastors and teachers;

For the perfecting of the saints, for the work of the ministry, for the edifying of the body of Christ:

*Till we all come in the unity of the faith, and of the knowledge of the Son of God, **unto a perfect man, unto the measure of the stature of the fulness of Christ.***"

(Eph 4:10-13)

The church will measure up to the measurement of the perfect man. The divine five-fold offices: apostles, prophets, evangelists, pastors and teachers is once again established in the last days. The true apostles and prophets will judge Christianity as the Lord beckons His sheep of the seven churches to come out of the Harlot church. (Rev 18:4).]

Rev. 21:18-21 [18] **And the building of the wall of it was of jasper**: and the city was pure gold, like unto clear glass. [19] And the foundations of the wall of the city were garnished with all manner of precious stones. The first foundation was **jasper**; the second, **sapphire**; the third, a **chalcedony**; the fourth, an **emerald**; [20] The fifth, **sardonyx**; the sixth, **sardius**; the seventh, **chrysolyte;** the eighth, **beryl**; the ninth, a **topaz**; the tenth, a **chrysoprasus**; the eleventh, a **jacinth**; the twelfth, an **amethyst**. [21] And the **twelve gates were twelve pearls**: every several gate was of one pearl: and the street of the city was pure gold, as it were	1, 2, 3

315

transparent glass.

[In the book of Exodus, Moses receives a blueprint for the four square ephod of gold that had twelve precious stones representing the twelve tribes of Israel (Ex 39:2-21). The twelve precious stones were to be worn by the High Priest of Israel. In the book of Revelation, the precious stones represents the spiritual priesthood manifested by the church of Jesus Christ, their High Priest.

In this chapter we see the church as a wife prepared for the Bridegroom. She is a city, with Old and New Testament roots fused together in its walls, foundations, gates, measurements, precious stones, and her name. The greatest mysteries collectively reveal how Jewish Christians and Gentile Christians become one in Christ and all inherit the promises of Abraham.

"For ye are all the children of God by faith in Christ Jesus. For as many of you as have been baptized into Christ have put on Christ.

There is neither Jew nor Greek, there is neither bond nor free, there is neither male nor female: for ye are all one in Christ Jesus. And if ye be Christ's, then are ye Abraham's seed, and heirs according to the promise." (Gal 3:26-29)]

Rev. 21:23 **And the city had no need of the sun, neither of the moon, to shine in it: for the glory of God did lighten it, and the Lamb is the light thereof.**	1, 2, 3
Rev. 21:24 And the **nations of them which are saved shall walk in the light of it: and the kings of the earth do bring their glory and honour into it.**	1, 2. 3
Rev. 21:27 **And there shall in no wise enter into it any thing that defileth, neither whatsoever worketh abomination, or maketh a lie: but they which are written in the Lamb's book of life.**	1, 2, 3
Rev. 22:3 And there shall be no more curse: but the throne of God and of the Lamb shall be in it; **and his servants shall serve him**:	
Rev. 22:4 **And they shall see his face; and his name shall be in their foreheads.**	1, 2, 3

Rev. 22:18 For **I testify unto every man that heareth the words of the prophecy of this book, If any man shall add unto these things**, God shall add unto him the plagues that are written in this book:	1, 2, 3, 4
Rev. 22:19 And **if any man shall take away from the words of the book of this prophecy**, God shall take away his part out of the book of life, and out of the holy city, and from the things which are written in this book.	1, 2, 3, 4

About the Author

Bishop Harris, Apostle to the End Time Church

Bishop Clarence B. Harris is the president of Alpha Omega Productions, Inc. and founder of Christian Fellowship Assemblies (1982), a national spirit filled ministry with a focus on end time prophetic studies. He is an international speaker, preacher, and educator who conducts training sessions and seminars worldwide, recently in North America, Europe, Africa, and South East Asia. As a graduate of the University of Miami (Florida), Bishop Harris majored in History and Religion and minored in Biology and Chemistry. In 1980 he was commissioned by the Southern Baptist Convention to serve as a chaplain for the University of the District of Columbia and Howard University in Washington, D.C. He also served as a chaplain at South Dade Federal Corrections Prison in Miami, Florida (1979) and founded the Open Bible Institute for Christian Apologetics in Coral Hills, Maryland in 1983.

Bishop Harris has been an educator, coach, and administrator in several of our nation's public school systems. He was Dade County's (Miami) Mainstream Teacher of the Year in 1991. He currently teaches Psychology, Sociology and History in Georgia. He has also pastored, been a community activist, and a promoter of racial reconciliation for three decades.

Bishop Clarence Harris was ironically, a former critic of the Christian faith in the early 70's. In fact, he attempted to prove the Bible to be false, because of Western Christianity's contradictory and hypocritical historical past. European anti-Semitism has for centuries rejected these biblical roots and therefore forfeited their ability to understand most biblical truths. However, after intense investigations of science, religion, and history, he became fully persuaded that the prophetic nature of the Jewish scriptures was amazingly accurate. He discovered that the Christian faith was valid; however, the practices of those who claimed to be Christian have been atrocious. Consequently, Bishop Harris became an apologist and defender of the biblical Christian faith. In 1980, after receiving the anointing that commissioned the First Century apostles, the baptism of the Holy Ghost, he began to fulfill his apostolic and prophetic calling to the Body of Christ. Having a great love for the Jewish nation and for the church, he has systematically proclaimed the restoration of the biblical Jewish roots of New Testament theology.

In 1981 Bishop Harris authored his first book entitled, "**Without Controversy, Great is the Mystery of Godliness**." Subsequent publications would include: "**Salvation the Bible Way**," "**A Divine Paradigm of the End Times**," "**Countdown to Global Governance**," and "**Tribulation or Triumph?**". Collectively, these books give a full disclosure of Jewish prophecy, Old Testament New Testament typology, and biblical progressive repetitious revelation. They were written for the purpose of unveiling the revelations of Jesus Christ in the last days. This is uniquely done from a First Century Jewish Christian perspective, supported by a history, science, and biblical research without a Western anti-Semitic bias. This collection of books were written to encourage and strengthen the hearts of true Christians, that they might comprehend the mysteries of God and be able to stand in the prophesied **Evil Day**.

The Jewish apostles' Gospel of the Kingdom was the gospel that was proclaimed by the First Century Church, John the Baptist and Jesus Christ. As an apostle and defender of the faith, Bishop Harris discovered that the Apostles' doctrines have been replaced by centuries of European cultural and theological relativism. However, according to the scriptures, the exaltation of the New Testament gospel of the Kingdom must be proclaimed globally in preparation for the return of the Jewish Messiah, Jesus Christ. Hence, the greater than 25,000 Christian denominational sects must be tried during the end times "showdown" between truth and error to see if they are in compliance with the word of God.

Bishop Harris has also produced a powerful End Time video documentary on the Book of Revelation, the 666 Antichrist kingdom, and the New World Order. It is entitled "**Mystery Babylon Exposed**."

Bishop Harris is an uncompromising preacher of truth and righteousness, who calls the Church unto repentance and holiness before the dreadful day of the Lord's judgement. "In the beginning there was only one Church. At the end of this age it shall conclude in the same manner." **Hear ye him** . . .

Alpha Omega Productions, inc
www.alphaomegapro.org
Athens, Georgia, USA

ORDER FORM

Name:_____

Company: _____ Church:_____

Address:_____

City: _____ State: _____ Postal Code: _____

Country: _____ Telephone:_____ Fax:_____

E-mail: _____ Church affiliation:_____

I would like to order the following items:

No. of Copies	Title	Price	Shipping	Total
	A Divine Paradigm of the End Times Unveils the hgidden mysteries in the Book of Revelations and Jewish prophetic books.	$19.95		
	Salvation the Bible Way A Systematic Old Testament - New Testament Study manual on the historical roots of biblical salvation. (10 or more $4.50 each, 50 or more $3.50 each)	$5.00		
	The Book of Revelation wall chart A beautiful 3-foot vinyl color wall chart that simplifies the Book of Revelation and the prophetic books.	$23.95		
	Without Controversy Great Is the Mystery of Godliness Examines the mystery of the Godhead, divine order in the church, body ministry, holiness, and walking in the spirit.	$19.95		
	Video: Mystery Babylon Exposed A two hour documentary on the book of Revelation and the New World Order.	$29.95		
	Countdown to Global Governance A detailed antidotal timeline of the movers, shakers, and organizers responsible for the New World Order.	$14.95		
	Tribulation or Triumph? A chapter and verse breakdown of the book of Revelation from a First Century Jewish Christian Perspective. Proves that the church is in every chapter of the book of Revelation. It also exposes anti-Semitism, ethnocentrism, and racism in Western European church theology.	$24.95		

Georgia residents 6% sales tax

Please call for bulk order rates

Total_____

Shipping Cost:
order of $ 50 or less = $ 4.00   order of $ 51 or more = $ 5.00

Please e-mail or call to check international rates.

Payment Method:
___ Check (Make checks or money orders payable (in U.S. funds) to

Alpha Omega Productions, Inc.
P.O. Box 6641 Athens, GA. 30604-6641

Phone: 706-769-8469